STRUCTURAL SURVEYS OF DWELLING HOUSES

STRUCTURAL SURVEYS OF DWELLING HOUSES

INCLUDING STRUCTURAL SURVEYS OF FLATS
AND NEW DWELLINGS

THIRD EDITION ENLARGED TO INCLUDE
A CHAPTER ON HOUSE AND FLAT BUYERS'
REPORTS, ADDITIONAL ILLUSTRATIONS AND
TWO NEW SAMPLE REPORTS

by
Ian A. Melville, FRICS
and
Ian A. Gordon, FRICS

with a chapter on the legal position
of the surveyor by
Paul G. Murrells
Solicitor

1992

Estates
Gazette

A member of Reed Business Publishing Group

THE ESTATES GAZETTE LIMITED
151 Wardour Street London
W1V 4BN

First edition published   1964
Reprinted   1965
Reprinted   1970
Reprinted   1971
Reprinted   1972
Second enlarged edition   1974
Reprinted   1980
Reprinted   1985
Reprinted   1987
Third enlarged edition   1992
Reprinted   2000

ISBN 0 7282 0163 1

Printed and bound in Great Britain
at The Manson Group.

Preface to the Third Edition

In the preface to the second edition of this book in April 1974, we expressed some astonishment at the "remarkable increase in home ownership that has taken place in the last decade". If asked at that time whether we would have continued to be astonished by such a trend we would have replied that we would not. Increasing home ownership was clearly here to stay and by 1987 had reached 14 million, well over three times the level of 30 years before. The extension of this, however, into the private acquisition of Council flats and houses would have left us both open mouthed with astonishment. Thus is hindsight ever humbling.

During the past fourteen years, the provision of dwellings in the private sector has, not unnaturally, followed demand. The need for smaller units has led to a revolution in the design of both new buildings and conversion schemes with variable results. The benign side is the enormous public interest and consequent sophistication of space layout, kitchens and bathrooms, while the depressing side is the poor quality of much of the construction and finishings to flats and houses. The fact that what is now termed "the housing industry" is now of such obvious importance to so many people that it attracts increasing attention from the media. This has resulted in much discussion, such as a well publicised television programme on timber frame housing. The recently discussed dangers of certain types of health hazards such as asbestos or lead pipes in soft water districts have also been generally made known although the problems emerging from earlier methods of construction in an ageing stock of buildings such as corrosion in steel frames or wall ties in cavity brickwork are still likely to be better known to the surveyor rather than his client.

Building control has reacted rather uneasily to change during this period, an obvious example being the requirement to insulate roof voids in order to save heat, followed by the disconcerting discovery that this regulation leads to condensation in low pitch roofs resulting in a hasty revision to provide for ventilation. This comment, however, is not intended to pillory those responsible but to emphasise the problems of legislation in a period of rapid change. The standards of the NHBC and TRADA have all, understandably, undergone fundamental alteration during the past fourteen years.

This period, also, quite apart from legislation affecting technical matters in buildings, has seen enormous extensions in civil law. The introduction of the Unfair Contract Terms Act 1977 is an obvious example, but the most notable changes are firstly in the interpretation of the terms of the contract between the surveyor and his client and secondly the extension of the doctrine of Tort. The writers consider themselves fortunate that they have received the benefit of advice from a leading expert in this field, Mr Paul Murrells, to illuminate this very important aspect of the surveyors' work and who has provided a completely re-written chapter on the legal position of the surveyor for this edition.

Against this background, surveyors, inevitably part of the system of conveyancing, have been accused, rather unfairly, of being too expensive and, rather more understandably, of being too self satisfied about the over duplication of work which leads to abortive expenditure on fees on the part of the general public. This has led to cries for "vendors surveys" or "log book inspections" which have diminished as the real problems of such seemingly attractive measures emerge upon more detailed analysis. Nevertheless, the need for speed in the production of reports is recognised by surveyors generally, if only to distance themselves from the criticisms of others in the stately process of house sale and purchase which has been so much under fire during the past decade.

But the surveyor could not comply with the demand for speedier reports without those indispensable modern aids, the hand recorder and the word processor. These have been the basis of the real shift in the surveyors' techniques since 1974. Also, although to a somewhat lesser degree, have been the increasingly helpful devices for testing and investigation ranging from more sophisticated damp meters to boroscopes and cover meters.

One of the most helpful aids of all however has been the production of the Guidance Note for surveyors on residential structural surveys published by the Building Surveyors Division of the RICS. While it is true, as one lawyer remarked upon its introduction, that "it nails our profession to the wall" it is nevertheless of inestimable value to have the surveyors' duty in this field clarified.

Finally, we must refer to the introduction of the "House Buyers" and "Flat Buyers" report forms produced by the leading institutions. It was never quite clear to practitioners, following their introduction whether they were valuations with extended comment upon condition or whether they were, in fact, mini structural surveys with an opinion as to value. Since the case of *Mr. and Mrs. Cross v. David Martin & Mortimer* heard in the Queen's Bench Division of the High Court in November 1988, however, the answer is now clear and the subject is within the legitimate scope of this book.

We have received an enormous amount of help, advice and encouragement during the years since the first edition of this book was published. Our thanks, in particular, go to Henry Stewart Publications who invited us to sit on the Editorial Board of "Structural Survey" a multi-disciplinary professional journal, when it first appeared. Stemming from this we have been involved each year with other Board members in the judging of the Structural Survey Competition organised by the publishers. This has given us a unique insight into modern practice in this demanding field.

Advice on the thoughts and difficulties of students in the subject of Structural Surveys has kindly been provided by Peter Huntsman, Principal of the College of Estate Management and his staff who have also extended much kindness to one of us on the occasion that he has been visiting lecturer.

Professional colleagues have been generous in their help and advice. Professor Malcolm Hollis, FRICS and Stephen J. Mika, FRICS MCIOB of Reading University for general and particular assistance on investigatory techniques, Anthony L. Poole, FRICS on health hazards and, for his unstinting help on a number of aspects, the late David Duke, FRICS. Our thanks are also due to John L. Barrow, FRICS FSVA ARVA and Barry R. Jackson, FRICS.

Our thanks are due to eminent members of other professional institutions, in particular Ian H. Reith, DIC CEng FIStructE FIMarE MConsE for help in connection with concrete and steel and Lawrence G. Hadley, OBE CEng FIMechE FInstE FCIBSE ACIArb MConsE for valuable assistance in connection with heating and electrical installations.

We have drawn upon two tables from Digest No. 251 issued by the Building Research Establishment and are grateful for the permission to reproduce the copyright material.

Finally, we owe an immense debt of gratitude to the late George Kirton whose sudden and unexpected death during the production stage of this book came as a great shock to everyone. As the Manager of The Estates Gazette Book Department he had given us a great deal of help and encouragement over many years.

London   IAN A. MELVILLE
September 1991   IAN A. GORDON

Preface to the Second Edition

The first edition of this book was kindly received when it appeared ten years ago and has been in constant demand ever since. In the late 1950s and early 1960s requests for structural surveys began to appear in increasing numbers and it was felt that a book on the subject might be both timely and useful for students and practitioners alike. It is doubtful, however, if even at that time anyone could have foreseen the remarkable increase in the trend towards home ownership that has taken place in the last decade. Tax allowances by successive governments coupled with a shortage of property available to let accelerated the trend but in recent years further impetus has been provided by a growing realisation of the need to conserve older houses. In April 1968 a White Paper "Old Houses into New Homes" was published which proposed that the whole system of providing grants for improving older houses should be strengthened. The amounts of such grants were substantially increased and the conditions attached were eased. Successive Acts of Parliament in the housing and planning field have encouraged this trend towards conservation and the general public has responded enthusiastically, the price of old houses in all parts of the country rising to unprecedented heights. We certainly cannot claim to have foreseen all that has happened but there is little doubt that there is a greater need for surveyors with competence in the field of structural surveys now than ten years ago and reports of Court cases have underlined the necessity for care on the one hand and the disastrous consequences of haste or inadequacy of knowledge on the other.

We have found it interesting to reflect on some of the changes that have taken place since the first edition appeared. For example there has been the increased efficiency of specialist techniques for the treatment of dry rot and wood boring beetle. Techniques for the eradication of rising dampness and for dealing with problems of settlement have also advanced and although none of the procedures mentioned in the first edition are in need of revision some change of emphasis becomes necessary as it is doubtful if, for example, any householder would now regard rising dampness with any degree of tolerance today. Earlier advice that it could, as an alternative to complete eradication, be kept "within reasonable bounds" is not likely to receive much sympathy. Times change and like any other professional man the surveyor must keep up not only with the latest developments in his own specialised field but also with the changing requirements of the public from whom the instructions are received.

In presenting lectures and talks to students and practitioners we have become convinced that one of the most difficult tasks confronting the structural surveyor is that of giving advice on newly constructed property. In the middle 1960s an enormous amount of publicity was given to defects which became apparent after completion in many new houses. The surveyor has always found in the case of building defects the reliance on such defensive measures as the Guarantee of the National House Building Council or the legislation of the Defective Premises Act 1972 rather depressing. We are, and always will be, firmly convinced that the time to recognise and take account of defects in any structure, whether old or new, is before the purchaser signs a contract. However cast iron the measures for restitution they are nothing like sufficient to compensate for the months of misery and uncertainty that have to be experienced before defects are put right in what to most people is their only capital asset, bought partly with hard earned savings and partly with borrowed money at high interest rates. The structural survey can be an indispensable aid to preventing such misery but the more we have considered the problem of new properties the more we have felt the need for the adoption of a slightly different approach from that recommended for the survey of older houses. A new chapter has therefore been added so that the difference in approach can be considered in detail and a sample report on a new house is included as an appendix.

One of the effects of the scarcity of accommodation is the trend towards the sale of flats on long lease, either purpose built and perhaps at one time let, for example those in the older mansion blocks, or converted from older properties now considered too large for their original purpose. The purchase of long leasehold interest flats is becoming increasingly common and the carrying out of structural surveys of such units posés quite different problems to those encountered in the survey of houses, particularly having regard to repairing liabilities. These problems are discussed in a new chapter and the appendix contains a report designed to illustrate the points which need to be covered.

The opportunity has been taken throughout the text to enlarge and elaborate on a number of aspects of the subject and to introduce metric equivalents and explanatory drawings. In particular even greater stress has been placed upon the need to clarify instructions with the client before embarking on the survey and to underline the necessity for tailoring the report to the property in question and to the requirements of the client. The problem of drafting the report itself has always been the subject of many questions to the writers and the opportunity has been taken of adding a further sample report on a simple two storey house.

The writers would like, in conclusion, to express their thanks to Mr John Sevastopulo, Assistant Director, and Miss M. E. Lowey, Manager of the Professional Indemnity Department of C. T. Bowring (London) Limited for the revision of the section of the book dealing with the all important subject of surveyors indemnity.

We hope that this new enlarged edition will continue to provide necessary guidance to the more advanced student and younger practitioner in a field which will always place severe demands on the surveyor's ability.

London   IAN A. MELVILLE
April 1974   IAN A. GORDON

It is becoming plain to those who are concerned with land and buildings that the prospective purchaser of a small house now instructs a surveyor as a matter of course where a few years ago he would not have contemplated such a step. A structural survey is now commonplace with the average house buyer and increasing numbers of small Georgian, Edwardian or Victorian dwellings are being subjected to close and detailed scrutiny very often for the first time since they were built. It is of some interest to reflect for a moment on the reasons behind this trend.

Let us consider the position of a young couple living in any of the great urban areas of this country a few years before the beginning of the Second World War, who wished to buy a house. They would, if they suffered the affliction common to most young couples through successive generations, have the difficulty of saving the deposit. They would accordingly turn their attention to the new houses being built on the outskirts of the town or city where they lived. The rapidly expanding *Building Societies* offered attractive terms to encourage prospective house purchasers to move to one of the newly built estates and there was little similar encouragement for the purchase of older houses in the inner suburbs. In any event most of these tended to be let.

In 1964 the picture has changed. Expense of travel to new development on the city outskirts is now very high and travel itself is not the simple matter that it used to be. In any event development on the outskirts of cities and towns is strictly limited by Green Belt, planning and other provisions and the shortage of suitable sites has limited the number of new houses available. Interest has accordingly turned to older properties. Government encouragement to local authorities and to *Building Societies* to grant mortgages in respect of older houses has made it possible for house buyers of limited means to purchase these houses. The offer of improvement grants and increasing publicity directed at the general public has resulted in a more favourable climate of opinion to older properties. Thirty years or so have passed in the meantime, however, and although prices of such houses will be high from the pressure of demand compared with before the war, the inevitable neglect from the war years and the wear of time will have searched out structural weakness or revealed poor materials for what they are. High, slender and unsupported walls now bulge outwards. The ruddy brightness in the bricks of the Victorian villa is now seen for what it too often is—the glow of ill health. The earlier felt damp-proof courses have perished and ugly wet stains are ignored behind the piano or chest of drawers while the crinkled appearance of the floorboards underneath is an irritating reminder of the ability of

Merulius lacrymans to flourish when damp is added to poor ventilation.

The 1930 semi-detached villas also have their troubles. The tiled roof may be a sorry spectacle after 30 years of frost. Damp has probably entered the structure of the houses at many different points, cracks along cornices show that unsupported flank walls are beginning to move outwards and sunken paving points to the inevitable discovery that the shallow drains have fractured.

This then is the picture, but only part of the picture. These houses can be made sound. Many of the older houses with careful treatment have taken on a new lease of life and are as comfortable inside as any man could desire. With discreet conversion they are as easy to run as most wives would expect. Diagnosis of the troubles and repair and improvement over a number of years is the pattern today. The readers of this book will be concerned with the next stage of the client's interview or the solicitor's letter of instructions and it is from this point that the book starts. Yet the background is of considerable importance. A growing population who have never paid doctor's bills now pay surveyor's fees.

Faced with lack of any guidance on the subject and the discouraging evidence of cases of negligence in the courts many surveyors have tended to turn away instructions for surveys and concentrate on other work. This is a pity as the surveyor in the eyes of the general public is still the man who comes to look at the house and whose advice affects the one or two really expensive transactions in the life of the ordinary man. The writers, when students, looked for a book on structural surveys and could not find one. It is hoped, therefore, that this small book will be found of benefit not only to practitioners who are principally engaged in other matters and accept instructions for the occasional survey but by the second or third year student. A basic knowledge of building construction must be assumed in the reader.

One final word. Properties such as factories, warehouses, offices, hotels and cinemas all receive the attention of the surveyor and have particular problems of their own. To cover these buildings adequately, however, would result in a different type of book.

Contents

A paged list of contents appears at the beginning of each Chapter.

CONTENTS

INTRODUCTION

THE TERM "STRUCTURAL SURVEY"

Scope of book

This book is strictly concerned with the duties of a surveyor when asked by the prospective purchaser of a house or flat to carry out an inspection of the property and to report upon its condition and state of repair. It deals with no other set of circumstances but these. It does not, for example, deal with those inspections and reports the object of which is to provide advice on value, or on insurance or town planning matters, or even advice on alterations or improvements to property though these may be mentioned in the text to point a contrast. The operation to be discussed is known as a "Structural Survey".

Technical inexactness but general acceptance of term

The term "Structural Survey" may be technically inexact and be a source of bewilderment to members of the engineering professions when used in the context of this book but, nevertheless, it has found such widespread acceptance with the general public and the legal fraternity that it can fairly be adopted as the correct descriptive term for this particular operation without further discussion or elaboration.

Nature of each survey varies

Of course the precise nature of each structural survey will vary. Surveys and reports will vary widely and consideration needs to be given to the effect that these variations will have on the basic operation, even apart from the difficulties imposed by the enormous range in the age and type of house or flat encountered. Furthermore, as the surveyor's inspection is often made in occupied and fully furnished premises belonging to someone other than his client, the circumstances usually preclude any major opening up or cutting away so that many of the structural features of the property remain hidden.

As we shall see these and other factors to be discussed make the operation a demanding task requiring skill in detecting what may be substantial defects from quite minimal evidence. It is therefore also necessary to give some indication of the field of experience and knowledge desirable in a surveyor proposing to carry out such work.

Instructions received from a variety of sources

Instructions for structural surveys are received by the surveyor from a wide variety of sources. Prospective purchasers of flats or houses may instruct a surveyor in private practice and call at his office for that purpose or the instructions may be received from the purchaser's solicitor in the form of a letter or telephone call. Many instructions are now received following the recommendation of a Building Society so that a nominated surveyor can carry out a single visit to complete both the structural survey and the mortgage valuation. Banks may instruct a surveyor to ascertain that the structure of a house is sound before they purchase it as Trustees and, a

2

growing custom due to increasing capital values and economic change, public companies may instruct a surveyor to inspect houses that they propose to purchase on behalf of employees. In the latter case instructions may be given to a surveyor outside the firm in private practice or to a surveyor within the organisation itself. The instructions received by the surveyor may be basically the same but the particular requirements of each client, taken in conjunction with the age and type of the house, may be completely dissimilar.

Types of instruction

The type of instructions received by the surveyor are likely to be reflected by the locality in which his office or offices are situated. An urban locality with many residential conversions may, for example, lead to a preponderance of flat surveys but generally the surveyor in private practice will receive instructions to carry out surveys in respect of private houses for family use. This, however, does not necessarily mean that there is any degree of similarity in the scope of the client's requirements any more than one house resembles another.

Purchaser's objectives

The surveyor's client may intend to occupy the whole house or he may also, or alternatively, have selected a large house with the idea of forming a flat, either self-contained or by means of furnished rooms, to provide a convenient home for the parents of either himself or his wife. It may be that he intends to provide a flat in part of the house only in order to let it and provide an income to assist discharge a mortgage. Again the surveyor's client may already live in the whole or part of the house as a tenant, either regulated or with the benefit of an agreement or lease for a number of years, and have provisionally agreed with the freeholder to purchase his landlord's interest subject to the advice of his solicitor and surveyor.

The surveyor's client may not be reliant upon mortgage funds for occupation. He or she may be a man or woman of marked views and definite tastes who may wish to completely remodel the interior of a derelict house and who will instruct the surveyor to give them full advice on certain specific points. He may be a man with capital to invest who wishes to purchase a house, convert it and let it in flats and derive an income from the transaction.

New houses, flats and maisonettes

Finally, in our brief list of prospective purchasers, which is by no means an exhaustive one, we might mention the case of two whose requirements warrant such totally different considerations from the normal that separate chapters are devoted to each. First are those prospective purchasers who require surveys of brand new houses or houses of comparatively recent construction, say up to ten years old, which have not perhaps yet had time to develop evidence of serious faults. Secondly are those purchasers requiring surveys of long leasehold flats or maisonettes (or freehold flats or maisonettes in the case of Scotland) where the purchaser's liabilities extend to the structure of the house or block in which the flat or maisonette is situated. The great variety of buildings both old and new means that such surveys are often the most exacting of all.

THE CLIENT'S REQUIREMENTS

Necessary attributes for the surveyor

The client who approaches a surveyor to advise him in respect of a house that he proposes to buy considers his own case to be unique and with some reason. He or she will seek out a surveyor knowing that the surveyor holds himself out to the general public to be skilled in giving advice in matters affecting property. Clearly, therefore, a surveyor who undertakes such work must have the necessary ability to do it since he is being asked to express an opinion on the exercise of his critical faculties. The surveyor's client at the outset will probably not know and certainly not care if the surveyor he chooses is an expert in other fields. He or she will certainly expect, however, that he is competent in the field of structural surveys.

Time and energy, knowledge and experience

Accordingly if the surveyor has doubts either as to whether he can devote the time and energy to the task that it will require, or doubts as to whether his practical experience or knowledge is sufficient in this particular field for the work involved he has the opportunity at this stage to refuse instructions. If the opportunity is not taken at this stage the surveyor may find that he has undertaken an onerous task beyond his capabilities or with insufficient time for its proper performance.

Discharging the duty

The surveyor's contractual liability to his client gives no latitude to the surveyor faced with this situation. The surveyor may perhaps have agreed on an insufficient fee. No part of his full obligation to his client is abated in consequence. A small house needs as high a degree of skill and care from a surveyor as a large one. Having accepted instructions and agreed a fee the surveyor must devote himself entirely to discharging his duty in the light of his client's requirements at whatever inconvenience to himself.

The client's expectations

Everyone will expect a surveyor to have a sound knowledge of building construction and, with this knowledge, to be diligent in finding defects and ascertaining if the defects are serious or not. Most lay clients will have seen the property, possibly on more than one occasion, and may not need a surveyor to point out obvious patent defects that anyone with eyes can see. However, the client will want to know more about the cause of the obvious defects he has seen and to be reassured that no other major defects exist.

More than the obvious

If damp stains are visible to the top floor ceilings most purchasers will expect more from their surveyor than to be told that the roof is leaking. They will want to know why the leakage has occurred. Most house purchasers will read with interest the surveyor's explanation of the major defects found in a house and the reason why they have occurred but if the surveyor stops here his client is likely to become impatient. The most important part of the report should follow.

Monetary liability warnings

The all important point to the surveyor's client is the result of the survey translated into terms of monetary liability not simply for the

4

repair of present patent defects but possibly for the repair of future defects of which only the first signs are apparent. Furthermore, warning is expected about faults in the design, layout, or construction of the property that may indicate latent defects not apparent to the eye but which can only be thoroughly investigated by opening up the structure.

The most exacting part of the surveyor's duties often lies in the last two sentences. Defects in buildings are many and various and the methods of repairing them equally varied. A purchaser reading a report will nod with complete sympathy with a surveyor who refuses to give even an approximate figure for the repair of such matters as bad dry rot since the extent and nature of the repair work required cannot often be ascertained.

The purchaser's wife will probably smile when the surveyor tactfully refuses to name even an approximate figure to cover complete interior redecoration on the grounds that the cost depends on matters of taste and personal preference. Both husband and wife, however, will be united in seeking in the report information as to the cost of repair work which they had not foreseen to the structure, where it is possible for this to be ascertained.

Defects, remedies and costs

The surveyor is expected to be skilled in finding defects, ascertaining why they are present, finding a remedy and, if possible, giving an idea of cost. Not only is the surveyor to be experienced in estimating the approximate cost of repair of defects in dwelling-houses but he must be able to suggest the most effective remedy for the particular defect under review.

An old definition of an engineer is someone "who can do with a shilling what any fool can do with a pound". The surveyor all too often is in the position of the engineer but there are times when he must discard this definition entirely from his mind since to attempt to tamper with bad rising dampness or flaking facing bricks with cheeseparing small amounts may lead to disaster and he must allow for an efficient long term repair ignoring cheap palliatives.

Familiarity with current costs

The matter of arriving at a possible cost for remedying defects is not, as it often thought, purely a matter for a quantity surveyor. As far as case law gives an answer, the courts do not expect a surveyor to be absolutely correct to the nearest few pounds but will take the whole tenor of his advice to his client into account. A surveyor used to repair work will be continually revising costs in his mind as the price of materials rises and labour charges increase so that he will be able to give surprisingly close estimates for common and frequently recurring items such as the renewal of defective pointing and perished flat roof coverings (with a careful proviso as to possible rot being present in the timber below).

Knowledge of houses of different periods

It is at this point that another attribute of a competent surveyor may be pointed out. It is, of course, the knowledge of characteristics of construction of varying types of houses of different periods. To recognise and diagnose the troubles in every type of house from a half-timbered Elizabethan cottage to a Victorian mansion is not solely a matter of textbook study but largely one of experience.

The surveyor's experience

It may well be asked how the surveyor is to acquire such experience without actually carrying out the work himself. Of course, assisting an already experienced surveyor in carrying out surveys on diverse types of property is probably one of the most useful methods of acquiring experience in this field, but equally a general interest in the history of building construction and a sympathetic understanding of the problems encountered in old buildings are vitally important attributes.

Even the most experienced of surveyors will be presented at times with details of building construction from past eras with which he will be unfamiliar. The surveyor's diligence and inquiring mind will be fully brought into play in these circumstances to ascertain the reason for the particular type of construction, to establish whether it is satisfactory or not and to trace the full consequential effects if matters have gone awry. Encounters such as this merely confirm that a surveyor's field of knowledge continues to enlarge throughout his professional career.

Tact and understanding for the occupants

Yet another attribute of the successful surveyor in this field of work lies in the degree of sympathy and understanding he extends to the vendor or the occupants of the property to be surveyed, as well as to the "bricks and mortar". As we shall see, the surveyor must be diligent and conscientious in seeking out all defects and all information necessary for his purpose, but this should not be at the expense of reasonable relations with those in occupation.

While the vendor has the desire to sell his property, the invasion of his privacy by a surveyor and hordes of specialists who wander everywhere can be most unsettling and difficulties will invariably be encountered at times. It is the mark of a good surveyor that his tact and understanding of the occupier's feelings will in the main resolve such difficulties without the unpleasantness which might subsequently damage negotiations between vendor and purchaser.

The reader of this book may be forgiven if he feels that the surveyor, having achieved all that has been set out so far, has done enough. In fact matters from this point on become worse instead of better. Let us go back to our hopeful crowd of purchasers patiently waiting on the first page of this chapter and ask them to step into the surveyor's office one by one for further discussion of their problems.

Likely consequences of purchaser's objectives

The couple who wish to provide a flat for the husband's parents in the basement of the Georgian terraced house have to be told that to comply with the requirements of the local council to remove a Closing Order is not just a matter of a few pounds to remove damp plaster. It will be a matter of some thousands, since the rotten wood flooring, the poor lighting and ventilation and the bad rising dampness are not matters that will disappear on redecoration.

The sitting tenant of part of a house may have to be informed that the demands of the local authority under the latest Housing Acts for premises in multiple occupation may involve him in heavy expenditure.

The lady who proposes to remodel the interior of a small Georgian terraced house and who has the cost of all her projected improvements accurately priced by a local builder, may be taken

6

aback to discover that the drainage system has never been modernised and provided with inspection chambers, air inlets and vent pipes. Also that the local sanitary authority is certain to insist on substantial drainage repairs particularly in view of the number of new sanitary fittings that she proposes to incorporate in the house. Furthermore, that a possible right of light to a window of an adjoining house may inhibit her plans for a new addition.

The investor may find that the shortcomings of the house that he proposes to convert into flats having regard to the requirements of the current Building regulations makes a mockery of his careful calculation of net yield.

Need for knowledge of local and national legislation

The surveyor must be aware of local and national legislation with regard to domestic property and be reasonably conversant with the law relating to such matters as easements of light and drainage. One does not have to look far for other fields of knowledge. The rights and duties of adjoining owners with regard to party structures, the spreading and possible damage from tree roots, a knowledge of planning legislation and an awareness of the beginning and end of the local authorities' obligations with regard to roads and services are matters that at once spring to mind.

It is considered perfectly legitimate for an ordinary lay client to expect the surveyor to give him the sort of information about the property outlined above. It is merely the standard of competence that one would expect from the surveyor who is considered by the lay public and their legal advisers as a specialist in these matters. The client before committing himself to the purchase will obviously not be able to obtain such advice from anyone else.

Costs may be dependent on detailed intentions plans etc

Clearly, however, this does not mean that the surveyor must produce a figure for builders' work on the spot like a conjurer producing a rabbit from a hat. Cases where the extent of the repair work cannot be ascertained have already been referred to, but other obvious cases occur where the interpretation of the local authorities' requirements are a matter of detailed and involved negotiation depending on the particular circumstances of the case, and perhaps requiring plans to be drawn before the extent of the work can be known, for example in the matter of means of escape in case of fire.

Need for full advice

Once the client is given all the requisite information obtained by his surveyor he is then able to decide whether his proposed purchase is a sound one or not. The surveyor seldom knows his client's precise financial circumstances and a thousand pounds may mean little to one man while to another it may mean an almost insurmountable difficulty in the purchase.

Bad bargains

The important point is that whatever the client's means he should be advised as fully and as accurately as the circumstances permit. This is because at the last resort he has the opportunity of withdrawing from the purchase if he cannot negotiate a reduced price in respect of formidable defects revealed by the surveyor, the presence of which hitherto has not been suspected. If he is not advised fully the opportunity for this is lost. The lay client comes to the surveyor for just that information which enables him to be

7

reasonably certain that he is not making a bad bargain and letting himself in for trouble and expense that will cause him endless worry due to his limited financial resources.

The client being a prudent man is ascertaining the facts before committing himself. In the words of Mr. Justice Hilberry in the case of *Rona v. Pearce* (1953):[1]

> "It is highly important to ordinary members of the lay public that a surveyor should use proper care to warn them regarding matters about which they should be warned over the construction or otherwise of a piece of property and that they should be told what are the facts."

Danger of assumptions in regard to clients

The surveyor must be careful never to assume that his client is knowledgeable in matters of property. His client may be expert in other fields but have only the most vague idea of the information that his surveyor can provide. It is therefore vital for the surveyor to put himself into his client's shoes and to assess his client's requirements in the light of all the information given to him.

Need to ascertain as exactly as possible what client requires

It is quite likely that a client will ask for a "structural survey" because a more knowledgeable friend has suggested the name to him but he may have no clear idea of what is involved. An interview with the surveyor will save both parties hours of wasted time and frustration.

The surveyor may jump to conclusions on reading a memorandum of a telephone call taken by his office that "Mr. Smith requires a survey" only to find that Mr. Smith requires some plans prepared. Indeed a misunderstanding of this very nature formed the substance of a case in the Court of Appeal where the surveyor assumed, when his client asked for a survey, that a measured survey and plans were required. Instead it was held that the surveyor should have realised that a report on the structural condition was what was wanted.[2]

On the other hand a message that Mr. Brown requires "a valuation of a house that he proposes to buy" may well on subsequent investigation prove to mean that Mr. Brown, who has been searching for a house for months, is perfectly willing to pay the price asked provided he can be assured that no serious structural defects exist.

FORMULATION OF INSTRUCTIONS

Instructions the basis of the contract

The need for clear instructions cannot be overstressed since this forms the essential basis of the contract between surveyor and client. Failure to spend some time on this important preliminary and to agree in advance the scope of the work to be carried out has caused disputes and loss of goodwill to experienced and competent surveyors and many hours have been spent in the courts arguing on

---

[1] Estates Gazette, 17th October, 1953, p. 380.
[2] *Buckland v. Watts* (1968). Estates Gazette, 30th November, 1968, p. 969.

this point alone. The surveyor must be prepared to assist his client in the formulation of instructions so that they are absolutely clear.

Need for surveyor to assist in settling instructions

The surveyor must realise that his client, quite apart from being able to appreciate what he expects from his surveyor, may well be in no frame of mind to specify his exact instructions. House purchasers are generally under pressure of the need to find and buy a property often from temporary or cramped accommodation and once they are satisfied with the new house and arrange satisfactory terms, it may be more a matter of irritation rather than congratulation for them when their surveyor finds a number of defects hitherto unsuspected. Plans to move the family before a certain time of year may be upset. The impending termination of the lease of their present residence may weigh heavily upon them.

Purchaser usually anxious for "good" report

The average family man may be forgiven for feeling that he has achieved much once he has found a home with the right number of rooms, that has a pleasing aspect, that is conveniently placed for his work and not only satisfies his wife and family as well but is offered to him at a price that he can afford. He may be perplexed and worried by matters that are new to him and by the time he is advised to seek a surveyor it is not difficult to understand that he is desperately anxious for a good report on the house.

It will be a strong minded man who will think out and issue the exact instructions that the occasion demands. Defects in the structure that might inconvenience him years later vanish into insignificance compared with the pressures surrounding him at the moment. He is more likely to be assailed by doubts as to whether a third bedroom will be sufficient for his family than as to doubts affecting the structure.

Once the purchase is completed and he is in occupation, however, the condition of the house becomes of greater importance to him. Troubles, other than financial ones, have generally passed and he is now preoccupied with finding out if the house can be run easily and if it is a sound repository for a large part of his capital.

Instructions to his surveyor several weeks ago when he was beset with trivial worries may be forgotten. His reaction on discovering that the covering to the roof is only likely to last for a few years is more likely to be "My surveyor should have informed me of this" rather than "I wish I had asked my surveyor to advise me as to how long the roof would last."

Need for surveyor to put himself in client's shoes

It is vital for the surveyor to bring a dispassionate mind to bear on his client's problems, think himself well into his client's shoes and envisage the fitness of the structure for his client's benefit for as far ahead as can be reasonably foreseen.

The importance of clear instructions is paramount since lax or sketchy instructions will not relieve the surveyor of his duty to his client. A request simply to "survey the house" will place a heavy obligation on the surveyor and this will certainly not be lessened if the fee is only a small one. This has been ascertained by litigation on several occasions and attention has already been directed to one case.

Interview or telephone discussion

Far from complicating matters some time spent in interviewing

9

his client or speaking to him on the telephone may clarify the surveyor's task. For example the more concrete instructions that may be formulated as a result of an interview could be as follows:

"To advise Mr. Jones as to the structural condition and state of repair of the dwelling-house and detached garage and work-room. To inform him whether any part of the structure is likely to cause him trouble over years to come as far as can be judged, particularly the crack over the staircase. Also:

To test the drainage system but

(a) Not to test the electrical system as Mr. Jones is himself an electrician

(b) Not to include the boundaries as they are worn out and Mr. Jones has obtained a builder's estimate which he is prepared to accept."

From this point the need of clear instructions is evident as a help just as much to the surveyor as to the client. It is then possible either for Mr. Jones to write his instructions on the spot or for the surveyor to confirm them to him in his conditions of engagement.

The value of the surveyor himself seeing his client is obvious. If he cannot arrange an interview he might try to speak to him personally on the telephone. Life may become so hectic in offices today that it is a temptation, to avoid wasting time in the office, to rely on a message taken by any member of the staff. This might simply be:

"Mr. H. Brown of 3 Vielas Road wants a survey of 93 Oak Avenue, Horsehampton. Will we arrange with Vendor Mr. Smith or his Agents Pendonbury Gaster & Co."

This information tells next to nothing. It is dangerous for the surveyor to proceed with the survey under such circumstances both from the point of view of the satisfaction of the client and also from the point of view of professional repute.

It is sometimes thought that a report without any tests or without undue attention to any specific points will meet the case, being a report that simply sets out the result of the surveyor's inspection and which states that no parts of the structure have been opened up and no services tested. The danger here is that the client would possibly have ordered tests of the services had he known of their value.

If ever a survey is carried out on such slender instructions the surveyor should consider that there is a burden on him to take the fullest steps in the matter that he can unless he has instructions to the contrary. Tests should be the rule not the exception in such a case. It is evident that should the client be informed of the value of tests to the services and the costs in each case and decided that he is prepared to forego them, only then is the surveyor's duty in the direction of tests discharged, although he must still of course advise his client as fully as he can on what he sees.

Instructions from solicitors

Instructions to surveyors to carry out surveys of the type covered

Vague or ill-defined instructions incur a heavy duty

by this book are often issued by a solicitor acting on behalf of a client. Solicitors are accustomed to condense a perhaps lengthy and rambling interview with a client into letter form using short crisp sentences and experienced solicitors take pains to see that the surveyor knows accurately the scope of his duties.

A solicitor often issues instructions to a surveyor after an actual interview with his client instead of a telephone conversation. Two solicitors may use totally different methods. The first may give his instructions by telephone giving a good deal of personal details and his client's fears and perhaps prejudices as well. The second may write a letter, often quite a long letter, setting out the information required in numbered paragraphs.

The value of a telephone conversation giving the following information is surely a sufficient rejoinder to the critical surveyor who wonders if all this ground work is necessary or useful.

"Mr. Black is the managing director of a well-known firm of roofing contractors, Messrs. Black and White. He has built up a good quality business from scratch, has direct uncompromising views and has no patience with scamped work.

He once employed a surveyor who let him down and against whom he had a successful action at law. The dispute concerned drains and woodworm. His wife suffers from rheumatism and has a horror of 'a damp house'. He has four daughters, two studying music, one studying to be a barrister and one married to a structural engineer.

He is buying 'The Limes' a large older type of house in Swivelsfield, Hampshire, part of which has been empty for a number of years. The house is listed as being of Architectural and Historic interest, the ceiling in the large ground floor reception room being of particular interest. The searches reveal that there is a closing order on the cottage in the grounds and the preliminary inquiries suggest that there is some dispute with the adjoining owner Major Bloom as to alleged damage caused by tree roots."

Whatever the reaction of the surveyor to this, his attitude is hardly likely to be one of indifference and his attention is sharpened to the salient points that his client is concerned about. If the points are difficult to obtain or if the surveyor's answers are inconclusive, he is likely to receive scant sympathy from Mr. Black or his formidable family.

The dangers of "Quick look" inspections and oral reports

Very often a surveyor is asked to have a quick look at a house or part of a house and advise his client orally or in writing for a relatively low fee as to whether it is structurally sound or not. There are a number of good reasons for refusing to entertain such instructions. The first is that it is impossible to claim that all the major defects have been found since sometimes a sign found after much investigation might be the only symptom of a serious structural failure. For example the case of a 50mm fracture in the party wall of a house found in the roof-space but hidden by new wallpaper in the room below.

11

The second reason is that with an oral report any subsequent dispute depends on the surveyor's word against his client's; a difficult position for a professional man and one that he should not risk. The third reason is that the client's instructions are bound to be incomplete from the very nature of the work so that the onus may well be on the surveyor to show that he explained all the disadvantages of such a survey to his client who nevertheless insisted on the work being carried out on an abridged basis. Usual experience shows that the client invariably wishes, once he has taken up residence, that he had obtained a full report.

Examples of the consequences

The chances of the surveyor's loss of reputation is unduly high under such circumstances. A survey carried out on a Saturday morning in 1½ hours under such instructions at a fee of seven guineas once cost an experienced surveyor £800 in damages.[1] In another case a surveyor was engaged to give a general opinion on a farm but was specifically told not to carry out a detailed survey. On reporting favourably his client purchased and subsequently found dry rot, woodworm and settlement. The court held that a competent surveyor should have been expected to discover dry rot when asked to give a general opinion.[2]

These examples should serve to drive home the point that such defects may only be revealed on the most detailed of investigation and that the surveyor should insist upon being empowered to do the job properly. It should be borne in mind, however, that the oral report is only stated as being bad so far as the ground covered by this book is concerned. There may be occasions in other fields of the surveyor's work where such a report may be justified. Within the field of structural surveys however quick surveys cannot be justified on any grounds and in the writers' view are fraught with danger for the surveyor.

Minimum basic requirements for a structural survey to produce a report which is satisfactory

There can really be no exceptions to the above rule however persuasive clients may be. Each surveyor should be quite clear in his own mind on the minimum basic requirements for a structural survey to produce a report satisfactory for the purpose. Beyond the minimum basic standards it may be, as we have seen, a matter for the client to decide whether to ask for additional work at that stage, for example unusual tests or perhaps advice on the possibility of alterations. Provided the surveyor is armed in advance with proper instructions, however, it may be legitimate for him to curtail his activities in certain circumstances.

Legitimate curtailment

A legitimate example of this may be when a client says "carry out a full structural survey – but if you find any signs of dry rot, I will not purchase in any circumstances as I have had an unfortunate experience before". The surveyor may be surprised at such dogmatism in his client but it would be sensible to cut short the operation in the event of finding dry rot and render an account on a reduced fee basis.

[1] *Sinclair v. Bowden Son & Partners* (1962), Estates Gazette, 14th July, 1962, p. 95.
[2] *Sincock v. Bangs* (1952), Estates Gazette, 16th August, 1952, p. 134.

Unacceptable curtailment

This procedure can be contrasted with the client who may say "have a quick look at the house for me and see if it is worth proceeding". The surveyor has a quick look and if he finds major defects he says so and his client looks elsewhere. If, however, on his quick look he finds very little wrong, many a client will proceed to purchase without having the "full structural survey" the instructions for which the surveyor had perhaps unwisely assumed would be coming his way after the "preliminary quick look".

The surveyor may find himself in some difficulty later on, if major defects appear in the house, in establishing precisely what he undertook to do for his fee and whether he entirely fulfilled his client's instructions. Experience shows that such arrangements are seldom documented in a satisfactory manner and in these circumstances the surveyor may find himself at a severe disadvantage.

THE "CONSUMERS" VIEW OF STRUCTURAL SURVEYS

General comments on surveyor's work

As home ownership has grown and news items relating to surveyor's activities have become more frequent comments are more often than not of an unfavourable nature. When a client considers he has been let down and manages to secure press or TV attention to his grumble the great many successful surveys, probably saving purchasers considerable sums of money, which are carried out, tend to be overlooked.

"Which?" articles "Getting a House Surveyed"
February 1970

The Consumer's Association however, through its monthly magazine "Which?" provides an overall and balanced view of what the public think about surveyor's activities.

The magazine first considered structural surveys in February 1970 in an article entitled "Getting a House Surveyed". At that time it found that 4 out of every 5 of the 1750 members sampled were pleased with the service that their surveyor provided. Even so some of the advice given to members in that article appeared to surveyors as somewhat odd.

For example it suggested that prospective purchasers should ask the surveyor if the purchase price is fair, which is really a matter of valuation, and indicated that a rewired electrical installation did not need testing when a surveyor would be wise to say that it did. Although there were also some ill-considered comments about surveyors not liking to be surveyed, in general the advice given to members as to their requirements approximated reasonably well to the views of surveyors on what could in the circumstances be provided. In particular the article advised against asking surveyors to do "quick look" surveys, advice which curiously is not carried forward into more recent articles.

May 1983

The most recent update on "Getting a House Surveyed" in May 1983 drew on the experience of some 3500 members who had moved. About 40% of the sample had had either a limited or full structural survey. Quotations from members sampled included "no point in spending a lot of money if all it does is recommend the engagement of other specialists" and "having seen a number of surveys they are not worth the money". Of those who had a survey 20%, about 28 of the sample, found further unreported faults in their property after moving in. Most common faults found later related to the plumbing, the roof and the windows with damp and electrical wiring problems being encountered to a slightly lesser extent.

"Which?" advice

Nevertheless the article recommended members to have a full structural survey except in the case of a fairly new property where it was considered that a "limited scope" survey would suffice. A study of Chapter 12 will provide sufficient reasons it is hoped to enable a surveyor to convince a prospective purchaser of such a property that this is not sound advice and that a full survey is really necessary to be of value.

The article stressed that it was not wise to rely on the report as a "legal document," presumably meaning that it should not be treated as a form of insurance, but to consider it rather as a means of alerting the purchaser to problems and for negotiating a reduction in the purchase price. Surveyors would fully endorse this advice to purchasers.

Comments in "Moving House" article of April 1987

In a more general article on "Moving House" in April 1987 which also dealt with estate agent's services and raising finance, one in four of the 500 sampled thought surveyors were not good value for money. Typical comments were that reports failed to mention major or obvious faults, reports were too short and lacking in detail, comments tended to be "non-commital", that they had too many exclusion clauses and that they were expensive.

Other references to surveyor's performance appear from time to time in "Which?" magazine since the Consumer's Association run what is called a "Which? Personal Service" dealing with members' problems some of which inevitably arise out of structural surveys. Recent problems have related to extensive woodworm infestation missed by a surveyor and severe rot in windows. It is interesting however to note that in August 1987 when reporting on problems encountered by a purchaser who relied on a mortgage valuation, it stated that it was still "worth spending the extra for a full structural survey".

"How surveyors measure up" article of February 1989

The most interesting article, however, for surveyors in "Which?" magazine appeared in February 1989 entitled "How Surveyors Measure Up." It contained advice to members of the Association on what to look for when choosing a surveyor and how to instruct him once selected and tells members what they can expect to receive from a mortgage valuation, a House Buyers report and a full structural survey.

The article sensibly makes the point first that there is no sense in proceeding if from the purchaser's own inspection he can see walls out of plumb, soft mortar, slates or tiles missing, cracks in the brickwork, signs of damp and "signs of leaks in the roof space" and that these would cause worry or that he did not have the financial resources to deal with them. It is not thought here that many prospective purchasers would venture into the roof space to look for leaks. They would probably be more visible on the top floor ceiling anyway and this was probably what was meant.

The article concludes in the case of mortgage valuations that purchasers would be taking a gamble to rely on the information in such reports as there is no "guarantee" that the property is structurally sound since they are based on a limited inspection. The article suggests that if the purchaser wishes to have more information than that provided by a mortgage valuation then a "home-buyers" report might be considered.

It points out that these are not available for old or large properties or purpose built or converted flats, overlooking the fact that even when the article was published a separate "Flat Buyers" report had been available for some time. It does indicate however that these abbreviated forms of report come on standard forms and are intended to provide concise, readable, fairly detailed accounts of properties where parts are reasonably accessible but do not provide detailed information on the services or minor faults. The main advantage to prospective purchasers as seen by "Which?" would seem to be that abbreviated reports of this type should be more readily understood. Against this they were considered to be not much cheaper than a full structural survey. Chapter 13 will suggest cogent reasons why this should be so.

The "Which?" view of what a structural survey should contain

From a full structural survey the article indicates that a prospective purchaser should obtain a detailed account of the structure, any major and minor defects and the likely cost of urgent repairs. It should cover all the main features from the roof to the foundations, information about garden fences and walls, any outbuildings and trees which might cause damage. As in earlier advice to members it stresses that a full structural survey is an inspection not a "test" and that while the surveyor should comment on items like the wiring, plumbing, central heating and so on he will not actually test them.

Where the surveyor would perhaps part company with the "Which?" advice relates to consulting a specialist. The article seems to say that if the surveyor thinks that the house needs to be rewired or that a new central heating installation needs to be installed the prospective purchaser should be told to consult a specialist. Here it is suggested that employing a specialist for a test would be a waste of money. It is, however, those in between cases, "not so old" or "near new" installations where the surveyor would advise consulting a specialist for a test as well as those new installations where doubts may exists on the reputability of the installer. Nevertheless the article stresses the importance of not hesitating to have tests carried out if the surveyor advises that they should be.

"Which?" concludes that a full survey should give a comprehensive picture and while it finds them particularly suitable for older properties it also points out that newer properties can still have their faults caused by bad design, neglect and so on. Whether a prospective purchaser obtains all that is suggested should be provided by a full structural survey depends, so it is said, upon choosing a good surveyor.

"Which?" on choosing a surveyor

"Which?" puts forward 10 tips to help the prospective purchaser find the "right" surveyor to do the job which is wanted and to instruct him accordingly. The 10 tips can conveniently be divided into two groups of 4 and 5 respectively with one to conclude.

The first group deals with the suitability of the surveyor to do the job. It is said he should preferably be recommended, he should be qualified, he should practice in the area where the property is situated and he should be insured. As to qualifications the article lists four surveyors' organisations and one for engineers but not the RIBA but does not distinguish between the different divisions within the RICS. On insurance it points out that members of both the RICS and the ISVA are required to have indemnity insurance. It is not thought that any surveyor would quibble with the advice comprising these 4 tips on choosing a surveyor.

On settling the instructions it suggests that members should seek out a surveyor who is prepared to do the job which is wanted, including if necessary commenting on the feasibility of any intended alterations to the property or commenting on special concerns, for example damp or means of escape. The surveyor should also be one who is prepared to explain and agree what he will provide for the estimated cost which it is suggested should be itemised to cover fee, VAT and expenses. The timing of the work should be established. This latter point is covered in the article by suggesting that the prospective purchaser complains about any delay but it is obviously better to agree when the inspection can be carried out and, barring undue difficulties, when the report can be expected to be delivered. These aspects on instructions cover another 5 of the tips leaving only the final piece of advice to be mentioned which is as equally sensible as the others and suggests that the instructions should be agreed in writing.

Other "Which?" views on vendor surveys and the measure of damages in negligence cases

Before leaving the "Which?" articles it is worth mentioning that the Consumer's Association, in its aim to simplify and speed the house buying and selling process, is a strong supporter of vendors having surveys carried out and these being made available to the prospective purchasers. It has been advocating these for some years and sees support for the idea in the more recent Law Commission proposal that vendors should be made responsible for disclosing all known facts about the property being sold thus reversing the current legal principle of "caveat emptor", let the buyer beware.

The Association recognises that a lot of work would need to be done before such proposals could be put into effect but it has also over the years investigated warranty and insurance schemes which could be tied into vendor surveys and are said to be available in other countries. These schemes on a superficial level are not unattractive but whether they ever get off the ground here remains to be seen.

So far as carrying out a survey for the vendor is concerned this would not necessarily be greatly different to carrying out one for a prospective purchaser although it would probably be necessary for the vendor to offer far more in the way of facilities for opening up than is generally the case on surveys for prospective purchasers. Indeed on the latter, positive obstruction by the vendor is not an unusual experience for the surveyor. As to the report, since it is intended to be shown to purchasers it too ought not to be unduly different. One can however envisage difficulties being experienced with some vendors who would possibly not like what they are paying for if the advice was unfavourable to the property they were trying to sell.

Another objective of the Consumer's Association is to change the way damages are calculated when awarded against a surveyor when found to be negligent. The current law dealing with the measure of damages will be discussed fully in Chapter 14 but the Consumer's Association wish to see the basis changed from the difference between the price paid for the property and its value if it had been correctly reported upon to the actual cost of repairs.

It has been demonstrated many times in Court hearings that while the cost of repairs obviously has to be taken into account, and may indeed be the appropriate amount in some instances, more often than not the award of that sum would put the aggrieved party in a far better position financially than he was before he contracted to have the survey carried out. It would seem that this objective could only be achieved if it was decided that in cases of negligence on residential property it would be appropriate to award punitive damages, possibly as an example to the rest. This seems unlikely to find favour even though the present rules cause hardship to house purchasers of limited means who cannot cope with the full cost of repairs and are only awarded the difference in value as damages.

Damages for negligence contrasted with negotiations when defects found on survey

The situation on damages can be compared with what happens when a prospective purchaser obtains a report which says that the property has defects. Normally by the time a prospective purchaser has found the house he wants and wishes it to be surveyed he has already decided that he is prepared to pay the negotiated price, subject to there being no serious defects of which he is unaware. The report will show whether there are any serious hidden defects and on its receipt the purchaser will either wish to re-open negotiations with the vendor using the report as a basis to reduce the price, or alternatively, in the case of a comparatively favourable report, will decide to accept the cost of putting right the defects found. On completion of his report, the surveyor may feel impelled to stress the need for the former course of action in some cases while accepting, in other cases, the client's decision to bear the cost of putting right the defects.

Surveyor's position on subsequent negotiations when defects found

It is probably best left to each surveyor to decide, in the circumstances of each case, whether at the time of settling the instructions he should explain to his client that if he finds hidden defects estimated to cost £10,000 to put right, it does not necessarily indicate that the purchase price should be reduced by that amount. Demand for the property may suggest that even with the knowledge of the defects ascertained, a purchaser may still be found at a figure much nearer the negotiated price than £10,000 below. Misconceptions should perhaps be cleared from purchasers' minds at the time the instructions are settled but it must be admitted that some purchasers are quite capable of asking for a reduction of £10,000 in the above

17

circumstances and getting it. Boldness can be rewarded when demand is slack and the vendor is desperate to sell, but it is questionable whether a surveyor would wish to become involved in negotiations of this nature. The risk of a purchaser losing a house under such circumstances is one for the client alone.

Client's presence during survey

Many members in the samples taken by the Consumer's Association stressed the importance of both accompanying the surveyor on his inspection and of discussing his report with him before acting on his recommendations. In regard to the former suggestion, perhaps there are surveyors who can chat to their clients and carry out a structural survey at the same time but they must be few and far between. Perusing the contents of the following chapters will, it is thought, suggest that the surveyor has quite enough to do coping with the survey without the distraction of the client's presence.

Value of client's visit at end of survey and later study of report

The client's presence would be one more distraction among many and experience suggests that it is the client who tires first on a structural survey. What is sensible, however, is for the client to visit the property at the end or towards the end of the surveyor's inspection so as to have some of the salient features of what will appear in the report indicated to him on site and so as to facilitate his understanding of the written word. Even more ideal is for this to be followed by the client's study of the report and a further visit to the surveyor's office to discuss the recommendations. There is much to be said for these two meetings with the client, first following the inspection and then secondly the submission of the report and providing an opportunity to iron out all points of difficulty that may arise. Given favourable circumstances, the wise surveyor will arrange for such meetings at the time the instructions are formulated and budget in his fee for the necessary time to be made available.

Long range clients and some difficulties arising from meetings

It should also be said, however, that lack of direct contact between the client and his surveyor does not imply apathy in either party. Many surveys are carried out at long range on the instructions of solicitors due to an obvious geographical difficulty in communication. Contact with the client can vary from the plain sensible and straightforward questions from a prospective purchaser that are already clearly relevant to the operation in hand, to the reiterated insistence on guarantees over the next ten years or so that reveal the need for a psychologist rather than a surveyor. There also comes a point where an interview with the client becomes difficult since this is used as an attempt to open a discussion over a wide range of other topics not mentioned before i.e. cost of alterations, furnished letting values, and so forth. It is always best therefore for the basic survey to be completed before the surveyor's energies are taken up in fending off such questions.

THE "PROFESSIONAL" VIEW OF STRUCTURAL SURVEYS

Up to now consideration has been given as to how surveyors

themselves have developed the professional service of carrying out the structural surveys required by the growth of home ownership over the last 40 years. Mention has also been made as to how this service has had to be tailored to the views of the courts on surveyors' liability to their clients and the views of the recipients of the service represented by the reports of the sampling carried out by the Consumer's Association.

The RICS Guidance Note

There is another source of authority which needs to be mentioned and that is the professional body representing surveyors. The Royal Institution of Chartered Surveyors came rather late in the day to the task of providing guidance to its members carrying out structural surveys of residential property even though the need for it was evident by reason of the many Court cases of negligence and the necessity in consequence to bolster the reputation of the surveying profession in the eyes of the public. Possibly spurred by the substantial rise in the premiums payable for surveyor's professional indemnity insurance the RICS Guidance Note on structural surveys was first produced in 1979 some 15 years after the first edition of this book was published and 6 years after the second. A second edition of the Guidance Note followed in February 1985.

Although not claimed as such must be considered mandatory

Produced by the Building Surveyor's Division of the RICS the Guidance Note claims to be just that and not a RICS Statement of Standard Practice, as might have been supposed. However, despite the words printed in the Note there can be little doubt that the courts would take the advice given and the views expressed as representing the minimum standard which the Institution would expect from its members in this field.

Accordingly any surveyor whose work is called into question and who is found to have performed below the standard set out in the Guidance Note would, it is considered, be in serious danger of being found to have been negligent. In other words the Guidance Note, despite any protestations to the contrary, has become mandatory.

The 1985 Second Edition of the Guidance Note takes the form of a slim booklet of some 20 pages which, nevertheless, contains a wealth of valuable advice regarding the settling of the client's instructions, the conduct of the survey itself and the preparation of the report, including a section at the end on leasehold residential property.

Mention will be made of the Guidance Note where appropriate in this edition by way of emphasis but whereas the Note provides a skeleton framework the intention here is to produce the necessary detailed advice to enable the professional task to be performed in a complete and satisfactory manner for the client.

THE FEE

Having agreed on the scope of the clients' requirements the next item to consider is the question of the fee since it is essential for various reasons, which will be discussed, for this to be agreed in advance.

Earlier advice on fee charging for survey work

Even in the days when a Scale of Professional charges was published by the Royal Institution of Chartered Surveyors structural surveys were to be carried out for a "fee by arrangement according to the circumstances". This was clearly wise since the variety of clients' requirements and types of buildings is infinite and has not been invalidated by the abolition of the Scale in 1982. However, it is as well for the surveyor to work out his own approximate basic charges since very often he will be asked to quote a fee at short notice.

Three methods of assessing cost of work

The amount of fee that each surveyor will charge will differ even for the same work. One surveyor's fees are found to vary from another's by the value he places on his time and will have regard also to his overheads, not only typing and secretarial salaries, but all that it costs him to run an office so that he has an organisation behind him while he is away. It is suggested that there are three ways which the surveyor might consider as possible methods for assessing the cost of the work.

1. By a rule of thumb method of so much per room.
2. By a percentage basis of the price on the same lines as a scale fee for, say, a valuation on the same property.
3. By a charge of so much per day or hour spent on the job.

1) By a rule of thumb method of so much per room

The advantages of this method are that it is easy to apply and that it enables the surveyor to approximate his fee to the size of the house. By number of rooms is meant number of bedrooms and reception rooms. Clearly, however, a disadvantage of this method is that two houses of the same number of rooms may be very different from the surveying point of view.

A nine room modern detached house may be an easier subject than a nine room rambling Victorian house where investigation of the structure may be a more difficult matter. The fee on this basis would be the same. This method therefore does presuppose that the surveyor knows that the houses in the locality of the survey are of much the same character.

2) By a percentage basis of the price on the same lines as a fee for a valuation

This also is a possible method but suffers from the disadvantage that a house in an exclusive area in strong demand would attract a high fee for the survey, while a similar house in a poor district would attract a much lower fee. It may well be maintained, however, that the higher fee is compensation for the added risk involved when a more costly house is surveyed since the measure of damages in case of negligence would be greater.

It is, however, a method of charging which brought forth complaints from members of the Consumers' Association who were sampled for the "Which?" report on structural surveys. It is strange that clients who will willingly pay a fee based on price for a valuation consider the same sort of basis of charging for a structural survey unreasonable, but it remains a fact that many do so. Of course, in discussing his fee with a client the surveyor need not necessarily quote the basis on which the calculation is made although it will be found that many purchasers do wish to have this sort of information.

Even if the surveyor is not told the asking price of the house to be surveyed, which might and indeed does sometimes preclude a quotation of a fee on this basis (for example a survey for a sitting tenant where the price may be the subject of negotiation or, if agreed, may reflect special circumstances), he should seek to have this information. A house known to be cheap for its type and area immediately puts a surveyor on guard and a valid argument against this suggested method is that there is no reason why the cheaper house in these circumstances should be the subject of a lesser fee as far as a structural survey is concerned.

3) By a charge of so much per hour spent on the job

This method is generally acknowledged as by far the fairest to both the client and the surveyor. Ideally a rate is agreed between the surveyor and client and the charge applied subsequently on the number of days or hours spent on the job by the surveyor himself, including of course all the time spent arranging for the survey, preparing the report and interviewing the client perhaps both before and after the survey as well as the number of hours spent at the property.

This method of charging is often acceptable where the surveyor is well known to his client or where, for example, he is often engaged by the same organisation to carry out surveys of different properties at frequent intervals and where the client is aware of the approximate level of charge for each survey. The agreement of a rate on its own could be dangerous, however, where the client is not known to the surveyor and if the surveyor failed to indicate the likely length of time which the work would involve.

Many inexperienced clients have no idea of the length of time which the operation may take and three hours on site for a small house can easily turn into a seven or eight hour operation when interviews, travelling and writing the report are included. An account four times the size of what was expected is not likely to be paid with pleasure. It is far better for the surveyor, in these circumstances, to find out in talking to his client all he can about the property and then to estimate in his mind the likely time involved and applying his normal hourly or daily rate quote a total inclusive fee.

Difficulty may sometimes be experienced in calculating a suitable hourly rate but it is essential for every surveyor in practice to be able to do this. The normal method is to determine overall annual net costs and then to add a percentage. Net costs must obviously include all the back up support required by the surveyor. Another suggested method is to base the daily charge on 1 per cent of gross salary. For example the daily charge to the client of an assistant earning £15,000 per annum would be £150, equivalent to £25 per hour if a productive day of 6 hours is worked.

This latter method has the merit of simplicity and can be related to all levels of gross income at any particular time having regard to the person carrying out the survey. It does, however, assume a reasonable size of organisation behind the surveyor by way of an office and supporting staff and allows for a reasonable return. It may not, accordingly, be entirely appropriate for very

21

small or very large organisations or for a surveyor practising on his own.

Indeed it is in the realm of charges that a rather facetious comment can be amply confirmed and entirely justified. One of the "Which?" reports said that the Association's members had found that the charge for a structural survey seemed to depend as much on the surveyor as on the property. Quite so, but the reason for that, it is suggested, should be obvious, particularly at a time when there is so much criticism of charges. The important aspect from the surveyor's point of view is that the work should be remunerative in its own right.

Need for ability to quote fee   If a new client asks for a total fee to be quoted beforehand and the surveyor replies that he is unable to state one since he does not know how complicated the job will be or how long the job will take him, this will produce an unhappy effect. The client is justified in asking how much the surveyor will charge so that he can budget for the overall expense. It is important to be able to say what the fee will be and not to be able to do so is apt to make the client feel that the surveyor is either unbusinesslike or is not used to this type of work.

It is appreciated that all three methods are open to criticism on the grounds that the calculation of the fee in advance is arbitrary or approximate, but the writers consider that the advantage of being able to quote a fee as soon as possible outweighs this by far. After some years of experience a surveyor soon becomes adept at knowing what his charges should be and some irregularities at the beginning will soon be ironed out.

Confusion between fees for structural surveys and mortgage valuations   The advantage of settling a basic charge for survey work in advance is not only that the surveyor's remuneration is agreed but also that any misconceptions in the client's mind in regard to the proper fee to be paid for a survey are removed. Such misconceptions do arise and it is understandable that some clients confuse fees for mortgage valuations with structural survey fees.

Bargaining on fees   It also removes the temptation from the client to indulge in the rather unhappy bargaining on the amount of the fee which sometimes arises when the account is rendered. The surveyor will find himself in a weak position if that happens. The time for bargaining, if there is to be any, is before the survey is carried out. If the surveyor quotes a fee for a small house and finds a castle he will have to accept the monetary loss philosophically, but the greater disadvantage is that he will have estimated the time spent in his dairy and possibly by the time he comes to carry out the work he may have other engagements immediately following and have to cancel them. The client may require his report before a certain date, for example before a sale by auction, and other visits some time later may not be possible.

Danger of cutting work to fee   The result may be that the surveyor will try to complete the survey in insufficient time and this will result in hurried and unsatisfactory work which will not be to the benefit of his client and indeed may result in neglect of duty to his client. However, if the initial procedure on formulating and agreeing the transaction is carried out as recommended this temptation should not arise except on very rare occasions. If such a temptation should arise owing to a misunderstanding or a mistake on the fee the surveyor will be well advised to remember that his duty to his client remains the same irrespective of the amount of the fee. If the surveyor skimps the work he cannot claim that his liability is limited by reason of a low fee.

Specialists' charges

Equally important in finding a suitable method to arrive at the total cost to the client is the question of fees of the heating, drainage, electrical and any other specialists. These will be engaged constantly by the surveyor and he must be able to have some idea of the cost of employing such specialist firms in arriving at a total cost, or be willing to ascertain the cost if his client wishes.

For larger houses, particularly country houses or large town mansions, the surveyor is well advised to employ specialist firms of good repute who are used to this work and well able to deal with it, or recommend such firms for his client to instruct. Each specialist firm will concentrate on its own particular field and should render a written report. This will relieve the surveyor of much worry and will result in a better overall survey. The fact that such firms should include an estimate with their reports is also of obvious value.

Knowledge of local builders

For smaller houses the surveyor may find it easier to make other arrangements. He may come to an understanding with a local builder for the loan of one of his men to assist with the drains who will bring the necessary equipment with him. At the same time some surveyors take their own electrical testing equipment while others prefer to use a specialist firm on all occasions. The advantage of knowing a number of builders in different localities is that their approximate charges for erecting ladders and providing men can be readily estimated.

Specialist contractors

Some surveyors and their clients take advantage of the fact that many of the specialist firms dealing with dry rot and woodworm control will carry out an inspection of residential property free of charge and provide a report with an estimate for the eradication of rot or the treatment of woodworm if necessary. They do this in the hope of obtaining work but although the presence of a representative of a specialist contractor on the survey can provide a useful extra pair of eyes, it should be stressed that his presence does not relieve the surveyor of any of his responsibilities.

However, should an attack of dry rot be found, the extent of which is ascertainable, or woodworm be present then an estimate for the necessary repairs or treatment can at least be obtained comparatively quickly. If dry rot is found the full extent of which cannot be discovered without works of exposure then an estimate for these works can be obtained which might be to the benefit of the vendor who will normally need to know the cost of putting matters right before he can hope to sell his property.

The formal agreement in advance of survey

Having agreed on the scope of the client's requirements and the fee for the work, the surveyor should now set up the formal agreement as the last step before making arrangements to carry out the survey. However, whether a letter is sent that confirms the terms of the contract or a covering letter encloses a set of Conditions of Engagement that are, perhaps, standard, but amplified or amended to suit the particular circumstances of the case, these are the terms upon which a Court will rely to decide whether a surveyor has fulfilled his duty to his client or not. Accordingly, the establishment of documentary evidence of the agreement as to what the surveyor is or is not to do in advance of the work being carried out is vital. Obtaining the client's signature to the terms of the engagement may be thought a part of this.

Earlier requirements by insurance companies

A primary requirement is for the surveyor to make it clear to his client that the inspection will be a visual one, that no opening up will be carried out, and accordingly he cannot be held responsible for reporting on parts of the building that he cannot see. Up until the late 1970's, it was customary for each surveyor to add a clause along the following lines at the end of his report;

> "We have not inspected woodwork or other parts of the structure which are covered, unexposed or inaccessible and we are therefore unable to report that such parts of the property are free of rot, beetle or other defects."

Provisions of the Unfair Contract Terms Act 1977

The exact wording of the clause would be agreed with the particular insurance company engaged by the surveyor to provide cover for professional negligence but, whatever the exact nature of wording employed, the procedure was deemed to be unsound with the advent of the Unfair Contract Terms Act 1977. Since the passing of this Act, it has been considered that, so to avoid any risk of the above clause being thought unfair, it should now be included in the surveyor's Conditions of Engagement as part of the contract. Whether the clause would, in fact, be considered unfair, has never been tested but if any client does in fact consider it so, he has at least the opportunity of cancelling his instructions. The reason for the need for agreement on Conditions of Engagement in advance can be a matter for explanation to the client and reference to this aspect can of course feature in either the covering letter or in the Conditions themselves if desired.

Use of 3 m ladder

One particular advantage of agreement in advance on the Conditions of Engagement is that they can set out the extent to which the surveyor can complete his visual inspection with the use of his 3 metre ladder. This provides an answer to any complaint if the surveyor is unable to report upon the condition of a high back addition roof, for example, where access is impossible except by long extension ladders. It is also as well for the surveyor to make it clear that he is not in the removal business and where vast or heavy items of Victorian furniture are concerned, he cannot be expected to move them. The same clause should cover the contents of fitted cupboards.

Floor coverings

Since the use of fitted floor coverings and carpets is now almost universal, there are many cases where the surveyor will be lucky if he sees any sight of floorboards at all and he should take care to include a condition that he cannot be expected to raise such coverings in the course of his survey. The absence of such a condition could lead to misunderstanding. Some clients genuinely think that the surveyor will rip up coverings to see what is underneath and that he should be oblivious of any wails of despair from the vendor.

Testing of services

Whether and which tests of services are to be carried out should be agreed beforehand and the appropriate clause inserted in the Conditions. For services not to be tested, it is advisable to say what will be done by way of visual inspection and that advice will be included as to whether further investigation is considered necessary.

The fee

The fee should be specified together with whether it is exclusive or inclusive of VAT and whether there is provision for additional charges for expenses such as travelling, meals, and the like.

Exclusion clause

A "for your eyes only" clause should be included to ensure that the surveyor's responsibility for his report extends only to the client to whom it is addressed.

Flats

If the property forms part of a block of flats it is necessary for it to be agreed that only the particular flat itself will be inspected together with roofs, elevations and common parts which are reasonably accessible and that it does not form part of a normal survey to inspect other flats without prior agreement.

Need for positive attitude in setting out Conditions of Engagement

The possibilities on what to include in the Conditions and what to leave out are almost limitless and each surveyor has to use his own judgement as to the length and content of any standard Conditions of Engagement. Whatever the format employed, the note struck by the surveyor should be a positive one in that he "will be pleased to carry out ... etc." rather than starting off the relationship by including too long a list of gloomy statements telling the client what he cannot do rather than what he can achieve by visual inspection without pulling the property apart and upsetting the vendor.

"Blanket" conditions can obviate need for many individual exclusions

Some surveyors go to great lengths, quite literally, in the documentation to attempt to cope with every type of contingency that might be encountered but it is believed that the Conditions of Engagement should preferably and, if possible, be kept fairly short. An obvious item of doubt as to inclusion might relate to the condition of the interiors of chimney flues. Problems have been encountered from emissions of gases and it is understandable that the surveyor who has experienced problems in this area will specify that he cannot answer for the interiors of such flues in his Conditions of Engagement. It is considered however, that this should be covered sufficiently by the general clause that he cannot be held responsible for reporting on parts of the structure which are "covered, unexposed or inaccessible ...". The same might be said for foundations, the interior of the cavity in cavity walls and structural elements behind panelling.

Limitations as to provision of repair costs

A general blanket condition of this nature would not however, suffice in some other instances where there might be specific agreed instructions from the client to provide an approximate estimate, for example, for repairs. The surveyor might wish to indicate the limitations involved in providing such a figure and sensibly make this a condition of its inclusion in the report. If a property has been newly built or recently converted, the surveyor might wish to have included in his fee an amount to cover attendance at Statutory Authorities to check on details and approvals. On the other hand if, as in normal circumstances, no attendance at building control and other local authority offices is likely to be required, he may wish to include a condition to the effect that if such attendance should prove to be necessary, an additional charge will be made to be agreed in advance at the time.

Chapter 2

The Preliminary Arrangements for the Survey

CONTENTS

ARRANGEMENTS WITH THE VENDOR

Time constraints

Once instructions have been accepted and terms settled the next step is to make the arrangements for the survey. The length of time to be allotted to the task must be judged as closely as possible having regard to the information so far received, with an adequate margin for travelling and meals. Inattention to such matters will lead to an exhausting experience which might have been avoided by a few moments of thought to details.

Another factor often overlooked is that in winter months the work may be severely limited by the number of hours of daylight. In summer any error in arrangements can be overcome by the surveyor staying later to finish the work, but in winter when darkness begins to descend about 4 p.m. the surveyor may be seriously inconvenienced if he neglects to consider this factor.

Presumably, of course, he will arrange to complete his inspection of the outside of the house first before he proceeds to the interior if there is any danger of the light fading, but this may not meet the case entirely, since there are many occasions when some interior detail of construction calls for a further look at the exterior so that a complete picture is formed in the surveyor's mind.

Need to advise vendor of estimated time

The question of the amount of time that the survey will take will also be important from the point of view of making arrangements with the owner or occupier of the house. It is irritating to arrive with a carload of specialists and equipment to be confronted by the lady of the house at the door saying that she is going out in 15 minutes time since the other surveyor (presumably from a Building Society) "only took ten minutes".

Investigations and tests

The owner of the house must be advised about whatever steps the surveyor proposes to take with regard to investigation of the structure and testing services. The importance of this last matter cannot be overstated. The owner of a property has the right to expect a surveyor to exercise reasonable care in his test or investigations and may claim for damage caused, in breach of such duty. The duty of a surveyor to take reasonable care when entering on the land of another cannot be ignored or shrugged off on the grounds that the client has asked for tests to be carried out. The best illustration is on the vexed matter of the water test of drains.

Water test for drains

It has long been considered by a number of surveyors, for opinion is divided, that a water test, when applied to a house drain of some age, is unnecessarily stringent and may cause damage. The reason advanced for this is that under normal use the flow of waste or soil in a house drain may never exceed one-quarter bore so that although the drain may settle slightly over the years or the cement joints of the sections of pipe become frail and corroded nevertheless the drain is sound so far as normal everyday use is concerned.

With the application of a water test, however, when the drain is filled full bore with a standing head of water in the inspection chamber, it is thought that the strain is increased on the drain to such an extent that the frail joints may fracture, thus causing damage. Against this may be put forward the answer that the water test is no more damaging than the result of a blockage in the drain which may happen at any time and that in any case the owner of a house is the recipient of a favour in being told that his drains are defective since leakage of water from frail joints in a drain may have very serious results in causing damage to foundations.

Justification for water test It may also be argued that if a house drain were in such a poor state that it could be damaged by a water test then the contention that it is not defective prior to the test is an academic one only. Unless the drain of a house complies with Building Regulation requirements at any one time it cannot be said that the drain is fully sound. If the jointing material between sections of drain fails under test it must have already been so porous and rotten that it would be unrealistic not to have called the drain defective prior to the test.

Warnings to vendors However the matter is viewed, the surveyor must give consideration to all possible dangers, however remote, and the recommended course is that he should fully warn the owner of the house that he intends to survey as to the full extent of any tests or investigations that he proposes to carry out that might cause such damage. It is not enough for the surveyor to say to the vendor that he proposes to carry out a water test to the drainage system since the vendor will not understand the full implications of this.

Obtaining the vendor's permission for opening up and tests The surveyor is wise to warn the vendor of the possible dangers of such a test under certain circumstances and this will involve a description of the process carried out. Some surveyors keep duplicated descriptions of the tests which they normally carry out so that these are readily available for dispatch along with the request to the vendor for his permission. Consent to tests or investigations likely to cause damage such as lifting areas of floorboards, the removal of expensive panelling or the testing of disused plumbing over expensively decorated rooms should be obtained in writing.

The need to obtain such permission is curiously omitted from the RICS Guidance Note. This states that the vendor should be informed of the extent to which the surveyor proposes to lift fitted carpets and floorboards and test drains, services etc. Merely informing the vendor and explaining the extent of the proposed testing in the detail as recommended here does not mean that the vendor will appreciate the full significance. If difficulties arise later the vendor will say that he did not appreciate all that was intended and if he had known he would not have given his permission. Obtaining that permission does not automatically absolve the surveyor from either risk or liability; that will depend on the reasonableness of his conduct on the test; but it will put him in a much better position.

At the same time as writing to obtain the permission the opportunity should be taken to request the vendor to have ready for inspection any plans of the property, guarantees for any work carried out and any planning or Building Regulation consents for any building work carried out.

The practical difficulty of warning the vendor adequately would seem to be that the whole operation is made to sound so terrifying as to lead the average house owner to withhold automatically his consent. In fact, however, it is encouraging to experience the fact that a large number of vendors know about water tests to drains and are cheerfully prepared to accept the risk of a test. Many owners, quite apart from adopting difficult attitudes about investigations, are quite willing, if approached tactfully, to strip floor coverings and help lift an occasional floorboard as well. One vendor on a survey became so enthusiastic that he crawled under a narrow sub-floor space and could only be extracted with some difficulty.

The surveyor's duty to leave matters as he finds them

The surveyor's duty of care extends to leaving matters at the property as he found them or, if that is not possible, of warning the owner or occupier of anything that may have happened. For example in an empty property in winter-time the plumbing may be drained down. If the surveyor fills the system to examine or test it, he must make sure that it is fully drained down again before he leaves. Floorboards which are lifted must be replaced properly or the owner warned of any possible danger.

One surveyor who could not replace a drainage inspection chamber cover as he found it, owing to breakage of the frame and surround when it was lifted for access to the drains on a survey, had to pay damages of £1,500 plus costs for injuries sustained to the vendor's wife who tripped over it some days later and who, it was held, had not been warned of the hazard.[1]

Notification of agent

If the vendor has an agent acting for him in the sale, as is usually the case, it is not only desirable that the surveyor should speak first to the agent but often a convenience for him to explain his instructions to the agent without the difficulty of being misunderstood. Some agents, if they feel that their client will raise no undue difficulty, prefer the surveyor to telephone their client direct for an appointment and to ask for the necessary facilities.

The status of the surveyor

The status of the surveyor is only that of "visitor" under the Occupiers' Liability Act, 1957. Accordingly the vendor is under no particular duty of care to ensure the safety of the surveyor in clambering over the house assuming that the vendor knows of no obvious traps or pitfalls. A word might accordingly be inserted at this point to suggest that academic interest does not outrun physical competence. It is tempting to risk the climb on to a roof without the delay of ordering ladders but hardly wise with leather soles on a wet day.

A good deal has been or will be talked about the surveyor's duty of care and here it might perhaps be restated in a different and more personal context. Passing, however, back to the interest of the vendor in the matter it is wise for the surveyor to carry insurance to cover damage caused by him to the vendor's property, as well as personal accident insurance for himself. A recent incident might serve as a warning where both could be involved and related to a flat roof covered with asphalt which was stated to be leaking and a builder walked on to it to inspect the cause of the leak. The whole

---

[1] *Skinner and Another v. Herbert W. Dunphy and Son* (1969), Estates Gazette, 24th January, 1970, p. 379.

30

roof then collapsed. The joists not visible from underneath were attacked to an advanced degree by dry rot. It could have been a surveyor instead of a builder and if it had been it would have been as well for the surveyor to know, even if the news was brought to him on a hospital bed, that the insurance companies were in touch with his solicitor.

EQUIPMENT FOR THE SURVEY AND CARRYING OUT TESTS

To carry out a structural survey the surveyor needs to have with him the equipment necessary for him to complete the service which he has undertaken to provide in the contract with his client.

The equipment needed will depend to a great extent on the property which he is to inspect, what he himself considers necessary to enable him to carry out his work and to some extent the nature of his practice.

The "ideal" inspection   Ideally perhaps all surveyors carrying out this type of work would wish to arrive at an empty house virtually empty handed, step out of the car and start to organise an entourage of assistants, a note taker, contractor's man and specialist advisers, all present with a vast array of equipment. He might be helped into his overalls to look at say the roof space and any other mucky part of the property but generally he would be free to peer while others did the physical work. The end product would be his because he would dictate the notes and put his name to the report having refined his assistant's draft. No doubt such ideal circumstances still exist but not unfortunately for the majority.

The more "normal" inspection   At the other end of the scale the surveyor will arrive at an occupied property on his own with a car stuffed full of equipment, wondering whether he has brought all he will need but prepared to do everything himself. If he is fortunate he might just have an assistant.

The RICS Guidance Note   In both situations the equipment taken needs to be only that necessary to do the job. The RICS Guidance Note speaks of the preferences of the individual surveyor and sets out a list of items he should consider taking. There is more to it than this, of course, but clearly a surveyor who said he could not fulfil his contract because he did not have with him one of those items would get short shrift from his client and from the courts if it came to that. Those items of equipment included in the list, or their "equivalent" as the Guidance Note puts it, are discussed in the following review of equipment and must be considered the bare minimum. Some other items not mentioned in the Note will be reviewed thereafter.

Note taking equipment   For note taking a good quality notebook with a stiff binding, such as a shorthand writer's book, is preferred by some surveyors. Others prefer larger sheets of paper clipped to a board with the advantage that when removed they can subsequently be retained on file with the report. As an alternative a hand held tape recorder can be used but problems can arise with these as will be discussed

31

later. For writing, pencil is preferred to pen for use at awkward angles and when taking notes in the rain.

Measuring equipment

For measuring, a folding five foot or two metre rule is essential, as is a small cased pocket flexible folding steel rule for measuring in confined spaces. A linen tape for the larger measurements of the site when required is indispensable. Chains, arrows and ranging rods would only be necessary if the grounds of the property are extensive. When the surveyor is on his own greater speed can be achieved with an electronic "tape" used with care. A crack gauge in the form of a small plastic sheet about the size of a credit card must now be considered essential for the reasons set out later in this book.

Long range magnifying equipment

The value of a good pair of binoculars or a small folding telescope not necessarily more than × 8 magnification is self evident for examining high inaccessible roof slopes and the tops of chimney stacks.

Lighting equipment

No surveyor would get far without his torch and there is some merit in having two for where there is no light in the roof space. Internal illumination to these hazardous places can be provided by a large lantern type lamp with a handle while a stout cylindrical rubber cased torch can be used for the darker corners, taking measurements etc. It is a wise precaution to have a spare battery and bulbs available. Sometimes the use of a wire guarded mains lamp with long cable and bayonet fitting for plugging into the staircase landing light is possible.

Probing equipment

For superficial testing of woodwork for the various types of rot and beetle infestation, scraping mortar and gauging the depth of cracks, a sharp metal probe is essential. Most surveyors use a bradawl but also take a screwdriver for removing and replacing access panels to plumbing etc.

Spirit level and plumb-line

Gauging whether floors are level is best done by the use of a spirit level than the eye or sensation. Some spirit levels have a cross level enabling the surveyor to tell whether walls are truly vertical or not. A plumb-line however is essential really for checking walls of any height when it can be possible to measure how much movement has occurred.

Hammer, bolster and mirror

Every opportunity should be taken to lift floorboards where possible and it is essential to raise the covers to all drainage inspection chambers. The latter seldom seem to have the handles remaining with which they were originally provided and the surveyor's finger nails will be preserved by the use of a bolster and claw hammer. The "claw" on the hammer will be needed to pull out the nails from the floorboards before they can be replaced. Having got the floorboards up the surveyor will find a mirror of reasonable size, not less than 100 mm square, useful for examining the underside of adjacent boards and the floor joists. If it is on a handle or long arm it can be even more useful.

Ladder

While it cannot be expected that a surveyor will arrive to carry out a normal basic structural survey equipped with a van and long builder's ladders the availability of the handy, lightweight, sectional variety means that surveyors with one of these can now get into the roof space of empty property on their own and gain access to most of the flat roofs of single storey extensions and the like to residential property. It is now considered essential therefore for all surveyors carrying out this work to be equipped with a type of ladder of this nature which when assembled must extend to a minimum of 3 m. These sectional ladders fit easily into the boot of even comparatively small cars and are a considerable boon to surveyors when the availability of builders assistance is scarce and expensive.

Moisture meters   Damp in all its manifestations features prominently in the work of all structural surveyors whose own observation and touch sensation for its ascertainment need to be supplemented with the appropriate equipment as confirmation and as an aid to the diagnosis of its cause.

There are a number of moisture meters on the market whether electronic relying on probes, surface contact or carbide. The former are in most common use and the more sophisticated types enable the surveyor to detect condensation. These are battery operated and measure the electrical conductivity of the material being examined. The larger models are usually provided with various calibrated scales for different materials, such as wood, brick and plaster and indicate levels of moisture in the material above the normal usually found in an occupied building, since the electrical conductivity of these materials is related solely to the level of moisture present.

A smaller handy pocket type of meter indicates moisture levels above the normal by a flashing light and this can be very useful in dark and restricted spaces and, for example, in roof spaces where the surveyor very often needs one free hand to steady himself. It is necessary for the instrument used on surveys to be fitted with deep probes to penetrate the material up to between 10 and 15 mm since surface readings are unreliable and can be rendered inaccurate by the presence of condensation.

Moisture meters are particularly useful in detecting the presence of rising damp in a property redecorated for sale but not provided with a damp-proof course, in detecting levels of moisture high enough to induce fungal growth in the depth of painted timber, as for example in skirtings, door linings or panelling where the surface is dry to the touch and the back surface is hidden or, again, in flooring covered over by fitted carpeting.

It should not be forgotten, however, that in the case of a lining to walls of metal foil below wallpaper or lining paper the meter can give an erroneous reading of maximum moisture content as the probes on penetrating the foil are short circuited by the metal. Since the maximum reading is obtained over the whole of the wall surface, an unlikely occurrence in the case of rising damp or any other damp penetration for that matter, it is not usually difficult to deduce what has happened in cases where this occurs.

Moisture meters are being modified and improved all the time and are now of enormous assistance to the surveyor in cases not only of rising and penetrating damp but also of condensation. Accessories should be acquired and maintained, such as the deep probes needed for examining timber framed structures.

33

Additional items

In addition to the foregoing basic essential items which must be considered mandatory as they appear in the RICS Guidance Notes there are a number of other items of useful equipment which could form part of the surveyor's armoury on structural surveys.

Compass

A compass is a great help in assisting the surveyor with descriptions where the property is comparatively isolated or even in more populous areas on an overcast day. It is far simpler to write "North boundary" than any other way. Again a compass will show the direction of other landmarks, which is a help in the opening paragraph of the report in giving a brief description of the property.

Pocket lens magnifier

A pocket lens with a magnification of about 6 is useful for identifying the frass left behind by the larvae of beetles which attack and devour timber and can also assist in identifying the beetles themselves if the survey is being carried out at the time of year when the beetles are active and emerging from the wood. If the magnifier is also fitted with a built-in light, as used by philatelists, it is also useful for peering into the exit holes formed by the beetles when they emerge from the timber to see whether the holes are well formed, clean and new indicating a recent attack or burred and with the dirt of years to suggest an attack long since extinct.

A lens is also useful for distinguishing between old cracks in brickwork and plaster and cracks which are of comparatively recent formation. Old cracks invariably contain dust and debris and in plasterwork, if the surfaces have been painted, it is often possible to detect the presence of paint in the crack itself, sometimes on both the "walls" of the crack and on the debris within the depth of the crack indicating the crack's existence at least at the time of the last redecoration.

Sometimes deposits on brickwork and plaster are difficult to identify as between the results of precipitation and evaporation or as fungal or mould growths and a lens is useful to see whether the typical crystalline structure is present which will confirm the presence of the former.

Lifting floorboards

Another most useful accessory is a patent claw and lever device for lifting floorboards. This exerts strong pressure on a sufficient length of board to overcome stubborn nails. One of the embarrassments of a surveyor's life is to stand exchanging small talk with a vendor while an enthusiastic carpenter attacks the floorboards with gusto and loud sounds of hammering fill the room. Often a board end will appear as the end of a sharpening parabolic curve with the carpenter getting steadily redder in the face. The final snap, proclaiming that the board, probably weakened with beetle attacks, has broken, also leads to a lowering of temperature in the relations between surveyor and vendor.

Photographic equipment

The advent of the idiot proof automatic 35 mm camera coupled with the almost instant processing and enlargement on colour film has brought the incorporation of photographs into reports within range of even the most unskilled photographically inclined surveyor. Although some defects in buildings, for example leaning walls and cracks in brickwork do not always appear as emphatic on

34

photographs as they do in real life, many defects can be made much clearer to the client utilising a combination of words and pictures. If with a little extra effort and the use of a word processor the photographs can be integrated with the text rather than appearing as a group at the end of the report the impression given to the client is even better. There is much to be said for including a camera of a type appropriate to the photographic skills of the surveyor as part of the basic equipment for survey work.

Sketches

The explanation of a defect is not something that can be expressed photographically but often a thumb nail sketch with features exaggerated can very often usefully supplement the written word. Photocopying makes for easy reproduction of such sketches and on site a pad of graph paper is useful for keeping such sketches in proportion.

Equipment for testing drains

If only a small property is involved the surveyor may be prepared himself to carry out a water test on the drains, assuming permission has been granted, without a plumber being in attendance. The equipment normally needed for this would include:

(a) A set of drain plugs, say three of 150 mm and three of 100 mm diameter.
(b) Two inflatable bag plugs, one each for 150 mm and 100 mm diameter drains and hand pump.
(c) A set of short telescopic drain rods.
(d) Overalls.
(e) Smoke rockets.

If instead of a water test permission is granted for an air test then in addition an air pressure drain testing machine would be needed.

Equipment for testing electrical installations

Similarly the surveyor, if competent to do so might also agree to carry out a test on the electrical installation. For this he would need insulation and continuity testers with varying capacities from 100 to 1,000 volts. These instruments comprise a constant pressure hand generator and a direct reading true ohmmeter with two terminals for connection, necessarily incorporating a fuse against an accidental connection to a live circuit. A separate earth tester is required.

In addition to the items already mentioned it is, of course, possible for the surveyor to extend his testing equipment to the point where he is almost completely self-sufficient and able to cope with any contingency. It is believed, however, that while it is perfectly possible and often desirable that the surveyor can equip himself for tests of the services of small houses, it is unnecessarily expensive to the client for the surveyor to undertake personally tests to larger house services.

A rather larger house will call for the aid of either one or two workmen to assist the surveyor with the drains and whose successive assistance on a number of surveys forming a convenient routine will be of the utmost benefit. With this size of house the team provided by surveyor, assistant to write down notes, workmen to help with drains and independent electrician to issue a report and result of his test is a most convenient one.

35

With a really large house it is considered that independent firms of specialists dealing with drainage systems, electrical installations and heating systems are best employed who will each issue reports and estimates from their own offices. Further discussion of this will be dealt with in a later chapter.

There is an ever continuing advance in the type and variety of equipment available to the surveyor for the detailed investigation of defects in buildings. Equipment such as optic fibre probes, for examining behind structural facings such as cavity walls, metal detectors for finding concealed metalwork such as inspection chamber covers under flowerbeds, cover meters for detecting the position and depth of reinforcement in concrete and anenometers for detecting draughts are however reserved for such investigations and are not normally brought into use on a normal structural survey of residential property.

SITE ARRANGEMENTS AND ORDER OF INSPECTION

Vacant property

The surveyor should not overlook the fact that a vacant house requires special arrangements. He should make sure that water can be turned on with the vendor's permission if a water test to the drains is allowed. Also that the collection and disposal of the keys is safeguarded. That electricity is connected if the survey is to be a long one and in winter. That he is supplied with all the necessary keys and that no parts of the property are separately locked – a not unusual occurrence in the case of houses let as investments or occupied in flats.

Occupied property

If the house is occupied and furnished the surveyor should leave himself adequate time to make the inquiries and gain the authorities that have already been discussed. He should leave plenty of time to instruct his specialists and make sure that they are supplied with adequate data. An enraged heating engineer turning up at the end of the day having been given the wrong address is not likely to give much sympathy to the surveyor.

Local conditions

Local conditions are worth a moment's thought. A survey in summer in a country district may be delightful and envious eyes may follow the surveyor from his chair-bound office colleagues, but the same task in the depths of winter may be a different matter. The surveyor should bear in mind not only local conditions in his travelling time but also the delays and frustrations caused by testing drains in cold weather and trying to investigate parts of the structure covered by snow, a dangerous matter from the surveyor's point of view physically and professionally.

Establishing a routine

Once the surveyor has arrived at the property he will be well advised to follow a set routine, so as to ensure that no part of the structure is missed. It does not particularly matter in which order the parts of the property are inspected and most surveyors rapidly develop their own set order.

Initial reconnaissance

Most surveyors find it sensible, before beginning the detailed inspection, to have a brief look around the property both outside and inside so as to get the "feel" of the house, without taking any notes. It is a good idea to allow 15 minutes to half-an-hour for this purpose depending on the size of the property. If the surveyor allows himself this sort of time in advance of the arrival of specialists it gives him a chance, in relation to an occupied property, not only to prepare the occupant in the gentlest possible way for the horrors to come but also to make a mental note of any particular features to which he would wish to draw the specialists' attention and to note the position of inspection chambers for the drainage test.

Suggested order of inspection

The specialists having arrived, having been introduced to the vendor or the occupant of the property, an essential act of courtesy, and set to their tasks, the surveyor may then start his inspection at the top of the house in the roof-space, then complete his internal inspection floor by floor and afterwards carry out his external inspection elevation by elevation and finally concern himself with the boundaries, outbuildings and site measurements, fitting in discussions with the specialists or dealing with tests of services himself along the way. Some advantages of carrying out the inspection in this order are that:

Advantages of suggested order

1. The inspection in the roof-space gives an experienced surveyor a knowledge of the house far beyond that suspected by the layman. The roof-space is part of the structure that is never "decorated for sale" and is not concealed with internal plasterwork, or panelling, by the original builder. Defects arising from settlement in foundations or movements in subsoil are far more pronounced at this level than lower down in the property.

   The surveyor can assimilate a surprising amount of valuable information from the roof-space and although his notes will be on specific points only, he will have some idea also if the house was originally well or shoddily built, if it was built cheaply, if it has been well or badly maintained and if the services have been modernised or neglected. The surveyor's inspection can then be completed in the light of this information.

2. The most important parts of the structure are completed first so that in the event of some extremely serious fault appearing that confirms his client's worst suspicions the surveyor may hasten to a telephone to advise his client there and then and cut the survey short. This may save his client money and the vendor wasted time.

3. The most exhausting part of the survey and that generally causing most upheaval and apprehension on the part of the vendor is completed first.

Some surveyors on the other hand inspect the roof-space as the last item before proceeding to the outside of the house on the grounds that the grubbiest part of the internal survey is best left to the end.

Suggested order for inspecting rooms

The order in which the rooms are inspected does not, of course, matter, but a set drill should be followed every time. In small houses it is, of course, comparatively easy to inspect each floor since the largest front room is the logical first step, the smaller front room or rooms, centre rooms and rear or back addition rooms being completed last.

In larger houses with rambling corridors with bedrooms and bathrooms leading from odd corners a rather more predetermined plan is desirable. It is recommended that in general a clockwise method of inspection is adopted with any wings or departures from the normal plan being described under the heading of "West Wing" or similar title. It is suggested that all the rooms are described as their position warrants or alternatively that the fixtures and fittings suggest a use rather than the furniture. These descriptions should be made with the surveyor standing in the floor described and facing the front elevation so that there is no doubt as to which room he has in mind. The way the surveyor is describing the property should be set out in the report to eliminate doubt. Measurements are a valuable aid to description and should be stated as being for that purpose.

The Schedule of Accommodation

The value of a full schedule of Accommodation should be self evident to a purchaser to enable him to check the vendor's particulars and be sure that he is getting what he has bargained for. It is surprising how many mistakes are made in the preparation of particulars and if the surveyor obtains a copy he may wish to highlight any significant discrepancies. The Schedule has other valuable uses which will be discussed later.

Schedules of Accommodation should be prepared in a manner which can easily be understood. For instance it has to be accepted that while the building industry and the professions connected therewith have been metricated for some years the lay purchaser of houses is still thinking in terms of feet and inches so that imperial dimensions are still a necessity. Whether metric equivalents are included can perhaps be a matter of choice. On the assumption that it is decided to include them a room might be described in the surveyor's Schedule of Accommodation as left centre bedroom about 15 feet 0 inches (4.57 m) by 12 feet 0 inches (3.66m), indicating that when standing inside on the left-hand side of the house when facing the front elevation the centre bedroom measuring 15 feet 0 inches (4.57m) by 12 feet 0 inches (3.66m) is under consideration.

Avoid descriptions of an impermanent nature

This is, it is submitted, a better method of description than for example "Mr Brown's study" or "Blue bedroom" as both these terms of description are clearly of an impermanent nature. It may well be that a surveyor's report is referred to long after it has been prepared and when the memory of the accommodation has vanished from his mind. If the property has been reoccupied and redecorated in the meantime it may have a very different appearance when compared with his notes.

Dealing with the vendor on site

It may well be wondered if all this attention to drill and method is necessary. Some reasons have already been given, but the greatest reason by far is that the surveyor is not often left to work undisturbed. He will often have to put part of his mind to dealing with, or soothing, awkward or over-anxious tenants or vendors, combating frenzied dogs that take an objection to the folding rule and saving small children from tumbling through skylights or falling into open inspection chambers.

Gaining understanding

The vendor may commence proceedings by saying "I will show you the dining room first as the daily help has not finished." If the surveyor has no predetermined plan he may soon find himself with the time far advanced and with no clear idea of the elements of the structure. Often a few moments spent in establishing relations with the vendor and explaining that he likes to inspect in a certain way and can survive the sight of unmade beds will result in complete understanding.

Vendors characteristics

While the many differing characteristics of purchasers have been mentioned it is as well to bear in mind that vendors also provide surveyors with an amazing range. While they all have one aim in common that of a quick sale at the maximum price they have differing ideas of the best way to achieve it.

Some vendors quite sincerely really wonder why it is necessary for the purchaser to have a structural survey at all. These tend to be less than wholly co-operative and clearly consider the less the facilities provided and the more difficulties put in the surveyor's way the less likely the surveyor will be to find anything wrong. Locked rooms, missing keys, relatives conveniently ill and not capable of being disturbed, night workers, or party goers similarly in need of quiet, following the surveyor's every move and chattering all the time are some of the ploys which will be encountered, which the surveyor must overcome with all the tact at his disposal.

At the other extreme are those who open the door to the surveyor, hand him a spare set of keys and say "I will leave you in peace to carry on. Help yourself to the tea and biscuits I have left in the kitchen and don't forget to lock up when you go. I am off for the day."

Perhaps somewhere between the two extremes lies the ideal vendor. Unobtrusive while the surveyor's work is in progress, who produces the tea at the right time and not the wrong, and who is around when you want to question him or her and who has the answers.

The RICS Guidance Note on questioning the vendor

The RICS Guidance Note recommends that the owner or occupier be asked questions concerning the history of the property to assist the surveyor to establish matters of relevance not apparent during the inspection. A warning is given that such verbal evidence as is obtained should not be regarded as a true statement of fact unless a full investigation has been made by the surveyor. Thereby, of course, lies the crux of the matter and much will be dependent on the quality of the information obtained and on the character of the person imparting it. It may well range from the downright misleading to the incoherent.

Checking information supplied by the vendor

Whatever information is obtained it will certainly need checking in all circumstances if it is to be relied upon but failing all other sources of information and the inability of the surveyor to check

Value of an assistant

with his own eyes it can be put forward if it seems to him reasonably likely to be correct provided he explains the circumstances fully. The value of an assistant is self-evident. An assistant with building knowledge is, of course, even better. Some surveyors maintain that an assistant is quite essential for regular work of this kind. Not only can he deal with some of the inevitable conversation and help with drawing back carpets and erecting ladders, but his chief value is that he leaves the surveyor free to clamber and climb, test, prod, feel, peer and generally get covered with cobwebs.

Methods of recording information

A number of different methods have been tried for taking notes and each surveyor tends to have his own preference. The principal methods are:-

1. To write or dictate to an assistant the full notes from room to room, as these are determined, in sequence under the various room headings.
2. To have a series of note sheets headed or specially printed to agree with the actual headings used in the report and for the notes to be written in the appropriate place.
3. To dictate sections of the report direct into a recording machine. These can then form the first or final draft of the report, depending on the circumstances.

The first method suffers from the disadvantage that it can lead to some difficulty in preparing the report as the notes are not in report sequence and may require an additional précis first. The second method is open to the disadvantage that it is rather inelastic and may lead to difficulty. Some surveyors extend these note sheets into check lists as an aide-memoire for use on the inspection and enter items under the appropriate headings as they go round the property. Such sheets, however, are difficult to organise for all formulae between a cottage and a mansion, so that very often they are found to be either too elaborate in detail or to contain insufficient space.

It is generally considered that a method of inspection that leaves nothing to chance provides a better basis for working, while the time spent on shuffling sheets of paper to find the right place to enter a note or to check every so often whether every item has been looked at (the method of inspection should take care of this) is better spent by the surveyor on using his eyes actually to inspect the property.

Method of inspection should become second nature

It is surprising how quickly a settled method of inspection can be acquired so that it comes as second nature to the surveyor and, of course, it will be found of use not only on structural surveys but for valuations, schedules of dilapidations or schedules of condition and, indeed, for any purpose requiring an inspection of property.

Disadvantages of hand recorder

The third method suffers from the disadvantage that it may be undesirable to dictate notes in the hearing of the vendor or any third party since a survey report at this stage is a personal matter for the surveyor's client alone. Just as awkward from the surveyor's point of view is that the vendor may pick up a contentious phrase and rush over to argue about it. There is the aspect also that in complex cases another operation is introduced between the inspection and the drafting of the report since the notes on tape have to be transcribed on to paper both for use in drafting and also as a record of the inspection.

For hand recorders to be used to their best advantage the surveyor needs to be able to leave the site with a complete report in draft virtually intact. This can only be achieved with a great deal of practice and certainly involves a change in procedure from the practice of taking handwritten notes; more time being spent on the site and all parts of the property being visited in the same order more than once.

A warning was issued to surveyors in the case of *Watts and Another v. Ralph Morrow* in November 1990,[1] where a hand recorder had been used on a survey but the surveyor was unable to produce transcribed notes or a draft report. The Judge criticised the report as being "lengthy and diffuse" and its conclusions as being inadequate. The report, said the Judge, was "strong on immediate detail but excessively, and he regretfully had to say negligently, weak on reflective thought".

Portable dictating machines need cautious use as exemplified by the experience of a surveyor who dictated notes in this way regarding a roof covering in a strong wind and was taken aback on returning to the office to discover that the sound of the wind was faithfully recorded but little else.

It will perhaps be gathered that the first method is recommended but the need for speed in the production of reports often requires the use of the third method on relatively simple or straightforward cases. The process of adapting from method 1 to method 3 is a painful one as those who have arrived back in the office with a mixture of part draft and part site notes needing much subsequent re-dictating will testify.

[1] Estates Gazette, 13th April 1991, p. 111.

Chapter 3
The Main and Subsidiary Roofs

CONTENTS

Relatively easy access to this felt covered flat roof which illustrates problems and the difficulty of modifications.

Determination of type of structure

make a close inspection. It is also considered essential that a purchaser should be warned in such cases of the dangers in proceeding to purchase without a close examination of the roof, the surveyor relating his comments to the characteristics of the roof and the age and general standard of maintenance of the property.

In order to emphasise the above point let us consider the two component parts of a roof, the structure and the covering to both pitched and flat roofs. With pitched roofs it is often possible to examine both covering and structure in considerable detail. With flat roofs, while it may be a simple matter to examine the covering, it is comparatively rare to obtain a sight of the structure. A surveyor might say in his report that the covering is defective and requires renewal and leave it at that. If a purchaser then finds that he has to renew all or part of the structure due to defects arising from previous damp penetration, he would have a very justifiable complaint against his surveyor.

FLAT ROOF STRUCTURES

Clearly the surveyor must not only report upon what he can see but also the effect on hidden parts of the structure of the defects seen and noted. We shall consider this aspect of close inspection and warnings of possible hidden defects in relation to pitched roofs later in this chapter. Continuing with the example of flat roofs, it may be asked how the different types of structure comprising flat roofs can be detected. Intelligent surmises from a sharp stamp with the foot on the roof can be made as follows:

(a) If there is a hollow sound, the probability is of timber construction. Occasionally, if the roof has little or no insulating properties and the rooms below have not been recently redecorated, pattern staining from the joists can be seen on the ceiling below.

(b) If the roof is not hollow sounding then the construction is probably solid. However it ill behoves a surveyor to guess whether this might be of concrete, filler joist and breeze concrete, hollow clay pots and concrete beams since there are many different methods of construction which would produce this sound.

On the whole it is better for the surveyor to limit his comment to saying that the roof is of hollow or solid construction and surmise timber construction only where pattern staining of the joists can be seen. In recent years other ways of forming hollow construction for flat roofs have been developed, such as lattice beams and metal decking, but these are rarely found in domestic buildings.

Dry rot in flat roof structures

The danger to a flat roof structure of timber should the covering have been leaking in the past is that of dry rot. The thought that the covering might leak one day never seems to have occurred to most of the original builders and there is seldom any provision for ventilation to the timbers of older buildings.

46

Damp penetration combined with lack of ventilation and warmth from rooms below are the ideal conditions for an outbreak of dry rot. This might well extend from the boarding to the joists and the plates on which these rest, eventually combining to render the whole flat roof structure unsafe. Signs of advanced failure can often be completely hidden.

It is not always appreciated that the inclusion of insulation, or the addition of it on renewal work, in a flat roof of timber construction can cause problems from rot. Provision must also be made for a vapour barrier and that barrier must be installed in the correct position to prevent warm moist air passing through the ceiling to condense in the space below the covering. Mistakes of this nature in new construction over the years since the 1960s, when combined with the use of chipboard instead of timber as a base for the covering, usually of bituminous felt, have been the cause of serious outbreaks of dry rot within a comparatively short period following construction.

In a reported case[1] relating to the survey of an upper maisonette in a converted 5 storey house, built originally about 100 years ago, the Court found that the surveyor had failed to warn the purchaser of the potential danger from a lack of ventilation to a flat roof terrace of wood, constructed about 6 years previously, and the very apparent poor construction of the upstands to the felt roofing by the omission of angle fillets and cover flashings. It transpired when damp staining and dry rot fungus appeared that the vapour barrier had been wrongly positioned and chipboard had been used in the construction.

Dry rot in the structure of a flat roof can also arise from an older type of common detail of building construction, that of building in the ends of joists into an unrendered one brick wall. If the roof is at high level, the supporting brickwork is exposed to driving rain and if the pointing is neglected, rain will almost certainly penetrate and affect the joists and plates. The collapse of a roof when walked upon, mentioned in the previous chapter, was an example of this happening. The surveyor must therefore be sure to give suitable warnings when timbers are ascertained or surmised in the circumstances of damp penetration.

Apart from failures caused by rot, total collapse in the structure of flat roofs seem to be relatively rare. Generally, those of timber construction follow the design of floors and very often the same size of joists is adopted as on the top floor. Since the flat roof seldom has to support the load that a floor has to carry from furniture, deflection is less common. If they can be seen the strength of timbers in a flat roof can be checked by reference to Tables B21 and B23 of Approved Document A "Structure" of the Building Regulations 1985 according to whether access to the roof is full or limited to only maintenance and repair.

Occasionally deflection is found to be due to other reasons, such as the formation of a trapdoor where none previously existed but

---

[1] *Hooberman v. Salter Rex* (1985), Estates Gazette, 13th April 1985.

Clear evidence of an overflow from a flat roof above the level of the damp proof course. What effect will this have had on the structure?

without proper trimming to the opening, or the positioning of a heavy water cistern on the roof, subsequent to its construction.

The presence of deflection in flat roofs can give rise to other problems. With rare exceptions, flat roofs should be provided with a fall to a suitable gutter or outlet, and any deflection can defeat the purpose by causing water to lie in pools, even to flow the wrong way and accumulate against a wall or a feature of the roof covering itself, such as a drip or roll. It must be remembered that with the coverings of flat roofs the tolerances are relatively fine when compared with the coverings to pitched roofs and what appear at first glance quite minor faults in design can lead to serious leakages. The surveyor may need his spirit level to confirm the absence or degree of fall if there should be the characteristic staining on the roof covering produced by persistent ponding. There is even greater need to check in this way if ceilings below have been redecorated shortly before the survey and stains from past damp penetration have perhaps accordingly been obscured.

FLAT ROOF COVERINGS

In regard to the covering of a flat roof this may be of a number of different types ranging from lead, copper, zinc and asphalt, through to various forms of bituminised felt with dressings. All of these particular coverings have their characteristic features in construction, departures from the recognised methods being fraught with danger. To describe the proper method of construction would be to cover points of building construction, comprehensively dealt with elsewhere.

However, few books dealing with building construction view the subject from the surveyor's angle, and the surveyor must not only examine the condition of the covering but also look for defects in design which might give trouble. Clearly the surveyor must have a thorough knowledge of the correct details before he can do this, particularly for rolls and drips for metal coverings and the details at abutments.

Age of roof covering

Irrespective of whether there are leakages, the surveyor must look at the roof and form an impression of the age of the covering, since with the coverings for flat roofs there is a generally considered and recognised useful life for the various materials used. A purchaser must be warned of the likelihood of complete renewal of the covering being required as this can be an expensive matter not bargained for.

Lead

Historically, the use of lead as a covering for flat roofs goes back over a long period being the traditional durable and reliable covering, its life depending mainly on the weight of lead adopted. Roofs have lasted for hundreds of years when covered in heavy cast lead with sound workmanship as evidenced by the roofs of some old houses and churches to this day.

In normal domestic work, however, it is common to find thinner, milled lead rather than the cast lead used on old churches

48

An old and defective lead roof. Note the characteristic rolls, the buckling, the long split and the badly aligned gutter.

Zinc

A fairly new zinc flat roof showing typical cappings and a generous upstand and flashing.

and 80–100 years appears generally to be about the maximum life of such lead. With properties of the late Victorian and Edwardian period therefore imminent renewal of an original covering must be anticipated. Splits and repairs with solder or bitumastic material are signs of obvious trouble in the past, but ripples on the surface, or a distinct impression of the boarding below, are signs that trouble may be expected shortly and that the time approaches for renewal.

Large areas of lead without rolls or drips will clearly cause trouble, by reason of thermal movement, in the form of buckling and splits as seen on the photograph on the left. Thus lead sheeting insecurely fixed on pitched roofs should be regarded with suspicion. Lead's resistance to atmospheric corrosion is considerable, oxidisation on exposure to the elements forming an insoluble coating of lead carbonate on the surface which has strong adherent properties to the metal below. No "aggressive" run off therefore arises from lead. However, if there is a run off on to the lead from another roof on which there is an accumulation of moss or lichens, or a pitched roof covered with shingles, the acid content of the rainwater may be increased to such an extent that the lead will be dissolved and holes or deep grooves formed.

It should be borne in mind that the Victorian builder would have employed what would now be the equivalent of heavy Code 6 lead sheeting. Lead is becoming popular again for detailing to positions which are of necessity exposed, but, since Code 4 lead is now generally employed the surveyor should still ensure that it is correctly laid and moreover is proof against lifting being that much lighter.

In Victorian times builders sought a cheap substitute for lead to be used on flat roofs and as a result zinc came into general use as a covering material on the less expensive houses. It is probably the most common material found on the flat roofs of Victorian and Edwardian houses at present, but zinc in acid polluted areas has a limited life of 20–25 years. With the reduction of smoke pollution in the air brought about by the Clean Air Act and the increased use of gas and electricity in industrial processes it had been thought that the life of zinc was being extended, possibly up to about 40 years for 14 gauge work (0.8 mm thickness) but the continuing vast quantities of sulphur dioxide still being emitted into the atmosphere suggest this is not now the case.

Zinc develops a carbonate on the surface by exposure to the air and the action of rainwater, but this is not sufficiently dense or adherent to prevent a steady attack on the metal. Eventually the zinc becomes extremely brittle, consisting at this stage mainly of zinc carbonate and the crusty look on the surface and the pitting indicate a covering of an age likely to need renewal in the near future.

Zinc caps should always be closely examined for splits, since these are a frequent source of trouble, usually through being trodden upon. As for lead, zinc can be rapidly corroded by the strongly acidic run off of rainwater from roofs with an accumulation of moss or lichens, from shingles or from copper roofs. Zinc cannot be

49

patch repaired to any degree of satisfaction and any signs of attempts to do this will probably indicate that complete renewal is required. Coatings with bitumen, with or without layers of hessian or canvas, indicate a similar necessity.

The surveyor will rarely see modern zinc roofs laid to correct principles. The scarcity of the zincworker has meant that zinc, where employed, is laid to a poor standard and the surveyor should be on his guard where renewals have been carried out in this material.

Asphalt

Since late Victorian times asphalt has become a popular covering for flat roofs but as it is laid in large areas without joints the condition of the boarding below the asphalt is of vital importance. Poor boarding, inadequately supported, allowing movement to occur in excess of what the material can accommodate as shown on the photograph below left will soon induce cracks and fissures. Asphalt has a limited life of about 25 to 30 years, and after this time it will become brittle and develop cracks through a lack of elasticity and an inability to adapt to continual changes of temperature.

Bumps will sometimes appear when moisture penetrates a crack, runs along below the asphalt and expands on a change of temperature, to cause a bubble. The top of the bubble will later develop a hole, allowing more dampness to enter. Signs of these defects suggest that the end of the asphalt's useful life is approaching provided that the true cause of the defects is diagnosed. This is said because in the laying of asphalt the trowel usually brings to the surface a thin skin, rich in bitumen, which tends to develop crazing owing to differential movement in relation to the main body of the material.

Inadequate support to asphalt roofing. Excessive movement in the boarding will soon induce cracks and lead to damp penetration.

Cracks found to be merely "skin deep" are generally, in consequence, of no importance in the absence of leakage, bearing in mind that the normal thickness of asphalt is to the order of 19mm. Surface cracking of this nature tends to develop a pattern similar to that of crazy paving and this can be distinguished from cracks due to structural movement which tend to form defined lines and, of course, usually extend to the full thickness of the material.

Blistering is a phenomenon with asphalt which may occur early on in its life as a roof covering and is due to the material's characteristic of being completely impervious to moisture and vapour and being continuous over the whole area of the roof. Any entrapped moisture in the structure either from condensation or from the process of drying out may, when subjected to the heat of the building or the warmth of the sun, turn into vapour, expand and cause a blister. This is particularly so in relation to concrete roofs covered in asphalt and is the reason why these are often fitted with small ventilators to permit evaporation through defined apertures.

In relation to hollow roof construction the effect is often to suggest damp penetration where none exists when the condensed vapour drips on to the ceiling. The traditional metal roofs of lead and zinc in contrast, allow a certain amount of water vapour to escape through the joints at rolls and abutments if condensation

50

Asphalt skirting beginning to creep due to inadequate support.

Copper

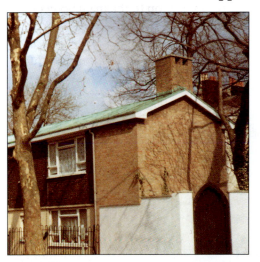

The characteristic green patina of copper roofing used here on the slope.

Bituminous felt

should arise in the structure, although this was less likely to occur in the past when ceilings were of lath and plaster than now, when ceilings are almost universally of plasterboard and skim with its poorer insulating properties.

For houses of fairly new construction i.e. over ten years but perhaps under twenty years old, the surveyor would do well to consider the implications discussed at page 402 in Chapter 12 on the subject of vapour and moisture barriers and insulation in relation to new or near new construction in flat roofs.

The airtight nature of asphalt can lead to another problem. Where this material is employed to replace the defective metal covering of a flat timber roof dry rot can occur when there is some residual damp in the wood and where insufficient provision for ventilation has been made.

Asphalt is also very prone to defects in design. When incorrectly laid on a slope or vertical upstand, it will creep as on the left. In this respect prolonged hot summers are asphalt's greatest enemy. It should not be laid to sharp angles and at junctions and changes of direction should be laid over tilting fillets, otherwise cracks will develop in the angles. Asphalt is not capable of withstanding loads and, occasionally, the surveyor will find that a water cistern laid on the asphalt or on bearers, will have caused it to spread. Impact from sharp heels and chair legs can also cause damage. Asphalt has the advantage that patch repairs can be carried out, always provided it is not too old generally to render these pointless.

Another lasting metal used for covering flat roofs which has a considerable history is copper, but this is not often found on the smaller domestic building. It is longer lasting than zinc but not so durable as lead, the sheets used being thinner. On exposure to the atmosphere the copper develops a highly protective patina on the surface which acts as a protection to the metal below.

However, eventually over a long period the metal becomes friable due to the continual movements caused by changes in temperature. Bulging and splits will eventually begin to appear. These defects will be fairly self-evident on a close examination, but care should also be exercised in the examination of the rolls to ascertain any physical damage due to foot traffic or impact. Standing seams in particular are prone to damage.

Provided the exposure of copper is to simple atmospheric conditions only, it will last a long time but this is not always the only degree of exposure. Increased acidity in rainwater due again to a run off from lichens, moss and algae and also from shingles can cause corrosion by way of holes and grooves in the metal and, as we have seen, the run off from copper itself can be damaging.

Bituminous felt applied in layers, bedded down in bitumen solution and with a surfacing of chippings is common in cheaper construction. It has a relatively limited life of probably no more than ten to fifteen years and many people regard it as a short term covering. A flat roof on a house fifteen to twenty years old or so, and covered with this material must be considered suspect and indeed in probable need of re-covering.

This attempt to provide an upstand in roofing felt may be well intentioned but the detailing is poor. The felt should have been taken up in a continuous sheet from the roof surface and a metal flashing incorporated below the tiling. Note also clogged gutter.

The chippings if not properly bonded to the felt in bitumen can often cause problems by becoming loose and being constantly washed down into gutters causing eventual blockage. Gentle removal of chippings on the joint lines will often reveal uneven

Fibre based tiles laid over the bituminous felt are designed to provide a wearing surface for foot traffic. Note blistering to skirting already commencing and absence of flashing. Is the top of the skirting tucked into the brickwork or does the pointing merely cover the gap? Safety has been totally ignored as has the possible effect of altering the position of the rainwater pipe, leaving a gap in the sill.

Ponding and growth on felt roofing.
Contrast between flat and pitched roof access

Most surveyors would find this type of detailing on a flat roof unusual to say the least. Chippings have been left off the felt roofing which is already showing signs of lifting with gaps appearing at the angles.

areas and poor bonding. Sometimes mineral surfaced felt is used without chippings and this is particularly prone to buckling and eventual splitting.

Unevenness, bare patches devoid of chippings, lumps and bumps and of course tell-tale splits are sure signs of trouble necessitating suitable warnings to a prospective purchaser that he must consider imminent renewal or replacement with a stouter cover. In particular, warnings should be given where cracks and splits occur to flashings or where flashings are simply dispensed with, as on the photograph at the bottom of the previous page, and the felt covering is taken up and tucked into the brickwork of the parapet walls, since these are the weakest point on this type of roof covering. Hot sunshine over a period, as for asphalt, causes a great deal more damage to this form of roof covering than continual rainfall. As with asphalt the question of vapour and moisture barriers is vital. With newly laid felt roofs the life of the covering is much reduced by a poor quality underlay or by detailing faults such as surface nailing.

Whereas with flat roofs it is often easy to examine the covering in detail while the structure remains hidden from view, the opposite set of circumstances sometimes occurs with pitched roofs, particularly in the case of pre-war semi-detached houses. Water Authority requirements to provide a water cistern and the fact that this, to be above the highest fitting, is often put in the roof-space, out of sight, has at least brought about the provision of more trapdoors in older properties. This is often combined with a further trapdoor giving access to the outside slopes of the roof itself.

A tiled appearance at the front, see page 279, does not always guarantee the use of tiles elsewhere. It is not often that felt is used on this degree of slope but it is already beginning to buckle and split. Other detailing is very poor.

PITCHED ROOF STRUCTURES

Double Lean-to Roofs

Probably the simplest roof to examine is that of the tall narrow fronted Georgian or Victorian terrace house of the inner suburbs, which often has a double lean-to roof with a central valley gutter at right angles to the frontage. This type of roof was provided to leave the designer a degree of freedom for elevational treatment with the use of parapets, cornices and band courses. Using slates the roof could be hidden from view because of its low rise. Most of these roofs have trapdoors to both roof space and slopes but if neither is provided the surveyor will be unable to comment on the coverings.

With pitched roofs it is a sound principle to examine the exterior in the first instance. From available vantage points the covering can be examined to detect those sags and unevenness in the slopes suggesting a defect in the supporting structure, often with additional evidence from uneven flashings, wide fillets and water lying in a valley gutter which help in the diagnosis of the defect to be carried out from the roof space.

With simple double lean-to roofs the main principle behind the construction is to provide adequate support at top floor ceiling level, along the centre line of the property, for the beam carrying the valley gutter and the lower end of the rafters, "A" on the cross and longitudinal sections at the top of the next page. Adequate bearing is also required for the top end of the rafters at "C". Irrespective of the adequacy in size of the beam supporting the

Parapets and cornices hide the roofs from the street on these terrace houses of about 1880.

54

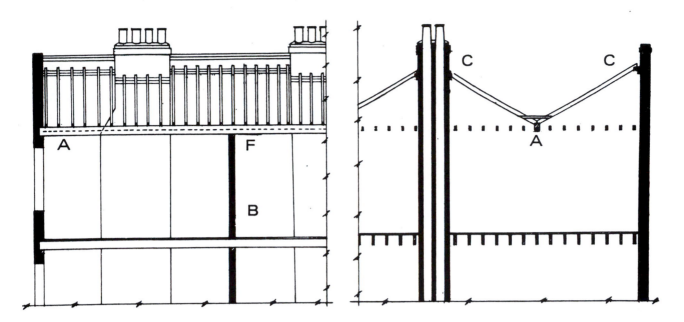

Longitudinal and cross section of simple double lean-to roof on narrow fronted terrace house.

central gutter, a point to be considered if defects are noted, settlement in the beam can arise through failure in the front or rear walls since these are seldom provided with any lateral restraint above the top floor level and are inclined to bulge as shown on the diagram on page 108.

Settlement in valley gutter beam

More often, however, settlement in the beam is due to settlement in a partition running parallel to front and rear walls "B" on diagram above which is often expected out of all proportion to its thickness and construction to carry half the total roof load as well as half the total floor loading. It follows that movement, for whatever reason, in the beam carrying the valley gutter causes the rafters to slip down from their support, probably a plate at the top. Varying amounts of deflection in the beam below the valley gutter cause unequal movements in the rafters resulting in a wavy effect in the tiling or slating.

Corbels

Another common defect in this form of pitched roof arises from breakage of the corbels supporting the wall plate carrying the top ends of the rafters. The corbels are often of brick and unequal pressure exerted by the rafters via the plate can cause the corbels to snap even when arranged correctly by modern standards, which is not often found to be the case in any event. Single bricks are often set projecting from the party walls for an alarming distance.

Span of rafters

When the frontage of this type of terrace property exceeds 4.8 m or so it follows that the length of the rafters on the slope is in excess of 2.4 m. In the good building practice of earlier times 100 by 50 mm rafters at 400 mm centres carrying tiles or slates would have been provided with additional support when this length is exceeded. This is not always found to be the case however. Other items being correct, the margin of safety in the rule of thumb calculation which provided this limit (i.e. span in feet over two giving depth of 2 inch (50 mm) rafter in inches) is sufficient in the majority of cases to cover the deficiency, and trouble from this cause alone is seldom found, provided always the span for the rafter is not out of all proportion.

Building Regulations 1985

Even now the limit of earlier times provided by the rule of thumb can be verified by reference to Table B13 in Approved Document A "Structure" issued under the Building Regulations 1985. The table shows that rafters of the above size and at these centres in the lower grade timber of strength class SC3 are allowed a maximum clear span of 2.42 m when carrying a dead load not exceeding 0.75 kN/m^2, sufficient for tiles and Welsh slates, at a pitch of between 22½° and 30°. The tables provided in this Approved Document can usefully be used for checking the evidence of the eyes in relation to other timber sizes, spans, centres and pitches in roofs of traditional construction where it is suspected that defects are attributable to overstressing of the component members.

Spacing of rafters

It is always important to remember when in the roof space to measure the distance from centre to centre of the rafters since the spacing governs the amount of load which each rafter can carry. Rafters, and the battens for that matter, can sag under excessive overloading from slates and tiles. However, where other defects are present, inadequately sized rafters or those positioned too far apart are often a contributory cause of further trouble when unequal pressure may cause an unsupported or inadequate rafter to sag in excess of a reasonable amount.

Purlins

Greater frontage width in the larger Victorian or Georgian houses with this type of roof, which, because they were more expensive, were often of sounder basic construction, result in longer spans for the rafters and the introduction of a purlin in each half of the roof, "D" on the diagrams at the top of the page opposite. This in turn has to be supported at each end, on the main front and rear walls and along its length. Support of this nature can result in trouble if the ends are built in for half the thickness of a one brick wall, when the exterior face is not rendered.

Driving rain, under conditions of a prevailing wind, will generally penetrate unprotected brickwork one brick thick, particularly if the pointing is defective, and this can have a damaging effect on the ends of the purlins, setting up wet rot and, very occasionally dry rot if there is a lack of ventilation in the roof space. If the ends rest on corbels then, as in the case of the support to plates previously mentioned, the corbels themselves can become defective. If of brick they can snap and if of cast iron, then over the years they can become rusty and fail.

Intermediate support is generally provided to purlins by struts "E" on the diagram opposite top right. These struts have in turn to be supported from something substantial, either the party walls or a load bearing partition. The supporting partitions, however, can settle in themselves causing the strut to drop and a sag to develop in the purlin which in turn is reflected in the rafters and the roof covering.

Lengths of purlin are often poorly joined and though joints are usually made where a strut provides support to the end of each section, a plane of weakness may be set up by excessive cutting

Wider frontage on terrace houses built in early 1800s require a more complicated double lean-to roof typically constructed as shown opposite at the top.

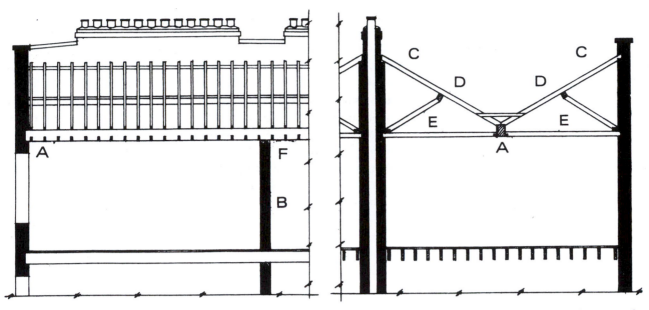

away where the sections overlap. Where there is an absence of a strut to support the halved joint between two sections of purlin then it is very common to find splits in the timber and sagging along the length of the purlin.

Single Lean-to Roofs

Frequently the Victorian terrace property with a double lean-to roof as described above has a back addition with a single lean-to roof. Here again the span on slope of the rafters is often excessive for their size leading to a sag developing as on the right hand half of the diagram below. These roofs, unless properly tied by the

The top ends of these rafters rest on a wood plate but wet rot is present in both.

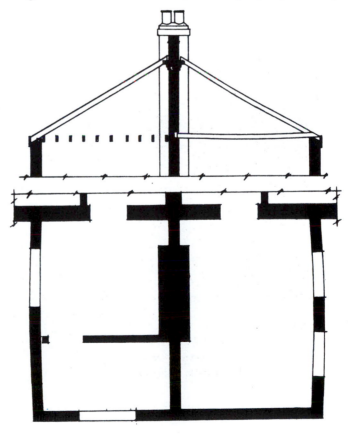

Single lean-to roofs usually provided for back additions in dwellings built in the 1800s and early 1900s.

presence of ceiling joists have a tendency to exert pressure on the top section of the wall at the foot of the rafters and it may be found that this section of the wall leans outwards. Fortunately in most cases the larger back additions, usually multi-storey, are provided with horizontal ceilings to the top floor so that this defect is found less frequently than it might otherwise be.

Lack of ties in single lean-to roofs

The defect is much more often to be found in the later and smaller two-storey terrace houses of the later 1800s and early 1900s where a small single storey addition may provide the original kitchen and toilet accommodation and have only a sloping ceiling. In the centre of the wall supporting the feet of the rafters, that is at the farthest point from any tie by way of bond to another wall a vertical bulge and a horizontal bow can quite often be seen coupled with a distinct sag in the roof above this point. On plan the effect could be as on the left hand diagram at the foot of the previous page.

Close Coupled Roofs

In late Victorian and Edwardian times smaller two-storey houses were built in great numbers and most of these are provided with a close coupled roof, with the ridge parallel to the frontage. It is unusual to find many inherent defects in roofs on this type of small house, since, basically, the design is of the soundest type. Trouble can arise, however, if the normal forms of construction are ignored or settlements occur in the supporting walls. These often occur as the front and rear walls providing the support are invariably broken up by window and door openings. The design being simple it is usually a straightforward matter to diagnose the principal cause of the trouble and there are often cracks and bulges in the walls supporting the roof to reinforce the conclusions drawn. External signs may also be sufficiently pronounced to put the surveyor on enquiry as he approaches the property to carry out his survey as on the photograph below.

The surveyor will need to establish the cause of settlement in these roof slopes. Advice to brace the roof structure may need to be coupled with a warning that it may disturb the attractive tiles which might be difficult to replace.

In its simplest form the close coupled roof is limited in use to spanning single rooms of about 4 metres in width. Although not very many houses are built a single room in depth nowadays, there are plenty still in existence from earlier times as in the sketch on the left with a simple close coupled roof as shown below in cross and longitudinal sections, while the form has always been popular for back additions. Designed to produce a rigid triangulated framework so that the weight is transmitted vertically to the walls, it relies on adequate nailing at the joints between the feet of the rafters and the wallplate, the rafters and the ceiling joists forming the tie (1) and the tops of the rafters and the ridge piece (2).

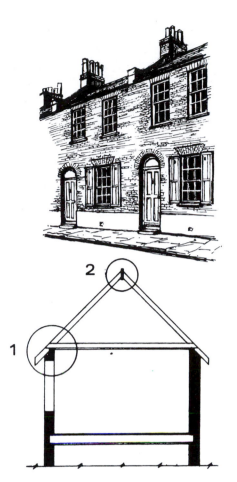

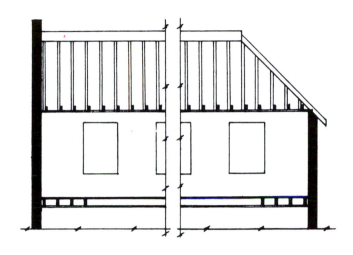

Couple close roof.

Collar roof   A version shown below and known as a "collar" roof permits a substantial saving in brickwork for the external walls by forming rooms partially in the roof-space. It is frequently found in cheap work but relies for equilibrium on the correct positioning and secure fixing of the collar to the rafters (3).

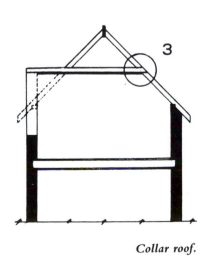

Collar roof.

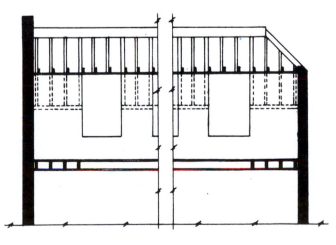

Close coupled roofs with purlin   A substantial increase in the length of rafter usually requires the introduction of a purlin (4) in the design to keep the size of rafters to a reasonable minimum. With a house two rooms deep as below intermediate support for the purlins can be obtained from a structural partition (5) parallel to the frontage.

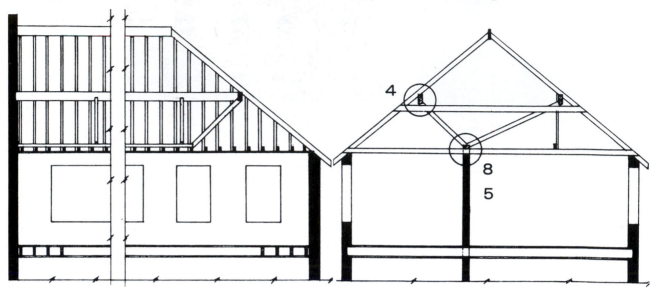

Close coupled roof with purlin.

If there are to be large through rooms then it may be necessary to introduce binders as at (6) on the cross section below if a hipped slope is proposed, and these might be carried on a structural partition at right angles to the frontage (7). In narrow fronted terrace housing, larger purlins can sometimes be used spanning from party wall to party wall and eliminating struts. In cheaper work the collar shown above and below is often omitted.

Close coupled roof with purlin.

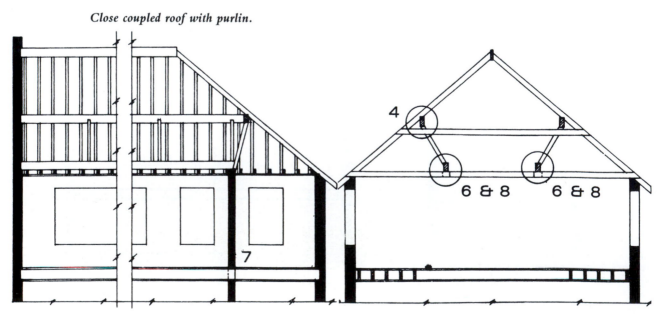

Large Victorian detached house with shallow pitch close coupled roof with purlins and hipped slopes.

Typical defects in various types of close coupled roofs

Except in cases where a property is built with the gable as the front elevation, it will be noted that in most examples the weight of the roof is carried by walls broken up by window and door openings. In all examples roof thrust is common forcing the tops of the supporting walls outwards due to inadequate nailing particularly at (1) in the close couple roof and at (8) in the purlin roofs where lengths of ceiling joists must be properly fixed together to act as effective ties.

With the collar roof, in better class work the joint of the rafter

A badly arranged joint to a purlin. Not only is one half left unsupported entirely but the top of the strut has been badly cut and provides inadequate support to the other half.

with the collar (3) is formed by a dovetail halved joint but in cheaper work nailing is relied upon, with the consequential thrust if the number of nails used is insufficient or the work ineffectively carried out. Little resistance to thrust is provided by the collar if this should be positioned above the half-way mark. Often with a hipped slope there is a tie for the front and rear slopes by ceiling joists but none for the feet of the rafters on the hip with consequent thrust arising.

Sagging in the rafters and purlins can occur if there is settlement in the load bearing partitions shown with the purlin roofs. Bearing in mind, for example, that the partition parallel to the frontage in the purlin roof is taking a load equal to twice that of the front and rear external walls, such settlement is not unusual. Frequently sagging arises when the ends of purlins have inadequate bearing on walls, lose such bearing altogether or when joints are badly made or lapped joints are not supported. Common to all, however, sagging occurs where economies in construction so common to speculative building arise.

Invariably in all except the very best work timbers will be expected to carry more weight over greater spans than most textbooks would recommend reducing the margin of safety considerably. For example the length of rafter below the actual collar in the collar roof while being stressed in compression is also subject to a bending stress, since over this distance it acts as a cantilever. Because of this rafters in a collar roof should be correspondingly larger, so as to be

An inadequately sized purlin and strut, the purlin showing signs of deflection. Provided it is not disturbed or additional weight added to it by, for example, recovering in a different heavier material than slate, all might be well.

Defective rafters cut off and new positioned alongside. How are they supported at the base? It seems curious with the evidence of new battens the opportunity was not taken to provide underfelt below the slating.

stiffer, than they would be in a close couple roof for a similar span, but this is very seldom found in practice. In consequence excessive deflection will produce substantial thrust at the top of the supporting walls.

External evidence of defects in roof structure

If there are no parapet walls separating houses in a terrace, an immediate indication of trouble may well be that the line of the party wall below the tiling or slating is readily apparent because the covering materials are at a slightly higher level at this point, than on either side. This may be caused by either roof thrust, from the spreading of the rafters at their feet, or, if it is more obvious in the centre of the pitched slope, by sagging in the rafters owing to inadequate size, too wide a spacing of the rafters or lack of intermediated support. Because of their character these defects are not only limited to terrace properties. Semi-detached properties of whatever age, particularly those of the inter-war period, without separating parapets, will often display defects of this nature and in precisely the same manner.

Support to purlins

Larger houses of this basic terrace type, provided with close coupled roofs, usually require a purlin for each slope at the front and rear. The purlins present little problem since support at each end can be obtained from the party walls on either side and intermediate support obtained from the top of a central partition by means of struts.

In taller houses these central partitions are often of timber stud and plaster construction. These have a tendency to settle in

63

A sagging purlin and bowed strut. Much evidence of past damp penetration from time before roof was recovered. Does the insulation at ceiling level and the bird's nest allow for adequate ventilation through the eaves. The felt above the rafters is fixed too tightly thus preventing moisture discharging below the battens into the gutter.

themselves, are often overloaded and invariably support floors as well. As a result they drop, letting both strut and purlin down. The situation is occasionally aggravated by the formation of an opening between rooms at a lower level. In the process a brace within the partition may be cut with dire results to its stability and ultimately that of the roof.

Collars

The importance of the collar in the construction of a roof must always be borne in mind particularly if the pitch is steep or the weight of the covering used is heavy. The collar provides the tie to prevent roof thrust due to the spreading apart of the feet of the rafters. The most effective position for the collar is for it to be fixed between the feet of the rafters as in the normal close coupled roof where it forms the ceiling.

In cheap two-storey construction or in larger houses, rooms are often formed partly in the roof-space so that a tie in this position cannot be obtained. The collar is then provided at a higher level, this type of roof being known as a "collar roof", as illustrated on page 59. If, however, the collar is positioned above the half-way mark it will be totally ineffective and ideal conditions will exist for roof thrust. A distinction must be drawn here between rooms partly formed in the roof-space with those totally in the roof. In the latter case, the joists forming the top floor will provide the tie between the feet of the rafters and this particular problem will not occur.

Steep pitch roofs

When roofs are of a steep pitch it may be necessary to introduce a second purlin for each slope. If roof spread is suspected it is impor-

64

Rooms partly in the roof space. The waviness in the patterned tiling suggests that the structural timbers having regard to the dormer windows may be inadequate.

Roofs for larger houses

Rooms partly in the roof space in a modern house requiring a thorough check on restraint provided by collar.

tant to check on the position of the collar since this has been observed on occasions below the top purlin, where it is found to be almost totally ineffective. The correct position is below the lower purlin where a much increased resistance to roof spread will be obtained. It may be necessary in such circumstances to advise the purchaser to provide an additional set of collars in this position.

In larger semi-detached houses the close coupled form of roof is often developed to provide hipped slopes down to the external corners from a central ridge. From this scheme all forms of variation are possible, to include the roof over the ubiquitous bay window beloved of the inter-war period. The importance of the framing and joining together of the timbers of the roof, in addition to the support provided by the structure below, becomes much more apparent with these more elaborate forms.

The load from the roof covering and rafters should be transferred down through purlins and struts to the structure below, all the timber being carefully framed together at the angles and hips with carpenter's joints of long tradition. Departure from the tried and proved details usually results in defects. Sagging in a roof of this nature, if not attributable to causes already discussed, can often be traced to a split in a timber weakened drastically by over-cutting to form a joint. A basic rule for any cutting is that it should not exceed one-third of the depth of the timber. An excess of this amount will weaken the member unduly and a split will be inevitable. The joint will then be unable to support the load it was intended to carry.

Complicated roofs must be considered as a whole by reason of the interaction of one portion or member with another. A defect in one length of timber or joint by over-zealous cutting will lead to widespread subsidiary defects. Occasionally undue economy in the original design to achieve a saving in the amount of timber used,

The formation of rooms in the roof space of this house has clearly upset the lie of the slating and may induce damp pentration in time.

Past alterations to pitched roof structures.

Trussed roof construction

perhaps by wider spacing of the rafters or by reducing the size of the purlins or struts, leads to widespread overall settlement. It is not often that this occurs on an individually designed house and fortunately if it does occur in one house of a terrace or line of semi-detached houses, then a glance at the remaining houses of the group will often suffice to confirm the basic cause of the trouble, since the pattern of defects will be repeated down the street.

A glance by the surveyor at the properties on either side in one reported case[1] might have spared him the embarrassment of being found to have been negligent by the Court. In advising the purchaser of a terraced house he failed to draw attention to the roof spread and the fact that the front wall was bulging. Evidence was brought to show that the same defect was affecting the other houses in the terrace and was visible at the time of the inspection. Three years later the local authority served a dangerous structure notice. Damages awarded against the surveyor in this case exceeded the original purchase price of the house.

Alterations in the structure of the roof in smaller houses are relatively rare but are on occasions found. The original builders probably built the roof around the cold water storage cistern, a not infrequent occurrence. When the cistern requires replacement it is found impossible to remove it from the roof-space, resulting in its replacement by a number of smaller cisterns. To position these in the roof-space, it is not unknown for the misguided to cut a purlin in the process. This may happen when a property without a cistern is converted, or improvements are carried out and these necessitate the installation of a cistern to comply with Water Company requirements. The effects of such cutting can be considerable.

In larger houses, where there are attic rooms, alterations are sometimes carried out with little regard paid to the total effect that these may have on the stability of the roof. The removal of partitions to increase room sizes may deprive roof timbers of their support. The installation of larger dormer windows without correct trimming around the enlarged openings and, in particular, without substitution of ordinary rafters by trimming rafters at least 25 mm thicker, or the doubling of the existing, leads to additional weight being placed on the old rafters nearby with resultant sagging. Though it is unusual, it has been known for the alterations to involve the cutting of the members of a roof truss. This will, of course, have dramatic effects on the roof in a very short period of time.

It may be thought that roof trusses of the King Post type are relatively rare and to be found in only the very largest of houses. However, in the days of cheap labour they were much more frequently adopted than they are today and roofs based on trusses of the King Post type have been found in comparatively small mews cottage type dwellings, the principal rafters supporting purlins, at about 900 mm to 1200 mm centres and boarding, instead of common rafters as shown opposite at the top and either zinc as a covering or very large slates.

[1] *Treml v. Ernest W Gibson and Partners* (1984), Estates Gazette, 6th October 1984.

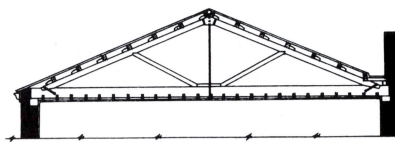

King Rod type roof truss on terrace of houses with covering of boarding and zinc.

An example of this form of construction encountered when more normal forms are expected can come as a surprise to a surveyor and underlines the importance of a close examination to establish the precise form of construction. Not that it is always possible to make the closest of inspections when the pitch is shallow. Then the report, of necessity, has to contain a statement pointing out the limitations of the inspection and advise the prospective purchaser of the danger of possible defects at the extremities of the roof. This problem of limited inspection at the extremities of shallow pitch roofs does occur on occasions and needs to be mentioned in the report in the same way as the hidden structure of flat roofs, particularly if there are signs of present or past roof leakages in view of the danger of dry rot where ventilation is limited.

Rooms in the roof space   In larger properties the presence of rooms in the roof-space, in the past usually the servants' bedrooms, is more often the rule than the exception. Properties with such accommodation will vary in regard to the differing forms of structure employed to support the purlins, rafters and roof coverings. From the point of view of inspection alone they present difficulties, particularly as mentioned above in regard to leakages, but also from the point of view of ascertaining the actual mode of construction.

Even if the surveyor can see the roof structure, not always the case by any event, he is often presented with a jumbled mass of timbers. Unless he is careful he may well come away from the property with little or no idea of how the roof covering is supported. It is suggested that a logical approach to this problem will assist the surveyor to decipher the jumble.

If the surveyor views systematically a section of the roof from the covering to a set of rafters, then through to a purlin and an examination of its support, if necessary by tracing any struts, it is thought that he will then be able to decide on the principle adopted by the architect or builder in the original construction.

Difficulties arise mainly in ascertaining the manner of support to the purlins. This may be from a stud partition separating the room from the roof-space, in which case there will probably be a beam in the top floor to support the partition in turn, or alternatively, the

67

purlin itself may be trussed with a series of braces, tie rods and a lower boom. An examination of the reverse side of the partition from the roof-space, if at all possible, is essential to differentiate the two methods of support.

The above arrangements may be adapted to support either the upper or lower purlin. In whichever case, it is still then necessary to follow the same systematic procedure to ascertain the support for the remaining purlin, or purlins if there are more than two all told, to any slope. Unless a clear understanding is obtained of the principles of the construction it is well nigh impossible to see how a correct diagnosis can be made of any defects found.

King and Queen Post roof trusses

Greater spans for the roofs of larger houses during the period from the middle of the 17th century to about the middle of the 20th century followed the patterns shown below for the majority of domestic buildings. Because the structure was not seen appearance had ceased to count, so that the softwood being imported at the commencement of the period could be framed into the rather inelegant, but efficient, King and Queen Post trusses, the joints being strengthened with metal straps and bolts. Such trusses reached their ultimate in design during Victorian times and comprised other variations and examples not shown here, although similar trusses to the King Post truss shown here with its slope suitable for tiling might well be found in 18th-century structures.

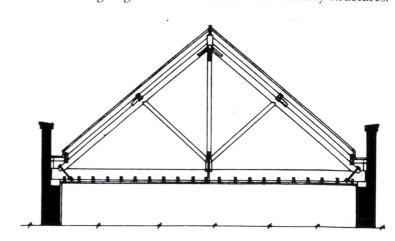

King Post truss.

Queen Post truss.

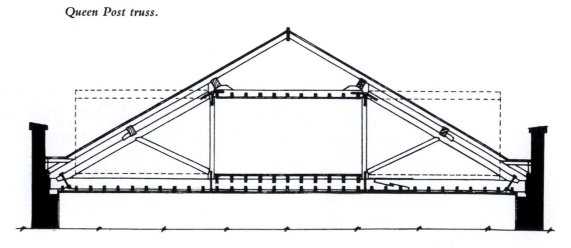

The Queen Post truss was useful not only for the larger spans but also for occasions when rooms were required in the roof-space, since the King Post was unsuitable for this purpose. Another form of truss, known as the Mansard, was something of a combination of the two types, a King Post truss on top of a Queen Post but with the lower roof slopes at about 60–70°. The version shown on page 67 known as a King Rod truss, replaces the central timber post with a long metal bolt, which is more efficient in tension. The example shown on that page with a shallow pitch has boarding carried on purlins, the common rafters being omitted, and is suitable for large slates or for lead, copper or zinc as a covering.

The Queen Post truss at the bottom of the previous page with a pitch for ordinary slates is typically found in the largest of Victorian houses. Houses of an earlier date with a need for a similar span of roof are morelikely to have variants of the Queen Post truss shown below. All these trusses are usually positioned at about 3.0 m centres unlike modern TRDA trusses which, being of much lighter construction, require much closer spacing.

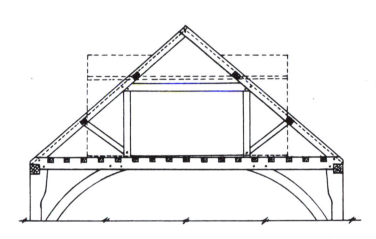

Early Queen Post truss.

Early types of trussed rafter roof

Early trussed rafter roof.

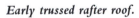

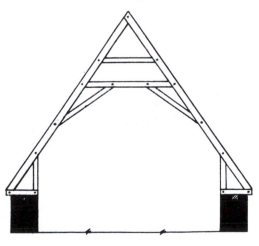

The roofs of medieval buildings developed in two ways depending on whether the building was wholly timber framed or not. For structures with strong mass walling and gable ends the trussed rafter type of roof was satisfactory. Each closely spaced couple was strengthened as shown left and the masonry gable ends protected the structure from wind pressure which, owing to the absence of longitudinal bracing, tended to cause undue racking effects when this type of roof was used on wholly timber-framed buildings.

69

Roofs of early wholly timber-framed
buildings

Initially wholly timber-framed buildings were based on cruck construction as on the left or a little later on the arcade principle and were successfully roofed on these designs since there were many points of support for the transmission of loads and much bracing inherent in the construction. From the arcade principle can be traced the evolution of the successful roof type shown below, once known as the medieval King Post roof but now known as the Crown Post type to distinguish it from the later version which is based on a distinctly different structural design. The Crown Post is a compression member and rises from the tie-beam to support a "medial", or longitudinal, purlin below the collar attached to each couple. It is not a truss as such since there are no principal rafters but it is the most frequently encountered of all medieval roofs on domestic property. Many differing arrangements will be found for the bracing. Sometimes bracings are taken from the tie-beam to the post, sometimes only to the purlin or alternatively to the collar but more often to both as shown here. Often the Crown Post will be elaborately carved as being originally part of an open roof.

Cruck construction.

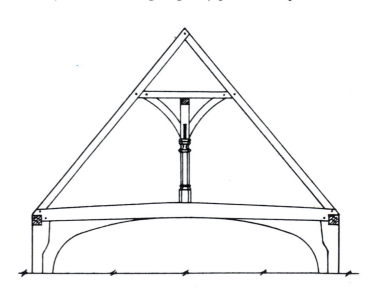

Crown Post roof.

Early types of truss

Trussing became much more common towards the end of the medieval period. The Queen Post shown on page 69 and the simple collar type with wind bracing shown opposite at the top respectively both provide room in the roof-space and like the Crown Post are both based on the main framing with tie-beam. Common rafters are shown dotted on the collar roof and it will be noted that the purlins are framed into the principal rafters (not carried on top as later), the usual medieval practice, along with the use of timbers broad side uppermost (as shown) instead of the reverse which is more sound structurally. Sometimes the purlins were held to the same depth as the principal rafters and the common rafters framed into the purlins.

An example is also shown at the foot of the opposite page of a small single Hammer-Beam roof developed from the earlier Tie-Beam and Queen Post roofs where open construction was required with a feeling of height.

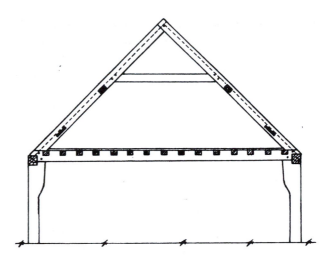

Simple collar roof.

A further method of forming rooms in the roof-space is to provide a mansard roof. As for the more complicated double roofs discussed above, it is important to ascertain principles of construction before diagnosing defects. In particular the surveyor must ascertain, if possible, whether the mansard is based on a Queen Post or similar type of roof truss, or if it is of simple framed construction, as in the smaller type of house. With simple framing the surveyor must again check back on support for the purlins if their length indicates that this is required, or if defects are apparent.

Dormer windows

Rooms in the roof-space are often provided with dormer windows. The coverings to these windows can be a frequent source of trouble and warrant particular attention. Often from a distance they appear to be in good condition but closer examination will reveal defective sides, particularly when these are covered with zinc, and defective roofs and flashings. The surveyor should examine the base of the cheeks which are a particular source of trouble.

The surveyor must also not forget that with dormer windows the timber construction of the roof and sides cannot be seen and that a prospective purchaser is entitled to assume that all is well if no comments are made. As to the condition and future life of the metal

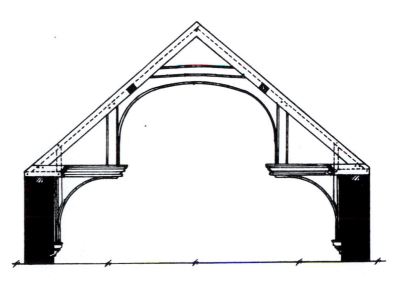

Single Hammer-Beam roof.

coverings to dormer windows, this should receive the same attention, the same remarks applying, as for flat roofs in general which were dealt with earlier in this chapter.

The fronts of dormer windows often repay equally close attention. Sometimes these are formed of brickwork as an extension upwards of the wall, as shown on the photograph on the left, or parapet, but are seldom provided with restraint to prevent movement at the top. At other times brickwork in narrow widths will be found built up off timber plates behind a parapet gutter and deflection in the timber or an attack of rot can lead to movement and consequential damp penetration, even apart from the dangerous structural condition that can arise.

Little has been said in the preceding pages in regard to prescribing remedies for defects found in the structure of pitched roofs. This is not an oversight, but in view of the varying nature of defects and conditions found it is not an easy matter to generalise on the advice which should be given. It may be a question of degree. The surveyor having described the defect and diagnosed the cause may well decide that settlement in a roof structure has taken place some time ago and the structure has now reached a new position of repose.

In properties decorated some years prior to the inspection, where making good to cracks in top floor ceilings has remained in position and where, on the roof, old cement fillets are still relatively sound the surveyor may feel confident that such is the case. On the other hand if the property has been very recently redecorated and repaired for the purpose of sale it may be dangerous to be dogmatic about this and the surveyor may have to state bluntly that he cannot tell whether movement will continue or has ceased. His warning that the movement may continue must be coupled with the advice that remedial work might prove costly.

Advice where defects found in pitched roof structures

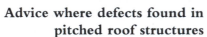

The danger of collapse is very real when the face is built up of unrestrained brickwork.

A neat arrangement of dormers in a close couple type of roof. However there appears to be a problem with the boiler flue on the right.

Dormers in the form of bay windows are commonplace in Scotland but less frequently found south of the border. Waterproofing aspects require careful checking.

The particular dangers to the surveyor of a house done up for sale were highlighted in a reported case where on an inspection said to have lasted 2½ hours the surveyor failed to draw the appropriate conclusions from filled cracks externally and cracks within a small cupboard where the back wall had not been decorated. Settlement continued and the damages awarded against the surveyor were almost half the purchase price of the house.[1]

There exist, however, many properties where the owners are perfectly happy to put up with bulged top floor ceilings and sagging roofs and these make little difference to their satisfaction in occupation. Their main considerations are that the roof remains watertight, that the ceilings do not crack and fall and that deterioration will not occur. If the surveyor is not confident that movement has ceased or if it appears to him that it is continuing, he must then devote some attention to the advice he should give.

If the condition is very bad the surveyor may feel obliged to point out that radical reconstruction is required on sound principles, but this will not often be found to be necessary. More often his task will be to evolve some method of restraining movement so that the roof, once repaired, will provide long service with the minimum of trouble. Provided that the surveyor states that he remedy is not designed to restore the roof to its original pristine condition but simply to prevent the existing condition worsening it is considered that this is perfectly legitimate advice. An attempt to push the structure of a roof back to its original shape would result in more damage being caused in the process.

In particular with the double lean-to roofs on the tall narrow fronted Georgian and Victorian properties little need usually be done with a sagging central beam if it has taken up a new position of repose. What is necessary, however, is to re-align the gutter, so that it falls evenly towards the outlet and to ensure that the top ends of the rafters are supported properly by a new wall plate, in turn supported on enlarged and strengthened corbels. With a lead flashing along the top edge of the roof covering which would allow for any slight further movement there is good reason to suppose that such a roof should remain watertight for many years.

Where rafters are of inadequate size or spaced too far apart the surveyor should advise the provision of a purlin to prevent the deflection becoming worse. If purlins are unsupported the surveyor may be able to suggest temporary support and the replacement of the existing by a stronger member. Alternatively a more practical solution in the circumstances may be the provision of a strut, always supposing that the surveyor can see a method by which it too can be supported. If ends of purlins are affected by rot due to being built in to external walls, the surveyor should be able to suggest splicing with new timber, the new ends to be carried on metal corbels or hangers well treated against rust.

Simple lean-to roofs with rafters lacking a tie can be provided with ceiling joists which would adequately restrain further

[1] *Hingorani v. Blower and others* (1976), Estates Gazette 19 June 1976.

movement. In these circumstances the surveyor may also have to advise the provision of a new wall plate properly supported to take the top ends of the rafters. Close coupled roofs, however, which are exerting a thrust on top section of walls will require strengthening by the addition of collars in the correct position and the surveyor must point out that this is essential before any repairs or partial rebuilding is carried out to the top section of the walls.

If settlement in a roof is caused through a drop in an internal partition the surveyor may be able to devise and suggest a method whereby the weight of the roof is transferred from the partition to a beam, carried on the main walls.

Poor jointing or excessive cutting of timbers causing splits can be overcome, depending on the circumstances, by the splicing of new timber alongside or the bolting on of metal plates. A purlin cut on either side of a water cistern can possibly be supported on each side of the cistern by additional struts.

These are some of the more familiar types of repair carried out to defective roof structures and which are open to the suggestion of the surveyor. There are many more but so much of the advice given by a surveyor in such matters will depend on the circumstances of each individual case.

The more experience a surveyor has in dealing with repairs of this nature the more likely the advice to his client will prove to be sound and economical. It is after all the question of the cost of implementing such advice that will govern a purchaser's decision on whether to proceed or not and having made recommendations the surveyor must have some approximate figure in his mind to complete the advice.

Modern trussed rafter roofs Although quite a number of houses are still being built with roofs of the rafter and purlin close couple type particularly if the shape is unduly complicated, many houses built since the 1960s have roofs based on the use of prefabricated trussed rafters. These use stress graded timber in relatively small sizes joined together by thin galvanised steel connector plates forced into the timber in special presses. Their use provides both a saving in timber and in the speed of construction since site work is confined to erecting, fixing and bracing the prefabricated components.

Bracing and connectors It is the latter aspect of bracing which over the years has proved to be one of the problems with trussed rafters. Initially reliance was placed on the battens to provide bracing but these proved to be inadequate. Many roofs became unstable because of undue racking necessitating major reconstruction. If the requirements for bracing set out in the 1988 amendment to BS 5268 Part 3 are not found to have been complied with advice needs to be given to a prospective purchaser to upgrade the bracing to the required level, provided all other criteria, such as spacing of rafters not exceeding 600 mm and adequate fixings, can be met. This is because movement can occur at any time after installation not just when there are severe gales. It may also be necessary to advise the taking of specialist advice on the practicality of arranging the bracing on site.

The effects of inadequate or a lack of bracing or of trusses being

Trussed rafters shown in course of erection. The surveyor can check on all aspects here but with older installations he must point out any shortcomings from the requirements of BS 5268 Part 3 as amended 1988 for bracing spacing, straps and connectors.

installed too far apart are likely to show themselves as deformations causing unevenness in the roof covering, possibly movement in the supporting walls and should there be combined pressure from the ridge and an adjacent truss, movement in a gable wall. Other serious movement can arise from the unauthorised cutting or modification of a truss perhaps at the original time of construction or subsequently for some reason such as the installation of a new water cistern or in an attempt to make some of the roof space usable. Serious defects of this nature indicate that the surveyor may well need to advise the purchaser to take further advice on the likely cost and the type of work needed to put the roof in good order before proceeding further with the purchase.

The important consideration is that all trussed rafter installations should have been designed by an engineer. Not all those found will have been and even if they were, the earlier requirements have proved to be inadequate over the years. Tampering even to carry out repairs by the unqualified is likely to cause more trouble than it solves and could put the surveyor at risk.

Another feature which has caused trouble with trussed rafter roofs is the connectors. The galvanising on some of these has proved to be inadequate against the condensation occurring in the roof space when an effective layer of insulation at ceiling level is combined with a poor level of through ventilation. The lack of ventilation may be due to poor original design or poor installation causing the material to block the airways. Whatever the cause the evidence should be clear from damp staining on the timbers as well as corrosion to the connectors probably leading to joint failure. It is possible that damp in the timbers in such a roof will reach levels of about 20% and accordingly likely to be conducive to outbreaks of rot.

Low pitched roofs

In modern roofs of low pitch it is vital to ensure that the coverings are in conformity with the degree of pitch. It is possible to construct a simple wooden scale to establish the pitch so that this can be compared with the claddings employed. It is also vital to establish the degree of ventilation balanced against insulation so as to avoid condensation.

Roof extensions

The 1980s saw the increase in popularity of roof extensions to existing dwellings. Ranging from the basic one room with perhaps bathroom and landing to quite extensive additional accommodation, such extensions are equally variable in terms of the quality of their construction. Many, particularly where constructed under professional supervision with established contractors are excellent but many more are not. Small commercial firms in particular, relying upon similarity of design for their profit element and upon casual or freelance tradesmen have found themselves in Court.

Since much of the structure will be covered or inaccessible the surveyor should press for copies of the constructional drawings since these will tell him a great deal; particularly the name of the professional or commercial firm involved and the date of construction. He should be able to establish whether the correct consents have been obtained and a chat with the local Building Inspector can

When the roof pitch is steep as here and covered with tiles an extension can be discreet and lit by new roof lights. Even so the necessary strengthening as carried out in this case is often omitted.

prove informative. The surveyor should then be able to compare the plans with his site notes, first considering the structure such as beams, padstones and timbers, secondly claddings such as asphalt, felt and mansard slopes, thirdly, detailing such as windows, parapet

Roof extensions to the average suburban 1920–1940s house tend not to fit in too easily.

walls and gutters and finally, the finishings such as plasterwork, joinery, sanitary fittings and decorations. By this procedure the surveyor should be able to give a satisfactory account not only of the quality of the work but of any future problems likely to prove troublesome.

Woodworm and rot in pitched roof structures

As many of the individual timbers as possible in the roof-space must be examined for evidence of attacks by woodworm, or for outbreaks of dry or wet rot. The former is astonishingly prevalent in roof timbers and if an attack is present the surveyor must not miss it or fail to advise the purchaser to seek specialist advice and estimates for treatment and eradication.

Dry rot in roof-spaces, though comparatively rare, might be found, for example, where a trimmer placed against a chimney stack has become saturated due to a defect in a flashing or, a more serious case, where rot has affected the battens and rafters on a roof of shallow pitch provided with underfelt stretched tight across the rafters. However the extent of the attack may be difficult to determine accurately. Consequently the advice given to a purchaser in this respect must be carefully formulated to cover what can be seen, a diagnosis of the cause and some indication of what may be found on opening up. Estimates of possible cost for the eradication of dry rot are best avoided in view of the difficulty in ascertaining the extent of the outbreak but the reasons for not giving an approximate estimate should be explained in the report. If a surveyor considers he should or can give an approximate estimate he should be familiar with all the dangers involved and should certainly err on the high side to cover the contingencies which may arise.

In regard to woodworm and dry rot which can be found in all parts of buildings all surveyors should equip themselves with the handy, pocket size, full colour BRE booklet "Recognising wood rot and insect damage in buildings" for use on survey work.

PITCHED ROOF COVERINGS

Need to examine both exposed and internal surfaces

It is essential to make a close examination of the surfaces, both inner and outer, of the slates or tiles covering pitched roofs whenever possible. Very little can be said about the actual condition of the individual slates and tiles from a distant view, apart from the general condition of slopes, missing slates or tiles, etc., and if the surveyor writes in his report that they appear to be satisfactory from a distance this could be misleading. Close examination will very often reveal the necessity for a complete stripping and a renewal of the covering which a distant view would fail to disclose.

Slates
Natural

With flat natural slates an examination of the underside will often reveal the principal cause of decay. Poor quality natural slates often indicated by blistering on the surface, fading of colour and excessive breakages contain carbonates in varying quantities and the sulphorous acids in the atmosphere and the rainwater of urban areas react with the carbonates to form calcium sulphate which can reduce the slate to the consistency of cardboard. Owing to capillary action acidic rainwater tends to remain under and between slates because of the lack of camber so that the decay commences from the underside. Often the sight of many slipped slates and numerous lead or copper tingles fixing former slipped slates, indicates that the decay has destroyed the area of slate around the nail hole, but this must be confirmed by an examination of a number of slates, as the defect may simply be caused by the rusting of a nail or merely a split in an individual slate due to impact. Hence the necessity to see the underside to confirm the diagnosis.

If the diagnosis is of the decay as described above, then it is only a matter of a short time before the vast majority of the slates disintegrate so that complete renewal will be required. It is most important to a prospective purchaser to be informed of this and not to be just told that a few slipped slates need renewal. Confirmatory evidence may arise on the surface of natural slates from flaking and blistering and, if this should be in evidence, the exposed edges should be closely examined to see whether the lamination is extending through the entire thickness of the slate. Surface flaking, however, may be entirely absent and the only evidence may be that observed from the underside.

Besides the carbonate content of slates, the amount of iron sulphide present also has an effect on the weathering properties. The sulphide oxidises to form hydrated iron oxide and sulphuric acid. Should the slate also contain carbonates then the effect will be to decompose the slate entirely. This defect can arise in country as well as town areas.

It is not suggested that a surveyor should necessarily differentiate

Defective slating and flashings. Note slipped slates below apron and exposed nailing.

The underside of slating should always be examined wherever possible for decomposition. Easy here, of course, because underfelt has been omitted when the roof was provided with new battens and slates.

The surveyor will need to find out why it has been found necessary to apply a waterproof compound to the slating of this property and advise a prospective purchaser appropriately.

Unsatisfactory detailing at the head of this slated roof slope leads not only to unsightly staining but also a risk of damp penetration. Steps have already been taken to provide a hip iron to prevent further hip tiles from slipping off.

These tiles show storm damage to ridge and verge. They are unsightly, being stained due to defects in manufacture and lichen encrusted.

Pantiles, Italian and Spanish tiling
Interlocking tiles

Old and defective pantiling.

numerous patch replacements will indicate the probable need for stripping and retiling.

Pantiles, Italian and Spanish tiling should be examined in precisely the same way as for plain tiling having regard to the particular features of each type. The tiles, if of clay, have the same properties in use as ordinary plain tiles and the same defects. In particular the surveyor should be wary of unusual forms of tiles, which are usually machine made. Many of the imported tiles of this type have been found to be lacking in durability, owing to under burning and to require replacement after a relatively short period. Even if the tiles are sound there is often the difficulty of securing matching tiles for replacement of breakages, which is an additional point which should be brought to the attention of a prospective purchaser.

The 1970s saw the introduction on a large scale of concrete interlocking tiles for both new and replacement domestic roofing. These tiles were heavy in comparison with the slate coverings that they were intended to replace and the rush to use them on replacement work, often without any analysis of timber strengths, has left a legacy of sagging roofs and associated cracks in the cement fillets to roof abutments. Their appearance, in spite of dark coloured sand faced finishes, was originally unaesthetic and has not improved with the passing years as the effect of weathering has led to staining and discolouration.

The large number of roofs re-covered with interlocking concrete

An extensively patched tiled back addition roof now requiring stripping and recovering. Note the partially renewed cement fillet at the top of the slope masking the joint between the tiling and the parapet wall.

tiles pays tribute to their cheapness in production and delivery rather than to any other factor. Apart from their great weight they were found to be difficult to cut and adapt to angles so that their use is preferably restricted to straightforward roof shapes and it will

An example of interlocking profiled concrete tiles used to replace slating with an untidy lead flashing, the top edge of which is merely tucked into a groove, cut into the rendering of the parapet instead of being stepped into the brick joints.

A good example of a laced valley in small limestone "slates". A careful examination internally will be needed to ensure all is well. If not the surveyor's estimate of costs would need to provide for near exact replacement not something which would be considered inappropriate.

stone slating. As its name implies the covering material employed is not slate at all, but slabs of stone of varying thickness. In Yorkshire, the stone is usually a sandstone and the slabs are very heavy and thick.

In the Cotswolds area limestone is used but the slabs are thinner. Limestone is also used in Sussex but the slabs are thick in comparison with the Cotswolds. The shape as well as the thickness of the slabs used can be irregular. In any event stout timbers in the roof construction are necessary in view of the considerable weight of the covering and close attention must be given to this aspect.

The traditional method of securing the stone slates in position is by means of wood pegs over the battens. As discussed under tiles, these are prone to decay, shrinkage, breakage under shear stress and insect attack, so that a close examination of the pegs is necessary. An alternative method which may still be encountered is for the slabs to be secured in position by bedding down in mortar on roof boarding. If this method is found the surveyor should be very cautious, since considerable troubles may exist of which he may not be aware, due to damp being retained below the slabs. This dampness may well cause the underside of the stone slabs to disintegrate and also be the cause of decay in the timbers. The surveyor must give appropriate warnings should such form of construction be found.

As to the condition of the stone slabs themselves reference should be made to the next chapter, where defects in stone are discussed, with particular reference to the weathering properties of various types of stone. A purchaser of a house with such a roof should be informed that works of renewal and repair to such roofs are expensive and difficult, in that the supply of skilled labour to carry out the work is dwindling. For that matter the discovery of such a roof may well be a case when a surveyor should exercise extreme caution in regard to the advice he gives his client. He might consider it an occasion which warrants recommending specialist opinion.

Such roofs are not in the everyday ambit of most urban surveyors and there is no disgrace in admitting this to a client. In fact, it is the professional duty to do the best for a client that should encourage a surveyor to be frank in such cases. On the other hand the knowledge that stone slates can last between one hundred and two hundred years and the oak battens perhaps a hundred should prevent the surveyor from being too hasty in condemning this form of roofing without due cause.

Shingles   A form of covering found on cheap construction and in country areas may be shingles. Roofs covered with shingles are rare and the use of this material has not found much favour, due to a lack of suitable wood, the ease of availability of other coverings and the risk of fire. Nowadays, Western red cedar is generally adopted, which shrinks less than oak or elm which were previously used and which is considered resistant to insect attack.

Undue warping, splitting or shrinkage in the shingles may mean that flat or plain sawn shingles have been used rather than the rift sawn used in the best quality work. Such defects should be looked for together with evidence of woodworm attack. In view of the danger of decay, close boarding or felt should not be used in the groundwork, which should be limited to battens fixed direct to the rafters. Oak shingles, however, were occasionally fixed to boarding so that the surveyor needs to be suitably cautious if this mode of construction is found.

Thatch To many purchasers a country cottage with a thatched roof has become their ideal, so that instructions may well be received to carry out a survey of just such a property. With the shortage these days of skilled thatchers a purchaser must be warned of the difficulties involved in owning such a property unless in an area where special measures are taken for preservation and to encourage the thatcher's skill. With thatch there is also extra danger of fire and of infestation by vermin. In regard to fire the surveyor should check the thickness of brickwork surrounding any flues passing through the roof, as half brick thickness is considered to be insufficient in the circumstances to prevent the risk of fire.

Length of life The surveyor should also endeavour to ascertain when the present covering was provided and the type of thatch adopted. Good quality reeds used in thatching, up to about 3 m long may last for periods of up to 60 years but the life of straw thatch is only about 20 years so that if the presence of the latter is ascertained, re-covering may be due fairly shortly. This may not provide such a problem as it did a few years ago as materials for this purpose are now more readily available and the new thatch can be dipped in fire-proofing solutions to satisfy insurance companies' requirements.

Thatch formed into dramatic patterns around the top floor windows. The section above the lower windows clearly requires some repair.

THE MAIN AND SUBSIDIARY ROOFS

Other forms of pitched roof coverings

Other forms of covering such as corrugated asbestos, coloured pink on occasions, or galvanised corrugated iron sheets are rarely found on domestic houses as such, but often on garages and sheds. Corrugated asbestos has been found, however, on terrace houses where it cannot be seen from the road, probably a war damage replacement of the original covering, but in one case as a measure of economy on a Georgian house of character. This only serves to stress the dangers of assuming conditions without looking. The principal point in regard to such coverings which needs to be made in the report, is that even if such a covering is in reasonable condition, a rare finding in itself, it can only be a relatively short time before drastic and costly recovering is required.

POINTS OF DETAIL

Ridges and Hips

Finally, in relation to coverings, the treatment of the ridges and hips requires mentioning, even if briefly. Very often ridge tiles are loose and the pointing defective which lets in damp to affect the ridge plate and the tops of the rafters. If pointing is defective to hip tiles the same troubles will arise but there is a particular point to bear in mind in regard to hip tiles. If the bottom tile is loose and not supported by a bracket, there is a danger that the loose tile may fall off and cause an injury either to the purchaser or a visitor with perhaps serious consequences for the surveyor if redress is sought.

Abutments—cement fillets

An important source of damp penetration into roofs is due to defects at the junction of roof coverings, be they flat or sloping,

Pointing to ridge tiles tends to be neglected and results in damp penetration to affect the top of the rafters and the ridge itself. When the pointing to the finial falls out a high wind can cause dislodgement.

An old and cracked cement fillet to patched natural slate roofing. Apart from shrinkage, slight movement in the roof structure induces a lengthwise fracture where one part adheres to the brickwork and the remainder to the slate.

with parapet walls, gutters, chimney stacks and other projections through roofs. Correct detailing and the use of more expensive materials at these positions can produce trouble-free joints, which will last for many years, but all too often cheaper methods are adopted in the original construction and when these become defective the problem is seldom reconsidered from basic principles, and the old materials are renewed to produce the same defects a few years later.

A common example of the cheaper method is the cement fillet, which although it has a historical basis going back to Elizabethan and Jacobean times, has been used for the sake of its cheapness ever since. If cement fillets are used in conjunction with soakers the result is slightly better than when used on their own in that even if the fillet does crack a little, water will often run down the soakers without penetrating to the interior. If soakers are omitted, however, it is highly likely that the fillets will need renewal every five to ten years at most, depending on the richness of the mortar mix originally used. All too often the enthusiastic handyman type of small builder considers that the more cement used in the mix the better, not realising that the stronger the mix the greater the shrinkage that will result and the sooner the fillet will become defective.

This cardinal defect of cement fillets should always be pointed out to prospective purchasers and their replacement with flashings of metal or at least the introduction of soakers, coated with

Lead flashing dressed down over new profiled concrete tiles and tucked in to slanting groove cut in brickwork and rendering.

Old but correctly installed stepped zinc flashing with, where the roof has settled, an unusual sight of the zinc soakers. A much neater installation than that on the left. Note many eroded bricks where exposed in stack.

91

Flashings and soakers in lead and zinc

A novel arrangement for disposing of rainwater from zinc covered dormer windows. More of a baffle than a gutter to divert the water into the unusually narrow parapet gutter.

Eaves, parapet and valley gutters

bitumen, should be suggested as a desirable improvement. To establish whether soakers are already in position is not always an easy matter, but an effort should be made to establish their presence as the point is of some importance. The difficulty arises if the underside of the covering is boarded, but even then it is usually possible to find a wide joint between boards which will reveal either a sight of the metal soakers or a direct view of the underside of the slate or tile indicating that soakers are missing.

The surveyor must bear in mind and warn his client against possible defects in soakers of zinc or lead which will not usually be visible to the eye. These defects arise when either metal is in contact with Portland cement or lime since both metals are subject to alkali attack. This can cause corrosion of the upstanding portion of the soaker and in particular in the angle between the two wings. Soakers combined with cement fillets are prone to this defect, hence the advice noted above, that the soakers should be coated with bitumen before fixing. Bricks with a high sulphate content in a damp parapet wall will have a similar effect particularly on zinc, owing to the highly acidic nature of any water coming in contact with the metal.

An ideal finish at sloping abutments is a combination of lead soakers and stepped lead flashings. A cheaper finish is the same detailing in zinc, but it is important that the two metals should not be used together, as sometimes does occur on repair work, since an electrolytic action can be set up in damp conditions between the two, causing corrosion.

Lead is obviously the superior material and much longer lasting. In both cases, however, tell-tale signs of splits, patching with bitumastic material and gaps will suggest that all is not well and demand further investigation. If possible it is useful to carefully lift a section of flashing and examine the exposed wing of a soaker here and there, particularly if there are signs of dampness in the parapet walls and in view of the possibility of sulphate attack on the metal.

Close attention should be paid to the type and formation of all joints between a roof covering and parapet walls, chimney stacks, roof lights, ventilating pipes, and other penetrations, since defects at these points are probably the most common cause of all roof leakages.

Particular attention should also be paid to the back gutters of chimney stacks, since these should not only be watertight but should also be designed to lead rainwater away from the stacks on to the general roof slopes. These gutters are not always accessible for easy inspection by any means and if they are not seen and inspected closely the point must be stated in the report.

The use of Code 4 lead in both new and replacement work which is lighter than the traditional material used for flashings, ridges, hips etc. has meant that increased reliance is placed on the fixings. These need close attention where there is any suspicion of skimping.

It follows from the above remarks that particular attention must also be paid to the type of gutter into which rainwater from the roof

Plastic guttering and rainwater pipes. Awkward detailing such as this near suspect flashings presents a risk of damp penetration.

A contrast in gutters between the highly ornamental on the left and the utilitarian half round on the right. Unusually snow guards can just be discerned.

flows. The normal eaves gutter of cast iron is of course the best to find for the simple reason that being normally fixed projecting from a wall, defects can be readily seen when it rains. Provided the defective gutter section is not left too long and by this we mean a few weeks, not months, little harm normally results from a leakage. If the gutter, however, is left for a long period to discharge water down the outside wall, the pointing becomes washed out, damp penetrates perhaps into a floor, and dry rot is set up, a point which the surveyor must always be careful to investigate if defective gutters are noted.

When on the roof, the opportunity must be taken to look at the inside of these gutters. Often they are painted on the outside just before the house is put on the market, so that from ground level all looks well. Closer inspection may reveal them to be practically rusted through, as the inside face is seldom painted or treated against rust. The alignment can also be checked from above since, if the fall is incorrect, water can often be seen lying in the gutter some time after the last bout of rainfall.

Accumulations of leaves and silt can also be noted and pointed out to a purchaser as being a prospective danger if not cleared. The adequacy of gutters to cope with normal rainfall should always be kept in mind. Sudden overflows from gutters in exceptional storms do not usually do much damage, if any, but an overflow from a gutter every time it rains because the gutter is too small for the roof area served can be a totally different matter. Stained brickwork in the area of guttering is an indication of continual trouble from this source.

The material and type of eaves gutter employed should be noted, as the varying types have characteristic defects. Heavy ogee gutters of cast iron are subject to cracking often at the back, where it is impossible to paint the metal once it is fixed. Such cracks can remain undetected for long periods causing dampness in the eaves and at the top of the wall. Should the eaves be closed there is a danger of dry rot in the timbers. On the other hand half-round light iron gutters and brackets are very often fixed out of alignment. Splits are less common than with ogee gutters since practically the whole of the gutter can be painted.

On older properties light ogee gutters in zinc will sometimes be found. These are invariably provided with horizontal stiffeners at right angles to the flow, which tend to assist towards blocking the gutters with leaves in the autumn. Zinc gutters of this type have a limited useful life, are easily damaged by ladders and, as with cast iron ogee gutters, are prone to split at the back.

Other materials in use include light metals, such as aluminium and galvanised steel and various types of plastic. The life of all three is much less than for cast iron and accordingly the surveyor must take even greater care to check whether gutters and pipes are in need of renewal.

For a period in the 1940s–1950s sectional concrete gutters combining a fascia and soffit for pitched roofs enjoyed a vogue. Difficulties with jointing the sections and thermal movement often led

On older properties the collection of rainwater was often rudimentary of the hit and miss variety if taken care of at all. As such the broken and sagging length of gutter might be thought of little consequence. However it concentrates the flow of water and is likely to cause problems.

to damp penetration and the surveyor should carry out a careful examination of both gutters and adjacent areas when this type of guttering is found on a building.

The almost universal use of plastic gutters has lead to a number of problems ranging from sagging or distortion due to the incorrect installation of brackets and accessories and, in the case of larger buildings, gutters of inadequate size. In one extreme case seen a gutter had melted from the heat of a projecting boiler flue below.

Parapet and valley gutters, on the other hand, being directly above an internal ceiling often give all too clear indication of defects by reason of damage to decorations. It is often, however, extremely difficult to locate the actual source of the trouble. Nevertheless, the damaged decorations can be covered up and a blob of bitumastic applied to the defect which will suffice until the house is sold. All the more reason, therefore, for the surveyor to examine the surface of the gutter itself, be it of lead, zinc or asphalt.

As for the use of these materials for covering flat roofs, apart from pointing out clear indications of old age and possible trouble, such as cracks, holes, splits, bumps and defects in design such as long lengths of zinc and lead with soldered joints and the absence of drips, the surveyor must try to make some estimate of the age of the material and of its possible future life and advise his client accordingly.

The danger of the effect of acid run off on to metal gutters from pitched roofs with an accumulation of lichens or algae and from

General view of defective slate roof with loose flashing. Note how easy it would be to overlook the central valley gutter and the roof slopes generally hidden.

Above, the type of gutter that is often forgotten and which if blocked by debris can cause untold damage as can a badly holed hopper head as shown in the photograph below.

Glazed roofs or insertions always repay close attention. Sloping glass should be wired for safety in case of breakage as in the top example but not in the lower where other examples of poor incomplete work also occur. Upstands and glazing bars are prone to leakage unless properly detailed.

A valley gutter prone to blockage and consequential risk of overflow. The surveyor would need to ascertain the means of disposal for rainwater. Even upon retiling the basic structure would remain.

Below, back gutters are prone to blockage from growth on limestone slates.

Secret gutters

The surveyor would expect to find rotted timbers if signs of damp penetration below a parapet gutter were observed to this extent. Suitable warnings would need to be included in the report.

roofs covered with shingles or copper should need also to be remembered in connection with valley and parapet gutters.

Inadequate outlets from parapet gutters are a frequent source of trouble. In heavy rainstorms water builds up and overflows above flashings to cause damage internally. A build up of melting snow can cause a similar problem. Provided a house has not been newly decorated, signs of this can usually be seen internally, but this is a point which needs always to be borne in mind. Dry rot can result from this failure of design as well as from the usual defects in gutters and since the timbers supporting both parapet and valley gutters are rarely seen, advice on defects should always be coupled with a warning of what may be found when the old gutter is taken up.

A particular danger for the surveyor when valley gutters are present is that if the roof of the property is in four slopes with a valley gutter parallel to the frontage, as shown in the photograph at the bottom of page 94, it is easy to assume from ground level that there are only two slopes, or, alternatively, that there is a flat roof on top. If there is no trapdoor to the centre slopes a clamber up the outer slope and down to the valley is necessary, where a close view can be obtained of the surroundings.

Disposal of rainwater from a central valley gutter in this position is an awkward problem and of necessity is usually through another type of gutter of dubious value, the secret gutter. Failure to ascer-

A secret gutter within the depth of a floor. Casing around the pipe and floor covering could make it difficult to detect.

A secret gutter in the roof space taking discharge of rainwater from a parapet gutter and showing abundant signs of overflow and rotted timbers below gutter.

tain the presence of such a gutter should it prove defective could be very serious.

Such gutters are a constant source of trouble in themselves. For one thing they seem to be seldom cleared out and are easily clogged with silt. For another they are often inadequate in size to cope with the heaviest falls of rain as evidenced by the gutter in the photograph above on the right. Both of these failings commonly arise, even apart from usual defects in the lining or the supporting timbers. All must be closely examined and the appropriate advice given on each particular set of circumstances.

Ingress of birds

The presence of a central valley gutter as described in the previous paragraph is a frequent cause of birds nesting within the roof-space, the birds gaining access by means of the outlet to the secret gutter. This can be a nuisance on account of the deposits and noise if nothing else so that such outlets should be covered by a wire mesh or balloon.

All gutter outlets for that matter should be protected in this way, not so much from birds, but from possible blockage by leaves and silt. If, however, any birds' nests are noted in the eaves or in the top of pipes or ventilators it is essential to comment upon them and strongly advise their removal. This is not quite so flippant as it sounds, as birds are particularly drawn to the warmth provided by the ventilators to gas water heaters. Blockage to these can cause

Electrical wiring

In looking at the ceilings of the top floor rooms the surveyor will hardly fail to notice the electrical wiring and as a result he may be able to confirm his electrician's views on its condition. The danger here is that if it looks new the surveyor might be tempted into passing an opinion on its condition when a test is not being carried out. The advice to the surveyor must be to avoid this temptation at all costs as appearance is no guide at all and comments suggesting that "the wiring is in good condition" may well land the surveyor in trouble. Only a test can give a reliable opinion as to the condition of the electrical wiring in normal circumstances, the only exception being when, in conjunction with very old switches and socket outlets, it can be seen to be so ancient that a test would merely confirm the obvious need for renewal.

Cisterns

The opportunity should be taken to examine cold water storage cisterns while in the roof space. This one is rusty and clearly in need of renewal.

Water cisterns, their condition, whether they are of adequate size and properly covered and insulated can also be dealt with while on the roof or more often in the roof-space, together with all visible plumbing, its material, position of stop cocks and whether lagged or not. These items cannot be dealt with in a few brief paragraphs and detailed consideration is deferred to Chapter 7 on Services.

Finally, it must be remembered that surveyors are not the only people who need to have access to the roof-space and the roof slopes. Such access is required for maintenance purposes and if it requires a long ladder just to renew one or two missing slates the cost of such work is likely to be high. Even the house owner may need to get into the roof-space to shut down the water supply to a fitting and if the surveyor has had a difficult time getting up and around, the prospective purchaser might be interested to know of the difficulties. Easy access to the roof can save both the purchaser's money and temper.

On page 67 the surveyor is advised to be logical in establishing how the roof covering is supported structurally. Perhaps the best advice to the surveyor when presented with an array of timbers as on the right would be "Don't panic!"

102

Chapter 4
The Main Walls

CONTENTS

Flank walls to end of terrace properties

terrace construction, on both front and rear elevations, where there is a lack of lateral support only above the level of the top floor, the floor joists in this case bearing not on the party walls but on the external front and rear walls. In such instances, only the section of the front and rear walls above top floor level may be found to lean outwards. The typical "V" shaped outline to the verge of a roof at the top of the rear wall seems particularly prone to this, as shown above, the condition sometimes being made worse by the point load from the valley beam. Again, on front walls, heavy cornices can aggravate the position.

In the foregoing instances, by the time the external inspection has been reached, an examination from the base of the wall should serve to confirm the surveyor's preliminary diagnosis made from the notes assembled internally, on the roof and in the roof-space.

Other instances of walls with little lateral restraint occur fairly frequently in end of terrace, semi-detached and also detached properties. Very often the flank wall, although restrained vertically for a proportion of its length by the bond at each end to the front and rear walls and possibly by intermediate partitions, is built without any lateral restraint from floor joists. If it is also carried up to a point as a gable, it is not tied at the top by the weight of the roof and only minimal restraint is provided by the ridge plate, purlins or any

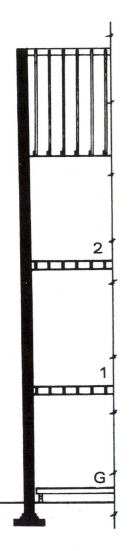

An almost totally unrestrained gable flank wall.

bedding down of slates or tiles at the verge. In these circumstances such a wall may develop a vertical lean in either direction, with its maximum at the top as shown alongside. Should the restraint, however, from the ridge, purlins or the bedding down be effective, the wall may tend to buckle, the change in direction occurring at eaves level and producing an unhappy effect. On plan a bow in the wall may also be apparent. A good example of this defect is shown on the photograph below in relation to a stone built house.

The gabled flank wall is one of a number of different variations of flank wall encountered. Such walls weighed down at the top by the roof but again without horizontal restraint from floors may curve vertically and horizontally outwards, the maximum movement taking place in the centre of the wall, perhaps adjoining window openings, always a plane of weakness in any wall. This condition may well arise in tall end of terrace houses of the Georgian and Victorian era, where the staircase is positioned against the flank wall. The circumstances often found in end of terrace properties and the differing types of movement which may arise in the flank wall related to the run of floor joists are shown at the top of the page overleaf.

Where in other properties of the same periods the stairs are positioned against the first party wall of the terrace, the flank wall is often combined with chimney stacks. These stacks may provide, in some instances, buttressing support to the wall, but as they are usually constructed of walling only one half brick in thickness

Distorted and leaning flank wall.

109

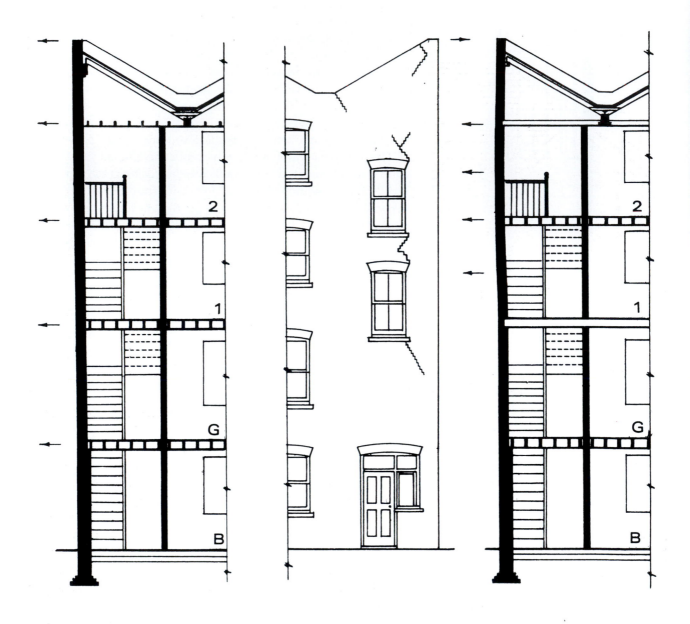

Tall chimney stacks

surrounding the flues, their movement tends to follow that of the wall of which they form part as shown on the photograph on the opposite page, top right.

If, as often arises in semi-detached construction of all periods, the roof at the top of the flank wall is in the form of a hipped slope and the stacks are carried up to a considerable height to overcome down-draught, the movement in the stacks may be eccentric compared with the wall below. Whereas the wall below may curve outwards, the stacks will probably lean inwards, since the top of the wall is restrained but not the top of the stacks. Should the top of the wall be subject to roof thrust the movement may be even more eccentric. With very tall stacks the effect can be dramatic to the eye, as on the drawing on the page opposite and on the photograph underneath, where an attempt has been made to restrain further movement.

Roof thrust pushes flank wall outward. Tall stack leans inward.

Again flank wall bowing out through lack of restraint and chimney stack leans inward.

Building Regulation requirements: ratio of height to thickness

In modern construction the question of lateral support is considered in greater detail than in former days and the Building Regulations and the British Standard Code of Practice utilised in the control and design of brick walls take this into account in determining the thickness of brickwork to be adopted. High, unsupported and thin brick walls often found in older buildings would not be permitted today and in assessing the suitability of walls in older buildings modern principles are useful to verify the evidence of the eyes.

In particular the recommendations as to the ratio of height to thickness form a useful guide. The example of the free standing wall used at the beginning of this chapter would have a ratio of height to thickness of 32 and the feeling of insecurity engendered would be fully justified. According to BS 5628 Part 3: 1985, "Use of Masonry", the maximum permitted height for a single brick free standing wall in wind zone 1 (South East England) would be 1.6 metres, a ratio of 8.5.

If the wall as part of a building, however, supported part of the roof loading and could thereby be considered restrained at the top, the ratio of height to thickness would be reduced to 24. For three-storey domestic construction the Building Regulations 1985 recommend that the ratio should not exceed 16 for each storey so that the wall is not satisfactory for its purpose unless restraint is present at both floor levels and at the top and the wall is built in a cement or cement and lime mortar.

111

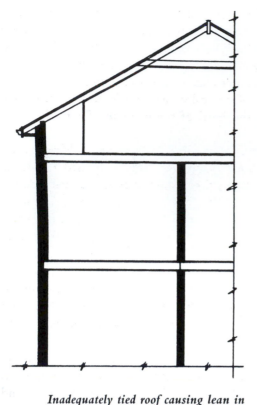

Inadequately tied roof causing lean in supporting brick wall.

Unfortunately many old buildings are constructed with lime mortar and the Building Regulations make no provision for this. Instead the Approved Document A "Structure" issued as part of the Building Regulations 1985 provides that a wall one brick thick when used in domestic construction not exceeding three storeys shall not exceed 9m in either height or length. Such a wall therefore forming the flank wall of a two-storey Georgian or early Victorian house and built in lime mortar might well be expected to buckle whether restrained at the top or not, since it falls short of modern structural requirements because of the type of mortar used.

Not all bulges and leans in brick walls are caused through inadequate thickness in relation to height or through a lack of lateral restraint, although this is probably the most frequent cause. A further common source of trouble of this type in old houses, however, is due to thrust from the roof, an example being shown alongside from an untied roof and on the two photographs below.

As we have seen from the previous chapter thrust from pitched roofs may arise through a lack of tie at the feet of the rafters or the absence or incorrect positioning of collars. It may also occur through the settlement of an internal partition which originally supported part of the roof load. Whatever the reason the tops of walls can be pushed outwards considerably and 50 mm to 75 mm is not an uncommon distance for the top of a wall to be out of upright from this cause alone.

Roof thrust causing a severe crack to the brickwork on the return wall of this outhouse.

Roof thrust causing a substantial lean to the front walls in this terrace of cottages. Note tapering reveals to windows and doors.

Deflection in floors

A further cause of localised bulges, often limited to a particular storey height, might be undue deflection in a timber floor either brought about by overloading or inadequacy of the original joists. Excessive deflection will result in the load from the floor being carried entirely on the inner edge of the wall exerting an eccentric thrust sideways instead of vertically downwards. As a result a bulge may well arise below the level of the particular floor which has deflected.

Bonding timbers

The surveyor should also not forget that in many old properties built before 1900 bonding timbers were frequently used within the thickness of the walls. These timbers are of course actually hidden by plaster or panelling so that they are never seen on a normal structural survey. If these are within a half brick or even a one brick distance from the outer face of the wall they may be affected by damp and cease to provide any useful support to the brickwork above. This can have a disruptive effect on the stability of a wall and is a further possible source of bulging. The drawing overleaf is devoted to the characteristics of the brickwork of much 17th- and 18th-century domestic building and shows how the bulging on the left below occurs.

Lack of bond between skins of brickwork

A practice also found at this time, but which extended right up to the present century, that of building facing brickwork in skins with little bond between the leaves is shown on the right below and this practice can also cause bulges.

Two causes of bulging in facing brickwork. On the left the rotting bonding timber causes the inner section of brickwork to settle fracturing the headers. Below inadequate bond to facing skin.

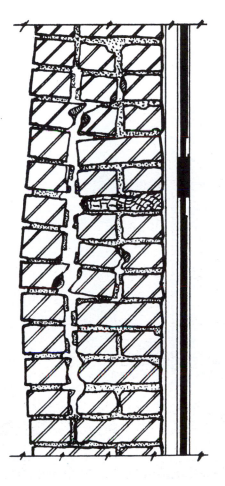

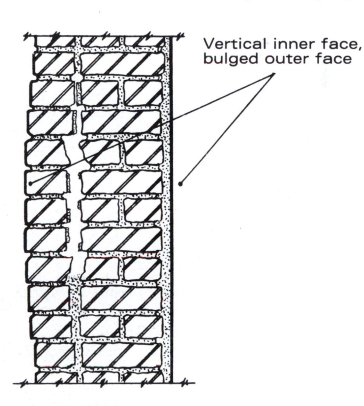

Vertical inner face, bulged outer face

The walls of the type of buildings at the top of the page built in the 17th and 18th centuries are typically constructed with timber ring beams supporting the floors and roof, bonding timbers within supporting the brickwork above, and very thin brickwork to the aprons below the windows. Wood panelling would provide the internal finish.

114

Movement below window causing cracked sill.

Movement above window causing arch to fail and fractures in the band course.

Below, a badly disturbed arch with pronounced outward movement.

The importance of windows as architectural features is illustrated in this attractive house.

Top right, a typical semi-detached house of the period 1920–40. Not surprisingly this type of house exhibits defects characteristic of its age, these being more prevalent in cheaper developments of the time. What is the surveyor to make of the house bottom right? The facing to the front elevation could be stone but it's regularity suggests the reconstituted variety and it's application could have been when the original windows were removed, the openings enlarged and new windows installed. Basically however it remains a "two up, two down" end of terrace house.

Defects produced by foundation failures or ground movements

Up to now we have considered leans and bulges, both horizontal and vertical, arising in walls through inadequacy in the original design by way of insufficient thickness in relation to height and lack of lateral restraint. We have also mentioned the effect, in particular, on such walls but also possibly on soundly designed walls, of undue thrust from floors or roof.

We must now devote some attention to the subject of defects observed in portions of walls above ground level which have their basis in faults of design in foundations or disturbing influences below ground. However, poor foundations for a house, in the writers' experience, have never been found in themselves to have been the cause of bulges and leans although it is quite possible others may have found such cases.

Poor foundations or disturbed support to foundations generally show themselves mainly by fractures through the brickwork, although it is appreciated that some form of a localised lean or bulge may also occur. This is not to say, of course, that walls, with a lean due to lack of restraint or other causes, necessarily have sound foundations. The reverse is usually the case and the temerity of builders of earlier days in founding a wall direct on soil or on two courses of footings is astonishing.

There are plenty of old houses with inadequate foundations by present-day standards remaining upright and erect, but this is due to the fact that the walls are of a reasonable thickness and the restraint from floors, partitions and such, sufficient. When such walls are disturbed, however, or other stresses are introduced, then troubles really arise, as we have seen, by way of leans and bulges.

Sub-soil and loading

Surveyors in the course of their training will have learnt that when loads are carried on a wall the foundations of the wall have to be designed to transmit that load together with the weight of the wall over a sufficient area of the ground, dependent on its bearing capacity. They will also have become familiar with the relatively simple calculations whereby the width of foundations can be ascertained knowing the condition of the sub-soil on which they are to bear. Having learnt all this from textbooks the surveyor is apt to be surprised when he finds that in dealing with the repair of older properties such foundations are rare. He might also feel rather smug in thinking that he knows a great deal more than his forebears. It is to be hoped that this feeling rapidly passes.

Contrast between older and newer practices

It is true that nowadays a greater knowledge and adoption of correct principles can be found but generally, however, rules of thumb and minimum requirements are followed slavishly without consideration of individual needs or a proper investigation of the sub-soil. Our forefathers were not always so foolish. This is easily demonstrated by the vast number of old buildings still standing perfectly erect while numbers of new buildings show every sign of significant failure.

A surveyor must retain a sense of proportion in the face of such contrary evidence and realise that in many cases for the weight of the structure and for particular soil conditions the rule of thumb and empirical standards adopted previously produced perfectly

117

satisfactory results in average cases. Nowadays there may well be numbers of houses with foundations far in excess of their requirements, but also many more where the same foundations are quite plainly inadequate.

Exposure of foundations · Unless the surveyor is especially instructed and has the vendor's permission, exposing a portion of the foundations is not a part of the procedure on a structural survey of an old house, by which is meant one that has been built for more than ten years. This might seem strange to some clients who consider foundations as vitally important in regard to the condition of a house. Even apart from difficulties in obtaining permission the necessary excavation would no doubt take some time.

Clearly if there are no defects visible in the walls attributable to the state of the foundations there is little point in the purchaser being informed of the nature of the foundations at a particular point. The statement that they may be presumed to be the same elsewhere and that they are satisfactory but do not comply with modern requirements is of little value. Irrespective of such modern requirements the purchaser could have been informed by the surveyor that they were satisfactory from the evidence of his inspection of the house under the conditions existing at the time.

The point about modern requirements is of interest only if alterations involving additional loading on the wall are envisaged or if the wall has to be taken down and rebuilt. It is suggested that the surveyor should always assume the non-compliance of foundations unless he knows from excavation that they do comply, or perhaps alternatively that the property is of such a date, having regard to the area, that compliance can be reasonably assumed.

A check on deposited plans with the local authority may assist the surveyor but very few properties built before the 1920s would be likely to comply with up-to-date requirements and furthermore there are many built since that period that do not comply. Even deposited plans only show intentions and nothing short of excavation all round can establish the precise construction of foundations.

Local knowledge important Generally over a period of time a surveyor will begin to acquire familiarity with types of property and sub-soil in his particular area so that when he is carrying out a structural survey he will be able to make reasonably reliable assumptions as to the type of foundation likely to have been employed by the original builders. A surveyor's local knowledge is clearly of great value to him and his client in this respect. This is one reason why some surveyors will not entertain instructions for a survey too far outside their own area, considering, in their view, that a client's best interests would be served by advising the client to approach a surveyor in the area where the property is situated.

Defective foundations As has been said before, the mere fact that an old property may have little or nothing in the way of foundations matters little so long as the structure is not adversely affected. However, in both new and old properties defects in the structure can at times be traced to mistakes by the original designers and builders. These mistakes may be by way of incorrect assumptions which they have made with regard to foundations. Loads may have been incorrectly judged or an optimistic view may have been taken of the bearing capacity of the soil with the result that the foundation to a wall is too narrow, or the foundations may be taken to an insufficient depth in the soil.

In such cases the foundations fail to fulfil their purpose and can be properly said to be defective. The evidence of such defects in foundation design will normally be visible in the brick joints in that these will be out of the horizontal and also in fractures in the brickwork. In particular where a wall is divided up in the nature of piers by windows all on the same vertical line, horizontal brick course joints may well droop in between the openings. Transverse fractures will also arise in the brickwork at the corners of the openings owing to excessive loads being transferred on to the foundations immediately below the pier. These loads are in excess of those existing generally at the base of the wall directly below the openings, with the result that a differential settlement occurs in the length of the wall.

Piers

Similar forms of misjudgement in allowing for greater loads at particular points arise in connection with piers attached to walls designed to carry loads over large openings. Hence in older properties with back additions a portion of the main rear wall may well be carried on a beam which rests on the junction of the side wall of the back addition and the main rear wall. Settlement due to a sinking of the foundation may arise at this point causing a fracture at the junctions and distortion in the line of brick courses.

Differential settlement

An example of differential settlement.

It is a well-known principle that foundations taking similar loads should be placed at an equal depth otherwise there is a danger of differential settlement. It is also recognised that all buildings undergo an initial overall settlement in the first few years of their life. However failure to appreciate these points and a desire to provide cellars under part only of a property often give rise to interesting conditions.

In some cases, pairs of semi-detached houses along a street are each provided with cellars for about half the width of the property and parallel to the flank wall. As a result the foundations to the flank wall were placed at a considerably greater depth than those of the party wall. As only to be expected, the initial settlement within a few years was greater on the party wall than on the flank wall, with the result that internally all floors sloped towards the party wall, the roof sloped in a similar fashion and brick joints on front and rear walls were out of the horizontal in the region of the party wall.

A similar condition in reverse has been observed in terrace houses where cellars were adjacent to alternate party walls and a defect of this nature is not uncommon in smaller houses built before 1910–1920 as shown on the photograph overleaf at the top. Even if there are no cellars the two end houses in a terrace are particularly prone to a similar form of defect. The circumstances here are that the first party wall is taking approximately twice the load than that taken by the flank wall. As a result there is greater settlement in the party wall and in consequence floors slope down

119

Cellars adjacent to alternate party walls may produce differential settlement in the remaining party wall.

towards the party wall and there are sloping sills, brick courses etc on the elevations. Two examples of this type of movement are shown below on the photographs.

Settlement in first party wall of a terrace due to heavier loading than on flank wall.

120

Additions

Fractures at the junction of the main walls with the walls of additions and bay windows will also often arise, since the foundations of the latter, being designed for smaller loads, are often placed at a shallower depth. As in the case of the cellars, described above, the fracturing may be due to differential initial settlement shortly after completion of the house or alternatively to subsequent continued settlement of the additions or bay windows in themselves. Reassurances can sometimes be given to a prospective purchaser if it appears that no movement has occurred since the initial settlement took place. Old decorations and previously repaired cracks which remain sound without further opening may assist in the diagnosis and the formulation of suitable advice in this respect.

Shallow foundations on clay and made up ground

Foundations generally placed at too shallow a depth will be prone to the effect of weather on the sub-soil on which they bear, particularly if this should be clay. Dry summers in particular deprive clay of moisture causing the soil to shrink and settle under the weight of the walls and inducing defects in the foundations and walls. Pavings around part of a house and even shaded areas on the north side can cause settlements to be of a differing amount since the ground is partially protected from the drying action of the sun. Differential settlement in such cases may be sufficient to tilt a whole house or merely cause a fracture in one length of a wall, usually at its weakest point, around window openings.

Shallow foundations on made up ground will also be subject to a differential settlement should the making up material be uneven in character over the site or where the filling material has not been properly consolidated. The design of foundations on made up ground is a difficult matter and failures are frequently found. A surveyor's local knowledge in such cases can be of great value to him.

Shallow foundations on sloping sites

On sloping sites, shallow foundations and, in particular, those of incorrect design will fail to hold the sliding tendency inherent in such positions. Settlement on hill sites is seldom uniform, with the result that corners of houses drop, one wall moves and even part of a wall can move. Houses built on sloping ground always require very careful inspection by the surveyor, particularly if the drains are found to be defective.

If the house is old, it is perhaps fortunate that time will bring the defects to light and make them obvious. If the house being surveyed is new, or near new, the greatest care is necessary to establish the construction from plans or evidence from the site, if at all possible, but this aspect will be fully dealt with in Chapter 12, together with the need for ascertaining the sub-soil, in relation to the different techniques required for surveys of new or near new properties.

Leaking drains

Extraneous matters can be a disturbing factor on the sub-soil causing settlement in foundations and walls and two aspects can be mentioned here in this connection. In particular, leaking drains have been known to cause serious settlement, sometimes relatively localised if from, say, a gully connecting to a main drain, but occasionally in a whole wall, where a badly leaking drain passes near

121

to and alongside the wall. If permission has been obtained to test the drains, the surveyor's suspicions of this cause of a settlement may be confirmed, otherwise the suspicion can only be stated with strong advice to carry out the test. If by process of elimination, the cause of a settlement cannot be ascertained the soundness of drains may well be a good line to follow as a possible solution to the problem.

Tree root damage

Another extraneous cause of settlements is tree roots. Roots of rapidly growing trees, particularly of poplar and elm, extract moisture from the soil causing settlement of the foundations. Houses with foundations on a shrinkable clay soil are in any event liable to settle if the foundations are shallow as we have already seen, but if there is a tree nearby the risk is doubly great and the risk extends to houses even with foundations normally deep enough for clay. It is very important for the surveyor to take particular note of all the trees on the site under review and also any trees on adjoining sites, or on the public footpath nearby. Bearing in mind that the roots of trees can extend in all directions to an extent equal to one-and-a-half times the height of the tree, the surveyor must have regard to the effect of the roots on the property being examined.

Having observed the presence of a tree in conjunction with clay soil, the surveyor will, it is hoped, quickly put two and two together if there are diagonal cracks in brickwork around door and window openings and on the corners of a property as for example on the photograph below since these cracks are typical of tree root action. The particular tree causing the trouble may be on adjoining land, in which case the purchaser may have a remedy at law in nuisance, but the surveyor should appreciate that not all purchasers

Severe cracking due to the effects of tree roots extracting moisture from the subsoil.

wish to become involved in litigation.

On the other hand consideration of the important factor of trees on the property being surveyed causing damage to other property nearby is dealt with in Chapter 8. An old house, containing no visible cracks in spite of a tree nearby may lull the suspicions but a prospective purchaser must be warned of the possible danger involved and be advised to remove the tree as a dry summer may produce cracks shortly after the purchase is completed. Because the pattern of cracks produced by settlement in real buildings as distinct from diagrammatic is complicated by the presence of windows, doors and other constructional features which divide walls into panels and introduce planes of weakness, it is probably best to consider diagrammatically first of all the patterns which would be produced if no such features were present.

Uniform settlement

The simplest form of settlement is, of course, uniform being the movement of the whole building from its original position on the left. This can either be total as shown centre below or partial as shown on the right. Some-such settlement usually occurs in all new buildings but if slight often remains undetected as there is usually no fracturing in the structure.

Differential settlement within a single structural unit

Differential settlement, on the other hand, within a single structural unit always causes fracturing, giving rise to vertical or diagonal cracks. It is sometimes said that the origin of the settlement lies below the highest point of a diagonal crack but while this is very often the case it is not invariably so and confirmation must be sought elsewhere. Cracks tend to follow a pattern consistent with a movement of a part of the building as a whole and there is often a rotational effect in panels of brickwork as they move about in axis.

With settlement in the centre of a wall cracks decrease in width with height. This is shown diagrammatically on the left and by way of two examples on the next page.

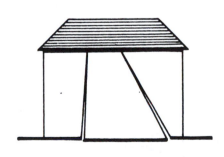

Settlement in the centre of a wall.

In the first example the provision of a large window and door opening at ground floor level in the original construction took little account of the loading from the roof and wall above. The pier between door and window is heavily overloaded. An asphalt damp proof course provides a slip joint and the cracks appear as two separate sections above and below the line of the asphalt and there is some oversailing at the corner as a result of the slippage movement. A leaking drain below the pier could produce the same effect in an otherwise sound structure.

123

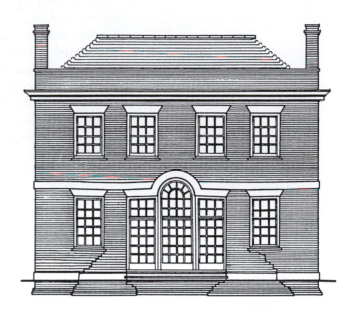

Settlement in the centre of a wall with the ends stable.

In the second example, the removal of the central pier to form an enlarged opening has thrown additional weight on the piers on either side, the foundations as a result settling. The cracks below the enlarged window opening would not be visible of course unless the ground was excavated.

When there are movements at the ends of a wall and the centre remains stable, the cracks increase in width with height as shown on the diagram on the left and in the example below. Here although the flank walls have settled to an equal amount the pattern of cracks varies at each end of the front wall. On the right the line of

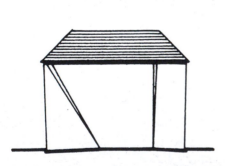

Settlement in the ends of a wall with the centre stable.

the crack is interrupted by the window where it takes the form of a gap between the frame and the brickwork. On the left, however, the large opening for the bay weakens the structure and allows the whole end panel of brickwork to move, resulting in a vertical fracture through the bay to the first floor window and upwards to eaves level. There will probably be appreciable loss of bearing for the purlin in the roof space where the movement will be at its maximum. Typical causes of this type of cracking are the effects of tree root action drying out a clay subsoil and again leaky drains running parallel to a length of wall.

Differential settlement between two structural units

Many houses are, of course, made up of more than one structural unit, for example a main building and a back addition as shown left, and centre below or a main building and a bay window as on the right. The latter although often appearing to be part of the main structure are usually a separate unit with thin walls and shallow foundations. Some examples are shown on the photographs.

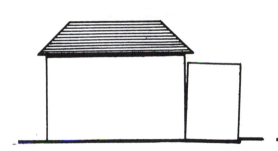

Above, differential settlement between two structural units.

Below, the shallower foundations usually provided to porches and bay windows often leads to differential settlement.

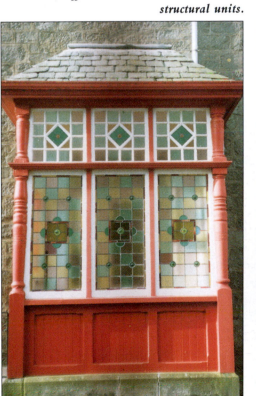

An elaborate version of the bay window.

Fracture in brickwork caused by differential settlement between main building and back addition.

The connection between the two units governs the type of damage which results when differential settlement occurs and more use of flexible joints rather than rigid connections would help to reduce the fracturing which commonly arises. Bonding, while it provides some restraint, is not sufficiently strong to prevent settlement occurring and although the bond might hold, fracturing will occur at the first plane of weakness, usually in the addition, as shown on the photograph above, it being the smaller structure, at window openings, but sometimes in the main structure instead.

Soil recovery

Because of the marked resemblance in the pattern of cracking to differential settlement in the ends of a wall it is appropriate at this stage to mention defects caused through soil recovery. Although it is the reverse of settlement there could be confusion between the two if little or no account is taken of site conditions. As the ground becomes swollen with moisture parts of the building are forced upwards and the cracks which form diminish in width as the height increases, as shown diagrammatically opposite at the top.

Tie Rods 'S' plates etc to restrain movements

Up to now in this chapter leans, bulges and settlements in walls as a whole have been dealt with. Two further points must be stressed in regard to these. The first is the presence of steel wall braces, steel channels, disc ties or "X" plates as shown on the photographs opposite which have already been added to a property by a previous owner to restrain further movement. These clearly indicate trouble in the past and must be carefully checked as to their effectiveness. If they appear to have been in position for some years and the sur-

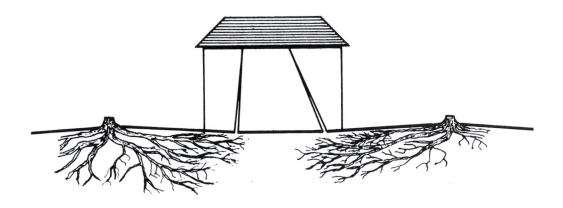

Effect of soil recovery following cutting down of trees.

Defects in bay windows: on the left outward bowing in overloaded piers: on the right settlement causing fractures due to differential movement between bay and main building.

Above an attempt to disguise the presence of tie rods. On the right the surveyor will be put on enquiry to ascertain how effective these very obvious tie rods are in restraining movement.

Advice in cases where settlement found

rounding brickwork remains sound and is not pulling away, indicating further movement, the prospective purchaser may have nothing to fear, but it is dangerous to be dogmatic about this.

One surveyor in a reported case[1] on a mortgage valuation where tie bars were present said that settlement had ceased. In the court hearing a structural engineer gave his opinion that there was a "fairly large risk of a substantial disaster" and damages of £12,000 were awarded against the surveyor. As to the second point, this concerns the advice in the report which the surveyor should give having found such defects as have been discussed so far in this chapter.

It should be clear that the surveyor's report must elaborate on a mere description of the defects found and an opinion as to their possible cause. The inferences to be drawn from their presence and the implication to a prospective purchaser must be made in a report, otherwise the surveyor has not fulfilled his duty. To draw these inferences is perhaps easier said than done.

There are many properties where bulges, leans and cracks have been in existence for years and have remained unaltered, the building having reached a new position of repose, albeit substantially different from its original position. Provided the building is not disturbed by outside sources or by imprudent alterations from within, it may well remain so for many years more. However, long term observation is required to establish with any degree of certainty whether such a position of repose has been reached and

[1] *Harris and Another v. Wyre Forest District Council* (1989). In this case the award was upheld on appeal but overturned in the House of Lords.

this would probably necessitate the use of tell-tales, periodic plumbing of walls and other forms of measurement.

The surveyor, on his one-day inspection of an entirely unfamiliar property, is at a disadvantage here and must on no account accept the results of any verbal examination of the vendor, however subtle the form of questions put. In the circumstances it cannot be said that on one inspection the surveyor need commit himself to a confident decision on the likelihood or otherwise of settlements remaining stable or becoming worse. He has not the information available to reach a decision of such importance. It is generally accepted that it would be unreasonable for the client to expect the surveyor to take such responsibility on the information to be derived from one inspection.

Clearly, however, a purchaser must be warned that there is an element of danger in purchasing a property with leaning and bulged walls and settlements. Here, we are assuming that the defects are not so serious as to be a downright danger to life and limb in which case the surveyor's advice can be much more positive. If the purchaser is prepared to take the risk of purchase, having sufficient desire for the property's other characteristics, then he does so upon his own responsibility. He must, however, be advised of the dangers involved and suggestions should be made as to the insertion of tell-tales, advice given as to the possible results of further movement, even involving the necessity for entire rebuilding or underpinning at a later date. If advice is given along these lines then in all probability the surveyor's duty is fulfilled. After all, some purchasers consider that leaning walls and sloping floors add to the charm of a house and if such purchasers buy, having been suitably warned, they have no cause for complaint if they have to dip deeply into their pockets to partially rebuild, repair, or prop the house up at a later date.

It may be that some readers will consider the recommendation given above on the advice to be written into the report rather negative and not very satisfactory from the client's point of view. The client's whole idea of having the survey carried out may have been to be reassured on the very points under discussion. This may be so but it does not alter the validity of what has been said before. The important aspect in the recommendation is that the surveyor "need not" commit himself on one inspection. It is not that the surveyor "must not" commit himself and circumstances may arise when he feels that he can give much more positive advice.

He may, for instance, already be familiar with the particular property or an identical property nearby. On the other hand he may consider, having weighed all the evidence, that the old making good to cracks visible in conjunction with the old decorations shows no signs of having been disturbed for years and that the property is in fact in a new position of repose. Provided that the surveyor is aware of all the dangers involved in expressing a confident opinion on such an important matter, and it is hoped that this aspect has been sufficiently stressed in the foregoing paragraphs, the writers see no reason why he should not proceed and give that advice.

Warnings of possible further movement

It might be difficult from the evidence of the crack taken alone to determine whether this is an example of the end of a wall moving out and the centre remaining stable or vice versa. Further evidence will need to be sought.

A damp proof course can provide a slip joint when brickwork expands. Note above absence of a dpc below the brick coping and damp stains at lower level possibly due to a blocked outlet from the flat roof.

here or under the main roof, if preferred, since they are normally seen closely from the roof and it is convenient to the purchaser or his builder, attending to items of disrepair, to have them grouped together in that section. Logically, however, in reporting on the main walls the finish at the top should be dealt with, even if only by a cross-reference to the section on roofs.

Eaves

If there are no parapet walls the construction of the eaves will be noted at this stage for inclusion in the chapter on roofs. It is important to make a close examination of the soffit to the eaves from windows or balconies, since, from ground level, it is not always possible to tell the form of construction at a glance. If the soffit is of plaster on lathing, as it may well be on earlier buildings, a closer inspection will often reveal cracks, looseness and bulged areas not easily ascertainable from ground level.

Match boarding can also easily be affected with dry rot or wet rot if gutters have been leaking through splits at the back. Other materials used for closing the eaves at this point include plywood sheeting, which may be laminating due to effects of damp and asbestos sheeting. If the surveyor cannot see the construction at the eaves closely he should not guess but say he cannot and say why. A guess will only make him look foolish if proved to be wrong.

Lintels and Bressummers

Following on downwards on each elevation, some consideration must be given to the formation of openings for windows and doors and the support provided to the brickwork above. Localised settlements will frequently be found in these areas. Every opening in an external wall is spanned by a lintel or arch, or perhaps both, to support the weight of the brickwork above.

In the past the combination of a wood lintel with a brick arch was very common. If the lintel is positioned in a wall only one brick thick, or even one and a half bricks thick where the pointing is defective, it is possible for driving rain to penetrate and affect the condition of the timber to such an extent, either by dry or wet rot, that sagging will occur and the brickwork above will be deprived of its proper support. Such a defect is found particularly in houses built

134

Besides parapets and their copings unprotected cornices are a source of frequent damp penetration. Vegetation growth as here is a sure indication of damp retention.

The bresummer above the bay window is often heavily overloaded leading to deflection aggravated, should there have been damp penetration, by rot. Even the roof here has settled but a glance by the surveyor will indicate here that the basic fault is one of design since the houses on either side are affected.

The surveyor will need to investigate what has happened here and what work has been needed to produce the uncharacteristic arch over the front door. No attempt has been made to repair the crack through the brickwork to the first floor window.

In properties built before about 1900 it is to be expected that brickwork above window and door openings will be supported on timber lintels. On exposure they are likely to be in the condition shown below with little, if any, strength remaining should there be indications as here of much damp penetration.

Deflection in lintel. Perhaps not as bad as it appears as the sill to the windows above is level. Nevertheless close investigation will be needed.

support for the brickwork above. This will not always be possible and there is absolutely no use in the surveyor saying that the brickwork is probably supported on a steel beam if he has not seen it. It is just as likely to be a wood beam or even constructed of re-inforced concrete.

A substantial timber lintel left exposed on the face of a stone building. The effects of exposure to the weather are becoming apparent.

139

The irregularity of the upper window openings and the mis-alignment of the cornice suggests a problem in the beam over the head of the bay window which holds up the front wall. Older properties often show signs of defects which may have been put right. The surveyor should check.

There is always a particular danger that a defective joint between the wall above and the bay window or other roof will allow dampness to penetrate and affect the beam giving rise to the depressing appearance as shown on the photograph above. Once again, care is necessary to open up the adjacent floor, if possible, to make a close examination.

It is good practice to examine any beams or lintels of importance from the floor above and if it is not possible to do this to point out the dangers of neglect should there be any signs of defects externally, particularly by way of settlement or defective flashings at the junction of the roof and wall.

In the small terrace house illustrated opposite at the top of the page in elevation and section about one quarter of the total load above ground floor level is carried on the beam over the bay window. Even apart from the possibility of overloading, which is not uncommon, damp penetration at the junction of front wall and bay roof can produce the effect if the beam is affected by rot.

Balconies

Particular attention should be paid to sills of windows and also thresholds of french doors opening on to balconies. Even apart from the fact that there may be settlement, it will often be found that window sills, if they are of stone or rendered brick, will crack. These cracks invariably allow dampness to penetrate to the wall below, to show signs by way of damp patches internally, although a stain can sometimes also be seen on brickwork externally. If allowed to continue such a defect gives rise to soft and loose plaster internally, possibly an attack of rot in the skirting, even apart from the damage caused to the decorations.

140

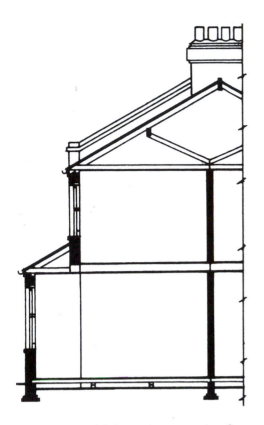

Indications of defective beam carrying front wall over bay window. May be due to over-loading or damp penetration.

Window and door mouldings

Very few canopies will be found as ideally protected as this with a copper flashing.

Should the apron below the window internally be panelled in wood, the position may be much worse and a more extensive attack of dry rot be set up, without the occupier being aware of it. If dampness below sills is observed but no cracks are apparent, the surveyor should check whether there is a throating on the sill. This is often omitted and causes water from the sill to run back along the underside of the projection to soak into the brickwork. Occasionally the throating will be found to be blocked and rendered ineffective by paint.

At the same time as lintels and sills are being considered when examining an external wall, the state of the reveals and any dressings should also be noted. Rendered reveals will sometimes be found to be cracked and loose. Stone or stucco mouldings and ornamentation to the surrounds may also be crumbling and loose. If these surrounds extend above the windows there is the possibility of damp penetration should cracks be allowed to develop. Even at the side, cracks to the surface of mouldings, particularly on top edges, permit the passage of damp to the interior. Any band or string courses and the like on an elevation also present similar problems if their condition is neglected for undue periods and these also should be examined, if necessary from a ladder.

Two points in particular arise in connection with mouldings and band courses. One is the danger of pieces falling and the other the possibility of rot in lintels, window frames and even skirting and floors. A case of dry rot extending to skirting, floorboards and joists

141

and also to the interior of a box shutter was traced to a defective band course, level with the skirting, on an external wall of a neglected Victorian terrace house.

We have now, in considering an elevation as a whole, looked at the top and the main area of the wall including any openings. This leaves the base of the wall. An examination of the base of the main walls will reveal a great deal about the structure and its ability to withstand damp and possible dry rot.

Damp proof courses

With luck, the surveyor will be able to see signs of a damp-proof course and, with even more luck be able to describe its type. A wide mortar joint near the base of a wall, ideally 150 mm or so above the ground level, will almost certainly prove to be a damp-proof course comprising two courses of slates. If settlement is present in the house the surveyor needs to check that fractures do not extend through the slates, which may make the damp proof course ineffective at that point.

An asphalt damp-proof course can very often readily be spotted, owing to its propensity to squeeze out under the weight of the brick wall above. Providing this squeezing out has not gone too far, it is not necessarily serious but the possibility of its continuance needs to be mentioned in the report.

If there was a damp proof course to this house it would be rendered ineffective by the earth built up against the base of the wall.

The tendency of brickwork to slide over an asphalt damp-proof course should also not be forgotten and this can be a serious defect in itself, if of more than 25 mm or so. An example of this sliding effect is shown in relation to a parapet on page 134 and also in relation to a ground movement problem on page 124.

Whether a property is likely to have a damp-proof course or not can often be gauged from its approximate date of construction. Damp courses became a by-law requirement around the turn of the present century. It is only in the very best forms of construction that a damp-proof course is found in a house of an earlier date. However, even with properties constructed after 1900 or so, one must never assume the presence of a damp-proof course.

Slates and asphalt, as described above, are fairly easy to spot, other forms such as lead, copper, bituminous felt with or without a lead core, or polythene, are more difficult, but with the permission of the vendor it may be possible to rake out a little mortar of the joint on which it is bedded and establish the particular type adopted.

Rising damp

The importance of establishing the presence of a damp-proof course and its type cannot be overstressed. The absence of a damp-proof course must always be clearly stated in a report together with a paragraph of advice regarding the type of troubles likely to be experienced owing to this absence.

If a property has been left vacant for some time, signs of rising dampness may well have disappeared. Few prospective purchasers realise that heating rooms will draw moisture up the walls and out to the surface of the plaster ruining the decorations. Particularly dangerous to the surveyor is the newly decorated or altered house, where it is easy to disguise the presence of rising dampness. To the chagrin of the purchaser this will only appear after he has moved in. The unwary surveyor can easily be misled in an old house, newly decorated or altered and "modernised" to fetch a higher price. The use of a moisture meter is here essential to probe deeply beyond the mere surface of decorated walls and externally readings can often be taken in mortar joints.

The extent to which a moisture meter must be used in the absence of visible evidence, or evidence to the touch, of damp was considered by the Judge in a negligence claim against a surveyor.[1] The case concerned a house built in 1975, surveyed in July 1979 and purchased the following September but where extensive damp was discovered by the new owner in October. Although the damp was caused by a leaking central heating pipe in the concrete floor it caused damp in the walls as well.

Evidence was brought to show that the damp must have been present in July when the survey was carried out, although not visible to the eye or discernible by running a hand down the wall. While the Judge agreed that the surveyor could not be expected to test the walls every "foot or so" nevertheless he decided that a more thorough use of the moisture meter would have detected the defect. Damages of £6000 were awarded against the surveyor contrasting with the £90 charged for the survey.

Unless the surveyor makes a practice of testing for dampness throughout every few feet he should keep a note of where the moisture meter was used on each survey and this might best be done by indicating the positions on a sketch plan.

If, on the other hand, a damp-proof course is provided care must be taken to ensure that it is of a sound type and not affected by movement in the wall itself or rendered ineffective by other causes. Lead, copper or a good bituminous felt membrane with a lead foil core, are sound materials being able to give a little to compensate for the inevitable slight movement in the initial settlement of a new building. However, large movements can cause a breakage in the continuity of the membrane, allowing dampness to rise in the wall.

Occasionally it may be found that insufficient lap has been allowed in the original construction at the joints of the strips and this also may permit damp to rise. Such a defect cannot be seen in the normal course of events without opening up, but it may be included in a report as an intelligent surmise for a defect causing an isolated patch of rising dampness if no other cause is apparent, with the appropriate recommendation to open up to establish whether the surmise is correct or not.

Thin lead damp-proof courses uncoated with bitumen when originally built into the wall may be affected by the action of lime and Portland cement particularly if the lower part of the wall is wet. This may cause partial or total failure over a long period, though such failures are rare.

In regard to bituminous felt and polythene, where employed, it is the surveyor's duty to indicate that these are materials originally introduced for economy, and that their long-term utility has not yet been proved to be as satisfactory as other more permanent

Laying new paving as here towards the front of the property with a disregard for the level of the damp proof course can cause bridging and result in rising damp appearing internally.

---

[1] *Fryer and Another v. Bunney and Another* (1981), Estates Gazette, 10 July 1982.

forms. Clearly one would anticipate that the sandwich layer of lead foil would extend the life of a bituminous felt damp-proof course over a type lacking this refinement.

The surveyor on inspecting older properties, may well come across earlier forms of damp-proof material, for example heavy paper coated in wax or pitch or canvas soaked in bitumen. Many of these older forms, including some of the inferior early and later cheap felts, will often be found to have become ineffective.

The presence of a plinth, or rendering to the whole of the exterior, may add to the surveyor's difficulty in ascertaining the presence of a damp-proof course. That such rendering or plinth should not, in correct building construction, span or bridge the damp-proof course does not prevent instances of this from being frequently found. The effect of this fault in design is to allow dampness to by-pass the membrane and appear above the damp course level. In such cases in order to check on whether a damp-proof course is present, it will be necessary to raise a floorboard internally and examine the inside face of the wall where it should be possible to rake a little of the mortar from the bedding joint, as already suggested for the outside face.

If isolated patches of rising damp are noted on the internal inspection, they may be due to a bridging of the horizontal damp-proof course at the same point externally. It is sound practice to follow the line of the damp-proof course in the external walls on all the exposed elevations to check whether bridging has occurred at any particular point.

Bridging due to the presence of a plinth or rendering has already

Bridging of Damp Proof Course

The surveyor would expect to find signs of damp penetration in both these situations. Raised flower beds on the left, a semi-basement on the right.

144

Overflow pipes projecting insufficiently beyond the face of the wall to throw water clear are a frequent source of damp penetration, as here, when unattended for a long period.

Typical details at the base of main walls from four houses of differing periods all suffering from rising damp. Internal plaster can be expected to be damp in both the stone cottage on the left at A and the late 19th century house at B built before dpcs became a requirement. Timber floors can also be expected to be rotted. In C and D for houses built between 1920 and 1940 at C and around 1960 at D the dpc has been bridged by a path externally and there is no connection between the dpc in the solid floor and the wall in C. Damp strains and rot in the skirting could be anticipated as it could in D where the ground has been allowed to rise above the dpc level and mortar droppings in the cavity bridge the dpc and provide a path for moisture to rise in the wall.

been mentioned in the preceding paragraph but soil allowed to build up against the wall, as in the photograph on the left below, a path constructed against the wall at a higher level than the damp-proof course, bridging by the construction of a solid floor at a higher level and, in cavity wall construction, an accumulation of mortar droppings at the base of the cavity are all frequent causes of this defect. Damp-proof courses stopped short of the external face of the wall usually for the sake of appearances, and subsequently pointed up with mortar, are also a cause of this trouble.

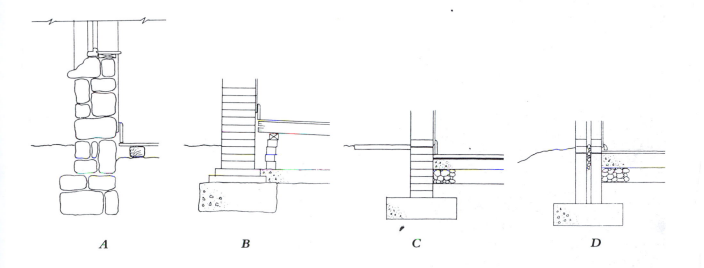

A	*B*	*C*	*D*

Ground Floor Air Bricks

Where the property being inspected has a ground floor constructed of timber joists and boarding, the absence of a damp-proof course in the walls makes this floor particularly prone to attacks of dry rot. There is, therefore, all the more reason at this stage to check, in addition, on the presence of and the number and position of air bricks which provide ventilation to the underside of the timber and the lack of which, combined with dampness, will readily set up conditions suitable for an attack. If no air bricks are present the surveyor must indicate the danger of this and recommend their installation.

If air bricks are present they should be examined to see that they are clear and unobstructed ideally from the inside as well as the outside. This can be done with a piece of wire. In particular, the air bricks should be positioned above the damp-proof course and on no account should soil be allowed to rise to within 150 mm of the damp-proof course and certainly never to obstruct the openings. Keen gardener owners have a tendency to bank up earth against the walls of a house, or to build a rockery, bridging the damp-proof course as a result, and obscuring the air bricks. They then wonder why they are troubled with rising dampness in the walls and dry rot in the floor.

Furthermore air bricks near ground level may allow water to run into the sub-floor space which is undesirable. Openings without gratings may also allow vermin to enter and easily become blocked with leaves. It should go without saying that the surveyor on encountering unsatisfactory conditions at the base of a wall will be put on guard and if possible will takes steps to investigate the presence of dry rot nearby but the full examination of floors will be dealt with in the next chapter.

While outside, a useful test can be made on whether the air bricks function satisfactorily by holding a lighted match against the grating. If the air brick is efficient the flame will be drawn towards the opening. The surveyor should take a note at this stage of the inspection of the number of air bricks and their position, as this information will be useful on checking whether they are sufficient and in the correct positions to fulfil their function satisfactorily in relation to the construction of the floor.

Advice on Rising Damp

Where surveys are carried out on houses built before 1900 which have no damp-proof course, the surveyor must be very careful in his report by way of anticipating a natural inquiry from a purchaser as to what he can do about it and in what way the rising dampness can be "cured". To say merely in the report that there is no damp-proof course and rising damp in the walls is not sufficient since it does not follow the precept of describe, diagnose and prescribe a remedy whenever possible, which it has been suggested should always be followed.

From the surveyor's point of view, reporting on rising damp in a structural survey report, is not so difficult as it may seem, although in a laudable desire to be helpful to their clients surveyors have found themselves in trouble in the courts on this very subject. The only complete method of eliminating rising dampness is the inser-

146

tion of a horizontal damp-proof course and this should be stated in the report.

Any palliatives, such as water-proof rendering on internal walls, water-proof lathing, skin walls, and the like are not methods of eliminating rising damp but merely serve to disguise it or cover it up. They are fraught with danger for various reasons. One important reason is the level of the local water table, a point on which it is considered a surveyor may not be able to familiarise himself on instructions for a survey and report unless in his immediate and well-known area.

If dampness is contained in a wall and cannot evaporate either externally or internally as is the case when a water-proof rendering or lathing is applied internally, it will rise in the wall until the level of the water table is reached. The water table may well equal the height or even exceed the height of the house. Since advice to apply water-proof rendering or lathing on the internal walls is usually limited to the lower floor, it should be clear that there is every possibility of the dampness rising to first floor level or higher, appearing on decorations where it did not do so formerly, damaging plaster and even affecting first floor timbers. The danger of this happening is considerably greater where the walls of a house are constructed of very porous bricks.[1]

The insertion of a damp-proof course is expensive. The methods of covering up rising dampness or patent methods of reducing its incidence are somewhat cheaper. In a desire to save the purchaser expense, the surveyor runs a serious risk of having to pay heavy damages if his advice is other than correct. If the client wishes to save money subsequently by trying an experiment with cheaper methods of combating rising dampness then he is at liberty to do so and run the risk of failure, but there is no reason why the surveyor should put himself at risk in offering such advice.

Having said this, however, it is recognised that if a surveyor is dealing with a property in his own area which he knows well, or with a property identical and near to another property with which he is familiar, he may well feel that the level of the water table and other factors in regard to the construction of the walls, such as the porosity of the bricks, are such that rising dampness is limited.

In such circumstances the other measures mentioned above may well keep it hidden and within reasonable bounds and there is no reason why he should not say so. The important factor is that the surveyor should realise the limitations of the methods of hiding rising dampness and bring these out in the report. Clearly in addition he must be sure of his ground.

Proprietary barriers to combat rising damp

A final point on the absence of damp-proof courses and rising dampness concerns the numerous proprietary methods which are claimed to provide a moisture barrier in old walls without the need to insert the traditional type of damp course. It is obviously necessary to consider these particularly where the existing walling is not

[1] *Hill v. Debenham, Tewson and Chinnocks* (1958), Estates Gazette, 14th June, 1958, p. 835.

147

appropriate for the insertion of the traditional type, e.g. a random rubble stone wall. The advice of the Building Research Establishment needs to be borne in mind here to the effect that the only non-traditional types suitable for use are those awarded an Agrément certificate. As recently as 1986 these were limited to the chemical injection type.

It is clear that the surveyor would be unwise to recommend any other non-traditional type until such time as it obtained an Agrément Certificate. Surveyors have a reputation for conservatism but this may not be a bad thing when there is a risk of a client wasting his money on the surveyor's advice with the corollary of a complaint. It is true that the proprietors of some methods offer a guarantee but the worth of this presupposes the existence of the company concerned in the years to come when a client may need to invoke its benefits.

The other side of the coin so-to-speak also applies in that when surveying a house which has had a new damp-proof course installed, either for the first time or as a replacement to a defective damp-proof course, he would have to report that it was not of a recommended variety unless it was of the traditional or chemical injection type.

Needless to say faced with the evidence of a fairly new installation of whatever type the surveyor would need to take particular care on his inspection to ascertain flaws and any areas where damp was beginning to reappear, a task made more difficult if the correct specification of hard rendering had been applied at the base of the walls internally to counteract any remaining hygroscopic salts in the wall.

Damp-proof courses installed at the wrong level and a loss of the chemical through cracks in the wall are not uncommon flaws in design and workmanship which are found.

If the installation was entirely new he would need to give advice on the type, comment on any evidence of bad installation but also have to point out that time alone would prove whether it was effective or not. Some reassurance can be obtained from examining copies of plans, estimates and guarantees which show that the whole of the necessary work was carried out by an established specialist firm but all too often the surveyor will find that the chemical injection work has been carried out by one firm, who may or may not be still in business, while the work of replastering has been carried out by a local builder.

Basements   The impression has been given up to now that the lowest floor of the property under consideration is the ground floor and no mention has been made of basements. The presence of a basement does not alter the method of inspection in regard to the external walls, the presence or otherwise of a damp-proof course and the ventilation to the underside of a timber floor. All these items are dealt with in precisely the same way, but there is an additional item of importance that requires attention.

Wherever walls enclosing rooms of basements or semi-basements are in contact with the surrounding ground a vertical damp-

Colourful but dangerous growth of dry rot fungus spreading rapidly in a basement.

Plinths and External Pavings

A brick plinth rendered ineffective by the absence of paving and a defective rainwater pipe.

proof course should be present to separate the two and prevent damp penetration. Since most houses with basements were constructed in the era of domestic servants, it follows that the majority of these houses date from times prior to damp-proof course requirements, so that it is relatively rare to find such an essential feature. In those days the staff were expected to take conditions of rising dampness in their stride without complaint.

All too often the absence of a vertical damp-proof course will be painfully obvious from the internal inspection, so that a surmise of the absence based on the visible evidence is reasonably certain to be correct. The reverse, however, is not so certain and the absence of damp patches is no indication of the presence of a damp-proof course which must on no account be assumed. If it cannot be seen the surveyor must report his findings, state what he would hope to find if he could see it and state why he cannot see it. If this should be due to the lack of opportunity for opening up, then the comments in the report should be completed with a recommendation that this should be done if it is considered vital to establish the true conditions.

It should not be thought that in the above circumstances vertical damp-proof courses will never be found. In better quality construction, prior to about 1900, slate vertical damp-proof courses were used at times and since then asphalt has been used extensively for this purpose.

The dangers when no examination is possible must be stressed in the report but on the other hand the surveyor must be careful not to libel a property by stating that it has no damp-proof course without being certain. After all it may be a house where a damp-proof course has been inserted at a later date and the closest of examinations may be necessary to detect its presence.

Very often at the base of the external walls there will be found plinths and either soil, gravel or some form of paving. These must be closely examined, particularly if the house is without a damp-proof course. Excessively cracked or loose plinths allow damp penetration and when this happens the very presence of a plinth prevents rapid drying out of the brickwork below.

If a plinth is provided it must be always well maintained, otherwise it becomes more of a liability than an asset. The surveyor should take particular note of the level of any plinth in relation to the damp-proof course. Sometimes if trouble has been experienced from excessive rising damp, a plinth is provided together with a coving at its base connecting it with the adjacent paving. Such paving should be provided with a good fall away from the base of the wall. If this is not done, then water will lie near the wall and find its way through fine cracks eventually into the brickwork.

The presence of moss and mud on the paving is often a good indication that the fall is inadequate. In such cases hacking up and reforming should be recommended, but at the same time it should be pointed out that these features are only present to prevent surface water getting into the brickwork and making the base of the wall wetter than it need be. They do nothing towards solving a

149

**Measurement of walls to establish
precise form of construction**

problem of rising dampness caused through the absence of a damp-proof course.

To conclude an examination of the main walls the actual components of the wall and their suitability for the task of keeping out the weather need to be considered. First the actual construction of the external walls must be established and here measurement will be of assistance. As previously mentioned, at each floor level the thickness of the external walls should be taken. This measurement will probably give some indication of the likely construction, when the outside face is of brick.

A one brick thick wall with plaster internally will measure about 248 mm to 254 mm. If also rendered externally about 267 mm to 280 mm; the figures for walls one and a half brick thick being respectively 362 mm to 368 mm and 380 mm to 387 mm. If cavity brick wall construction has been adopted, these figures will be increased by about 50 mm in each case. Cavity wall construction has only become common since the 1940s so that on arrival an estimation of the date of the house will enable some idea to be obtained of whether such construction is to be expected. If so, then the measurements of the thickness of external walls should confirm it, or at least be sufficiently odd to rule out traditional solid construction. The absence of headers on the external face is also a useful confirmation of cavity work.

Care, however, must be taken not to assume that because a wall seems by measurement to be odd and therefore of cavity construction, that both leaves are of brick. Suitable blocks for use on the inner leaf may measure from 76 mm to 114 mm in thickness. Unless they can be seen either by opening up at ground or first floor levels, the surveyor should not guess at the construction of the inner leaf. Instead he should point out in the report that by measurement and possibly by stretcher bond visible on the external face, that the wall appears to be of cavity construction, but that he is unable to say of what form of construction the inner leaf takes.

With the need for energy conservation the prospective purchaser may himself have some particular knowledge on this point and the surveyor must be wary not to lead him astray if he does not know for certain. Needless to say the surveyor should point out the disadvantages of brick inner leaf construction as against the use of concrete blocks with a higher insulation value.

Solid construction and cavity work

It is to the point here to consider the purpose behind cavity wall construction. The principle was, of course, not particularly new but in the 1920–1940 period of expansion to our cities, the two-storey non-basement house was the ideal of the speculative builder and the newly married couple. Many thousands of such houses were built at prices well within the reach of a vast number of people.

Structurally, all that is required for such a house are main walls one brick thick. It was, however, well known that a solid one brick thick wall by itself was not proof against the penetration of rainwater, particularly when in exposed positions and subjected to driving rain under the force of prevailing winds. A knowledge of

150

this fact was the reason why a considerable proportion of the dwellings of this period had rendering applied to the brickwork, even if only at first floor level, where the walls are more exposed to rain. To say this is not to overlook the fact that many houses were built one brick thick without rendering, to be even cheaper. But such houses are now in many instances badly affected by damp penetration.

To obviate the necessity for rendering, the cavity wall was introduced. The slight additional costs of constructing a cavity wall could be amply covered by the omission of rendering and a saving would then be achieved on the use of facing bricks, since the outer skin could be constructed in stretcher bond. Furthermore the inner leaf might be constructed of some form of concrete block at a considerable saving over brickwork, at the same time improving the insulating properties of the wall.

Cavity insulation   The oil crisis of the early 1970s which led to a sharp increase in fuel prices also led to a considerable increase in the number of houses where the owners have filled the existing cavity with either granular insulating material or urea formaldehyde (UF) chemical foam.

Although it is now said that about 1.5 million homes have been insulated with UF foam the early days saw some problems with damp penetration and the effect of fumes on the occupants when the treatment was provided, in some instances, without regard to whether the property was suitable to receive it or not. There are a number of requisites which need to be satisfied before such work is carried out.

These pre-requisites were eventually incorporated in the 1982 amendment to BS 5618: 1978, a "Code of Practice for Thermal Insulation of Cavity Walls (with masonry inner and outer leaves) by filling with urea formaldehyde foam". This was an endeavour to ensure that from then on the work would only be carried out on suitable houses.

These for example would exclude those houses in exposed positions, houses where the inner leaf was fair faced or dry lined, houses of framed construction unless all gaps were sealed, and those without trunking across the cavity for floor ventilation etc unless appropriate work was carried out to seal the cavity from the occupied parts of the house before it was filled with foam. These pre-requisites apply, of course, in effect to all forms of cavity insulation incorporated after the building's construction.

Around the same time as the Code of Practice was issued the Building Regulations in England and Wales were amended so as to require notification to Local Authorities before such work is commenced. Provided it is to be carried out using material approved by the British Standard and by one of the contractors registered under the British Standards Scheme of Firms of Assessed Capability no objection is normally raised unless the local authority has reason to consider that there is a potential risk.

Cavity insulation work is now governed by Approved Document C4 of the Building Regulations 1985, paragraphs 2.13 and

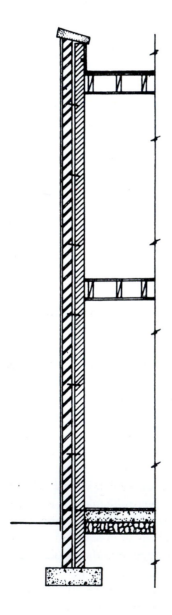

2.14. Suitability has to be assessed in accordance with BS 8208 Part 1, 1985 for existing traditional cavity construction. Materials and installation have to be in accordance with either British Standard or Agrément Board schemes which represent good modern practice against which earlier installations can be judged. Note, however, that in Scotland and Northern Ireland different regulations apply and in the former the use of urea formaldehyde is not permitted at all, as is the case in some States of North America.

Surveyors inspecting houses with cavity walling need therefore to ascertain whether the cavity has been insulated or not. In most cases vendors consider insulation a selling point and will only be too happy to show the surveyor the papers to enable him to check the details of what has been provided.

However, if the installation has gone wrong and defects have arisen as a result it is unlikely that the vendor would say anything. It would be up to the surveyor himself to check whether insulation had been installed, if so of what type and what the problems had been and then, if necessary, provide appropriate warnings for the prospective purchaser. Tell-tale signs of installation would be any oozing of the material at gaps internally or externally around openings at the top of the cavity in the roof space and any signs of making good in the brickwork where the nozzle of the pump had been inserted. If the installation had gone wrong there may be damp patches on walls and perhaps signs of rot in floors deprived of ventilation.

The earlier furore regarding the effect of the fumes on the occupants produced by the urea formaldehyde curing into formaldehyde has died down. Installation in houses suitable, or made suitable, for the purpose generally prevents the discharge of fumes, to parts of the building occupied, for more than a short period. If it does happen and continues to cause irritation to the eyes, nose and throat a registered contractor will return to track down and seal any leak from the cavity.

In any event the levels of concentration are normally so low and normally fall off to around the same levels as in an uninsulated house within a year or so so that there is no danger of any detriment to health beyond the irritation. Even so this can sometimes be overcome by increasing ventilation initially to the external air for a while. UK construction practices are not so prone to this problem as are buildings for example in Canada and the USA where most domestic construction is timber framed.

Earlier, one particular defect of unrendered one brick walls was highlighted. In driving rain they are not proof against penetration of damp. There are many positions where such brickwork will not be affected, but certainly at high level there is a serious risk of damp penetration should the wall be facing the direction from which the prevailing winds blow. Usually, however, diagnosis is simple. If damp stains are seen internally on a wall at high level, it is an easy matter to check on the aspect and thickness of the wall at that point and ascertain whether the cause is due to this or some other defect, such as a cracked rain-water pipe.

Defects in cavity walls

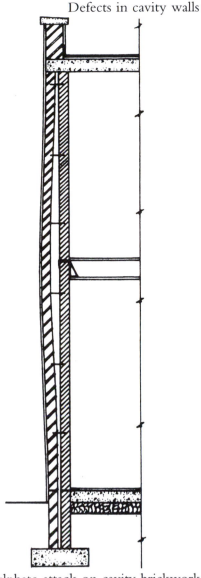

Sulphate attack on cavity brickwork

Although the use of cavity walls has solved some problems in relation to damp penetration, their introduction has brought a number of others. Cavity walls need careful detailing and careful supervision at the time of construction. There is a danger that the cavity may become bridged with mortar droppings on the wall ties, or of the cavity filling rising above the damp-proof course and making it ineffective and the necessity for the provision of correct damp courses around openings where they are essential to seal the cavity may not always have been realised.

Unfortunately basic knowledge of this sort was not always available to the builder and his workmen at the time of construction and many cases where the essential features of cavity wall detailing have been ignored will be found. Even architects and surveyors do not always detail cavity wall construction correctly. If the house being surveyed is a few years old it should be possible to attribute dampness internally to defective design or construction according to the position of the stains.

In the section earlier in this chapter covering leans, bulges and fractures in solid walls, no mention was made of cavity wall construction in relation to these defects. In domestic two-storey construction, where cavity walls are most frequently used, loads are not considerable and such defects as are found are essentially due to specific causes. The surveyor should bear in mind the radical departure from traditional methods that cavity construction involves. Undoubtedly the effects of leaning and bulging and of eccentric loading will be more serious with cavity than with solid walls as the stability of the former depends essentially on the effectiveness of the wall ties, particularly when most of the load from floors and roofs is carried on the inner leaf. Should a lean or bulge occur in the outer leaf, the anchorage of the ties may be disturbed and there is good authority for considering that if a cavity wall be as little as 25 mm out of plumb in a storey height its stability may be seriously impaired.

Sulphate attack on the mortar of the brickwork has been known to increase the height of the outer leaf in a two-storey house by as much as 50 mm.

In such circumstances if the roof load is carried on the inner leaf alone or the condition arises in a gable wall, severe disturbance to the anchorage of the wall ties would occur and as a result the outer leaf would in effect be virtually a free standing wall half a brick thick and two storeys high, with little or no lateral support at the top as shown on the left of the page opposite. On the other hand if the same circumstances arose where the roof load was equally distributed over both leaves, there is every likelihood of a bulge occurring as the upward thrust of the wall would be resisted by a downwards thrust from the roof as in the example on the left of this page. The omission of a damp proof course below the coping would tend, in these examples, to aggravate the sulphate attack.

A further cause of disturbance to the anchorage of the ties may well arise if there is excessive shrinkage in the inner leaf where concrete blocks have been used. Fracturing of the brickwork and

153

near the ceiling internally of the top floor rooms and probably a crack in the asphalt allowing damp to penetrate.

In the second at the top of the previous page, a terrace of houses built of sand lime or concrete bricks with a high shrinkage rate will rapidly develop vertical cracks at about 2-metre intervals particularly between ground and first floors in the long unbroken brick panel. The crack might extend down to damp course level but, as its cause is shrinkage, not below.

CHARACTERISTICS OF BRICKS

The composition, manufacture and characteristics of bricks varies considerably and the correct choice of brick for the position in which it is to be used is of considerable importance. All too often a brick which is reasonably suitable for external facing work between damp course and eaves level is used in parapets, chimney stacks and retaining walls, where it may be affected by frost and continual saturation during long damp periods. Similarly the same brick may be used below damp-proof course level where the degree of dampness is greater.

Local knowledge

For the construction of houses in the past bricks were usually purchased from within a reasonable distance so that in particular areas there is often a predominance of similar bricks in use. This enables surveyors to be familiar with the types of brick commonly used within their own area and in this respect they have an advantage over surveyors unfamiliar with the local conditions. Irrespective of such an advantage, however, an examination of the bricks used in exposed or damp positions, such as parapet walls, chimney stacks and retaining walls or below damp-proof course level, will very often provide a guide of their type and possible failings under severe conditions.

In several positions it is useful to scrape the surface of a few bricks with a penknife or a coin to ascertain whether the surface is hard or soft and crumbling. Many types of red facing brick used during and since Victorian times, together with some modern bricks, have hard smooth outer surfaces but relatively soft interiors. The modern rustic facing brick is a good example of an applied surface treatment to a common brick with a soft interior. Underburning, even in good quality bricks, will have the same effect of producing a hard surface and soft interior. Furthermore all clay bricks have varying degrees of frost resistance which affect their performance in exposed conditions and in addition contain a proportion of soluble salts, usually sulphates of sodium, calcium and magnesium.

In the exposed positions of a house such as parapet walls, chimney stacks, retaining and free standing walls and occasionally below damp course level, if this is some distance above the actual ground level and in particular where pointing has been neglected in these positions, moisture may penetrate behind the hard surface of the brick and, on freezing, expand to dislodge the outer face. Should this occur the soft interior of the brick will be exposed which has little resistance to the weather.

156

Soluble salts

Soluble salts in the brickwork cause efflorescence. This produces the white powder familiar on the surface of new brickwork while the bricks are drying out following construction and as such is harmless and unimportant apart from the aspect of appearance. The real danger from sulphate attack occurs when brickwork is being continually saturated. This may arise in parapet walls and chimney stacks without damp-proof courses, in free standing walls, below sills which are defective or where any other defective projection allows water to penetrate in quantity.

It can also arise above ornamental details, such as string courses, where the brickwork is continually splashed during rainfall, and near ground level from the same cause, or if the brickwork is continually damp, below damp-proof course level. In these positions the salts in the bricks are continually brought to the surface by the evaporation of the moisture in drier periods to be deposited there and to crystallise causing the surface of the brick to disintegrate. Should the interior of the brick be soft and crumbling this will rapidly deteriorate on exposure to the weather and the brickwork may take on the appearance as in the photograph below.

It is appropriate at this stage to mention that bricks, in themselves containing small amounts of soluble salts, may also be affected by salts derived from other sources such as the soil behind retaining walls, the condensation from flue gases, or from adjacent stonework such as sills which because they are porous and may be dissolved by acid in rain-water cause the run-off to affect the brickwork. The effect on the brickwork will be the same whether the salts are within the bricks or are derived from elsewhere.

Spalling brickwork. Note how the defective bricks are more in number along the line of the chimney flues indicating that the brickwork is not proof against the penetration of the condensate from flue gasses.

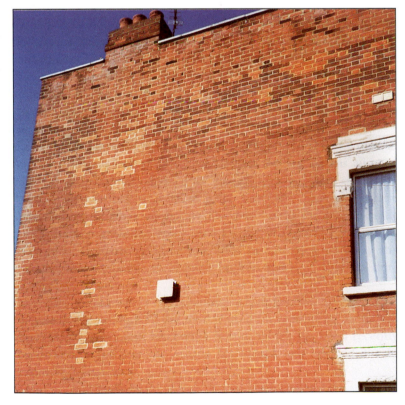

Defective pointing.

being too rich in cement. A further defect often found is where new pointing has been carried out but the old joints have been insufficiently raked before the work commenced, so that the key of new to old mortar is poor and the new work drops out.

As mentioned in the immediately preceding section on bricks, mortar to brickwork in conditions of severe exposure and where the brickwork remains wet for long periods, as in parapet walls, chimney stacks, retaining walls and brickwork below damp course level, is liable to be affected by frost damage. It can also be affected by the action of soluble sulphate salts derived either from the brickwork itself or from some other source, such as the soil behind retaining walls.

Frost will cause the surface of the pointing to spall off as well as causing the surface of the bricks to disintegrate. Sulphate attack on cement and cement lime based mortars leads to cracking along the length of the joint but the surface may remain firm for a while. Later, however, if very wet the mortar will be reduced to a soft paste. Usually the mortar affected by sulphate action will appear whitish in colour, often less so in the centre of the joint compared with the parts in closer proximity to the bricks. Considerable expansion occurs in the bed joints and this may cause cracking and bulging of the brickwork. It can also cause spalling on the edge of the bricks and occasionally the stability of the brickwork may be impaired as, for example, in parapet walls and chimney stacks.

Defective pointing, as on the photograph above left, be it from old age and neglect or the causes described above, needs to be renewed, since it is a frequent source of damp penetration through external walls. It is perhaps wise for the surveyor to suggest, where the brickwork is old, the use of cement lime and sand mixes for repointing, although this information may properly be thought more suitable for a specification. With both frost and sulphate attack on mortars it is essential to advise a purchaser to remedy the cause of the excessive dampness in the brickwork, usually by the provision of proper damp-proof courses, which gives rise to these forms of attack.

Rendering
Rendering walls has always been a popular form of external treatment. At one time the purpose of rendering was to produce the same impression as building in stone but by using cheaper bricks and covering them with an imitation stone rendering. The architects of the Regency period frequently adopted this subterfuge, which has been extensively followed ever since, though it is doubted whether the practice has ever really fooled an onlooker. It has, however, been a convenient cover up for all sorts of cheap-jack construction below the rendering and has, of course, a long history going back to the time when daubing the framework of timber buildings was common.

The efficiency of a structure which has been rendered is to a great extent governed by the condition of the rendering. In past years an efficient art in stucco rendering came into existence but nowadays the materials which were formerly used are no longer manufactured and the standard of plastering has generally fallen so

160

low that it is well nigh impossible to obtain the standard of finish that used to be commonplace at one time. As a result patching is difficult on old buildings and replacement of whole areas has very often to be carried out in a different manner.

The general replacement of Roman and other forms of cement formerly used in stucco renderings by Portland cement has been the principal cause of the trouble. Portland cement while having many excellent uses in concrete and mortars is generally employed in much too great a quantity for satisfactory smooth external renderings, with the result that excessive shrinkage causes cracks and a failure of adhesion to the backing. However, the work of the Building Research Establishment in recommending suitable mixes for varying degrees of exposure may hopefully lead to an improvement in future.

The surveyor needs, of course, to be able to identify the various types of finish adopted, from the stucco mixes based on Roman or other proprietary cements of Regency and Victorian times, to the pebble-dash, rough-cast, scraped or textured finishes in common use today based on Portland Cement, together with the standard floated finish. Nowadays a number of machines are available which can be used to apply a characteristic textured finish.

Smooth dense finishes containing Portland Cement are prone to surface crazing due to excessive shrinkage and the development of hair cracks. Should such rendering be applied to brickwork containing a high percentage of soluble sulphate salts and water penetrates these cracks, it cannot escape and there is a serious danger of the dissolved sulphates attacking the alumina in the cement. This causes considerable cracking in the rendering, in the first instance along the horizontal lines of the mortar joints.

Later the rendering may fall off in sections of considerable area. In these circumstances it would be unwise for the surveyor to advise new rendering of the same type, without advising thorough drying of the brickwork and the use of sulphate resisting Portland Cement. This should be applied in an open textured cement lime and sand mix, which, by having greater porosity, will allow evaporation from the surface and reduces the risk of hair cracking. Alternatively it might be better to advise the entire replacement of the rendering with some other form of weatherproofing, for example tile hanging, slate hanging or weather boarding either of timber or PVC.

The surveyor should always examine rendering closely, wherever it is found and in whatever form, for surface cracks and hollow and worn areas indicating a need for renewal. In particular, cracked and loose areas on projections, such as cornices and mouldings, should be noted in view of the danger of injury should portions drop off. Although recommended, very few projecting details are provided with proper flashings, which would help to prevent deterioration, a point which should be noted in advising on the repairs that may be required.

As an alternative to rendering, many one brick walls are vertical tile or slate hung as a protection from driving rain. Clearly in

Identification of different types of rendering

A bold treatment at the eaves. The rendering to the deep overhang is carried down around the bay and oriel windows and on the front wall at first floor level. There is little or no sign of cracking which raises the question of the construction of the front wall above ground level.

Tile and slate hanging

A large amount of tile hanging is on timber framing in the sprandrils of bay windows as here.

Battens and Nails

Tile hanging is not often found in this position because of possible damage. Defective slate hanging on the right.

examining a wall finished with vertical tile hanging the same defects as on tile roofing may be expected and the covering should be examined from this same point of view. It may be possible, from the gap left by a slipped tile, to see the method whereby the tiles are hung. A particular point in regard to this is that unless wood battens are well treated with preservative they are very prone to decay in this position.

On the other hand, tiles nailed to coke breeze concrete blocks are liable to failure as the sulphur corrodes the nails. Another method, used in former times, was to nail the tiles to a mortar joint but the hold on the nail as a result is very uncertain and in conditions of high exposure there is a danger of the tiles being blown off. An unusual use of tile hanging is shown on the photograph below left.

Slates may be hung vertically by precisely the same methods as tiles and the same dangers arise as exhibited in the photograph below right. When either are used on timber studding, found at times on gables and bay windows, it is most essential that felt and some form of insulation is provided to prevent draughts and excessive heat losses. In one house it was found that the insulation panels were absent and cold water pipes had been placed between the studs, an example of defective design that speaks for itself.

When the surveyor encounters tile or slate hanging he needs to be cautious and, if there are any indications that the battens or nails are rotten or corroded, he should warn his client of what may be found when the tiles or slates are removed. The same difficulties, however, arise as with the inspection of roofs, only to an even more

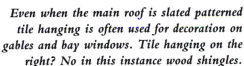

Even when the main roof is slated patterned tile hanging is often used for decoration on gables and bay windows. Tile hanging on the right? No in this instance wood shingles.

Artificial stone facing

frustrating extent, as it is very rare to obtain an opportunity for close examination. Numerous missing tiles or slates, or evidence of considerable patching, may be an indication of a need for more basic repair than the mere replacement of the missing tiles or slates.

Application to existing walls of rendering or slate or tile hanging is designed to keep the weather at bay. An application to existing walls for a different purpose of more recent introduction is artificial stone. This is applied solely so that one property can be distinguished from another and set it apart from the rest.

The artificial stone is often made up with pulverised fuel ash with a colouring agent and being impervious can introduce dampness problems where none existed before. Any slight cracks will allow water to enter and become entrapped behind the facing. As likely as not this will evaporate towards the interior instead of the exterior as formerly and may even freeze, expand and disrupt the surface.

Inadequately considered applications may leave windows unopenable, airbricks essential to under floor ventilation covered over and damp proof courses bridged. Poor preparation of the existing surface could also cause sections to fall off through lack of a good bond between the two surfaces and with possibly dangerous results.

Extreme caution by the surveyor is indicated when this type of applied covering is found.

TIMBER FRAMED WALLS

Modern form with cladding

Apart from houses built with cavity walls utilising two leaves of masonry the period 1960 to 1980 also saw a substantial increase in the number of houses built with a timber frame, a cavity and a cladding of brickwork. To all intents and purposes such houses are indistinguishable at a quick glance from those built entirely of masonry.

Identification of timber framed construction

In view of the problems encountered with some timber framed houses and the reputation, whether justified or not, which they have acquired it is important to identify such construction.

Measurement is not a great deal of help as an aid to distinguishing timber frame construction because the vertical studs are usually about 100 mm × 50 mm and accordingly when in position measure about the same as the blockwork often used for the inner leaf in a cavity wall of all masonry construction. Fortunately there are other indications which without the need to open up the structure should help to determine the construction.

In the first place the windows are commonly fixed to the timber frame not the brickwork of the outer leaf and this gives a deeper reveal. Internally, tapping the inner wall surface of an outer wall in a number of places will indicate dry lining if the sound is hollow. The dry lining could be either on timber frame or on battens fixed to masonry blockwork so that it is vitally necessary to go a stage further and borrow a pair of steps or a kitchen chair from the vendor and tap above window and door openings. Here paradoxically a solid sound will indicate timber framing due to the presence of a timber "lintel" in contrast to dry lining on brick or blockwork which will still sound hollow in this position.

Another indication in relation to a terrace house would be from the roof space when the separating party wall is found to be faced with plasterboard. It is almost certain in these circumstances that the house will be of timber frame construction. On the other hand the opposite is by no means the case. If the party wall is of masonry, timber frame construction for the front and rear walls cannot be ruled out. While still in the roof space it might be possible to crawl into the eaves to verify whether the plate on which the rafters bear is planed or not. If it is then timber frame would be indicated as wall plates in the normal course of construction are left as sawn.

Probably the soundest evidence is that derived from tapping internal surfaces but if doubts still exist then raising a floorboard internally adjacent to the end of a joist and ascertaining the bearing should confirm whether the construction is of timber frame or not.

Checking for differential movement

Apart from the normal checks for damp proof courses, weep holes, underfloor ventilation etc necessary with any form of cavity construction it is essential to make a thorough check for differential movement between timber frame and cladding. Normally an allowance of 5 mm per storey height is made for shrinkage in the timber frame which is expected to be completed in the first year or two. In newly constructed dwellings this essential allowance can normally be seen by way of a gap around window and door openings and at the eaves. If, however, the house is older any inadequacy in the allowance will manifest itself by way of distorted sills to openings and cracking and bulging of the brick cladding, the latter more easily ascertainable at window openings. Sometimes internally there will be popping of the nails holding the plasterboard, due to excessive strain, and cracking at ceiling and wall junctions. The surveyor needs to differentiate the latter, however, from the normal shrinkage cracks often found when a skim coat of plaster has been applied to plasterboard.

Possibility of dry rot in timber framework

Of course the main cause of alarm over the use of timber frame construction for dwellings arose from cases where bad detailing involving the incorrect use of vapour barrier and breather papers led to outbreaks of dry rot which spread through the framework. Pattern stains or mould growth need to be assiduously looked for and should they exist advice must be given to the purchaser to seek permission for a thorough opening up and investigation before any commitment to purchase is entertained. Even if such signs do not exist it is essential to take moisture readings with the vendor's permission in the studs and top and bottom rails of the timber frames. For studs the readings should be taken 200 mm above the floor level and a deep probe moisture meter with insulated prongs and hammer action will be required to penetrate the plasterboard. Readings of between 10% and 20% would be considered satisfactory. Anything appreciably above this amount would necessitate the surveyor recommending further investigation before a client proceeds with purchase.

Earlier forms "Half-timbering"

Earlier timber-framed walls generally known as "half timbered" are not found very frequently in towns except, perhaps, where there is still a central core of such buildings which have escaped the ravages of fire. They may, however, still be encountered in country areas.

Mock-Tudor

Again as with all forms of walling it is important to establish the precise form of construction. It is to be hoped that no surveyor will get taken in by examples of mock-Tudor, even although the more elaborate and expensive one-off houses in this style can be deceiving to the unwary. Normally there are plenty of tell-tale signs to enable the true construction to be established although it is unlikely that any structures of this type will give themselves away quite so blatantly as the example shown on the photographs at the top of the page overleaf. Of course, in this case the timberwork being only a treatment applied for cosmetic effect can be repaired comparatively cheaply to restore the pristine appearance.

Rendered or Plastered Timber framed

Presenting a greater difficulty are those buildings which have been entirely rendered, generally to keep out the draughts penetrating between the frame and the infilling panels. A good example is shown on the photograph at the bottom of the page overleaf and without cutting away the only real clue to the true construction is likely to be provided by some form of Crown Post or Simple Collar Roof of the type shown on pages 70 and 71,

The attempt to provide a half timbered appearance is now spoilt by the lack of adhesion. If sound it might catch out the unwary.

although there may be other evidence from internal bracing or exposed timber on internal partitions.

What is the construction of the walls to the house below? Rendered brick or stone? In fact they are of half timbered construction.

Even greater care than normal must be taken when such buildings are encountered and the slightest signs of prospective trouble need to be brought out in the report backed up if possible by photographic evidence. Firm recommendations on opening up are needed not only for verification of constructional details but also for establishing whether all is well or the surveyor's fears are realistic.

Where timbers are in fact visible particular care is necessary in examining exposed framing for attacks of woodworm, exemplified by the small flight holes and for attacks of rot, particularly at the base of storey posts. If necessary rather more opening up should be carried out than with a brick building, provided permission is forthcoming; if not, then particular care should be taken to explain any doubts which may exist in the surveyor's mind in view of the multitude of dangerous points that exist.

In particular and even more so than with brick buildings, the framing structure of walls, floors and roof must be examined as a whole, since each is dependent on the other and the infilling panels of bricks and plaster are merely provided to keep out the weather. Very often in older buildings first floor joists are cantilevered out to carry first floor wall framing and the timbers of the roof. Extreme care is necessary in such circumstances to examine the first floor

At some time in the past part of the corner post of the above half-timbered dwelling has been removed and replaced with brickwork. Nevertheless some distortion of the frame is evident.

A hot potch of brickwork, tiles and timber where one side of a party wall has been exposed. Would the surveyor have realised the wall was of half timbered construction if it had not been exposed. Care will be needed to ascertain the construction of other walls.

Plastering on timber frame.

Decorative plastering on timber framing.

since unwise cutting, perhaps to form an opening for a staircase or a trapdoor, can be disastrous.

Fortunately most timber-framed buildings are old and have had many years in which to reveal their defects. A sense of the tumble-down seems to many people their main source of attractiveness but the main danger is that that actual state may be reached earlier than anticipated. It will often be found that the edges of beams carrying the infilling panels are so eaten away by worm, that there is a serious danger of the panels falling out. To the surveyor such houses can be a headache and possible source of danger. The report must clearly point out the surveyor's doubts about such a structure and he should be adamant in refusing to guess at the likely condition of timbers that are completely hidden and where there is no possible way of obtaining information as to their size, nature or condition.

It should be remembered however that some timber-framed buildings now have a degree of care lavished on them that would have seemed strange some years ago and the surveyor should not lightly assume that substantial repair work is necessarily an in-superable barrier. Detailed study of the exterior can often repay the surveyor and can be regarded as time well spent, since minor signs of disrepair can often give a much more detailed picture than is generally realised. It is recommended that the detailed study is best concentrated not necessarily at the front elevation, which is gen-erally the most spick and span, but the rear elevation or alternatively the elevation most exposed to the effect of the prevailing wind and weather. On these elevations the structure will be seen where it is least cared for and accordingly not touched up and where the ravages of time and dampness are seen at their worst.

STONE WALLS

Identification of stone

Stone walls can provide the surveyor with some difficulty in certain circumstances. If the surveyor practises in an area where a local stone is a common building material, he will no doubt be familiar with it's properties and its capabilities of withstanding the local atmosphere. The first task of the surveyor however will be to identify the stone used. This is not easy since it can be wrong to make assumptions about local stone in the absence of exact knowl-edge. Sometimes approximately similar stone is taken from quarries in other districts.

Having decided on the identification of the stone, and a visit to the local museum may assist in this, the surveyor must decide on the construction of the wall and whether it is entirely of stone, or of some facing with a brick backing. Here again, as for cavity wall construction, examining the wall in the sub-floor space at ground level or the wall within the thickness of the first floor may be helpful. From his knowledge of building construction the surveyor should be able to give a name to the walling, be it random rubble, uncoursed or built to courses, squared rubble of either of the two sub-divisions as for random rubble, regular coursed, or one of the other forms of rubblework such as polygonal, flint walling or

168

even Lake District masonry. Alternatively in the very best class of work ashlar will be found, but here the surveyor will have to be careful to ascertain the backing to the stone, since these walls are usually compound and the backing may be of brick or of rubble-work.

Characteristics of Building Stones

It is well known that nearly all building stones are attacked to a greater or lesser degree by acid in the atmosphere depending on the chemical composition and structure of the stone. It may be thought that such attacks would be limited to stone dwellings in cities but this is not the case and buildings in country areas are affected in much the same way, since air pollution is widespread, particularly from sulphur dioxide.

Limestones consist mainly of calcium carbonate and are all subject to the effect of acids in the atmosphere. However, the degree of weathering depends on the structure of the limestone used. Some are durable, some not so. Sandstones comprise particles of sand bound together by a cementing material, in some cases consisting of carbonates. Such sandstones are affected by the atmosphere in the same way as limestones, but those that have a binding agent of silica or iron oxide are not affected. Other sandstones contain considerable amounts of clay and these particles are washed away by the softening effect of water. Granites on the other hand are not affected by the action of the atmosphere or rainwater but they may be affected in other ways as described below.

The crack in this stonework may be due as much to poor bonding as to any settlement.

The detailing of the sill/ bandcourse on this property results in damp penetration to the stonework below causing the surface to flake.

Defective and cracked hood moulding on right and defective brick arch above in stone buildings. More than likely the cause in each would be a rotted timber lintel behind each feature.

Defects in stone walling

All building stones which are porous are subject to the effects of salt crystallisation from soluble sulphate salts in a similar manner to the defects arising with bricks. The salts may be contained within the stone itself or deposited on the stone from another source by the evaporation of rain-water. The degree of resistance to such attack depends upon the pore structure of the stone and not its composition.

It follows, therefore, that for a surveyor to be in a position to give a report on a stone-built house he must establish the type of stone used and must know something of its properties. Few surveyors would profess to carry such information on the chemical composition of stones in their heads, but most would recognise that some research may be necessary to provide suitable advice and comments.

Having established the type of stone used and armed with a knowledge of its properties, the effects on it by the atmosphere or other agents, arising perhaps through poor detailing, can be considered. Smoke and sulphur dioxide from solid and other fueled fires and boilers dissolves in rain-water as sulphurous acid. This acid tends to dissolve limestones continually and while softening details and sharp edges at least keeps limestone clean by carrying away unsightly deposits. On sandstones, however, with a binding of carbonate it tends to dissolve the binding agent. In such cases where dampness extends to a deeper level, as on cornices, band courses and sills, the moisture may evaporate at the edge leaving a hard crystalline deposit, depriving the stone farther back of its binding material and causing a loss of adhesion. This may result in spalling

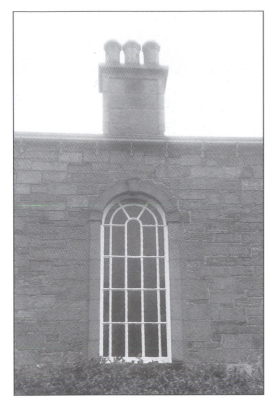

Is there a fireplace behind and below the window or is the window a dummy? No doubt the designers little joke but the surveyor will need to solve the mystery.

Badly eroded stonework around window opening and to surfaces below.

Soluble salts

Frost damage

on the edge of the projection. This is a particular feature of porous sandstone construction and sills and copings in this material, even on otherwise brick-constructed buildings, will often be found to have this defect.

Defects in construction resulting in attacks by soluble salts causing severe staining, efflorescence and decay may be due to lack of a damp-proof course or bridging of the damp-proof course, particularly where this is stopped short of the outer face of the wall. It may also arise when external paving is built up above damp course level or through salts being carried over from other materials, such as brickwork or concrete lintels, by reason of defective parapet construction or the top edge of projections allowing water to penetrate.

In coastal areas in particular, stone surfaces will be affected by the action of salt in the air causing decay. Each time salt-laden rainfall or sea spray penetrates the surface, the resulting evaporation deposits salts which cause decay in the stonework. Sometimes with stone mullions, jamb and transoms, the evaporation is towards the interior, where higher temperatures prevail, with the surprising result that the decay is to the inner faces and outer surfaces remain comparatively free.

Frost damage to porous stonework may also arise where moisture is allowed to penetrate unprotected projecting surfaces and eventually freezes. The expansion of the moisture will tend to blow the face off such projections. Renewal of the member affected with

Support from hollow timber structural partitions

walling above the beam, as mentioned in the previous chapter.

It should always be remembered by the surveyor that partitions which sound hollow when tapped are not necessarily devoid of structural significance. In older houses it is rare to find a brick partition and one or other of the hollow stud partitions found internally will usually be found to be carrying not only floors but a proportion of the weight of the roof structure as well.

These partitions rely on the framing together of their principle members for their strength, either with or without trussed formation construction and the misguided cutting of openings will not only cause settlement in the roof structure, as we have already seen in Chapter 3, but also in the floors. The correct diagnosis of a defect such as this expressed succinctly in a paragraph is so much better than a series of bald statements that this or that floor has a slope.

However, at this point it needs also to be stressed that even though a partition is of solid construction it is far from immune from settlement. The reasons for this will be dealt with later. Sufficient to indicate here that such settlement may cause floors to develop a slope in the same way as with stud partitions which become defective.

Deflection in floors

Particularly in older properties, floors may be found to have deflected in the centre but to be relatively level at the extremities. This is due, usually, to inadequately sized timbers which are often to be found in Victorian terrace houses of cheaper character. This defect in the original design appears to have been particularly aggravated by the tremendous weight of furniture in use in Victorian times. Joists will be found to have deflected under the weight and failed to return at later times when the load has been removed.

Herring-bone strutting. Excessive cutting

The provision of herring-bone strutting would have assisted in preventing deflection to an extent, but this seldom seems to have been considered necessary in cheaper domestic construction. Its installation nowadays is a useful palliative and, for the purchaser, has a more direct value in preventing the unseemly and sometimes disturbing "rattle" of an unbraced Victorian floor. Even moderately well-constructed floors may reveal a similar defect often due to incorrect cutting to install electrical conduit at a later date. Notching or cutting timbers excessively for this or any other purpose can cause deflection.

Ends of joists built into external brickwork. Joist hangers

Where the ends of joists are built into brickwork at upper floor levels, they may be subject to dampness if the wall is facing the prevailing wind or if damp conditions arise through defective pipes or blocked rain-water hopper heads. These conditions can well cause an outbreak of rot, which could spread like wildfire since builders in the past seldom considered ventilation to the upper floor necessary and it will seldom be found to be provided.

Since the rot will commence in the ends of the floor joists the support to the floor will immediately become affected and the condition could become serious if not dealt with quickly. Nowadays, it is not permitted to build timber into external or party walls and all supporting joists must be placed on some form of corbel or joist hangers of sheet steel built into the brickwork. Perhaps in

188

future years surveyors will find defective floors due to rusting of the joist hangers, but to date such a case has not been recorded. Thankfully this defect probably lies some years ahead.

Sleeper walls

With wood ground floors, the support is usually provided by sleeper walls and also in older construction by the external walls since the joists are often built into the walls, either on the brickwork itself or on a wall plate. Accordingly the support to ground floors may be disturbed by attacks of dry rot affecting the timbers and occasionally by the joists slipping from their position on the wall plates.

Detailed examination of structure of floors

We have now dealt with the inspection of hollow wood floors, room by room, and paid sone attention to their support by other parts of the structure. We must now pay some attention to a detailed examination of the structure of the floors themselves. This presents difficulties for the surveyor even more so than in the past with the present vogue for stuck down floor tiling and fitted carpet. Even when the house is entirely unfurnished, the entire structure of the floors cannot be examined since clearly this would involve taking up nearly every floorboard and the surveyor would be at the house for days.

Action by the surveyor when "put on inquiry"

Even the most stringent decision of the Courts does not suggest that it is necessary to take up every floorboard. Court decisions have suggested, however, that the surveyor is "put on inquiry" by any sign that might indicate that all is not well and that a competent surveyor would follow in such circumstances certain courses of action. If he could not follow such courses then the surveyor is expected to say so in his report and give advice that such steps should be taken and couple this with suitable warnings to a prospective purchaser of what he might find should it be possible to take the appropriate action. In accordance with the guidance laid down by the Court's decisions, it is suggested that a surveyor should follow the procedure set out below.

Taking up floorboards and carpets

In upper floors it is necessary, albeit subject to the vendor's permission, for the surveyor to take up floorboards wherever there is reason to doubt that all is not well, for example where there are signs of rot and woodworm,[1] or where it is necessary to establish some form of doubtful construction, such as beams supporting upper walls and again reason to suggest that these are defective.

At the level of the lowest floor it is considered essential, even if there are no reasons for supposing anything to be wrong, to take up at least one or two floorboards so as to establish the form of construction below floorboard level.[2] This area cannot be inspected in any other way unless the surveyor is fortunate enough to find a cellar. It will moreover be all the more necessary should floors be present in a basement.

Warnings if boards cannot be lifted and surveyor "on inquiry"

Defects can exist below ground and basement floors of which very little sign may be apparent above floor level, making the

---

[1] *Hill v. Debenham, Tewson and Chinnocks* (1958), Estates Gazette, 14th June, 1958, p. 835.
[2] *Grove v. Jackman and Masters* (1950), Estates Gazette, 4th March, 1950, p. 182.

inspection doubly necessary. If the vendor's permission cannot be obtained to raise the boards this should be clearly stated in the report. If this is combined with reasons to suspect trouble, then the surveyor must add to his advice the warning for the purchaser to anticipate expenditure unless such an operation can be carried out that will prove that all is well before he completes the purchase.

Assistance from builder

The surveyor may consider lifting carpets and raising floorboards himself. Alternatively, a jobbing builder who might also assist on the drain inspection and bring a ladder could be employed under the supervision of the surveyor. For one thing it is easier for the surveyor and for another it allows the surveyor to consider other matters rather than exhaust himself. Besides, most builders will be able to raise boards very much easier than a surveyor and probably do far less damage. Once the boards are up, the surveyor will find his torch very useful and a mirror held at an angle will also enable more to be seen under the floor without the necessity for the surveyor standing on his head.

Checking span and size of upper floor joists

With upper floors, a check on the size and span of the joists together with their spacing and a comparison with Table B3 in Approved Document A "Structure", to the Building Regulation 1985, can lead to a rough calculation for their adequacy. If the answer is ridiculous in relation to the actual floor seen it may be necessary for the surveyor to check that there are no beams within the thickness of the floor dividing the total span into lesser units.

It will often be found that floors are not quite up to the recognised ideal. This should be pointed out in the report, but if the property is old and no serious deflection has occurred it is probably reasonable to point out that the margin of safety is such that no cause for alarm need arise. Comments, however, should be limited to only what can be seen and advice should be given to investigate floor strengths before purchasing if considered necessary in particular cases where loading is critical.

Infestation from wood boring beetles

If flight holes of wood boring beetles can be seen the surveyor is recommended to examine the underside of the floorboards where many more will probably be found. He might also examine the joists for flight holes and use the prodder to clip off a piece from the edge to see if the wood is channelled. Actual beetles may be seen on the floor during summer months. It is not wise for the surveyor to give an opinion on whether the woodworm is active or not unless he is absolutely certain. The presence of beetles, little piles of bore dust looking clean and fresh, clean new flight holes, particularly on newly painted woodwork, are indications that the outbreak is active.

Active or inactive infestation

Remembering that the flight holes are signs that the beetle has emerged and the damage has been done the surveyor should be extremely wary in advising that the woodworm is an old attack and inactive. At the time the surveyor is writing those words the grubs may well be consuming the wood and tunnelling away actively in the timber without anyone being the wiser since secondary and tertiary infestations are quite common.

Furniture beetle

The most common type of woodworm met with in ordinary

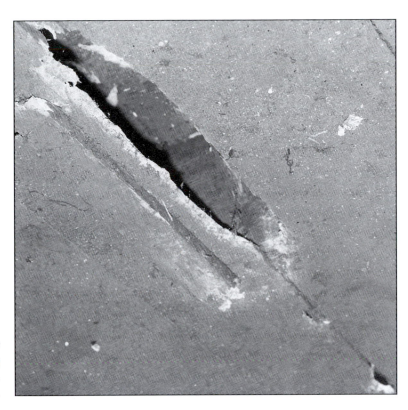

Holes in floorboards of this nature are a sure sign of heavy infestation by wood boring insects, usually the common furniture beetle. Floors can become very dangerous.

domestic construction is the common furniture beetle (*Anobium punctatum.*) The flight holes of this pest are round and about 1.5 mm diameter. If the beetle is present the flight holes are often found around the trapdoor to the roof-space and under the stairs and more often than not in floorboards as well. In damp conditions the development of the grubs appears to be faster and the damage therefore greater.

The grubs of the common furniture beetle have a considerable liking for wicker work and it has been known for an infested laundry basket, bathroom stool or similar item brought into the house to be the cause of the attack. Similarly second-hand furniture can also be a source of infestation. The grubs also have a great liking for plywood. Generally the common furniture beetle will attack the ordinary softwood carpentry and joinery of the average house, though hardwood timbers are not immune. An attack will often be found in conjunction with an outbreak of dry rot.

Death-watch beetle

On the other hand the death-watch beetle (*Xestobium rufo-villosum*) attacks hardwood, particularly oak and can be a danger to timber-framed dwellings and other larger dwellings where hardwood may have been used for roofing work, staircases or flooring. Those who enjoy looking around buildings will no doubt have seen beams so far eaten away by the grubs of this beetle that there is very little left. It is perhaps encouraging to see these, as it shows that the attack has to be very serious indeed to affect structural stability.

A word of caution however is necessary in regard to historical buildings since all may not be as it seems. The surveyors and architects in charge of these buildings are masters at the art of taking the

191

weight off beams and transferring it elsewhere, leaving the beam in position, the idea behind the exercise being solely to avoid its replacement. The flight holes of the death-watch beetle need not be mistaken for those of the common furniture beetle since they are nearly twice the size, being about 3.0 mm diameter. Damp conditions encourage the activity of the grubs making the wood easier to digest.

Powder post beetle

Common furniture and death-watch beetle are the most likely form of woodworm which the surveyor will encounter but two others deserve mention and these are the powder post beetle (*Lyctus* family) and the house longhorn beetle (*Hylotrupes bajulus*). The former attacks hardwoods only, such as oak, ash and elm, the latter being particularly favoured, but in all cases only the sapwood is attacked. The larvae reduce timber to a fine flour-like powder. The elimination of all sapwood from building timbers is an essential to avoid trouble from this pest, which can be distinguished from the common furniture beetle by its bore dust which is powdery compared with the granular material of the common furniture beetle.

House longhorn beetle

The house longhorn beetle confines its attack to seasoned softwood timbers. It is a particularly serious menace and notification of an attack is a requirement in certain areas. We are learning by the experience of continental countries in dealing with this beetle since it has caused vast damage in Northern Europe. The flight holes are oval shaped 3.0 mm by 9.5 mm. Roof timbers particularly around flues will be attacked first. This pest is particularly dangerous for the surveyor since it can consume the interior of the wood leaving only a shell, which may or may not be marked by blisters and its presence is accordingly difficult to detect.

Bark beetle

The surveyor should not confuse any of the beetles described above with one which may be encountered particularly on the edges of rafters and purlins in roof-spaces. This is the bark beetle which confines its attention to any bark remaining after the timber has been converted. The holes made by this beetle are about 3.0 mm diameter, sometimes oval in shape, but once the grub has consumed the bark and the beetle flown away the attack can be said to have ceased.

It is rare in any event to find bark beetle present and if it is, the quantity is very limited. The presence of the beetle flight holes may, however, raise alarm with a prospective purchaser and it is satisfactory to be able to give some reassurance for a change.

Estimates of cost of treatment. Specialist contractors

Unless a representative of one of the specialist contractors accompanies the surveyor on his inspection he would be ill advised to attempt an estimate of the cost of treatment for woodworm, since its full extent can seldom be gauged on a structural survey, particularly if the house is occupied and fully furnished and with floors covered with linoleum, vinyl tiles or fitted carpets. The surveyor must see as much of the floors as he can, explaining in the report why he cannot see the whole area. A recommendation should be given in the report that the full extent of the attack be ascertained and an estimate obtained, coupled with a guarantee, from a reliable specialist firm carrying out woodworm treatment and that the estimate should be obtained prior to the exchange of contracts. With this to hand the purchaser will be able to budget for the expenditure involved.

Dry Rot in upper floors
Leaking joints to fittings

Completed repairs following dry rot. Has enough been done? What enquiries should the surveyor make?

Diagnosis of cause and remedial work

Outbreaks of dry rot are occasionally found at upper floor levels but their cause is usually fairly easy to trace. Defects which give rise to such attacks are cracked or blocked waste, soil, or rain-water pipes and hopper heads, defective roofs of projecting additions and, from within the house, leaking joints to soil pipes, flush pipes and water closets, and the joints to waste water fittings such as baths and sinks. Fittings and pipes should always be closely examined for these defects and the floors around the fittings inspected for rot, since it is surprising how long a small leak can exist without anyone noticing it. Since there is normally no ventilation in upper floors once an outbreak starts it can spread rapidly and before long will affect not only the floor but also the timber within the interior of stud partitions. Eradication can be extremely costly in such circumstances.

If, on opening up, dry rot is found to be present in any part of the structure, the surveyor will perhaps notice a characteristic pungent musty smell indicating its presence and which will frequently be encountered in closed up basements or where floors are attacked in cupboards beneath stairs. With experience the surveyor will soon be able to detect this smell very easily. Crinkling on the face of timber is another indication of dry rot together with the tendency of the wood to take on a cubical appearance, due to shrinkage and the extraction of moisture. White or green strands and silky threads of snowy white cotton wool tinged with yellow will also be encountered, together with brown and red fungi with white edges to the fruiting bodies and a reddish powder of spore dust. When prodded with a penknife or sharp prong the timber presents no resistance either to the prod or to the withdrawal of the implement.

It is not suggested that a structural survey report is the proper place for long descriptions of remedial measure to deal with the afflicted timber and it is unwise of the surveyor, for obvious reasons, to attempt to value the cost of such work. It is however the proper place to diagnose the cause of the attack if at all possible.

Depending on the cause, the surveyor will be able to indicate to the purchaser whether it is due to a localised defect, the lack of rectification causing the outbreak, or due to an inherent defect in the structure. With dry rot in upper floors the cause is almost invariably localised and provided the defect giving rise to the attack is put right, the defective timber cut out and renewed in accordance with the correct procedure and the surrounding areas sterilised, there is no reason, given proper maintenance on the structure, why there should be a further outbreak in the same place.

Dry rot in ground and basement floors

With timber floors at ground and basement levels, however, the cause is very often due to inherent defects in the structure, such as rising dampness in the walls, where there is no horizontal damp-proof course coupled with the lack, or inadequacy, of ventilation to the sub-floor area. The sub-floor area is most important and, as

Early forms of construction. Inherent defects

How dry rot can develop in lowest floors

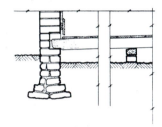

The typical growths of an outbreak of dry rot in timbers within a damp and unventilated cellar.

Advice to prospective purchasers

previously stated, warrants examination by the surveyor whenever present in a property.

The Building Regulations and by-laws provide for proper construction nowadays, in the general interests of health, so as to cover the sites of buildings with concrete of a minimum thickness. Long before the current regulations were introduced, however, wood joists were often laid over the bare earth or on rudimentary supports laid on the earth to separate the joists from contact with damp, but this aim was often defeated by the rubble such as broken bricks, pieces of plaster and bits of timber left under the boards.

The warmth of the house will forever draw moisture to the surface of this earth below the floor and always maintain damp conditions. At a later stage still sleeper walls would be constructed, a plate run along the top and the floor joists rested on this and built at their ends into the external walls and partition walls as on the drawing on the left. As the damp-proof course was omitted from the external walls, it certainly never occurred to the builders to provide a barrier against damp below the plates, so that more often than not the sleeper walls are saturated with moisture, more so than the external walls since these at least have one face exposed to the air, allowing a certain amount of evaporation from the surface.

If there is a short distance between the underside of the floor-boards and the earth and the ventilation to this area is poor, then ideal conditions for an attack of dry rot are present. All too frequently this is found to be the case. This is not to say that any rot will invariably be found as given good ventilation to the underside of the floorboards and a low water table in the locality, it may be avoided. No apparent signs have been found in some houses where these conditions in fact exist. The owners of such houses are indeed fortunate. Provided the purchaser is not intending to proceed to carry out alterations and in the circumstances he should be warned to take advice if he is proposing to do so, he may be given some assurance that trouble is highly unlikely to develop from dry rot.

The absence of a damp-proof course and the consequential likelihood of rising dampness in the walls to the detriment of the decorations, has been dealt with in the previous chapter on the main walls, but an even more serious result is its effect on wood floors at ground and basement levels. The presence of an extensive attack of dry rot in such floors coupled with this inherent defect is a serious matter and the two cannot be divorced. There is absolutely no use advising a purchaser merely to replace the floor attacked. This is downright bad advice as the conditions for a further outbreak of dry rot remain.

If the purchaser wishes to retain a wood floor at this level, it must be pointed out to him that radical reconstruction of the floor and sub-floor structure is required, together with the provision of proper damp-proof courses and adequate sub-floor ventilation. The only alternative is the provision of a concrete floor with an adequate damp-proof membrane. These alternatives so as to drive home the full effect of the conditions found should be included in the report. It is not sufficient merely to describe what is found since

194

differing interpretations will be put upon the words used and differing inferences drawn, depending upon the reader. The implication of the findings must be expressed in the most unequivocal fashion, albeit without undue elaboration of detail.

Ventilation to the sub-floor area

Even where a damp-proof course is present in the walls, the supreme importance of adequate ventilation to the sub-floor cannot be overstressed. The point is that earlier by-law requirements did not specify that site concrete be waterproofed, or be provided with a damp-proofing membrane. If there is no ventilation or, for that matter, if it is limited in extent, moisture will still be drawn by capillary action through the pores of the concrete with the result that atmospheric conditions in the space below the floor may be humid. In such circumstances the conditions for an outbreak of rot are present.

To combat such conditions the ventilation in the first place must be overall and there must be no pockets of stagnant air. Ideally for this purpose all houses should be square, with a sizeable depth for the sub-floor area and many air bricks in the front and rear walls, about 150 mm above ground level. Quite a number of the pre-1939 semi-detached houses fulfil this description and, provided they remain as built, it is seldom that the surveyor finds trouble with these. However, it must be recognised that the vast majority of dwellings fall far below the ideal.

Provision in terrace housing

One of the more common types of house falling short of this ideal is the simple terrace house with front and rear rooms, entrance hall and staircase, with a passage to the back addition. The provision of an air brick or grille below the front entrance door, although common, is not universal, and, if the back addition room has a solid floor, then the whole area of entrance hall, passage and below the stairs will not be provided with through ventilation and the likelihood of an attack of dry rot in the area shown hatched on the drawing alongside is considerable.

The surveyor will find many houses where the initial construction is at fault in this manner and also where the through ventilation is completely interrupted by the presence of a solid floor for a kitchen or scullery, another example being shown below.

The surveyor will also find many cases where old wood floors

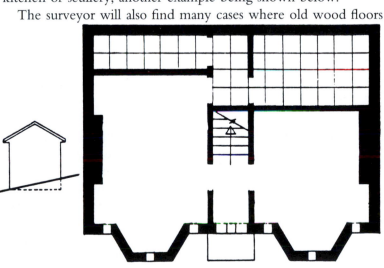

195

Ventilation to basement sub-floors. Testing air bricks

The sight of concrete adjacent to wood flooring should immediately put the surveyor on guard. What about the ventilation to the wooden floor?

Comparison of ground and floor levels

Through ventilation

have been removed and replaced with concrete in part only, with dire effects on the ventilation to the remainder of the wood portion which, deprived of such ventilation, rapidly deteriorates.

Dry rot appears to be even more prevalent to wooden floors in basements. The reason for this is not difficult to appreciate since the height of the sub-floor space is usually very limited. There are usually much larger areas of the sub-floor where the air is stagnant owing to the presence of entrances at ground floor level with cellars below. It must also be appreciated that basement areas seldom experience the gusty conditions found at ground level, with the result that there is often very little air drawn into the air bricks. The simple test with a lighted match already mentioned will demonstrate this and the surveyor should carry out this test on all air bricks, bearing in mind that on a very still day there may not be very much reaction on the flame. Even so there should be some.

The surveyor should check that there are sufficient air bricks provided to fulfil the purpose for which they are intended. Very often along a whole frontage it will be found that only one or two small gratings equivalent to one air brick in size will be provided and with most of the holes partially clogged with rust and earth, it is hardly surprising that they are inefficient.

Air bricks should be at least 225 mm by 150 mm, positioned at each extremity and at intervals not exceeding 1.5 m. Anything less must be considered inadequate and the purchaser's attention directed to it. Needless to say openings in the grille should be absolutely clear and at least 150 mm above ground level where possible. Grilles should not be allowed to remain broken since they may allow vermin to enter the sub-floor area.

On closer inspection of a wood floor at ground or basement floor levels, the surveyor must first pay particular attention to the level of the floor in relation to the level of the ground outside. Clearly if the floor is below the ground level and it is wellnigh impossible to provide an adequate ventilation, a solid floor is really the only adequate type of floor in the circumstances, and the surveyor must at all times say so.

Secondly the surveyor must check on the provision of through ventilation, having regard to the presence of solid floors in some compartments. In regard to this a check may be necessary, if doubt arises, on whether pipes have been laid below the solid floor in order to maintain through ventilation to the wood floors. Sometimes this is done but more often than not it is forgotten when a defective wood floor is replaced with concrete by inexperienced workmen.

Thirdly, the adequacy and condition of the air bricks provided should be checked, together with the provision of openings in sleeper walls to maintain the current of air through the sub-floor to corresponding air bricks on the opposite wall. Adequate through ventilation cannot be achieved if the openings are not in an opposite wall, but in a wall to one side. This will often be found to be the case with back addition floors, if these are at a different level from the remaining floors in the house. As a result there is a greater

196

tendency for dry rot to arise in the back addition floor than might have been the case had adequate through ventilation been provided.

From the foregoing remarks it will be seen that the surveyor will not be able to give a report on a hollow wood floor at basement or ground floor levels without taking up boards and examining the sub-floor area. This must be the rule, not the exception, even where there is little reason to suspect defects, but definitely so where there is suspicion.

Advice to purchasers where taking up of boards is not permitted

If the vendor is unco-operative and will not permit boards to be raised the surveyor should not take the responsibility of advising a purchaser on the condition of the floor if this is to be based on mere surmise. Guesswork on the construction and condition will only expose the surveyor to extreme danger in negligence at a later date.

It is, after all, the vendor as well as the purchaser who wants the sale to go through and he cannot blame the purchaser for assuming the worst if he is not prepared to allow an inspection to prove it otherwise. Often a recommendation to the purchaser to assume that extensive works to the floors will be required, with a suggested figure as to the cost likely to be involved, is the best that the surveyor can do if the vendor will not allow any boards to be raised at all and the conditions are suspicious.

SOLID FLOORS

Difficulty of opening up

At least sub-floors have the merit that they can, given co-operation by the vendor, be examined, but what is the surveyor to make of solid floors? The answer is very little in many cases without cutting a hole. In surveys, this would be too much to expect unless instructions were especially expressed to effect such an operation and the vendor had given his permission, which is thought would be given very reluctantly to say the least. There may be occasions however when opening up the floor might have to be recommended.

Much as always will depend on the results of the initial survey inspection, but it is important to be aware of the substantial problems experienced with solid floor slabs installed in new houses over the last 30–40 years.

Problems over the last 30–40 years

During this period, as discussed in greater detail in Chapter 12, covering surveys of new dwellings, sites which would previously not have been considered suitable for house construction have been brought into use and there is much evidence to suggest poor workmanship and a lack of supervision in the placing and compaction of fill over poor ground.

Spate of defective solid floors

These factors have combined to produce a spate of solid ground floor slab failures and even as recently as 1983 the National House Building Council paid out approaching £1 million in that year alone in settlement of claims for repairs to defective floor slabs. Even so that sum was said to have been lower than the amounts paid in previous years because higher standards had been introduced in 1974 requiring a suspended floor in cases where the depth of fill exceeded 600 mm. Although the average cost of the repairs was in the region of £2,500 per house for the most favoured type of repair, pressure grouting, costs as high as £7,500 per house were quoted for excavating and replacing fill for the more serious cases.

BRE Digest Classification   In a similar manner to its classification of cracks in the superstructure, the Building Research Establishment has produced a table in Digest No. 251 in an attempt to bring some uniformity to the way damage to ground floor slabs is described and this table is set out below:

BUILDING RESEARCH ESTABLISHMENT DIGEST 251

FLOORS

Table 2 Classification of visible damage caused by ground floor slab settlement.

The classification below attempts to quantify the assessment of floor slab settlement damage in a similar way to that for superstructure damage, given in Table 1. It has not yet been used extensively to determine its applicability. It should be noted that the categorisation may be qualified by the possibility of progression to a higher category; this should arise only when examination has revealed the presence of voids or areas of loosely compacted fill (or degradable material) beneath the floor slab such that more settlement can be expected.

Category of damage	Degree of damage	Description of typical damage	Approximate (a) crack width (b) 'gap'[1] mm
0	Negligible	Hairline cracks between floor and skirtings	(a) NA (b) up to 1
1	Very slight	Settlement of the floor slab, either at a corner or along a short wall, or possibly uniformly, such that a gap opens up below skirting boards which can be masked by resetting skirting boards. No cracks in walls. No cracks in floor slab, although there may be negligible cracks in floor screed and finish. Slab reasonably level.	(a) NA (b) up to 6
2	Slight	Larger gaps below skirting boards, some obvious but limited local settlement leading to slight slope of floor slab; gaps can be masked by resetting skirting boards and some local rescreeding may be necessary. Fine cracks appear in internal partition walls which need some redecoration; slight distortion in door frames so some 'jamming' may occur necessitating adjustment of doors. No cracks in floor slab although there may be very slight cracks in floor screed and finish. Slab reasonably level.	(a) up to 1 (b) up to 13
3	Moderate	Significant gaps below skirting boards with areas of floor, especially at corners or ends, where local settlements may have caused slight cracking of floor slab. Sloping of floor in these areas is clearly visible. (Slope approximately 1 in 150). Some disruption to drain, plumbing or heating pipes may occur. Damage to internal walls is more widespread with some crack filling or replastering of partitions being necessary. Doors may have to be refitted. Inspection reveals some voids below slab with poor or loosely compacted fill.	(a) up to 5 (b) up to 19
4	Severe	Large, localised gaps below skirting boards: possibly some cracks in floor slab with sharp fall to edge of slab; (slope approximately 1 in 100 or more). Inspection reveals voids exceeding 50mm below slab and/or poor or loose fill likely to settle further. Local breaking-out, part refilling and relaying of floor slab or grouting of fill may be necessary; damage to internal partitions may require replacement of some bricks or blocks or relining of stud partitions.	(a) to to 15 but may also depend on number of cracks (b) up to 25
5	Very severe	Either very large, overall floor settlement with large movement of walls and damage at junctions extending up into 1st floor area, with possible damage to exterior walls, or large differential settlements across floor slab. Voids exceeding 75mm below slab and/or very poor or very loose fill likely to settle further. Risk of instability. Most or all of floor slab requires breaking out and relaying or grouting of fill; internal partitions need replacement.	(a) Usually greater than 15 but depends on number of cracks (b) greater than 25

Note: 1 'Gap' refers to the space – usually between the skirting and finished floor – caused by settlement after making appropriate allowance for discrepancy in building, shrinkage, normal bedding down and the like.

Contrast of "Severe" and "Moderate" damage

It is significant that the National House Building Council only recognises the damage described as "severe" or "very severe" as qualifying for reinstatement under its warranty scheme. Gaps between skirting and floor of 19 mm and cracks in slabs or partitions of 5 mm width coupled with clearly visible sloping to the floor (approximately 1 in 150) and some voids below, are classed as "moderate" and do not qualify for reinstatement. It is not considered that many purchasers would tolerate or be prepared to live with this degree of damage.

Evidence of defective floor construction

The surveyor needs to be very diligent when inspecting houses with solid floors to look for gaps below skirtings, cracks in applied floor finishes indicating possible cracks in the slab, sloping floors, or depressed areas, utilising his spirit level. It is also necessary to pay particular attention to cracks or ill-fitting doors in partition walls, because so often these are built off the slab and such defects are more often attributable to settlement in the slab rather than faults in the partition itself. Indeed these partition cracks may be the most immediately apparent indication of slab settlement and emphasises again the need to relate one part of the structure to another both on the survey and in the report.

Case reports

The failure by surveyors to spot defects in concrete floors has featured in a number of reported claims against surveyors. In one case[1] the surveyor on a valuation missed a big crack in the floor indicating subsidence in the fill to the old quarry on which the house had been built and resulting in it slipping downhill. Here the damages awarded were £29,000 on a house costing the purchaser £14,850. In another case[2] the surveyor missed a 20 mm gap below the skirting to rooms on the ground floor of a house which had been built off too thick a bed of inadequately compacted rejected building material and was progressively settling. Damages of £5000 were awarded. In a third case[3] the surveyor missed the expansion in the concrete floor due to sulphate attack which resulted in displaced brickwork as well as a large crack in the floor. The concrete had been laid on a bed of colliery shale. In yet another[4] the surveyor failed to relate the evidence of sloping floors and doors out of alignment to the serious degree of settlement in a house built on a sloping site.

With solid floors another very important item is the damp-proof membrane. In modern construction this would be a Building Regulation requirement, but in the event of poor construction and total failure of the membrane, evidenced by wet floors or areas of tiles lifting or being exceptionally hollow sounding, the surveyor must assume the worst and advise the purchaser to envisage total reconstruction of the floor.

---

[1] *London and South of England Building Society v. Stone* (1983), Estates Gazette, 2nd July 1983.

[2] *Westlake and Another v. Bracknell District Council* (1987), Estates Gazette, 16th May, 1987.

[3] *Davies and Another v. Parry* (1958), Estates Gazette, 21st and 28th May, 1958.

[4] *Cross and Another v. David Martin and Mortimer* (1989), Estates Gazette, 11 March 1989, [1989] 1 EGLR 154.

199

Older solid floors

On the other hand there are many solid floors in older houses where one may doubt the presence of a damp-proof membrane on the score of age alone. Such floors, often in kitchens and sculleries, were no doubt laid on thick beds of hardcore and concrete and perhaps covered with quarry tiles, which in themselves help to keep dampness at bay. Beyond saying that the floors are solid and finished with a particular surfacing, it is hard to see that the surveyor can be expected to say more. If the tiles are cracked, the concrete or other surfacing damp, or the floor settled, however, further investigation must be recommended, but the proviso must also be to envisage complete relaying as the only proper remedy.

FLOOR COVERINGS

With solid floors, occupiers' habits of laying linoleum vinyl sheet or other impervious coverings will assist the surveyor in establishing whether such floors are damp, since if damp does penetrate it will collect below the surface and has a tendency to rot the covering.

Fixed sheet or tile coverings

Sometimes the floor covering is of either linoleum or carpet and can easily be raised for partial examination of the original floor immediately below. Increasingly there are times, however, when the surveyor will come across various forms of fitted sheet or tile rubber, plastic tiles or even sheets of hardboard pinned to wood floors. These render the surveyors' task more difficult so that he must indicate their presence in the report, comment on their condition if they have become a part of the premises and point out that they obscure the floor below, so that no comments can be made on its condition unless the surveyor is put on his guard.

In the same way, the limited nature of an examination of floorboards carried out in a house which is fully furnished and with floors entirely covered with carpets, tiling or linoleum should be pointed out in a report. It is clearly impossible for the surveyor to examine every part of the floorboards in such circumstances, though it is important that he examines those that can be seen with ease.

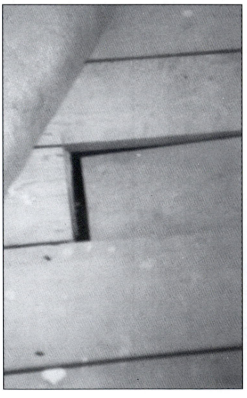

The careless cutting of floorboards, in this case to install central heating, and inadequate subsequent fixing can present a dangerous hazard when a new owner has not been warned in advance by his surveyor.

In dealing with older property, the surveyor should bear in mind the possibility of new floorboards having been fixed over old worn or beetle-affected boards. If boards are seen butting against the skirting this may indicate that this undesirable practice has been adopted. In these circumstances the surveyor would be put on his guard and would no doubt raise some boards to ascertain whether his suspicions were true. Unequal floor levels from one room to another may be a further indication. If no such indications are present, it may well be that the presence of woodworm elsewhere will be of sufficient warning to the surveyor to suggest that all is not well.

On solid floors, vinyl, plastic and rubber tiles may again be encountered, together with all varieties of clay, marble and other floor tiles. Again the surveyor should comment on their condition.

200

If tiles are old he should indicate the difficulty of matching them for replacement, possibly necessitating entire renewal unless the purchaser is prepared to put up with a patched effect on the floor.

Parquet   Other types of flooring may be encountered. For example a thin layer of hardwood parquet over a softwood floor produces the same effect as a fitted carpet so far as the surveyor is concerned. The surveyor certainly cannot say that the softwood timbers are not affected with beetle or dry rot since the hardwood parquet covering may not be affected and yet conceal the outbreak. Investigation is usually not possible since damage would only be caused to the parquet by opening up an area and it would not be reasonable in most circumstances to expect the vendor to grant such a request.

Accordingly, close inspection should be devoted to any slight signs in the parquet indicating damp or other defects, slight curling of the edges of the parquet strips or discolouration of the grain of wood. The surveyor should always warn his client that the softwood carcassing of the floor is more liable to be affected with rot or beetle and give an outline of other matters vitally affecting his client's decision, such as the nature and state of the damp-proof course and sub-floor ventilation.

Woodblock   Another example would be wood blocks which form a hard-wearing floor if the type of block is carefully selected and efficiently laid. Two main defects are apt to occur. The first is that the grain of some blocks is apt to splinter and disintegrate which is not a happy defect if the purchaser has children, or even if the adult members of the purchaser's family are in the habit of going around barefooted. The second defect is that where there is an inadequate damp-proof membrane the blocks are apt to lift, particularly if the water table is high and the blocks as a result may sometimes be affected by dry or wet rot.

The surveyor should indicate that to repair a part worn vinyl floor gives a patched effect and that it may be better to renew the whole floor.

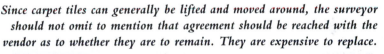

Since carpet tiles can generally be lifted and moved around, the surveyor should not omit to mention that agreement should be reached with the vendor as to whether they are to remain. They are expensive to replace.

Chapter 6
The Interior

CONTENTS

THE PARTITIONS

The internal structure

These chapters have so far dealt with most of the principal structural elements of a building, the roof, main walls and the floors. There remains one main structural item still to be dealt with, namely, the primary internal partitions and these will be considered in this chapter together with the remainder of the interior finishings, such as doors, staircases and fireplaces before we pass on to a consideration of the services.

Thickness of partitions

In examining the house room by room in detail, as we have stated previously, the surveyor should note the thickness of the external walls at each floor level. In a similar manner the thickness of each partition should be ascertained. This can be done on leaving a room by measuring the thickness in the door opening and, by dint of measurement between openings, the thickness of internal partitions without door openings but separating rooms, can also be obtained.

An initial gentle thump with the side of the fist to gauge the condition of the plaster on the partition can be followed, if all is well, by a hefty thump. The contrast between the sound of this and an equally forceful thump on a nearby external wall should indicate to the surveyor whether the partition is of solid construction or not.

Construction of partitions

Clearly with a partition plastered on both sides the surveyor cannot be positive of the construction unless the floor is opened up alongside and he can see an unplastered section. However, with internal partitions it is possible to make intelligent assumptions and provided they are stated as such no harm need arise necessarily. A one brick thick partition will measure overall, with plaster, about 265 mm and will sound solid when struck. Such construction can be safely assumed when these circumstances are encountered.

Similarly solid sounding partitions 150 mm thick are almost invariably of half brick construction with plaster on both sides, particularly in properties built prior to the First World War. A particular feature however of older properties, usually pre-1900, is a form of construction consisting of timber framing with brick infilling panels. The timber is often undetectable without opening up, but such partitions are very prone to defects particularly at the base.

Since the 1920s all types of different partition blocks have come into use, the most frequently encountered being breeze blocks and hollow clay blocks. These may produce partitions varying in thickness from 75 mm to 140 mm, depending on the thickness of the block employed. The most common, however, is a 75 mm block resulting in a partition 115 mm thick with plaster both sides. With partitions below 115 mm it is unwise to state the construction categorically without checking, and it is suggested that the description "block partition" of the appropriate thickness might be employed.

Hollow sounding partitions will be found frequently in older properties. These are seldom less than a total of 127 mm to 140 mm being constructed basically of 100 mm by 50 mm studs, generally with lath and plaster both sides. In smaller buildings of more recent construction thicknesses of 100 mm overall will be found made up of 75 mm by 50 mm studs covered with plasterboard and a skim coat of plaster. Again the surveyor must avoid being dogmatic about the construction since variations are possible, particularly with newly erected partitions, as there are numerous types of patent methods in use to form complete partition units. For that matter the lath and plaster may turn out to be metal lathing and plaster and the surveyor is not usually able to tell the difference.

Internal structural partitions

Having dealt with the possible construction of partitions during the inspection of the house and if necessary, or considered desirable, ascertaining the actual construction by examination from the floor space or sub-floor area, the surveyor must then proceed to ascertain which partitions are of structural importance or of no structural significance at all. Noting the direction of floorboards and joists will assist in this respect since clearly if joists bear on a partition, the partition must be carrying the weight of the floor.

Similarly partitions at a lower level directly below another in a room above must at least be supporting the upper partition if nothing else. Invariably one or other partition in a property will be carrying a proportion of the load from the roof but it may not be clear which one until the roof-space is inspected. Having ascertained this from the roof it may be necessary for the surveyor to make further examination of the partition below should settlement be found in the roof structure.

Loading on partitions

It is not always appreciated that many internal partitions, in fact, carry loads considerably in excess of those carried by external walls. Problems of excessive loading may perhaps not arise but the load on a partition carrying floors both sides and a proportion of the roof loading as well can be very high indeed.

The foundations of partitions

The foundations and construction of partitions which have structural significance are important, having regard to the load which the particular partition is intended to bear. Brick partitions should, of course, have foundations appropriate to their thickness and height in a similar manner to the main external walls. In older properties, before the advent of building regulation and by-law control, the foundations may be minimal or non-existent and the partitions will be found to have the same form of defects as external walls of similar age and construction.

These defects may be due to settlement or partial failure of the foundations. In view of the protection afforded by the house itself, settlements due to tree roots or poor foundations on a clay soil may not be so marked as in the case of external walls, but settlement due to defective drains passing under a house may be more severe. Differential settlement between external and internal walls can, however, create havoc with the internal condition due to its twisting and distorting effect.

205

Failure in structural partitions

Failures and defects of the above type in partitions can readily be ascertained from settlement observed in roof structures, floors and staircases and in particular around door openings. It will often be found that doors have had to be planed down to fit a door frame twisted out of true by settlement and that transverse cracks are in evidence from the corners of the frame. Internal door frames and doors should, as of routine, be closely examined for these indications of movement and the doors inspected from both the closed and open position.

Timber stud partitions

Surveyors may sometimes fail to realise that the hollow stud partition can have a great deal of structural significance. Behind the hollow sounding lath and plaster in older properties stands a complicated network of struts, braces, tie beams and stiffening members all carefully framed together and capable, given good support at the base and sound design, of withstanding considerable pressure. Some can even function without support over comparatively wide spans being trussed and framed up in the manner of roof trusses, three examples being shown below. If surveyors and architects fail at times to realise this, it is hardly surprising that the layman or less experienced builder can also make mistakes.

Cutting of members

Door openings often provide evidence of structural movement in partitions when they become out of square requiring adjustments to the door itself.

The increasing amount of alteration work, often unsupervised, in older buildings can give rise to the detrimental cutting of vital members in these partitions to form door openings, sometimes of considerable size. This point has already been touched upon in earlier chapters, dealing with the roof and the floors, but it does no harm to stress its importance again in view of the ever increasing tendency to alter and adapt older buildings.

*Examples of trussed partitions. At **A** the upper half supports the lower. The partition at **B** also with centre door carries both floors above and below. At **C** there are door openings at each end and metal rods are used for the members in tension.*

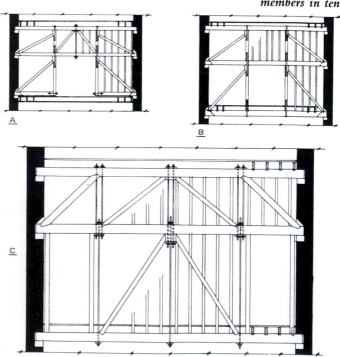

Formation of openings The formation of openings in solid partitions, if inadequately formed, can also cause damage to the structure above. This sometimes arises if the person making the alteration has mistaken a structural partition for one with no structural importance and provided the opening with an inadequate lintel. The effect of this may not be so apparent at the particular floor level where the new opening is formed but will be more noticeable as the height of the partition increases.

Where a large house has been extensively altered, the tracing of a settlement fault can be a complicated matter as it may be due to the formation of large openings in old structural partitions combined with the addition of new partitions to form smaller rooms. Settlement in a partition of a non-structural character, added at a later date, may, of course, be due to the inadequacy of the support provided. This, however, can usually be traced and diagnosed fairly easily, since the floor on either side may well have settled in addition to the partition and there may also be additional signs by way of cracks to the ceiling below.

Block partitions In properties built since about 1920 the increased use of partition blocks built directly off the site concrete often causes cracks to develop at the junction of partitions with the external walls due to differential settlement between the two. Such cracks, although unsightly, are not of a serious nature and can usually be filled. Once repaired and the initial movement having ceased, the cracks are not likely to open again unless the making good has been incorrectly carried out.

Large partitions constructed of concrete blocks are also subject to cracks induced by shrinkage. These blocks tend to absorb considerable quantities of moisture on building sites unless well protected, even assuming that they are fully matured on delivery, which is by no means always the case. More moisture is taken up when the blocks are laid and plastered. The drying out process may take well over a year to complete and during its progress some shrinkage in the blocks occurs causing fractures. These fractures may be coupled with a differential shrinkage, both between the blocks and between the undercoat and plaster finishing coat. Such a defect can usually be diagnosed by a series of short cracks, nearly parallel, along the top of the partition coupled with vertical cracks at the end of the partition.

Changes in the internal structures of buildings are now commonplace. Whatever the type of construction the surveyor should investigate the implications of the removal or alteration of load bearing partitions. He is also advised to warn his client of the implication of any changes and to recommend that enquiry be made by his Solicitors to establish whether the construction work was carried out with the consent of the appropriate authorities and approved by the Building Inspector at the relevant time.

We have now completed our consideration of the main structural elements in the average sized dwelling-house but there remain one or two further elements deserving mention, which although outside the definition of structure are no less important.

207

CEILINGS

Potential damage by heavy plaster ceilings

Longitudinal cracks roughly parallel to an adjacent wall in plaster ceilings often indicate outward movement in the wall while a diagonal crack as below may be evidence of settlement in the walls at the corner.

Cornices

One of these concerns heavy plaster ceilings in old houses and is most important in that neglect to give a suitable warning could land a surveyor in serious trouble. Such ceilings can suddenly drop, sometimes as a result of heavy vibration, and if this happens could result in a new owner or a member of his family sustaining an injury. For this reason, in each room the surveyor should look closely at the ceiling for cracks and bulges.

Extensively bulged ceilings or those with severe cracks, should be noted down for renewal, since the key may well have become loosened and sections easily collapse. Bulged ceilings should be tested with the tip of a broom handle or similar pole and, if the plaster moves, should also be immediately noted down for renewal. The surveyor should take no chances with such ceilings in view of the possibility of injury.

Plaster over the years, particularly when applied as thickly as in Victorian times, shrinks and continual vibration on the floor above may well cause the key on the lathing to snap, inducing the bulge. Defective key to plasterwork of ceilings can usually be ascertained by an examination from the floor above, by raising the floorboards. It may well be considered necessary to do this particularly if the ceiling is ornamented, where replacement in an identical form would be very costly and where it would be preferable to retain the original.

In such cases a bulge could be mistakenly thought to be due to defective key to the laths when it may, in fact, be due to a bowed condition in the floor above. Without care, an incorrect diagnosis could be given in these circumstances, but this would be preferable to failing to warn a prospective purchaser against the possibility of collapse

If there have been serious roof leakages in the past, or a serious overflow from a water cistern, considerable bulging may be caused to ceilings and the key to the lathing can be completely destroyed. Sometimes the laths will be pulled away from the underside of the joists. Particular care should therefore be taken in examining a house which has been neglected or where there is evidence of such occurrences and it will be necessary, in order to be sure, to raise the floorboards and examine the condition of the laths in these cases.

Laths should, of course, be examined themselves in any event whenever boards on upper floors are raised in other investigations. A serious attack of woodworm can directly affect the ability of laths to support a heavy plaster ceiling. In addition should there have been an attack of dry rot in the floor, the laths, being the lightest of members, will almost certainly be seriously affected and lose their strength.

As a corollary to the examination of ceilings in each room, the condition of cornices should be noted. Severely cracked cornices can also drop without warning and it therefore ill behoves a

208

surveyor to fail to warn an intending purchaser of cornices in poor condition. In particular, sectional plaster cornices with heavy decoration, often found in Georgian houses, may be loosened by settlement of the structure and be ready to drop at the slightest vibration.

THE STAIRCASE

A further item of importance in a house is the staircase connecting the various floor levels. Staircase troubles are more often than not associated with, or caused by, other more serious defects in a property. A staircase does not in general settle by itself since the flights rely for their support on other structural members, such as partitions or floors and more often than not it is defects in these which cause the trouble.

It is considered here that the surveyor's examination of the house as an entity and not as individual bits and pieces will assist him in avoiding such vague statements as "the staircase has settled towards the flank wall", given without any reason whatever and will encourage him to ascertain the actual cause, for example movement in the flank wall due to the lack of lateral restraint. Occasionally, however, a pure staircase defect will be found, such as a split string or carriage or weakening of the members due to woodworm attack.

Fortunately the underside of at least part of the staircase can be seen in most houses which will normally assist in a diagnosis. If not, then the condition of the plastered soffit may well add weight to the defect observed above. The surveyor should also always examine and warn against loose handrails, shaky balustrades and missing balusters. Most surveyors will have learned that it is wise not to lean on handrails and balustrades but laymen do just that and children can, of course, easily fall through the opening left by a missing baluster.

Safety Since it is recorded that there are something like 200,000 accidents a year in the home involving staircases including 600 or so fatalities the surveyor should give some consideration to the safety aspect of the original design as well as apparent defects due to neglect. A check should be made on the headroom, overall width, distance between balusters and height of handrail and balustrade. In addition a warning should be given if there are winders at the top of the stairs and unprotected glazing which could prove a severe hazard if someone slipped.

JOINERY

The general condition of joinery should be noted on the room by room inspection. It is not suggested that every chip on skirtings, door frames and windows should be painstakingly written down in a vast schedule of internal defects. The surveyor must use common

Movement causing staircase landing to part company with supporting wall.

sense. In a house where considerable ill usage of joinery has occurred, a paragraph covering the point should be included to draw the purchaser's attention to the condition and an indication given that repairs will be necessary which might increase his costs to some extent.

In a well-cared-for house it may, on the other hand, be appropriate to mention specifically a split door panel, chipped window sill or the like. The same considerations apply to window and door furniture. If generally in very poor condition, the surveyor should say so, but if only a few items require renewal he might indicate their position. This will show the client that the surveyor attends to detail in his work as well as to major items.

Schedule of defective joinery

In some cases notes taken on the site contain numerous items of a small nature referring to the internal condition of joinery and fittings. These reflect the nature of the property. It is undesirable to burden the report with these items but, apart from the general paragraph, a detailed schedule could be provided if the client wishes. The writers have never had any offer to supply a schedule of this nature accepted; the reader can guess why.

Although the fire parts do not meet current requirements, most purchasers would wish to retain as attractive a surround, interior and hearth as this.

Gas and electric fires and stoves

FIREPLACES

During his inspection the surveyor will note the absence of chimney breasts in relation to his notes on the brick gatherings in the roofspaces and the chimney stacks above roof level. This will enable him to record those areas where chimney breasts have been removed often with dire results to the structure above.

The condition of fireplaces should be noted room by room, including surrounds and hearths and the type of appliances. The description is best included in the Accommodation Schedule and the details of any defects included in the body of the report. Clearly old kitchen ranges, the original Victorian register grates, or even the pre-1939 open fire, are out of date and do not conform to modern requirements.

The modern slow burning open fire or convector stove, however, are suitable to modern requirements but the condition should be noted. If the fireplace has been adapted to take an electric fire the surveyor is recommended to check whether there is a flue. This is not always the case. A fireplace surround provides a focal point to a room but nowadays there are an increasing number of "dummies". The openings of other fireplaces may also be blocked and gas fires fitted, the fire parts having been removed.

The presence of gas and electric fitted fires and also slow burning stoves will often be encountered when a survey is carried out in occupied premises, particularly with the increase in "log" or "coal" gas fires but these fittings may sometimes have vanished when the new owner takes possession. If the surveyor is describing what he sees, he might warn his client to establish whether such fittings are included in the sale or not. Lack of agreement on this subject can lead to friction on completion and the purchaser may

210

well consider that he has been let down if not warned of this point.

A clause in the report might say, "You should establish whether fittings such as fires, water heaters, etc., are included in the sale and agree a list with the vendor." The surveyor should avoid the laudable, but misguided, temptation to agree such a list at the time on behalf of the purchaser, since the vendor may quite easily turn round and say subsequently that he agreed to no such thing. At the time of the survey, the vendor may not have realised how useful a particular gas fire would be when he moves.

Hearths

The Building Regulations are stringent in regard to the provision of adequate hearths to fireplaces. In older properties hearths will often be found to fall far below these standards and the surveyor may well consider it necessary, at times, to draw a purchaser's attention to such hearths if they appear to him to be unduly inadequate and there is some prospect perhaps of an open fire being used. Hearths will also on occasions be found to be cracked excessively, such cracking often associated with settlement in the floor. It may be necessary in such circumstances to advise complete reforming of such hearths.

Blocked openings

If fireplaces have been removed or if openings have been blocked up, the surveyor should check that through ventilation is provided to the flue from both top and bottom and, when on the roof, check that adequate precautions have been taken to exclude the entry of rain. All too often these points are neglected and the flue not swept, with the result that rain soaks into the old soot on the gatherings and ugly stains appear on chimney breasts and adjacent wall surfaces. Even more serious however can be the effects of condensation in a sealed up flue producing much staining from treacly percolations through the brickwork surrounding the flue.

Fireplace and boiler flues

Fitting of pots of this height invariably mean there have been problems of down-draught.

The flues from fireplaces and boilers should not be ignored, but a great deal cannot usefully be said about them. The surveyor cannot tell by visual inspection whether a flue is satisfactory or not and there is no equipment readily available or that is easy and straightforward to use for testing the average brick-built domestic flue. On occasions, there will be clear indications that all is not well by the presence of stains on plasterwork, but the absence of these will certainly not indicate that a flue is blocked, or that a fire, when lit, will smoke offensively, or that the parging and mortar of the bricks has disintegrated to such an extent that fumes leak out, or even that a flue has collapsed completely so that fumes from one flue discharge into an adjoining flue. These conditions require extensive and elaborate investigation should troubles arise, and a structural survey is not the time to carry out such investigation. The surveyor must, however, state that he cannot comment on the condition of the flues since he cannot see their interiors and also that these were not tested.

The writers are not aware of any legal cases involving the negligence of surveyors in connection with defective flues. This seems surprising since, to the writers' knowledge, no surveyors ever test flues and if it came to the point it may be possible that a judge might decide that a surveyor should give an opinion on a point of this importance. Clearly, one must warn a purchaser of the dangers involved in flues should they be defective and of the expense involved in repairing or lining flues should this be necessary. In particular the prospective purchaser should be warned of the necessity to check the soundness of any flue before any attempt is made to use it.

If the purchaser, having been warned, requires further investigation then he is entitled to ask for it, but at present it would seem to involve an additional element of work for which a further fee would become due. If a judge should decide subsequently that a close examination of flues should form part of a routine structural survey, then clients will have to pay for the additional time and labour involved by way of increased fees. It is possible that a successful defence to a charge of negligence, should such a case arise, might be that it was not normal surveyor's practice to examine flues closely on a structural survey.

Danger of condensation in flues

Particular care should be taken in warning purchasers of the danger of slow burning solid fuel and gas appliances in relation to condensation of gases in the flue. Attacks by the fluid of flue gases which is produced on the parging, mortar, and brickwork lead to undermining of the flues' stability, quite apart from the nasty nature of the stains that may arise on the plasterwork. The subject of boiler flues will be dealt with again in the next chapter.

PLASTERWORK

Mention of wall plasterwork leads on to the general condition of wall plaster in the house. This must be dealt with, however briefly, since extensive replastering can be costly. Severe cracks in wall plaster will, no doubt, have been mentioned earlier in the report, when their cause has been discussed under the particular structural defect. However in old properties it is often found that plasterwork is generally loose or soft due to old age, or damp penetration on previous occasions. Often walls with plaster in this condition are lined or papered with a heavy wallpaper, such papers in effect holding the plaster in position.

On stripping the paper to redecorate, the new owner may well find that the plaster will come away with the paper, greatly increasing the cost of his decorative work. A purchaser is entitled to be advised if this is likely to arise. If the condition is general throughout the house, a paragraph of advice will be sufficient as an all-embracing note, otherwise the client should have his attention drawn to specific compartments which may have been unduly neglected.

Plaster affected by rising dampness

An important point does arise in connection with plasterwork which has been affected over long periods by rising dampness. The water in the wall invariably contains dissolved salts derived from the ground which are left on the surface of the original plaster when evaporation occurs. These salts are usually hygroscopic in character and therefore absorb moisture from the atmosphere when damp and humid conditions arise.

Accordingly, the surveyor should always indicate to the purchaser the necessity for renewing plaster affected by rising damp in addition to the advice given to eliminate the cause, otherwise there is a danger that the purchaser's new decorations will be ruined. He should also make it clear that specialist work in eradicating rising dampness will entail the removal of the old plasterwork to a specified height and its replacement in render. The surveyor will often find soft Carlite plaster has been used even when so called specialist work has already been carried out.

Dampness on plasterwork due to condensation or rain penetration in flues is similar in character and, even though the cause is eliminated, the decorations may again be damaged if the plaster is not cut out and renewed. In all circumstances the walls should have sufficient time to dry out before replastering is carried out. Purchasers often do not realise how long a period this should be and need to be warned that the time relates to the thickness of the wall, the rate being 9 months to a year for a one brick thick wall.

Plasterwork in new property

In relatively new built properties careful examination of the plasterwork for cracks and tapping to detect hollow areas is necessary, as the surveyor will often find such defects exist. As mentioned in the chapter dealing with the main walls, the standard of plastering has deteriorated considerably over the years and the incorrect application of the top coat on the undercoat can lead to differential shrinkage between the two. Cracks and hollow areas are the inevitable result. All too often an insufficient time is allowed for drying out, both before plastering and between coats, and cases have been seen where, due to this cause or to an inadequate combination of materials, complete breakdown of the whole of the wall plaster has occurred.

INTERNAL DECORATIONS

Internal decorations can be dealt with in the report in a similar manner as plasterwork. The surveyor will have noted decorations in each room as to type and condition. If both type and condition are widely varying, it may be necessary to set out the notes to the various rooms in a schedule in the report, but often a paragraph will be sufficient to the effect that some rooms are in fairly good condition, but specific rooms are poor and in need of redecoration.

Cost of redecoration

The surveyor should always exclude the cost of redecoration to internal compartments in any estimate to the cost of repairs, since purchasers' tastes vary considerably in the standard and type of decoration required. The surveyor's figure is almost certain to be wrong and most purchasers have a fair idea of the cost of redecorating a room to their own requirements or in these "do-it-yourself" days may be proposing to do just that.

It is said, often correctly, that with some houses the decorative state hardly affects the value. This is not always so by any means, since white paint that has yellowed is considerably easier to

213

redecorate than acres of dark brown paint that is flaking. It is considered that a purchaser would appreciate his attention being drawn to extensive areas of flaking paint that requires stripping, as against areas of a light shade requiring a mere wash and rub down preparatory to repainting.

MISCELLANEOUS ITEMS

Various miscellaneous items will fall to be dealt with in the report under the heading of "Internally" to complete the survey of the property. Such items, for example, as fitted cupboards, bookcases, panelling and wall tiling will require description in the accommodation section, but any special features or defects will be noted under this heading as the case demands. Dado panelling in basements requires particular attention in older properties as it is often used to hide rising damp and is therefore very prone to outbreaks of dry rot.

Wood adjacent to external walls in the form of panelling as here or shutter boxes is always prone to attacks of rot.

Similarly in larger properties which have been neglected, wall panelling may well be affected by dry rot in cases where cracked rainwater pipes, defective gutters or continual overflows from fittings have allowed water to run down walls. Shutter boxes in all properties repay particular attention by the surveyor, as small openings around the frames of windows and french doors can permit damp to enter under conditions of driving rain. The interiors of shutter boxes lack ventilation and, as we have seen, damp and a lack of air lead to outbreaks of dry rot which, commencing in such places, can spread to adjacent floors.

Recent renewals

Surveyors should always examine areas around newly replaced or repaired timber very thoroughly, as the evidence of recent renewals suggests that troubles of some sort may have arisen, possibly dry rot, and it may well be that exposed timbers only have been renewed, without a thorough investigation into the root cause of the trouble. In such cases the surveyor may consider it necessary to open up the surrounding area and if this cannot be done, warn the purchaser of what may be found when exposure work is carried out and recommend that this is done before the purchase is completed.

In examining basement rooms and in particular cellars and W.C.s under entrance steps, the timber of doors, windows and frames will often be found to be affected by wet rot. The base of door frames in particular are often affected. If windows are elaborate, with linings in wood, often attacks of dry rot commence at the back of the linings to spread later to the frames.

Legal requirements

To conclude this section of the report three important matters require careful consideration in certain circumstances depending on the property. These concern legal requirements which can be made by local authorities in respect of fire escapes, basement rooms and houses in multiple occupation of which the lay purchaser may be totally unfamiliar.

It could be said that perhaps these matters are not particularly apt in a structural survey of a house, which essentially deals with physical conditions as they exist. Taking a limited viewpoint on these aspects is incorrect however, since future possibilities must be covered and who but the surveyor is going to advise the purchaser before he commits himself to buying a house on which such requirements may be made? It is often, furthermore, when a purchaser moves in and commences a little judicious alteration that these points emerge. This is one of the reasons why it is essential when settling the instructions with the client to establish as far as possible what the client's intentions are in regard to the future of the property.

Means of escape in case of fire

The first of these matters concerns means of escape from the house in case of fire. The legal requirements in regard to this are set out in the Building Regulations 1985 as mandatory rules applying to new or altered dwelling houses of three or more storeys or to a building containing a flat on the third storey or above. This, however, is to place too restrictive a view on such an important matter and, irrespective of any legal requirements, a purchaser's attention should be drawn to the methods available, or lack of them, of escape from the upper floors should a fire occur.

In two-storey properties the point need not be too laboured since it is relatively easy for most people to escape from a first floor window and probably the worst that could happen would be a broken limb. Even here, however, if the surveyor's client is elderly or infirm it may be a point that he or she may like to consider. For properties above two storeys in height and for those in multiple occupation, the necessity for comment is even greater and some form of protected staircase or easy escape to an adjoining roof is absolutely essential. It is a matter of great regret that the authorities are lax in using or cannot always afford to use their existing powers of requiring such works to the full. The increasing number of people trapped by fire each year is a depressing reminder of the lack of attention to this matter.

Basement rooms

The second consideration arises where basement rooms occur and these are, or are intended to be, used for habitation. As every surveyor knows, the local authority has power to make regulations in respect of such rooms, to cover lighting and ventilation together with protection against damp. Again for various reasons, local authorities have been hesitant in the implementation of their powers. In many cases the powers are not brought into action until there is a change of ownership, so that a purchaser who had in mind to use a basement previously occupied, without complaint from the local authority, may have a shock when he is served with a closing order.

Non-compliance with regulations

He will at least think unkindly of his surveyor, if the surveyor has failed to warn him that the rooms do not comply with the regulations and that a closing order is likely if certain works are not carried out. Depending on the basement, the works required may well be very costly indeed. If a closing order is already in existence this will probably come to light in the searches carried out by the purchaser's solicitors, but even so the surveyor should draw his client's

215

attention to the difficulties that may arise in carrying out works to secure its withdrawal.

It is essential for the surveyor to familiarise himself with and keep abreast of any changes to the Building Regulation requirements and with the definition of a basement room in his own immediate area and the works acceptable to the local authority to satisfy the regulations. He should, however, bear in mind that not all local authorities have the same standard of acceptable works.

Property in multiple occupation

On the final point instructions may come from clients purchasing the freehold of a house with sitting tenants, obtaining in the process one flat with vacant possession. If such a client has limited means, he will almost certainly not realise the expense involved and possible consequences which might arise should the property fall short of the requirements of the Housing Acts and the local authority decided to operate the powers vested in it under the sections dealing with premises in multiple occupation.

Chapter 7
The Services

CONTENTS

INTRODUCTION

Purchasers' attitudes to services

Having completed his examination of the structure of the building and the internal finishes, the surveyor must devote close attention to the services. This chapter will deal with the examination and testing of the services within the house connected to the public utilities, water, electricity, gas and the drainage system together with the system of heating hot water for domestic purposes and also for providing warmth.

It may be that a purchaser, in giving his instructions for a survey, has the structural condition of the premises uppermost in his mind at that time. However, it must be obvious that a basic structure is of little utility, by itself, without those services that make for comfort and satisfaction in occupation. House owners tend to take services for granted and give little thought to what happens when a tap is turned, a switch depressed, or a plug or chain pulled. These operations are of everyday routine occurrence and all that most people ask is that the various taps and switches function when operated and that when a plug is pulled whatever is to be disposed of, vanishes without trace.

Increasing importance of services to purchasers

More recently and particularly during the past decade it is true to say that the services have assumed an even greater importance than formerly. Little more than fifty years ago the installations comprising the services in the smaller property were often rudimentary. The average small house had a cold water tap and a gas point in the kitchen, generally electric lighting throughout, though many still had gas, but almost certainly no electrical power installation. Slightly larger properties might also possess an elementary hot water system, operated from a back boiler behind the dining room fire or a small and generally inefficient solid fuel boiler in the kitchen.

Even today there may not be much improvement over this standard in many properties but the modern housewife in particular expects to find a great deal more. She will expect to find in the kitchen electric power for her washing machine, points for her refrigerator and mixer, to say nothing of a constant supply of hot water. The male purchaser, to whom the task of feeding the boiler was once delegated, will not wish to be continually running to and fro, trying to satisfy a boiler's voracious and expensive appetite for coke which possibly is one reason for the present enthusiasm for gas fired boilers. Nowadays, boilers are expected to look after themselves and require occasional attention only. Needless to say, very few houses are quite up to date with the latest fashions and even some brand new houses give doubts as to whether they will be as comfortable and as efficient as their sellers would have us believe.

Failure by the surveyor to indicate in his report deficiencies in the services is not likely to remain unnoticed for very long. The purchaser may fail to notice an outbreak of dry rot or a settlement for some while. A defective hot water system, on the other hand,

219

will be noticed almost at once and it would not be very long before a purchaser discovered why a fuse blows every time an electric fire is used. The purchaser may well be thumbing through the surveyor's report, a few days after moving in, to see what is said about these particular items.

The importance of tests

In order to be in a position to pass an opinion on the adequacy of services we must stress again the importance of tests as the rule rather than the exception. In the case of the drainage, electrical, gas and hot water installations, no opinion as to the efficiency, safety or economy in running characteristics can be given without tests. Phrases such as "appears to work satisfactorily", or "the system was in working order during our inspection" are little more than worthless and should not be included because they give the impression that all is well when it may not be.

For example, electric lights will work satisfactorily on an old installation until such time as the defective insulation on the cables causes a short circuit and probably a fire into the bargain. However inefficient, most hot water systems can be made to produce some hot water at a basin, if only for the surveyor's benefit. In regard to the drainage system, running a tap and watching the water disappear down the drain from the inspection chamber gives no information at all on the soundness of the drain. A test is necessary before any opinion can be expressed as to whether it is watertight or not.

It is a great pity that pressures of time and money often rule out tests of services to smaller dwellings. Such factors however do not diminish the desirability of such tests and their value to a purchaser particularly when money is tight. It follows therefore that a survey where no tests are carried out must be considered inadequate in many instances and rather limited in scope. If no tests at all are authorised and therefore the surveyor is in no position to comment upon the condition of the services, a wide field remains where expenditure could be incurred by a purchaser. It is perhaps not too much of an exaggeration to state that of the total value of a house excluding any element of land cost, at least one-quarter may be attributed to the services. Total renewal therefore of all the service installations in the worst of cases, can be a very costly matter indeed and a purchaser must be warned in such circumstances of the risk of such expenditure being required even, perhaps, before he moves into the house.

The value of specialists

Many surveyors consider that the interests of their clients are best served by the employment of specialists to carry out tests on the electrical, gas, hot water and central heating services. In view of the complicated nature of the installations in some houses, this is a course which can be recommended. On the other hand, it is realised that those surveyors who consider that they have a detailed knowledge of these matters may well prefer to carry out such tests themselves.

In employing specialists, a surveyor should seek his client's authority, preferably in writing. Provided he has such authority and attaches the specialist's report, complete and on the specialists'

220

headed notepaper, to his own, it is considered that the specialist would then be in the same position as the surveyor in regard to responsibility to the client for the views expressed in the specialist's report, should they be incorrect. The client's remedy would lie against the specialist and not against the surveyor. On the other hand, if the specialist is employed without authority, it is probable that the surveyor would be held liable for any errors that may arise direct to the client. In the circumstances, it is essential, of course, to make sure that the specialist is well aware of what is expected from him and what might transpire should an incorrect or careless report be submitted.

The selection of specialists

The surveyor should choose his specialists carefully, if necessary taking advice on their selection from the various professional institutions. These institutions are usually only too happy to oblige with a list of appropriately qualified advisers in a particular area. If the tests are to be on electrical or gas installations than the appropriate companies will very often carry out tests for a fee but it may be unwise to employ either of the companies for this purpose, since they would have a duty to ask for the remedy of any serious flaws in the installation that might be a danger and if the surveyor's client did not proceed to purchase, the vendor certainly might have some cause to grumble in the circumstances.

The Electricity company also maintains a list of approved contractors, authorised to carry out electrical works and tests of installations and it is probably best to employ one of these. Contractor's charges for carrying out tests are usually less than those of the supply company, but as they are primarily in business to carry out electrical works they may not, unless told clearly, appreciate their responsibilities in submitting reports. There must also be no suspicion in the surveyor's mind that the report is being used as a vehicle for obtaining work and the surveyor must have complete confidence should a contractor be chosen for such tests.

Estimates of cost for specialist's work

It is essential that all specialists be instructed to give an approximate estimate for the cost of putting right any defects in the system tested, since the report is of little real value without this. It is, of course, permissible for the surveyor to comment on this figure and to add it to his approximate figure for repairs in his own report, but, beyond drawing attention to the specialist's report, it is suggested that other comments should be avoided as these might be misleading and tend to confuse.

Specialists' technical jargon

Specialists generally talk and write technical jargon with great facility, even to the extent of confusing surveyors. The surveyor must therefore persuade the specialists who are employed either to write entirely in an understandable fashion or, alternatively, to add a few paragraphs of general explanation at the end of their report and to bear in mind always that although they have contact with the surveyor and send the report to him nevertheless it will be a layman who will ultimately read the report and have the most direct interest in it.

COLD WATER SUPPLY

Mains water It would seem logical to commence the review of the services with the simplest and possibly the first essential, a pure water supply. Thanks to the efforts of our Victorian forefathers, there are relatively few properties without a piped supply of water generally fit for drinking. Many properties even now, however, have one tap over a sink for this purpose and very little else. It is always wise for the surveyor to assume, in such a case, that the prospective purchaser will have in mind some improvements. In which event, unless he is duly warned, it will come as a surprise to a purchaser when the Local Water company requires him to install a storage cistern.

Requirement for storage   Water companies in most districts in order to relieve demand at peak periods, permit only one tap from the main supply at the kitchen sink, all other fittings having to be supplied by distribution pipes from a cold water storage cistern. The cistern also provides a small emergency supply if, for some reason, the main supply has to be turned off. The installation of a cistern can be a costly matter for a purchaser of limited means, since it often involves the formation of a trapdoor to the roof-space, the provision of adequate support to the cistern and alterations and re-running of pipes, together with lagging against frost.

Cold water storage cisterns In areas where there is a requirement for a cistern the surveyor must check thoroughly for the presence of a cistern and if this is absent, must warn the purchaser that the provision is a requirement of the Water company's by-laws and that he may be called upon to install one at any time. In making allowance for the approximate cost of installing a cistern, the work to provide support, pipe alterations and ancillary matters, as above, should be included.

It should be borne in mind that a cold water storage cistern need not necessarily be in the roof-space and provided it is above the highest fitting to be supplied, any position will do. Hence, it is not uncommon to find a cistern on a flat roof, in a cupboard and even above a false ceiling. It may be necessary for the surveyor to do some searching and tracing of pipes to locate it. Having found the cold water storage cistern the surveyor must examine it thoroughly if this is at all possible.

Galvanised steel cisterns   The most common form of original cistern encountered in older houses is the galvanised steel type. Cisterns of this material do not last for ever and if there are extensive signs of rust internally, the surveyor must advise the purchaser to have it renewed without delay. If there are only the slightest signs of rust perhaps around the outlets these should be indicated in the report and coupled with a warning that the cistern, although it may last for a few years, may fail at any time and cause damage.

Ball valves and overflows   The surveyor should examine the ball valve and float and see that it is working efficiently and also look carefully to ensure that the cistern is provided with an overflow pipe, to discharge in an easily

222

observable place, where the overflow of water can cause no damage. The surveyor is advised to check the size of the overflow pipe, as against the size of the mains inlet. The overflow pipe should be double the size of the inlet pipe in order to provide a good margin of safety should the inlet valve at any time become faulty. A useful additional point to be checked is that the overflow pipe is fitted with a hinged flap at the outlet end, since this will reduce the possibility of freezing due to a cold current of air from the outside passing up the pipe, but it is not very often that such a flap will be found to be fitted.

Covers to cold water storage cisterns It is a by-law requirement that all cold water storage cisterns be fitted with a cover to protect the water from contamination. If the cover is missing, the purchaser must be advised to have a new cover fitted. If the cistern is in the roof-space or exposed entirely on a flat roof, it must be provided with adequate insulation against freezing, together with all the exposed pipes. The lagging must be adequate and if there are doubts on this according to the material used, the point should be made in the report.

Lagging of pipes Care should also be taken to see that pipes near exposed or open eaves are properly lagged. Pipes are often difficult to reach in such positions with the result that lagging is often omitted. A mistake often made when the ceiling of the top floor is insulated against heat loss, is to carry the insulation below the water cistern, thus depriving it entirely of the beneficial warmth of the house and leaving it, probably, more susceptible to freezing than before. This point should always be checked.

Other types of cistern Other original forms of cistern may, of course, be encountered but are relatively rare. In older properties, wood containers with a lead lining and also slabs of slate fitted together to form a cistern may be found. Such cisterns even apart from the possible pollution aspect of the former although possibly giving satisfactory service at the time of the inspection, should be condemned since it is well-nigh impossible to gauge their condition and they could well burst at any time to the extreme annoyance of the purchaser. A further difficulty, however, often arises in connection with these cisterns of lead and slate, in that they are often built into the structure. As a result it is usually difficult to remove them. Often they have to be left in position and their size may preclude the easy positioning of a new cistern to take their place. Asbestos cisterns occasionally encountered should also be replaced.

Size of cisterns During the examination of the cistern, the size should be taken as a matter of course. This actual size need not be given in the report, since it will mean nothing to the layman. Instead the length, breadth and height should be translated into the capacity in gallons and litres and this figure given as the nominal size of the cistern. The water level should also be measured and this used, with the length and breadth, to give the actual capacity.

This is important, since Water company by-laws specify a minimum actual capacity for storage cisterns for a given number of fittings as distinct from nominal capacity. Where a domestic hot water installation is also provided, the cistern has to have a larger

An inadequately lagged glassfibre cistern and associated copper tubing. Note the balance cistern for the central heating system which is totally unlagged.

actual capacity. It is up to each surveyor to obtain a copy of the relevant by-laws of the company, in whose area he practises, and to familiarise himself with the requirements in this respect, in order to advise the purchaser whether the cistern is of the correct size or not.

Rising mains   In the course of the inspection of each room in the house, the surveyor should take note of the position of the rising main to the cold water storage cistern. An important matter in regard to this is that it should be fitted with a stop valve, in a readily accessible position, in order to turn the supply off in the event of a defect in the ball valve to the cistern. The stop valve should be free in operation and its position and condition covered by the report.

The rising main position should also be considered from the point of view of freezing in cold weather. If it passes through the sub-floor space, or an unheated cellar, it should be well lagged. Often the main will be found to rise against an outside wall in a larder at ground floor level, a popular position in the speculative building of the inter-war period.

Such a position could hardly be worse from the point of view of freezing and in this position the main should be lagged from below floor level to the cistern, for its entire length. Lagging for the total length, however, is not always a practicable proposition, since the main, being on an outside wall, will almost certainly pass into the roof near the eaves, just about the coldest spot imaginable and one where it is almost impossible to reach for the purposes of lagging a pipe. In such cases, appropriate advice to move the main to a less exposed position may be essential if the purchaser is to avoid trouble in the future.

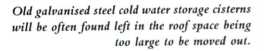

Problems with cold water cisterns

Increasing use is now made of plastic or fibreglass cisterns either rectangular or circular. These are often set up on inadequate platforms or supports and appropriate accessories such as covers are missing. Long unsupported plastic overflows too are often suspect.

In older properties, the surveyor will often find a large old disused storage cistern in the roof-space, this having been replaced by two or more smaller cisterns connected in series. A glance at the trapdoor access to the roof-space will provide the reason as to why this has been necessary in most cases. Often in new houses as stated in Chapter 3, the roof is, to some extent, constructed around the cistern and no thought is given to the ease of replacement through the trapdoor.

The alternative of smaller cisterns, connected in series, is practicable but often plumbing alterations have to be made as a result which increase the cost of the work. However, to carry the example to the extreme, it has been found in some houses that the trapdoor access is hardly large enough for the surveyor to pass through let alone a cistern, in which case a renewal of the cistern would involve the enlargement of the opening. Sometimes

Old galvanised steel cold water storage cisterns will be often found left in the roof space being too large to be moved out.

225

however it will be found that there is sufficient flexibility in a poly-thene cistern to allow it to be squeezed through far smaller trap-doors than would be the case of a rigid cistern of similar capacity.

Cold feed pipes to fittings and stop valves

The remaining point to check is that all cold feed pipes, coming from the cistern, are provided with stop valves, whether to fittings or to a hot water system. This is important for ease of rewashering taps to fittings and for any attention that may be required to the hot water system. Surveyors do not think highly of those stop valves placed in the roof-space, since these can hardly be considered easily accessible.

It is better if they are positioned somewhere below the top floor ceiling level, albeit out of reach of little hands that may not be able to resist the temptation to twiddle. Comments on the inaccessibility of such stop valves do show that the surveyor can pay attention to the smaller details, which can be an irritation to a purchaser should something go wrong. If the surveyor makes sure that all valves operate he will have the peace of mind in knowing that his client will not suffer flooding through a jammed or ineffective control valve.

Mains drinking water

It is important to ensure that a supply of mains drinking water is available at the sink in the kitchen. If the tap at this point cannot be seen to be connected from the rising main, then running the tap should indicate, by the pressure of water, whether it is from the main or from the storage cistern.

It is not correct to assume that mains water is always available at the sink, since alterations in the past may have left the main tucked away some distance from the sink and it may be all too easy to make a connection to an adjacent cold feed pipe from the cistern. A particular check on this point is necessary where a house has been converted into one or more flats, so as to ensure that each unit has drinking water.

Adequacy of supply to fittings

In larger houses, or again where alterations or conversions have been carried out to form multiple units, care is not always taken to ensure that an adequate flow of water is provided at all fittings when a number are being used at any one time. The usual domestic size of 19 mm main cold feed pipe to the bath with 12 mm branches to basins and W.C., is normally quite sufficient for a house with one bathroom, but if there is more than one bath in a property, or numerous basins such as in a small boarding or flatlet house, then it is essential that the cold feed is increased accordingly to give the recommended flow in litres per minute at the fittings.

In houses with numerous fittings it is a wise precaution for the surveyor to turn on as many taps as possible and establish whether there is a reasonable flow. Cases have been known where taps produce little more than a trickle, when those elsewhere are giving an adequate supply. A full investigation of inadequacies in a cold water system can be lengthy and is generally not necessary on a structural survey of a small dwelling-house. It is important, however, that the surveyor should be aware of the existence of this problem and draw attention to it should the need arise since instructions are often received from clients proposing to purchase houses with part possession only, for conversion purposes and even, of course, for letting rooms.

In this respect all surveyors should be familiar with the contents of BS 6700: 1987 "Specification for the design, installation, testing and maintenance of services supplying water for domestic use within buildings and their curtilages", to enable a comparison to be made between the ideal and the building being inspected.

HOT WATER AND CENTRAL HEATING SYSTEMS

Having dealt with the cold water supply, some consideration must be given to the means of heating water for domestic purposes and perhaps to provide full or partial central heating. At a time when, to some surveyors, the full small bore copper pipe, radiator, pump and gas fired boiler installation seems to be universal it is as well to remember that there are two principal systems for this purpose commonly adopted. These are termed the direct and indirect systems.

The direct system   The direct system is the cheaper to install and is to be found mainly in smaller, older houses, where there is only a domestic hot water supply or at most partial central heating to the limited extent of one or two radiators or a towel rail. Even so, the system is not particularly suitable for hard water areas, owing to the tendency of the boiler and the flow and return pipes to become furred by the continual circulation of fresh water in the process of being heated and drawn off.

The direct system takes its name from the fact that the flow and return pipes are taken direct from the boiler to the hot water storage cylinder, which comprises a single unit where the hot water is stored. From the cylinder hot water is drawn off at the fittings and it is only when there is any left over that radiators or a towel rail are heated. The disadvantage is clear in that if hot water is greatly in demand, then very little heating is provided.

At one time boilers in the cheaper ranges provided little over the output normally required for domestic hot water, although a towel rail could usually be added. The efficiency of boilers has, over the years, been greatly improved and there are numerous types of slow burning solid fuel domestic boilers, and also fires with back boilers, which are claimed to have sufficient output to heat up to three radiators and a towel rail in addition to domestic hot water.

Even so the disadvantages of the direct method must be stressed in describing this type of system, when found in a house. Particular care must be taken when there is evidence of a new boiler installed in an existing direct system, since the efficiency of the system must always be in doubt owing to the possibility of furred pipes. A test is necessary, however, to prove the point one way or the other.

The indirect system   The indirect system is more expensive to install and, as its name implies, the hot water for domestic purposes is heated indirectly, by means of a calorifier contained within the hot water storage cylinder. The calorifier is connected, by primary circulation flow and return pipes, to the hot water boiler.

All radiators and any towel rails are supplied from pipework on circuits direct from the boiler or from the calorifier, so that the heating of radiators is entirely separate from the domestic hot water and is not affected by the drawing off of hot water from the taps. Also, as no water is drawn off from the heating circuits and the same water is continually circulating, the incidence of furring in the pipes and boiler is considerably reduced.

Balance cisterns

It is necessary with the indirect system to have an additional small storage cistern, of not less than 15 gallons (68.2 litres) capacity and usually positioned in the roof space, to supply water to top up the calorifier and heating circuit. The presence of this balance tank, as it is often called, will very often indicate the use of an indirect system, which is the only gravity system which should be employed where any pretence at the provision of adequate central heating by hot water is attempted. It is, of course, essential that a valve be provided, so as to shut down the heating circuits during the summer months leaving just the hot water system functioning.

Hot water storage tanks and cylinders

The surveyor should examine any galvanised steel hot water storage tank or cylinder closely for signs of rust. Its size should also be taken, for conversion into gallons or litres, in order to assess its suitability to fulfil the household requirements, on the basis of an assumed average consumption of about 10 gallons (45.5 litres) per head.

Insulation

If the cylinder is not lagged, together with the flow and return pipes, the fact should be indicated in the report, since for very little expense economies in fuel consumption can be achieved. If the cylinder is lagged, the surveyor should be wary of commenting on its condition but should, instead, point out that it could not be closely inspected owing to the covering. There is always a danger, in such circumstances, that the cylinder has rusted without anyone being aware of it.

The surveyor should also check whether the cylinder is fitted with an electric immersion heater, or preferably two, for use in summer months, a small heater for sink and basin water and a large heater for baths. During these months a boiler is unnecessarily costly to run and a back boiler served by a fire in the living room can be an inconvenient arrangement.

The cylinder should be closely examined to ensure that it has an expansion pipe, taken from the top of the cylinder to discharge over the top of the cold water cistern and through an opening in the cover. If the system is an indirect type, the surveyor should also note whether the calorifier and heating circuits have an additional expansion pipe to discharge over the small balance cistern provided for topping up.

Boilers

During the inspection of the interior of the house the type, method of firing, size and approximate age of the boiler should be noted. The surveyor should also always note whether a boiler is fitted with a safety valve, which is particularly important in hard water areas where furring in the pipes can cause blockages and result in highly dangerous explosions. This safety valve is omitted on

228

occasions with direct systems, where a back boiler is used in connection with an open fire or closed stove. This is a very bad practice and may be a source of danger.

Tests of hot water and central heating systems

Only descriptive items in regard to hot water and central heating systems have been dealt with so far. As mentioned before, tests of the system should be the rule rather than the exception, but where no instructions for these are given, or where for some reason or other tests are impracticable, the surveyor should at least be able to give an intelligent description of the fittings that can be seen and to describe obvious visual faults. These may range from signs of rust corrosion and faulty valves to radiators, poorly fitted pipe layouts, sub-standard pipe joints and accessories and, in particular, unsatisfactory boiler compartments. The surveyor should also note where radiators are obviously of inadequate size or where, due to complications in the structure they have not been provided at all thus presenting obvious deficiencies in the system.

What he must avoid, however, at all costs is extending such a description to phrases such as, "the system was working during my inspection and appeared to be in order". Such phrases are liable to give the impression that there is no possible doubt that all is sound and this may well mislead a purchaser.

Only a test to the system will give any indication at all as to the efficiency of the boiler to supply hot water to the fittings, the system's economy in running, its safety in operation, whether surfaces are adequate or not for the heating of the rooms in question and finally whether pipes are furred up or not. The tests involve starting from cold and noting the time taken to reach certain temperatures, together with the amount of fuel used. While the system is heating up the heating engineer will inspect the system and calculate the adequacy of the radiators. A full report can then be given, to include an estimate for rectifying any faults. Nothing short of this can be considered at all satisfactory as a basis for forming an opinion.

Arrangements for testing

In making arrangements for such a test, as described above, it is essential to secure the vendor's co-operation in shutting down the system the night before since the engineer will not appreciate finding the system in full blast when he arrives. This will amount to a wasted journey for him and for which a charge will generally be made.

It is particularly essential to have tests where hot water heating systems are in any way elaborate and where they are oil or gas-fired or of the small bore type where electrical pumps are involved and in many cases automatic and thermostatic control is adopted. While a surveyor may have a working knowledge of such systems, he is treading very dangerous ground by trespassing into the world of a specialist and by endeavouring to give opinions on such systems. Unfortunately, many clients will be forceful in pressing their surveyor to give assurances, without incurring the expense of additional fees, but such pressure should be resisted.

However, the surveyor, even when instructed not to commission a test, must fully present the result of his visual findings in order to discharge his duty to his client. Points to highlight might be where parts of a new boiler are missing or where an old and obviously suspect boiler serves a newly installed pipe and radiator system. Another cogent reason for comment is where the primary flow and return pipes and possibly the main service pipes are lagged with asbestos. It should be reported that not only does this material need replacement but that its removal must be carried out in controlled conditions.

Gas fired boilers and boiler flues

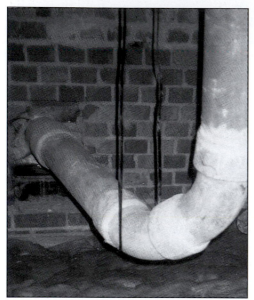

Not surprisingly this gas flue pipe was found to leak fumes.

Dangers of warmed air systems

Oil fired heating systems

The mention of gas-fired boilers introduces again the subject of linings to boiler flues and the dangers involved in ignoring the necessity for these in the report. It is essential that when a gas boiler is installed to discharge its fumes into a brick-built flue that such flue is lined with vitrified pipes or one of the types of flexible liner to prevent the condensation of the flue gases attacking the lining or parging to the flue and the mortar and brickwork.

Unfortunately, this is not a point that can always be checked adequately or even at all. The surveyor must, therefore, indicate the necessity for the lining in the report, point out that he cannot see it without extensive cutting away and indicate the dangers should this work not have been carried out.

Precisely the same remarks apply in the case of oil-fired boilers, but these in addition must have their flues provided with an insulated lining, in view of the high temperatures appertaining in the flue. Again, the surveyor is unlikely to be able to check on this point and, as above, must explain why and warn of the dangers of the omission of the insulation. There is always a possibility of a purchaser becoming involved in a protracted argument and perhaps litigation with a neighbour should the unlined flue be incorporated in a party structure.

In the case of warmed air heating systems it is all the more necessary to advise an inspection and report by a specialist in view of the distressing cases that have arisen where occupants have been asphyxiated owing to errors on installation whereby the products of combustion have been passed into the heating ducts instead of the flue.

Oil-fired systems involve the storage of oil, on the premises, in a fuel tank. Besides the question of capacity, which can easily be measured, local authorities have regulations for the installation of storage tanks for this purpose, covering their position in relation to the remainder of the premises and the question of safety in use.

Here again the surveyor may have a working knowledge of these regulations and may be able to comment appropriately, but generally it is advisable to instruct the heating engineer to deal with the entire installation, including the tank, since this is a specialist field. The heating engineer should, of course, test all safety measures, such as the operation of any valves controlled by fusible links to stop the flow of oil to the boiler in the event of fire. It is considered that, in the case of the more complicated installations, the little knowledge possessed by most surveyors in general practice can be a dangerous thing.

PIPES AND FITTINGS FOR COLD AND HOT WATER SYSTEMS

Requirements

Little has been said up to the present, in the consideration of the hot and cold water services, of the pipes which carry the water from the storage cistern and cylinder to the various fittings and from the Water Company's supply point at the boundary. Originally any installation of the pipes should have followed consultation with the local Water Company and the local council, since depending on the area certain pipes may be unsuitable.

Lead pipes for instance are not suitable for soft water areas, since the lead can be dissolved in the water which is now recognised as presenting a health hazard. This risk is much reduced and is considered generally acceptable in hard water areas. In other areas where the soil is of peat and the water is of acid reaction, the use of galvanised steel pipes is not allowed owing to the corrosive action of the water. On the other hand, galvanised steel pipes are suitable for hard water areas since they are stronger. As a result they are able to withstand the hammering sometimes required to remove the scale formed by the deposits, even when a solvent is used, but it is desirable, in these areas, to use a pipe the next size above the normal to allow for this. The surveyor's local knowledge will have to be relied on in respect of the wrong material used for plumbing installations, as no hard and fast rules can be given.

In soft water areas, the dangers of bi-metallic corrosion should be borne in mind where copper pipes and a galvanised cistern are used in the same system, since the water acts as an electrolyte and copper, carried in solution from the pipes, can attack the zinc in the galvanised surfaces. It is sound practice to utilise pipes and fittings of the same material, but this precept is not, by any means, always followed.

Materials for pipes
Lead and copper

In the past, lead was universally used for pipes owing, principally, to its ease of working. When galvanised steel pipes were manufactured to be much cheaper than lead, these came into common use. Copper has for some time been available and has many merits, being fairly easy to bend, available in long lengths, with a good resistance to corrosion, possessing considerable strength and not in need of painting. Joints of the capillary type are easy to form and when freezing does occur it is often only the joints which need reforming. A possible health hazard has been publicised due to the lead element in joints but it is thought that this is remote.

Polythene

Polythene tubes for cold water services are also now in common use and these have many advantages, though with the cardinal disadvantage that they cannot be used for hot water services in view of excessive thermal movement. In the first place, they reduce the risk of freezing, owing to the possession of better insulating properties than other pipes. Again, polythene tubes can be bent easily and resist corrosion.

Aluminium and stainless steel

If the surveyor should come across aluminium pipes in the water

231

supply system, there are good grounds for suggesting that these pipes will have a very limited life, and their use, at present, cannot be recommended. Stainless steel pipes are becoming more used for both hot and cold water services but are still comparatively expensive. Ideally the pipes should be of a stainless alloy all through, not merely surface treated, and a sure way of distinguishing the former material is that it is non-magnetic whereas steel, which is only stainless on the surface, remains magnetic.

More often than not, however, the surveyor will find the more traditional plumbing materials in use. Should the piping be in a mixture of lead, copper and galvanised steel, the surveyor should indicate the possibility of corrosion arising from dissimilar metal contacts, since a number of cases of defects due to this cause have been reported.

Problems with old lead pipes

In many old properties, the cold and hot water installations will still be found to be mainly in lead. Arrays of pipes will be found performing the most fantastic contortions, many lengths being practically unsupported and sagging between the brackets while others are, wholly or partly, buried in walls. Those surveyors with experience of property maintenance will know that such installations are a constant source of annoyance and leaks a frequent occurrence.

Many leaks are difficult to trace and where pipes are concealed, pinhole leaks can cause damage over a period before becoming apparent. Very often the main cause of the trouble is due to the effect of lime on the lead, causing minute holes by corrosion which, in pipes carrying mains water, are eventually enlarged by the pressure. Lead becomes brittle and stretched with age and, accordingly, less and less efficient the older it becomes. In the circumstances, a purchaser moving from a house with a fairly new installation, all in copper pipes, may feel disgruntled if the surveyor does not draw his attention to the inadequacies of a plumbing system with a number of old lead pipes or the health hazard in soft water localities.

Water supply other than from the main

Finally, before we turn to a consideration of the sanitary fittings, it must not be forgotten that not all houses have the benefit of a mains water supply. The surveyor will at times come across properties where the supply is from a well. Surveyors in rural areas will be more familiar with such properties than those practising in towns and this once again serves to illustrate the desirability, in general, of surveyors confining their attention to properties in their particular locality.

Wells and pumps

Where a well supply is found, the construction should be compared with the desirable recommendations and any faults noted for correction. The method of delivery may still be by a hand pump and not every purchaser may appreciate the hard work that this may entail. Alternatively, raising the water may be by means of an electric pump, perhaps controlled automatically. In such cases the electrical engineer should cover the pump's condition, efficiency and safety in his report.

A surveyor's local knowledge may assist him in gauging the depth of the well and in knowing whether it is ever likely to dry up

232

in long spells of drought. If the surveyor has no local knowledge then he must make strenuous efforts to ascertain this information from independent local sources. Finally, the presence of a well is, without doubt, a case where a purchaser's authority should be sought to engage the services of an analyst to report upon the suitability of the water for drinking purposes.

SANITARY FITTINGS

Water closets
In the room by room inspection of the house, particular care must be taken in bathrooms, W.C.s and kitchens to note the type, age and condition of sanitary fittings. Water closet fittings, in particular, require close attention, since some of the old obsolete short and long hopper types will still be found, which are now considered inefficient and insanitary. Cased-in W.C. pans, whether of the old valve-operated type or in conjunction with a flushing cistern, are also to be noted for replacement as they are, nowadays, considered insanitary.

Wash down closets are satisfactory, but their efficiency does depend on the shape of the pan and its ability to channel the water from the flushing cistern into a suitable force to push the contents of the pan into the soil pipe. Single-trap syphonic pans can cause trouble through blockages in the constricted waterway, on which depends the action. In this respect, two-trap syphonic pans are altogether superior and increasingly common, but it is important that the correct matching cistern, made for the pan, is employed.

W.C. pans and their joints to the soil pipe should be closely examined for cracks and chips. Earthenware closets which are cracked or chipped absorb water and are therefore insanitary and may harbour germs and the surveyor should note these for replacement. Cracks in the base of the pan, or on the outlet, or defective joints to soil pipes particularly with the increasing use of plastic pipes and special connectors can cause a slow leak of water and these are a frequent source of outbreaks of dry rot in the floors of W.C. compartments. The surveyor must therefore take particular care to feel around below the junction of fittings and pipes for any tell-tale drops of water and also examine carefully the floorboards around the fittings.

It is always essential to flush all water closets as this will not only indicate the leakages mentioned above but will also indicate the efficiency of the flushing particularly if half a dozen pieces of newspaper 150 mm by 50 mm are first thrown into the pan. Many of the old high-level cast iron cisterns, operated by means of a cast iron bell, will be found to be so rusted as to be incapable of delivering a fast effectual flush. In the circumstances, the surveyor may well advise their replacement by a cistern with a piston-actuated syphon which functions with less noise, requires less force for its operation and is more reliable. Plastic, vitreous china, or even the old porcelain enamelled types are preferable in all respects to the cast iron.

Wash-basins
Wash-basins are usually made of earthenware or vitreous china.

233

Earthenware is an absorbent material, so that when a basin made of this material becomes chipped or cracked so that water can penetrate the glaze, it rapidly spreads to cause a large stain. Vitreous china basins do not suffer from this unsightly condition so that minor chips on the glaze are not so serious. Unfortunately, it is all too easy to drop jars or bottles into the bowls of wash-basins, with the result that many will be found to be cracked. These cracks can allow water to drip on the floor and sometimes penetrate to the joists.

Where basins are cased in, leakage can continue for a period without the owner noticing, so that a surveyor should closely examine the flooring in the area of cracked basins. Cracks can also be caused by over-tightening of the nuts securing the taps to the basin. Occasionally wash-basins will be found made of porcelain enamelled steel. These, if subjected to heavy usage, can become chipped so that water penetrates to the metal causing rust marks and, eventually, perforation.

Sinks   White glazed sinks are made of fireclay or earthenware, the latter suffering the same faults as W.C.s and basins made of the same material, when chips or cracks occur. Sinks should be of an adequate depth, usually not less than 250 mm so that the old shallow London pattern sinks are now considered obsolete and suitable only for replacement. Stainless steel and vitreous enamelled sinks will also frequently now be found, but aluminium sinks, where used, have in many cases been found to be unsuitable and have corroded rapidly where the taps are connected below the bowl, under the rim and also directly below the outlets of the taps.

All basins and sinks should be checked to see that the waste pipe is correctly trapped. In older properties, or where an unauthorised additional fitting has been installed by an odd-job man, untrapped fittings will occasionally be found. These fittings contravene the Building Regulations and should be provided with proper traps, otherwise there is a danger of foul air penetrating into the room. Where traps are found, the depth of the water seal should be noted, as this information will be useful when the drainage system is under consideration. As for the fittings themselves, traps can be defective and allow water penetration into a floor below, which if permitted to continue over a period may possibly lead to an outbreak of dry rot.

Baths   Little is usually called for, by way of remarks, in connection with baths in the report. The most common material is porcelain enamelled cast iron, but nowadays reinforced glass fibre and plastics are found and in the more expensive older properties occasionally ceramic materials. An unduly short bath should be noted since taller purchasers may have got used to a long bath and be annoyed to find only a short bath in their new house. The type, material and condition and, in particular, whether the enamel is heavily stained, worn or chipped should also be noted.

In older properties the roll-top edged bath will be found as against the more modern rectangular bath suitable for use with side and end panels. Where old baths do have panels these may be of heavy wood and may well have become insanitary over the years and sometimes will be found to be affected by rot and woodworm.

Modern bath panels may be of vitrolite, enamelled hardboard plastic or even marble, but of whatever type they obscure a sight of the trap and the arrangements for the overflow. In such circumstances, there is always the possibility of a leaking trap causing defects in the floor which cannot be seen, a point which should be borne in mind by the surveyor and which should be added to the report.

As the surveyor examines each basin, bath, or sink, he should check that the taps are connected to the water supplies and note in general terms the condition of taps and any defects, such as worn washers or loose fittings.

Showers
The provision of showers is on the increase due not only to the obvious convenience of this facility but as an alternative to baths in confined spaces. The surveyor should always take great care in checking the fittings, enclosures and bases of showers as these are a frequent cause of damp penetration. Good quality fittings, a well tiled enclosure and a ceramic tray mounted on a rigid base with a space for inspection below will reassure the surveyor while a flexible tray in a sub-standard enclosure with obvious making good at the joints and a part redecorated ceiling below will obviously not.

SOIL AND WASTE CONNECTIONS

Anti-syphon pipes
With one exception, we have now dealt with the room by room examination in so far as it covers sanitary fittings and their supplies of hot and cold water and the method of trapping the outlet. However, in addition to examining the trap and taking its depth of water seal, the surveyor should also note whether any connection is made to an anti-syphon pipe. This will be important in relation to the soil and waste pipe installation to be considered later, but also in regard to the connection of the anti-syphon pipe itself with the trap.

In some cases it will be found that the connection is made on the wrong side of the trap, so that the anti-syphon pipe does not fulfil its function. In such cases there is a danger of the water being syphoned out of the trap and foul air in consequence entering the room. On the other hand, of course, the traps provided may be of the resealing type, obviating the necessity for anti-syphon pipes and this point should also be noted, together with the type of resealing trap employed.

Investigation of pipework
Whereas it may seem logical to proceed next with a consideration of the disposal of waste water from the sanitary fittings by way of the waste and soil pipes externally, this method will be found to have certain disadvantages. As in the case of the larger roofs, it is easy to become confused and the profusion of timbers in the roof of a large property can be compared with the tangle of soil, waste, rain-water and anti-syphon pipes often encountered on the elevations.

Since the examination and testing of the drainage system usually comprises a completely separate operation at some point during the survey, it is suggested that by following a set routine in regard to this, so that it includes the waste and soil pipes, the surveyor will avoid confusion and will be able to take his notes and draft his report upon the drains in a clear and logical fashion.

This will be a difficult matter if he endeavours to trace the waste pipe of every sink, bath and basin and the outlet from every W.C. in turn. Such a method would result in considerable duplication of effort. On the other hand, a procedure of inspection, commencing at the head of the drainage system and embracing a description of each branch drain and its purpose, together with a description of the purpose of each gully has much to commend it.

DRAINAGE SYSTEMS

Before proceeding with a consideration of the problems encountered in the house drainage system, it may be desirable to devote a few paragraphs to the differing types of system adopted for private houses. These differing systems will have some bearing on the scope of the examination and may well limit the degree of testing that can be carried out. They will certainly govern the purchaser's liability for repairs, should the drains be defective.

Drains and sewers

Pipes which carry foul water and rain-water are called either "drains" or "sewers". Whether a pipe is a drain or sewer depends on a number of factors. The rules to apply differ for properties in the London area as against those in other areas.

Outside London, any pipe taking foul water or surface water from within the curtilage of one property is a "drain" and as such is in private ownership. All other pipes are sewers. The responsibility for the repair and maintenance of a drain does not end, however, at the boundary line of the property but extends up to the point where the drain connects to a sewer.

Sewers, however, fall into two categories, public and private. Private sewers can only be found outside London with groups of properties constructed after 1st October, 1937. In every matter of maintaining, renewing and cleansing, private sewers are the responsibility of the owners concerned, the proportion of liability being fixed at the time of construction by the local authority. This, is, therefore, a point which can be checked by a solicitor on behalf of a purchaser.

All other sewers are now public sewers, be they below land owned by the local authority or below private land. However, where such sewers before 1st October, 1937, were classed as "combined drains" the local authority, although responsible for carrying out the work, can recover from the owners of those properties which utilise the sewer any costs of repair, renewal or improvement, but not the costs of cleansing.

The position in London

In London, the position differs slightly in that a "drain" not only

236

includes a pipe used for the drainage of premises within the same curtilage, but also a pipe used for draining a group of buildings, provided the drain was constructed after 1848 with the sanction of the appropriate authority. Thus, it will be seen that any "combined drain" serving properties constructed before 1848 has become a sewer and is the responsibility of the local authority, both as to any works required to it and to the payment of costs. After 1848, any pipe constructed by private owners to drain a group of properties remains a combined drain, repairable by those owners unless taken over by the local authority.

Since 1937, the local authorities in London have been empowered to make an order requiring new groups of properties to be drained by a "combined operation", in which case the combined drain, so constructed, remains the responsibility of the owners concerned. However, the order does not specify the proportion of liability as between owners for the cost of any necessary work, leaving a wide margin for possible dispute. There are no "private sewers" by definition in London, pipes in this category within the London area being known as "combined drains".

Considerable litigation has ensued, in the past, on whether pipes are "drains" or "public sewers" and the surveyor should be aware of the difficulties that can arise in determining this point. On a structural survey, it may be unwise for the surveyor to be dogmatic on repairing liabilities as the straightforward answer, which may seem apparent on the site, may not bear legal investigation. If there is any element of doubt in the surveyor's mind he should warn a purchaser to make further inquiries, preferably through his solicitor.

Small drainage systems Probably the simplest drainage system to describe and examine and the most frequently found, is the single house with its own main drain, connected to a local authority sewer in the street. In such cases, there may be two separate main drains, one for foul and waste water and one for rain-water only, both drains connecting to separate sewers below the street. Both variations of this system commonly occur where streets have been laid out first, followed by the construction of houses. The streets and sewers may have been constructed by the local authority or alternatively privately built and then taken over.

Sewers below estate roads In the development of estates of houses outside London, particularly before and since the end of the Second World War, individual houses may be connected to "sewers" below the estate roads which remain in private ownership, either collectively by the house owners or by the original developer, if the houses are leasehold. It may well be that the purchaser will have additional liabilities for the upkeep of the private sewer besides his own length of drain up to the sewer. It is likely, however, that the searches undertaken by the purchaser's solicitor will bring to light such circumstances, which is fortunate, since the distinction between a private and public sewer will not always be readily apparent to the surveyor.

Private sewers Where a small group of houses has been constructed on a plot of land, perhaps surrounded by existing houses and an existing pattern

237

should an obstruction occur. It is considered that there is little force in the argument that drains of old houses should not be expected to withstand the pressure of a water test, since obstructions are equally likely to occur with old drains as with new. There is, in fact, more likelihood.

Degree of leakage

A drain which is not watertight is clearly defective, but, in advising a client, consideration must be had to the degree of leakage and the position of the drain. In properties where the drains are very defective, the surveyor will find on occasions that the length of drain under test just will not fill, the leak being so considerable that the water promptly passes into the sub-soil, at some point along the length. This would be an extreme case of a leaking drain necessitating advice to excavate in order that further tests and examination can be carried out and which might entail, at worst, the need to grub up and re-lay the whole drain.

Identical advice would be necessary where the drain leaks to the extent that the water in the upper chamber visibly drops when the test is commenced and rapidly vanishes from the chamber, that is, within the space of ten minutes or so. On the other hand, cases occur where after a period has been allowed to elapse, say fifteen minutes for absorption by the cement work of the chamber, the water level will drop very slowly, perhaps six inches in thirty minutes. In such cases, it is considered that the leak can be classed as slight and advice given that a patent method of repairing the drain could possibly be adopted, which avoids the necessity of grubbing up and re-laying. This will be discussed, however, later in this chapter, since other considerations have to be taken into account before the correct advice can be formulated.

Water tests to drains

It is not considered necessary to describe here, in detail, the method and procedure for carrying out a water test to the underground drainage system, since such information can be obtained from any one of the many books on drainage and sanitation, and most books on building construction. The method usually described and invariably adopted of commencing from the chamber at the head of the system commends itself on a structural survey, since during the course of the testing much other useful work on the drainage installation can be carried out by the surveyor starting his notes at the same point.

Acceptable pressure

As to the head of water to be adopted during the test on old drains, it is considered that 600 mm, equivalent to about 0.007N per mm, as both the minimum and the maximum should be aimed for whenever possible. As stated previously, 15 minutes may, of necessity, have to be allowed for absorption in the chamber, and drains left under test for about half an hour, testing to be carried out between chambers, in as short lengths as feasible. Often with old drains, it will not be necessary to leave each section under test for so long, since the water will have vanished long before that time has elapsed.

Plugging drains for testing

It is important, on testing, that the plugging of the lower end of the drain should be satisfactory. The surveyor will find, in many cases, that a cracked pipe or collar at the lower end of the drain will

240

render the use of a disc plug impracticable and, in this respect, inflatable bag plugs will be found more satisfactory on many occasions. If the condition of the channels, benching and rendering in the upper chamber is so defective as to make reliable measurement of leakage impossible, then recourse must be had to the method of plugging the length of the drain at the top end, topping up from a container set at the required height and measuring the drop in the level by means of a rubber tube and glass gauge attached to the lower plug.

The surveyor should always remember that he is responsible for carrying out the test and for measuring the drop in water level in the inspection chamber. The surveyor should, therefore, take the measurements and timings himself, and not rely on someone else to do it. This would be particularly important if the surveyor was employing, as assistant, a plumber not known to him. The surveyor should also bear in mind that marks indicating water level of chalk or wetted paper can easily be disturbed. Wax crayon marks are preferable, but the use of a Beattie water test gauge has a great deal to commend it.

Smoke tests to drains   If a water test on the underground drains is not permitted by the vendor, permission may be granted to carry out a smoke test. In such circumstances, it is considered essential that the surveyor should weigh in his mind whether such a test is really worth the trouble. The pressure available from a smoke testing machine is so low that the test is in no way comparable to the water test, which does reproduce the conditions of actual blockage in the underground drains.

Air tests to drains   The same remarks apply to the ordinary air test, using the same type of machine but without smoke. Furthermore, unventilated branch drains, with either test, can only be subjected to a pressure of about 0.0007N per mm^2 before the smoke or air pushes the water forming the seal, out of the trap.

Drain lengths between manholes can be subjected to an air test, under pressure, with an air pressure testing machine, but in such circumstances the test may be more severe than a water test since the usual pressure applied to stoneware drains is 0.02 N per mm^2 equivalent to a standing head of water of 2.13 m in the upper chamber. The difficulty with an air pressure test is that the full implications would have to be explained to the vendor and it is thought unlikely that permission would be granted for such a test, if already previously refused for a water test, in view of the fact that the pressure that can be adopted could exceed that available on a water test in normal circumstances.

Vendor's reluctance   It is possible for the surveyor, at times, to overcome a vendor's reluctance to agree to a water test by the exercise of tact in personal discussion where his client may have insisted on a test perhaps due to a bad experience in a former house. Very often, if the reasons for wishing to carry out the test are carefully explained to the vendor he can be induced to agree. It is not usually necessary to proceed to the next stage and inform the vendor that if he will not agree to the test being applied, the worst must be assumed in regard to the condition of the underground drains and the purchaser advised to budget accordingly for virtual renewal. Discussion along the latter lines is not conducive to good relations and it is, perhaps, wise to leave the exertion of this sort of pressure until after the survey is carried out, and to direct contact between the purchaser and vendor. Clearly, in the absence of permission to test, the surveyor must warn his client fully of all the implications of untested drains and stress these warnings. The surveyor has no other alternative in the circumstances.

Preliminaries to testing

Assuming, however, that the surveyor has permission to carry out a test and the testing is under way, the surveyor can then proceed with his examination of the external visible features of the drainage system.

Visual inspection of channels, benching and drain connections

At each inspection chamber it is customary to note various details in regard to the construction and the condition of each part. The type of channels used and whether they are cracked or not should be noted. Concrete benching should be examined for cracks and whether it is correctly formed, so that when rodding operations are necessary it is sensibly shaped for the plumber's feet. The material of the main drain and all branch drains should be noted where they join the chamber, together with the size.

In regard to the sizes of drains, however, it should always be made clear in the report that these sizes apply only to the visible connections, as seen in the chamber. Elsewhere below ground the sizes and the type of drain may vary. This, however, is a point which cannot be verified without opening up the ground along the whole length of each drain, although indications of differing sizes may be obtained by using a mirror.

Inspection chambers

It is always advisable to take the invert depth in each inspection chamber as a matter of course, so that on pacing the length of drain between chambers the fall can be gauged and checked in relation to the size of drain adopted. Rendering in each chamber should also be examined for cracks and hollow areas. Defective rendering can drop off and cause either total or partial obstruction in the system. If chambers are deep, they should be of an adequate size and provided with sound step irons for easy access. Existing step irons should always be examined for rust as it has been known for a plumber to be left helpless in a deep manhole when the lower steps have snapped off.

Interceptor traps

Where a chamber is fitted with an interceptor trap, the surveyor should always check that the rodding eye is fitted with a stopper to prevent foul air passing from the sewer into the house drainage system and also to prevent the ingress of rats. It is always advisable to recommend the fitting of a brass lever stopper with arm, handle and staple if this is not provided, particularly if the chamber is deep. Blockages, as likely as not, arise at weekends when plumbers are not available or if they are, at fearsome cost and at the risk of damage. For the purchaser to be able to release the stopper without donning his thigh length waders is a considerable advantage. At the very least the stopper should be provided with a chain to secure it to the chamber wall.

Is this internal inspection chamber adequately sealed? At least it is not hidden.

Branch drains

Is this connection adequately airtight? The surveyor should endeavour to check.

In relation to each chamber the cover deserves attention. For chambers within buildings, it is necessary to check whether covers are fitted with a double seal or, as will often be found in old buildings, with only a single seal thereby permitting the likely entry of foul air. Externally, covers may well be found to be broken and these are a danger in themselves, should anyone tread on them. Covers will also be found to be exceptionally rusty together with their frames, sometimes beyond saving. Covers with broken lifting handles can be tiresome to a purchaser and should be noted for renewal. Light covers positioned in garage drive-ins should be replaced with covers of a heavier type suitable for private vehicles.

Moving from the inspection chamber under review, the surveyor should then follow each branch drain, taking note of its purpose and, utilising the notes taken internally, noting which fittings it serves. At this stage, the surveyor will be able to decide whether rain-water is taken separately to surface water sewers under the road or even, possibly, to soakaways. If no access is provided to a separate rain-water system, it may be necessary to check on the plans deposited with the local authority before an answer can be given to the eventual disposal of rain-water and surface water.

With an absence of access, it would be unwise for the surveyor to assume discharge into public surface water sewers, since soakaways are by no means unusual. It should not be forgotten that soakaways too near a house can be a possible cause of settlement in the main structure. In the diagnosis of the cause of a settlement this may be a possible line of investigation to be followed if rain-water is disposed of in this manner and there are no other apparent reasons for the movement. As for other drains, however, without access, the surveyor will be unable to pass any opinion on their condition.

With soil branches to W.C.s on the lowest floor, few complications arise, since the connection is made direct and the test will reveal the condition of the drain. With a branch to serve upper floor W.C.s, a connection at ground level will be made to the soil pipe fixed to the wall of the building. Soil pipes should be checked as to their material and condition. On older properties, the surveyor will find lead or light iron pipes. The former may still be found to be entirely sound, but the latter will often be found to be split and to have defective joints. Light iron is not acceptable under modern regulations for soil pipes and their replacement on older buildings with heavy iron, although not a requirement unless defective or alterations are made, is advisable.

In recent years there has been a vast introduction of plastic pipework. The surveyor should always look for the British standard mark and note whether the full set of accessories have been provided or whether, due to haste, unacceptable substitutes have been employed or, as in the case of the photograph on the left, left out entirely.

Venting of traps

When there is more than one W.C. connected to a soil pipe, it is essential that traps to all the appliances be fitted with anti-syphon

243

pipes, with the exception of the top fitting in certain circumstances. As the surveyor will be aware, the anti-syphon pipe must either be carried up to above eaves level or, alternatively, connected to the soil pipe above the highest fitting where the soil pipe itself is carried up as ventilating pipe. Occasionally the surveyor will find that where a W.C. has been added to the property, a connection is made to the soil pipe without providing ventilation to the trap of the new fitting or, alternatively, to the existing fittings.

While the surveyor is still at the chamber near the head of the drainage system, it might be appropriate, before passing on to other matters, to mention the standard test for the vertical soil stacks by means of a smoke rocket. When the soil pipe is connected to the highest chamber the test serves two purposes. Firstly, the soundness of the soil pipe is tested by means of the smoke together with all joints, but in particular any joints internally which are the most important. Secondly, a check can be obtained on whether there is through ventilation to the drainage system, evidenced by the emission of smoke from the top of the ventilating pipe.

A further point to check in regard to ventilating pipes is that these are taken clear of any windows, in accordance with the Building Regulations, to prevent nuisance from foul drain air. Under the 1990 edition of Approved Document H to the Building Regulations 1985 a ventilating pipe must extend 900 mm above any opening into the building nearer than 3 m and be fitted with a cage or other perforated cover.

Soil branches are, of course, the only branches which should be connected direct to the underground drains in the ordinary two-pipe system of plumbing, which is the most frequently encountered. All other branch drains should terminate in a trapped gully, the waste water or rain-water discharging over the top of the water seal, either by means of a back inlet or by means of a shoe or, if necessary, via a channel. Apart from checking that no waste or rain-water pipes are connected direct to the drains, the gullies themselves repay close examination by the surveyor.

In the first instance, the surveyor should check that they are in fact trapped gullies and not rain-water shoes of the trapless gully type. If the surveyor is not wary, it is easy for the two types to be confused. Secondly, the water seal from the gully trap should be forced out to enable an inspection of the bottom of the trap to be carried out. On occasions, when testing a branch drain in the usual way by filling up to the gully top, it will be found that the leak is not due to a defect in the drain, but due merely to a cracked gully. In these circumstances, if the gully condition is not checked before the drain is tested, it may be necessary to re-test.

The treatment of the area around the gully should be noted by the surveyor, together with the mode of discharge from pipes. All too often the surveyor will find that pipes, instead of discharging below the gully grating or by means of back and side inlets, will terminate some distance above the grating and will splash the surrounding area and the base of the wall. This, although not found

244

Poor detailing around a gulley with shoe missing to rainwater branch. The many wastes etc. discharging into it cause splashing and dampness internally.

frequently, can be the cause of dampness internally, which in turn may lead to an outbreak of dry rot.

Waste water and rain-water pipes

Waste water and rain-water pipes should also be noted in regard to their material and condition. Normally, these will be in light

At least this rainwater pipe is taken properly to connect with the back inlet on the gulley. A pity about the hole in the pipe.

A contrast between the original and inappropriate plastic replacement hopper head and rainwater pipes. Note damp staining and eroded pointing in area of upper rainwater pipe (effect internally?) and eroded bricks on main rear wall and flank wall of back addition.

iron, but occasionally lead stacks will be found and also, on more recently built properties and old properties which have been converted, heavy iron or plastic for waste stacks. For rain-water pipes zinc, galvanised steel, aluminium and plastics are nowadays found,

Mixed lead and plastic waste pipes taken to a large replacement plastic hopper head. The hopper would need cleaning regularly with a bath and two basins discharging into it.

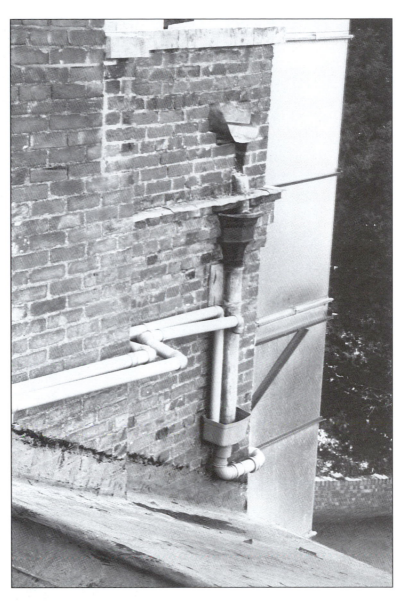

The work on the right is appalling. Note the gutter outlet at the top which allows water to splash everywhere and the distance between the lower hopper and the outlet of the plastic waste pipe supposedly meant to discharge into it. Someone has also taken the lead flashing to the lower roof slope.

but, as elsewhere in connection with internal plumbing and gutters, their use tends to be as a cheaper substitute for cast iron. Needless to say cracked pipes need noting for renewal and as mentioned previously their presence may necessitate investigation to ascertain defects internally which may have arisen, should the cracked pipes have been leaking for a long period.

Traps to fittings

Where more than one waste fitting discharges into a waste stack, it is necessary for the traps to the fittings to be ventilated in the same manner as already discussed under W.C.s and soil pipes. Often to avoid the necessity for the additional pipes, waste from fittings is taken to discharge into a hopper head, but this is an undesirable practice as the hoppers readily freeze in winter-time, tend to become clogged, harbour scum, and as a result give off offensive smells, which can cause annoyance if they are situated near windows.

This practice has not been allowed in the London area for some time, but will be found frequently outside London and on older

247

Buried pipes are more subject to corrosion and more difficult to renew. Often too they are the unsuspected source of dampness with its attendant troubles of defective plaster, dry rot, etc.

Wire balloons

Loose fixings

Incorrect connections

Ventilation to drainage system.

properties within the Metropolis. This is an additional point for the surveyor to note and should the purchaser be intending to add to or alter the existing arrangements, it is likely that a local authority in the London area would insist on work being carried out to make the whole installation comply with the present-day requirements.

As for soil pipes, waste pipes into which a number of fittings discharge should be carried up as ventilating pipes. It is important with all ventilating pipes that the surveyor should indicate the absence of wire balloons, as these are essential to prevent blockage by birds' nests.

In connection with all vertical stacks on houses the surveyor should pay attention to any loose fixings. Top lengths of pipes, in particular of ventilating pipes, often have minimal fixings with the result that in a high wind a whole six-foot length may come crashing down.

As a final matter in regard to soil, waste and rain-water pipes, the surveyor should always be on his guard to notice incorrect connections made, often by the handyman, without the knowledge of the local authority. A good example is shown on page 247. Instances are found of waste pipes connected to rain-water, soil and ventilating pipes. In one instance, it was noticed that a waste of polythene tubing had been led to discharge through the grille of a fresh air inlet, the mica flap having been removed to facilitate entry.

Mention of fresh air inlets introduces the subject of the necessity for through ventilation to the underground drainage system. It has already been mentioned that a soil stack from a branch drain to the highest chamber may be extended to roof level as a ventilating pipe for the top end of the system. Similarly at the lowest end there should also be either a fresh air inlet or alternatively, as these are not now permitted in the London area in close proximity to a building, a ventilating pipe taken to the full height of the front elevation. A combination of these two pipes should provide adequate through ventilation, but very often the pipe at the top end of the system will be missing or, alternatively, run from an intermediate chamber leaving part of the system above that chamber unventilated. .

At the front of the property the small fresh air inlet with a grille and mica flap can become buried, or if set in a wall become covered over. Sometimes the fresh air inlet is just removed, but in either case there can be an accumulation of foul air in the lower part of the system. Even if a fresh air inlet is found, the mica flap and grille are often broken and missing and the inlet may then become an outlet for foul air from the drainage system.

Advice on drainage systems
Having completed the testing, so far as is practicable, and the inspection of the drainage system the surveyor will then give some consideration to the advice which he will provide in the report. Before we consider this, however, it would be as well to state that although a drain may be watertight it may not necessarily be satisfactory in every respect. Drains should be self-cleansing, but the surveyor will come across instances where this is far from the case, either through too large a drain being used or, alternatively, the drain being laid at an incorrect fall.

Self-cleansing attributes
An accumulation of solids in the chambers will give an indication of this type of defect, but the check which the surveyor takes on the fall and size of the drain will be more useful as confirmation. In such circumstances blockages may be more frequent, a troublesome matter to any house owner, and the drains may be insanitary unless regular cleaning is carried out. It is, perhaps, a matter for preference whether a new owner would wish to put up with this irritation, or whether he would wish to re-lay the drains in these circumstances. He should be made aware of the problem, however, by his surveyor, even though the surveyor would hardly wish to condemn the drains outright and advise re-laying in the report for this reason alone.

Alignment
Even though a drain be watertight, there is still the question of badly laid drains which are out of true alignment and cases where jointing material has been left around the joints within the pipes. Both defects are a cause of blockages and possibly a continual source of annoyance to an owner and it can be an expensive matter to open up a length of drain and re-lay a section to overcome this problem. There are means of detecting defects of this nature, by means of mirror and ball tests, but tests are not normally carried out by surveyors on structural surveys where they involve special equipment of this nature.

Special tests
However, there may be occasions, for example where a surveyor is instructed to give special attention to the drainage system, when such equipment should be brought into use and the tests carried out. Such tests would increase the time taken on the survey and thereby the fee. It is considered that a client should, perhaps, be

given the opportunity of deciding whether the additional cost of such tests is justified, having regard to all circumstances.

However, it is considered that most clients would be satisfied with a water test, certainly in the first instance, since the results of this will indicate to the purchaser, through the report, whether a really substantial sum of money is required to remedy a leaky drainage system. Should a leaky system be found, the defects which might have been exposed by the additional tests will automatically be brought to light at a later date by the preparatory investigation necessary to locate the leak before it is remedied.

It is considered desirable, however, that the report should make it clear where a water test only is carried out that such a test does not form a full investigation of the drainage system. A water test only provides evidence as to whether the drains are watertight or not.

Having established that the drainage system leaks, whether in part or wholly, the surveyor should endeavour to proceed, as has been suggested throughout this book, to diagnose the cause and to give some consideration to prescribing a remedy. As to the cause, in the first instance, the surveyor should be as certain as it is possible to be that it is the drain that is leaking and that the water is not escaping through defects in the chamber or gully, or for that matter leaking past the plug due to a broken collar at the lower chamber. Testing in the proper manner will assist the surveyor in avoiding errors of this nature.

Advice on drain repairs
Lining

Within a particular length of drain, slight leaks may be caused by relatively minor defects in the jointing material, due to old age alone or aggravated by minor movement on settlement. In such circumstances, a purchaser may well be advised to consider further investigation and the possibility of repairing the drains by the patent internal lining process, which avoids digging up the ground to carry out the repair in the traditional manner. This process, carried out by a number of companies can show a very worthwhile saving in costs, but the surveyor should, before including such advice, be sure that the company would recommend that an effective and long lasting repair can be carried out by this method.

Traditional method

If the surveyor is not sure then he should advise the purchaser to be prepared to meet the estimated cost of work by the traditional methods. Such an estimate must clearly be very approximate only and stated to be so. The surveyor should also allow a good margin in his figures to cover all eventualities. By a slight leak, the writers mean a drop of say not exceeding 150 mm in half an hour, after allowing a period for absorption of 15 minutes if measurements are being taken in a chamber.

Slight leaks

Slight leaks of this nature occur in old drains running at a reasonable depth of not less than about 600 mm below ground level and in good bearing soils other than clay, in drains not subject to vibration and in drains well away from trees. In particular, drains passing below buildings with basements and on occasions below buildings without basements, suffer from slight leaks of this nature and are often suitable for repair by the patent method discussed above.

250

Serious leaks

On the other hand, the surveyor will encounter drains where it is not even possible to fill them full of water, or where the level drops visibly at a rapid rate. In these circumstances, there may well be good reason to advise not only further investigation preparatory to possible entire re-laying, but also remedial measures to combat the cause of the trouble. Clearly, drains laid in shallow ground subject to vibration or to seasonal movements of the soil when repaired from the inside, will remain subject to the same pressures as before. These pressures will probably cause the drains to become defective again in a relatively short period of time.

Tree roots

Furthermore, drains which pass near to trees can be affected by the action of the roots in a number of ways. In the first place, the roots increase the shrinkage of clay soils in dry weather. Secondly, the presence of moisture attracts the tree roots, so that if seasonal movement of the soil has induced cracks to occur at the joints, fine roots will penetrate these and flourish within the drain. In the third instance the roots themselves may exert sufficient direct pressure on the drain so as to disturb it.

Other works may be involved

In cases where drains have serious leakages and the cause can be attributed to settlement, either from the causes mentioned above or from inadequate foundations, or the action of tree roots, they require more than simple repair or renewal. The surveyor must allow therefore in his approximate cost for the additional work that may be required to remodel the system, by running the drains on new lines, or for providing additional foundation work together with flexible joints to ensure that when relaid, the drains remain stable in the foreseeable future.

Sewage disposal

Up to now it has been assumed that the eventual disposal of sewage from the building being surveyed will be, via a public sewer, to the local authority sewage disposal works. However, not all houses have the benefit of this facility, which most of us tend to take for granted. The surveyor may be instructed to survey a house in a country area which is too remote from a public sewer and, consequently, either has to store sewage in a cesspool for subsequent collection, or, if the house is large, may be provided with its own miniature disposal system.

Cesspools

With cesspools the surveyor should check as far as possible that the installation complies with the Building Regulations. In particular, the position of the cesspool in relation to the house should be considered. Ideally the cesspool should be at least 15 m away, on the downwind side of the house and in ground which slopes away. It will be necessary also for the surveyor to look around in the area of the cesspool to ensure that it is not within 18 m of a well or spring used as a source of water supply. The cesspool must also have ready means of access for cleaning and for emptying the contents, without the contents having to be carried through a building. In this connection, a paved drive to within about 9 m is essential to enable the local authority emptying vehicle to approach within easy distance.

Size and construction

As to size and construction, the surveyor will obviously have some difficulty in checking on the details below ground and will

251

therefore have to consult plans at the offices of the local authority or, if plans are not available, point out that the details cannot be checked. Should plans be available for consultation, the surveyor should be able to gauge the adequacy of the capacity from the normal allowance of $2.8\,m^3$ per person which allows for an emptying interval of 100 days (although the Building Regulations 1985 in Approved Document H require a minimum capacity of $18\,m^3$ for new construction), assuming that all waste water and rain-water is excluded from the cesspool and taken to soakaways, a point which can be checked on the site.

Emptying
While at the offices of the local authority the surveyor should also make inquiries regarding the frequency of emptying, the normal charges for this and the charge that would be made if an additional emptying to special order was found to be necessary. The local authority may also assist the surveyor in connection with any past history of nuisance arising from the cesspool.

Ventilation and cover
While still at the site, however, the surveyor can check for certain matters in connection with cesspools that should be visible. For instance, the cesspool should be adequately ventilated by means of a fresh air inlet and ventilating pipe normally at least $3\,m$ above ground level. Furthermore, the cesspool should be provided with an adequate air-tight inspection cover and the remainder of the drainage system separated from the cesspool by an inspection chamber fitted with an interceptor trap.

Warnings
In preparing the report, the surveyor should remember to indicate that he was unable to check details of construction not visible to the eye. Obviously, should there have been settlement in the base or the walls, allowing pollution of the surrounding ground, a serious nuisance would arise possibly involving total reconstruction of the cesspool. As a result the house would be out of action during the course of the reconstruction. A warning of this possibility should be included in circumstances where a cesspool is found, as the surveyor will not be able to check for such defects. A prospective purchaser needs to be advised that such are the hazards of owning country properties with cesspools. Those retiring to country cottages may well have become somewhat rosy eyed and overlook such considerations.

Individual soil disposal systems
Where the surveyor is instructed to carry out a survey of the larger type of country house, which has its own disposal system, there are excellent reasons to seek the client's authority to instruct a firm specialising in the design of these installations to carry out an inspection and to supply a report. There are many differing types of installation working on various principles and although most surveyors are aware of both the principles and the systems, it is not considered that knowledge of the principles alone enables a surveyor to recognise a sound system requiring the minimum of regular attendance from a system that is likely to be a continual source of trouble.

Flow rates
Apart from the maintenance factor, many of the systems installed in the larger country properties are of some considerable age and may by now be considered to be outmoded. Although the total

quantity of sewage from one house may be small, it should be remembered that the system has to be adequate to cope with a maximum rate of flow considerably in excess of the average rate, to avoid undue disturbance in the system. The sewage may also, nowadays, be more complicated to deal with, due to the use of detergents.

Specialist advice   The specialist familiar with the everyday workings of sewage disposal units, will be able to examine the system with these factors in mind and to report accordingly. There may, of course, be a contracting firm responsible for regular maintenance of the existing system, but it is suggested that the report of an outside professional firm of design consultants is to be preferred. A professional firm of this character will bring the same critical approach to the problem as that adopted by the surveyor in dealing with the structure.

GAS INSTALLATIONS

Not too long ago the average person was inclined to consider gas, apart from its use for cooking, as a source of power that was in decline. Recent years have brought about a reversal of this trend, due to the strenuous efforts by the suppliers to improve the efficiency and appearance of appliances, coupled with the tapping of the natural gas resources below the North Sea. Unfortunately the much increased use at a higher pressure now than previously with coal gas has also produced a much higher incidence of accidents.

Age of installation   The high cost of electricity for heating coupled with the uncertainty and high cost of oil supplies in difficult times, has also persuaded many people to turn again to gas. However, the gas installation in many of the houses that the surveyor inspects will be as old as the house itself, but even if not, may well be 80 to 100 years old. Over the years gas pipes rust and may become paper thin, or alternatively the pipes may become clogged giving poor pressure. Nowadays, when a client is intending to install a gas-fired central heating and hot water system, it is almost a certainty that the main supply from the Gas company's pipes below the street will be inadequate.

Increased pressure   Surveyors have not always, as a matter of course, carried out tests of gas piping or have even asked their clients whether they would wish such a test carried out. This may have been due to the fact that defective and dangerous gas piping was a comparative rarity. Furthermore, blowing out pipes to improve pressure or hammering to clear rust was a relatively cheap operation and the need for a larger main is fairly obvious, where intended improvements are known of in advance. Compared with the frequency of dangerous and defective electrical installations, faults in gas systems were rare. However, the occurrence of defects has been noted more frequently in recent years and it is highly probable that their incidence will increase in view of the average age of gas installations in dwelling-houses and the fact that natural gas is delivered at twice the pressure of the manufactured coal gas which used to be supplied.

A rather patchy quarry tiled path possibly replacing an earlier more ornamental pattern or mosaic version. If there is wood flooring to the entrance hall the surveyor will need to check that there is adequate ventilation to prevent dry rot in the sub-floor area. There is no ventilator apparent.

PATHS, GATES AND RAILINGS

Tiled entrance paths

The surveyor should also make a note of the condition of paths and gates immediately surrounding the house. He will probably find, if he is engaged in a survey of a house built in say 1890, that paths are formed with small geometrical coloured tiles often of impressive complexity and design, laid on a concrete base. The base may well have fractured with the result that the tiles above have become loose and broken. Unhappily it is often not possible to find replacements for these tiles, except at considerable expense and the only alternative is for the whole path to be relaid to a finish of the new owner's choice, as perhaps happened above.

Gates

Gates, particularly leading to garages, are often found to be a source of trouble since the weight and span of the gate is often too much for its fixing and the resultant sagging makes it a source of exasperation and difficulty as in the case of the gate shown opposite at the top. Oak gates will take indefinite wear but softwood gates, if neglected, will absorb moisture and are apt to rot and very often a coat of paint will be applied to conceal this fact. The surveyor will soon tell with his probe, however, if a gate should be replaced.

Metal railings

Metal railings are worth more than a casual glance. Such railings, which were extremely popular prior to 1914, may often be formed very elaborately of wrought or cast iron, often supported by back stays. Over long periods the railings are generally covered, layer

266

Wooden gate to garage driveway. Even if not rotted it would still be a source of annoyance because of the continuous need to reduce the depth of the bottom rail as the gate settles on its hinges.

upon layer, with paint and may appear deceptively sound. Any weakness, however, will generally appear at the base of the railings due to rust. The chief defect with metal railings is that moisture is apt to penetrate the sockets at the base, where contact with the iron

Elegant wrought iron metal railings in need of very close examination when the safety of users is at stake. Rust at the base can render them unsafe.

The immediate environs to a house can present hazards as well as the expense of repairs and renewals. Dangerous steps here and weak balustrading and railings all need renewal above.

causes rust which expands and fractures the plinth, besides affecting the strength of the iron itself.

Better quality older railings were fixed in lead and modern railings are fitted with brass or gun-metal bushes to prevent this defect arising. The surveyor will soon ascertain, by scraping the paint at the base and examining the cast iron and also testing the stability of the railings with his hands, if any immediate repairs or renewals are likely to be needed. Metal railings often enclose open areas and may adjoin a public way so that some care on the inspection is necessary in view of the dangers of collapse under pressure. The same remarks apply to the balustrades of any steps.

THE OUTBUILDINGS

The next task of the surveyor is to examine and record the state of repair of the various outbuildings adjoining the house and within the periphery of the grounds. The first outbuilding of consequence that will require inspection may well be a garage. Garages will vary from small asbestos structures at the rear of a terraced or semi-detached house built in the 1920s and 1930s to a large detached imposing structure of brick and tiles, perhaps with a flat or playroom above. Inspection of the garage will, of course, follow in the same way the rules for the inspection of its parent structure and does not require any exhaustive description at this point.

It is worth mentioning, however, that any defects in materials, for example facing bricks or roofing tiles, which the surveyor has found in the main structure may well be repeated on the garage and outbuildings. It is prudent for the surveyor to take some pains to find defects that are likely to be caused from neglect. Outbuildings are never maintained with the degree of care given to the dwelling-house itself and it is commonplace to find advanced attacks of

Is there a garage for the house below or is the door for show? What has the crazy paving covered? There might not be a garage for long on the right.

268

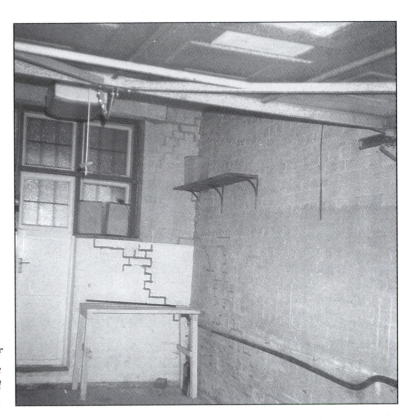

The extensive signs of cracking to the inside of this garage suggest something wrong in the area of the rear right hand corner which will need investigating.

beetle in the timbers that have never been treated, or troubles from dampness caused by blocked gullies and fractured gutters that have never received attention.

The consequences of skipping lightly over outbuildings when carrying out a structural survey on a comparatively modest 3 bedroom detached house were brought home to the surveyor in a case[1] concerning the separate garage used as a utility room.

The surveyor described it as "brick built in 9″ brickwork and in a satisfactory condition". The judge found that the garage should have been described as of "breeze block construction with an asbestos sheet roof which was brittle and fragile, likely to split and crack, scantily supported, much repaired and at the end of its useful life".

The judge concluded that "if the roof had been accurately described . . . the plaintiff would never have been in peril of suffering the injuries which he did in fact suffer" when he fell through the roof on investigating a leak. In this case damages were awarded not only on the basis of diminution of value on account of the wrongly described garage but also in respect of the injuries suffered by the plaintiff.

Fortunately for the surveyor, the plaintiff's injuries were not as severe as they might have been. It matters not that every surveyor knows, or should know, that it is unsafe to walk on any asbestos roof, new or old. The plaintiff in this case was not told.

[1] *Allen and Another v. Ellis and Co.* (1990). The Estates Gazette, 17th March, 1990. Page 78.

The surveyor is also advised to look for faults of design that can cause trouble, due to insufficient attention to detail when the garage was built. Even although an architect may have devoted every care in designing the dwelling-house, the garage might not have received the same degree of attention. Alternatively it might have been erected after the main house was built and such matters as awkward roof gutters that are not adequately drained and no provision for wash down gullies might be mentioned. For smaller garages lack of drainage is no particular disadvantage since a barrel underneath a single downpipe will provide a satisfactory source of rain-water for garden or domestic use.

Other exterior structures, varying from summer houses and tool sheds to detached barns, will rarely have any common characteristic apart from the fact that they are usually constructed partly of timber and that this will be generally neglected. A thorough soaking in preservative may extend the life of these structures for a surprising period, but very often they are beyond repair and can be remarkably costly to replace.

Summer houses, tool sheds, etc

THE BOUNDARIES

The surveyor should now turn his attention to the boundary fences. This is an important matter since the boundary fences not only define the plot and should perform this function adequately, but they exercise some restraint from the marauding instincts of small boys and animals. The surveyor will find, in the case of most

Below left: the surveyor should take no chances with free standing boundary walls which are leaning. They can collapse unexpectedly causing damage and possibly injury. Below right: brick walls often separate terraced house gardens built before 1920. If maintained well and repointed when required they will provide long service but not if built of a poor quality brick as here.

270

Sulphate attack on the rendering to a brick boundary wall.

surveys, that the site is enclosed and defined by a wide variety of types of fences and a thorough inspection of the boundaries is necessary. The surveyor should describe each length in turn and a description of its position in relation to a compass point is also desirable. The surveyor can then note the condition of the boundary and ascertain who is likely to be responsible for its upkeep.

Boundary Walls   Prior to 1900 brick walls were most commonly provided to form boundaries some five or six feet high and the local brick of the

The surveyor should check carefully that features such as this are soundly bedded. Sudden detachment could be dangerous.

271

district was invariably used even if not always wisely, see photograph on page 270. It is a tribute to many of the local bricks produced that considerable numbers of these boundary walls, if carefully maintained, are in as good condition today as when they were built. When neglected, however, they can prove troublesome. Insufficient foundations and the absence of damp-proof courses, together with lack of pointing and long unstiffened lengths of brickwork can cause leans, bulges, fractures and settlements to a spectacular degree. The surveyor must carefully determine whether a boundary wall in such a condition can be saved or whether it is essential to rebuild on the grounds of safety, perhaps reusing the old bricks.

Retaining walls

In hilly areas the boundary will often comprise a retaining wall holding back the soil of the garden. Indeed in such areas retaining walls may form a feature of terracing in the garden itself. Collapse of such walls can be a very serious matter particularly if they adjoin a public thoroughfare.

The surveyor does well to err on the side of caution when reporting on retaining walls. Old walls rely on the mass weight of stone or brick to prevent the soil exercising an overturning motion. The foundations, if any, and the thickness of the wall at its base are just those items which cannot be seen. The surveyor must therefore use his eyes to make a careful inspection along the full length for cracks and fissures and use his plumbline to check whether the wall is upright or not. A fractured and leaning wall must be a candidate for rebuilding and even a severely leaning wall without a fracture must be considered ready for rebuilding; the appearance of a fracture would probably be coincidental with collapse.

The cost of rebuilding a stone boundary wall can be considerable but the owner will be liable should it collapse and cause injury to a passerby.

A case[1] relating to one such wall concerned the survey of a house in Somerset purchased in 1977 for £27,000. This had a 200 year old random stone boundary wall 55 m long. Over 17 m it retained a patio some 3 m above the adjoining roadway. There was a partial collapse of the wall in 1980 and engineers were called in. They established the rate of movement in the wall, which by then was leaning 155 mm out of plumb, and the judge considered half this amount would have been visible in 1977. He decided that the surveyor should have mentioned this along with the bad condition at two points and should have advised a partial repair which would have cost £5,900 at that time. This would have provided the purchaser with a better wall and accordingly he reduced the damages to £4,425 plus £500 for distress, vexation and worry. The trial took 12 days and costs in addition must have been considerable.

Ownership of boundary walls

Plain brick boundary walls to the gardens behind terraced houses built before 1900 are often deemed to be shared between the respective owners on either side. This is usually so in fact, since they are, in the majority of cases, built on the line of junction of the two properties. Measurements can often ascertain if this is so or not.

[1] *Bolton v. Puley* (1983). Estates Gazette, 24th September, 1983. Page 1160.

Use of a straight joint incorporating a vertical damp proof membrane would have been so much better than the bonding to the main house wall as used here.

In any case of doubt, however, the surveyor is advised to draw the attention of his client's solicitor to the matter so that he may add a note to his preliminary inquiries in an endeavour to clarify the point.

Piers and Pointing

Sometimes stiffening piers indicate likely ownership since these are invariably built on the land of the owner of the wall, in which case the actual boundary line may be the far face. Notwithstanding the question of liability, however, repointing to the internal faces of brick boundary walls is often a matter that is neglected and it is an item that the prospective purchaser should know about. Such re-pointing can, in large areas, be an expensive matter and the surveyor should compute the approximate area of repointing needed. Often such calculations amount to a sum that will surprise the surveyor, let along his client.

Copings

The surveyor should take some care in observing details of brick boundary walls. Two points in particular may arise, firstly, if the top two courses of bricks are green with damp, unsound in consequence and likely to fall, or again where a tree root passes under a brick boundary wall, whether a small relieving arch is formed in the brickwork to allow room for growth.

Boundary walls abutting dwellings

Another and more vital point that the surveyor should always look for is where a brick boundary wall joins the structure of the house itself. It is extremely rare for old garden walls to be provided with damp-proof courses and rising dampness may be transferred to the main structure, often with unhappy results if the two are not separated by a vertical damp-proof course.

273

A fine newly erected close boarded fence, the posts and rails showing that ownership lies this side of the boundary.

Timber fences   The timber close-boarded fences, beloved of builders between the wars for their comparative cheapness, are by no means an inexpensive type of boundary to replace today. A note should be taken of the age and probable life of any such fences. The surveyor

A fence such as that above would present a similar appearance to this from the opposite side although not for only half its length as here. The wind has removed the other half but it is the neighbour's fence and for him or her to renew or not as there is no legal requirement to do so.

should ascertain whether the rails of such fences are bowed and split with age or coloured green with moss and dampness, since in either event the strength is adversely affected.

The most common defect with fences of this type is that the wooden posts have become rotted at their bases and the surveyor should slightly rock the fence to see if it is stable, as it will have to withstand gale force winds and driving rain. The surveyor may consider that the provision of concrete spurs is sufficient to extend the life of the fence for a number of years ahead or he may feel that more radical repair work is required. Very often an apparently safe-looking close-boarded fence may be on the point of collapse.

The traditional method of ascertaining the ownership of close-boarded fences is still valid. The visible posts and rail supports as on the photograph at the top of the opposite page will be found on the side of the fence to which it belongs, since the face of the fence defines the boundary line. It is always prudent to advise reference to the deeds in case of doubt, however, since often such fences have been repaired from time to time since the house was built and may have been erected in the wrong place, for example in the case of joint garage extensions. Interwoven wood fencing panels between wood supports however provide little indication of ownership.

Chicken wire, chain link and trellis fencing

Boundaries formed with chicken wire or chain link fencing or light trellis are best described to the client as being of a more temporary nature, although standards of galvanising chain link fencing have improved immeasurably and plastic coated wire is now also much used.

The typical do-it-yourself flimsy fencing panels often found as replacement for more sturdy originals.

THE GARDEN

Trees and clay soil

No description under the heading of this chapter will be complete without some mention of the garden itself. Usually some general note is sufficient to describe the condition of the garden, but considerably more attention is desirable where trees are present and it may well be necessary for each of these to be described separately, even apart from cases where spreading roots exert a pressure on the house or outbuildings under review. The chief danger with trees is that they absorb the moisture from the sub-soil and, in the case of a survey in an area of clay soil, the surveyor should take great pains to gauge the probable effects of any trees he may find on the site or nearby.

Building Research Establishment advice

The Building Research Establishment say that while any growing tree can affect the moisture content of shrinkable clay and cause movement, broadly speaking rapid growing broad-leafed deciduous trees present the greatest risk, while evergreen conifers present the least. Other types of trees are somewhere between the two. In the vicinity of fast growing trees the drying effect of the roots may cause shrinkage down to such depths as about 3 m. A large tree may absorb 50–60,000 litres of water each year from the ground and the root distance of isolated trees generally spreads to a radius greater than the height of the tree.

The surveyor needs to be on guard when the familiar silhouette of the poplar presents itself within the tree's height of any building. Groups are even more dangerous but even comparatively small trees when as near to a house as that below right can be the cause of settlements.

Accordingly it is not difficult to see that trees such as poplar, elm and willow may be lethal to structures within quite a considerable

distance. The Building Research Establishment give an interesting and useful guide to the characteristics of different types of tree in Digest No. 298 to assist surveyors to assess the likelihood of damage to buildings. The need to identify tree species is stressed and typical distances of tree to damage are given with a view to replacing the older rule of thumb suggesting that an investigation was needed if a tree or shrub is nearer to the building than the distance of its mature height (1½ tmes the height if there is a group of trees). The rule of thumb however should still be applied if it is not possible to identify species on a survey.

Many trees take a long time to reach full maturity and there are many cases where young trees were originally planted in suburban gardens, often in Georgian terraces or between semi-detached houses built between the wars, which have grown to a formidable height, some of the later trees still growing rapidly. The roots of such trees dry out the clay below the foundations of the nearest part of the house and the cracking internally to the structure can be widespread, particularly if the roof is braced and stiffened.

Trees on boundaries

Very often such trees were planted on the boundaries of the gardens and it is where these occur that the surveyor must take particular care. It is not enough for him simply to inspect the structures comprised in his client's own plot of land. He must carefully observe if any damage is being caused to any adjoining houses or if there is any likelihood of any damage occurring and if so he should point this out in his report. Very often there is no option but to advise felling a tree within a dangerous distance of a dwelling-house and taking steps to poison the roots.

Other trees apart from poplars can cause problems and this tree in close proximity to old houses built at a time when construction tended to be somewhat basic could well be the source of trouble—the bay window for example has had to be tied in. On the right physical pressure pushes the wall outwards.

277

There are many reported cases of trees planted by local authorities in the thoroughfare causing damage. Is this one doing so?—the surveyor will need to check.

The danger to the purchaser is that he may be faced with a heavy claim for damages from an adjoining owner if the roots of a tree on his land are causing damage to a neighbour's house. Many purchasers would rather not have the risk of such claim hanging over them should the possibility be even remotely present. If a purchaser was not advised of the possibility the surveyor might be placed in a difficult position should the claim be made and damages successfully recovered.

MEASUREMENTS OF THE SITE

Reasons for measurements

The last task for the surveyor before he leaves the site is to take the measurements. These will be used in his opening preamble of the report in order to assist in the description of the property. The reader may wonder why some pains are taken and time spent on taking measurements that do not have any other value than that of description, but there is one clear factor in their favour. This is that the surveyor will often be instructed to provide a report to a client or his solicitor who may be many miles away.

Sometimes, and one might instance the case of a company buying houses for employees or trustees making an advance from trust funds, the man who reads the report may not have the slightest idea of what the property may look like and obviously some description set out briefly in the form of the measurements is going to help him. It is obviously going to be an even greater assistance to a solicitor, who does not know the property, to be able to form

278

some comparison from the surveyor's report with a deed plan that he might have on his desk.

A number of surveyors believe that there is no great benefit in providing descriptive measurements in the case of reports of small simple dwelling-houses and accordingly do not provide them. It is not possible to argue with sufficient conviction that measurements are always vital, nevertheless the procedure is recommended.

There is clearly no point in setting out rigid rules, and attempting to describe what measurements should be taken. The object is to take such measurements as will provide a clear picture to the reader. Obviously a frontage measurement to the road is of value since this will probably not only be marked on a solicitor's deed plan but figured as well. If the property is approximately rectangular, a depth or average depth might be taken and a frontage to a side road or rear frontage, if there is one, is of obvious value.

The main shape of the plot or ground in which the house stands might be described as in the form of a rectangle or triangle if it is capable of such description but any fields forming part of the land conveyed are best dealt with separately at the end of the opening paragraphs setting out the situation and description of the property.

FINAL RE-CAPITULATION

Perhaps just before leaving the site, the surveyor might pause for a few moments to re-capitulate in his mind whether everything necessary to prepare the report has been thought of and that the

In an unusual house such as this the surveyor should be at pains to distinguish between structural and decorative timber.

notes are complete. It is irritating to have to return to the property merely for something that has been forgotten. If it is perhaps wondered how it is possible to remember all the points covered by the foregoing chapters, it might be a consolation to indicate that not every point arises in connection with every house. Depending on the circumstances, certain areas of knowledge will not be required with some properties and can safely be forgotten, even if only for that day.

The more experienced the surveyor the less likely the necessity for a second visit, either to check again on some doubtful point or take account of something omitted from the notes. The importance of adopting a method of inspection should have been made obvious by now and the young surveyor having found his method satisfactory, should stick to it, provided it gives him all he wants. There is no disgrace, however, in having to return for a second visit to any property and the most experienced of surveyors will find occasions when this is essential to fulfil the duty to the client. After all, to lose a few pounds on one survey in order to do the job properly is far more profitable in the long run than perhaps to be faced with a heavy claim for damages with the loss of reputation that such a claim entails.

It is at this point also that a check list can be useful. Pro-formas are not recommended for the reasons given elsewhere in this book but it can be good practice for the surveyor to look swiftly through a check list before leaving the site. The list need not consist of more than key words sufficient to jog the memory.

A sylvan setting. However there could be problems depending on the nature of the sub-soil and the type and proximity of the trees to the house. Is the surveyor sure of his tree identification?

280

Chapter 9

The Report

CONTENTS

hand some surveyors tend to describe features of properties in glowing terms and although these may gratify the client they may lead to an unbalanced judgement of the report. Plain factual descriptions are best.

The need for care in drafting

Care in setting out the facts, however, is also essential so that the facts serve a purpose and do not fall into the category of irrelevant material. No surveyor who has drafted structural survey reports will have any doubt as to the alluring nature of red herrings in this respect. However, in collecting information to comply with his instructions the surveyor takes pains to ensure that his information is complete and regards the facts ascertained as pieces of a puzzle, that, when fitted together, give a complete picture.

Relevant information

The structural survey report, as we have said before, differs from other types of reports in that it states facts and then draws inferences and, if necessary, gives a warning. The danger where other factual information of no particular value is given is that the lay client may assume that an inference is meant to be drawn. He may then draw the wrong inference. Further correspondence on the matter may, instead of clarifying the position, diffuse the purpose and nature of the report and lead to exasperation on both sides.

The client is naturally over-eager to grasp the advice given and will give weight to any information his surveyor provides. Accordingly the surveyor has a duty not only to be accurate in what he writes but to include any factual material solely for a purpose. If some fact comes to the surveyor's attention that is ancillary to the object of the survey but nevertheless which he feels should be brought to his client's attention, a possible solution to this might be in the form of a covering letter attached to the report:

"Mrs. H. Black
Dear Mrs. Black,
6 Honeysuckle Cottages, Henge.

I now enclose my report which I trust you will find quite clear.

During my inspection the occupant of the adjoining cottage Mrs. Blake, informed me that the field to the rear of the terrace of cottages is used in the summer for motor cycle meetings and the noise is intense. Although this information is not a matter that affects my report, I thought that you might like to know about this fact in case you had not already heard of it.

Yours sincerely,"

It will be seen therefore that it is necessary for the surveyor when drafting his report to confine himself solely to his instructions and to avoid setting out irrelevant facts, expressing biased personal views and, most important of all, giving opinions where such opinions are not required. This principle should be borne in mind during the actual process of drafting but under rule 2 a further aid to this necessity will appear in that the instructions require setting out at the commencement of the report.

(2) Have the framework of the report clearly in mind

The need for a relevant framework

The requirements to form a good framework for a report are exacting and do, to some extent, conflict with each other. First, there is the necessity at all costs for the report to deal in full with the ground that the surveyor must cover so as to give his client full information and advice and also to discharge the surveyor's legal duty. This means, of necessity, that the report in the case of a large house is, in all probability, likely to be a long one.

Again, in the case of a relatively small house with a number of troublesome defects the report cannot, by the very nature of the ground to be covered including fact, opinion and warning, be a short one. Clearly, in either of these cases the report is not likely to be easy to draft. In the first place there will be a considerable volume of factual material to marshal in a clear manner and in the second considerable space will have to be devoted to describing the cause of defects and dealing with possible remedies.

Completeness

The next requirement is that the report must be complete in itself and must have no gaps. It must debate fully each problem raised. It must not assume that telephone conversations have been recorded in detail and thus omit confirmatory information. It must, in the last resort, be capable of being examined in detail on any facet of the survey.

Against these requirements, however, the surveyor has a duty to produce a human document. With the continual increase of individual house ownership greater numbers of the general public require surveys than ever before. A large number will have never seen a surveyor's report and their whole attitude to the profession will be conditioned by the reports produced.

Need for understanding of client's problems

It is, accordingly, at the present time just as urgent as it ever has been for a mutual understanding and sympathy to exist between the surveyor and his client. If the surveyor gives the impression in his report that his client's problem is important to him, that he deals with every aspect of the matter fully and helpfully and that he has carefully weighed an expenditure of even a minor amount, he is likely to have gone a long way towards achieving this understanding.

The framework of the report will to a large degree govern the extent of the impact which the document will have on the client. Diffused and rambling documents with information set out under inappropriate headings where it is never clear from first to last which are the main defects will be a poor foundation for understanding, even if every particle of the information is somewhere contained within the report. Conversely, a brief report will be the easiest for any client to digest, but brevity is not to be considered an end in itself. Such a report may refer only briefly to important matters, leave the client in considerable doubt and the surveyor's duty undischarged.

Even the term "back addition", which would appear to be essentially self-descriptive and eminently fit for use, has caused a good deal of misunderstanding. Whereas the surveyor thinks of a house in terms of its external appearance his client usually thinks of a house in terms of its internal layout. The surveyor is recommended never to give up trying to find new and accurate methods of description. If he can convey, in crisp terms, an accurate description of a fault in a structure his client, probably without knowing it, will give him credit for technical ability.

Continual efforts by the surveyor to improve his powers of description will have a further benefit in that the re-appraisal of sentences involves the opinions expressed which may, in consequence, be made more precise.

(5) Keep the English clear. Keep sentences short, use simple words and take care with punctuation

The need for clear plain English

The chief disadvantage of bad or verbose English is that it wastes time, since it obscures the meaning of the report. The client will puzzle over conclusions that should be plain. The man who pays for a structural survey is entitled to have a document that he can understand. Not all clients will be as familiar with documents as the Queen's Counsel, who is used to sifting and interpreting a great number of papers in a limited time.

Advance thought

In order to achieve a well written report the surveyor should, before he puts pen to paper or starts to dictate think out in advance what he is trying to say and then set it down as simply and clearly as possible. He should try to make his English serve the meaning that he desires and not to use the report as a method of disposing of a set of notes collected at the house. The report is not a paraphrase or extension of the notes but a separate operation to be commenced with a clear and uncluttered mind and with the feeling that style is as much an objective to achieve as the practical part of the survey itself. Slavish adherence to the notes will result in such passages as:

> "The glass to the window in the left front room is broken, one pane of glass is cracked to the right front room and a further pane of glass was found to be broken in the kitchen adjoining."

This could either be replaced by "some cracked and broken panes of glass throughout the house should be replaced", or if more detail is required the information could be included in the form of a schedule.

Impersonal phraseology preferred

The English used should be impersonal to remove any impression of partiality since the surveyor is dealing with facts. Such a phrase as "we regret that the main flank wall is bulged" sounds insincere. On the other hand the writer should try to write simply enough to sound like a human being.

The impersonal passive should be used with care. Sentences such as "it is thought that you will have seen the interior decorative condition for yourself" has a slightly insulting flavour. It is better to write "I expect that you will have already formed your own view of what redecoration you will require."

The surveyor should strive not only for an impartial style but a form of report that explains accurately what he has discovered or ascertained without introducing unnecessary fears in his reader. Although brevity is to be admired as a general rule, undue brevity can have an unfortunate affect. A phrase such as:

"All floors, where inspected, were found in good order" might make the client wonder if the surveyor has done more than stroll round the ground floor while:

> "Following your instructions boards were taken up in the ground floor living room, dining room and hall and the joists were examined underneath. The fitted carpets were stripped in every case and the furniture carted into the garden ..."

makes him feel that his surveyor is thorough but he may well wonder uneasily if he should have stopped him in time to preserve sufficiently good relations with the vendor before exchange of contracts. The expression "following your instructions" in this context although exact is not tactful.

Clients often unaware of "normal" practice

Few prospective purchasers have sufficient experience to judge what is usual or unusual and the repetition of the phrase in this context has the effect of causing the purchaser to wonder if he has asked too much. A faint suggestion of truculence on the part of the surveyor may creep in of which the surveyor may be quite unaware. A phrase such as:

> "As a result of your instructions a considerable time was spent in examining the floorboards"

may mean that the surveyor considers his client's thoroughness in making sure that the floors were sound was a prudent step, but the meaning that the client may read into the phrase is unfortunate.

It is as well to recall that the average purchaser usually relies on the surveyor's opinion of what is thorough or customary practice and any deviation should be explained.

> "Signs of dampness were found over the skirting of the bay window to the ground floor left front room. Since we were concerned that fungal attack might have affected the timbers of the floor at this point, permission was obtained from the owner to raise two floorboards. The timbers underneath were found to be satisfactory and the boards were replaced."

This passage, although long, will have the ring of a well managed operation while the prudence of the surveyor will be made modestly clear.

Avoidance of "hedging" phrases and un-warranted caution

The surveyor should avoid hedging phrases where these are not necessary and steer clear of excessive caution where this is not justified. A frank admission that an answer cannot be given is better than a paragraph that looks at first sight as if it means something, but really does not. The surveyor should also try to avoid the sort of foolish sentences which tend to creep into hasty drafts. The

303

statement that "the chimney-stack is fractured and I advise that this be looked into" hardly inspires confidence.

Verbosity

One of the most compelling errors in drafting a report is excessive verbosity. This is an easy trap for the surveyor whose mind may be on the facts of the defect and who may easily write phrases such as:

> "Although the floor timbers cannot, due to the particular circumstances, be examined it is permissible to state with some confidence that attacks of beetle may be present" ... and "The desirability of ascertaining the exact condition of the floor joists is of considerable importance from the point of view of repair cost."

Common words

So far as words are concerned, common words are to be preferred to the less common. An expression such as "We would acquaint you with the condition of the roof structure" may have been written since the use of the word "acquaint" may be thought to give a formal and impersonal flavour. All it does, however, is to make the client wonder if his surveyor has any human qualities whatsoever. Adverbs and adjectives should ideally be reserved to make the meaning more precise and not included where they have no force. This is always an easier matter to specify than observe. All surveyors are familiar with such phrases as:

> "The cracking is relatively slight."
> "This will inevitably mean that the cost of repair will be increased."
> "There is a serious danger of an attack of dry rot."

Perhaps just as common is the adverb or adjective that changes the meaning. To write "the cracking is not unduly serious" is by no means the same thing as "the cracking is not serious". In the former case an uncomfortable note of uncertainty is generated which may not be intended in the case of, say, a plaster ceiling.

Short sentences and punctuation

The surveyor should also take care with punctuation. Sentences should be kept short in order to assist the reader grasp the meaning of a complicated passage without having to read it several times. Commas should be used liberally, in the first place in their purely grammatical quality and, secondly, in the value that they provide in giving force to the important part of a sentence. Accuracy is always important.

The Appendices to this book comprise four specimen reports. The first is in respect of a simple two-storey house and is provided with a series of photographs at the end which are referred to in the text.

The second report deals with a block containing two self contained flats being marketed for conversion back into one house. Here the photographs are integrated with the text and in this report emphasis is given to suggestions for dealing with rather more complicated defects.

Thirdly, a sample report is provided in respect of a purpose built mansion flat principally to show the way in which the examination of the lease from the surveyor's point of view and the partial examination of the structure can be undertaken.

Finally, in Appendix 4, a report on a newly built structure is included in order to illustrate the basic difference of approach in the survey as against an older building as recommended in Chapter 12.

In the third and fourth reports reliance is placed entirely on words to convey the content apart from the provision of a photograph by way of frontispiece to set the scene. It has to be recognised that when dealing with and contrasting sole and shared liabilities incurred by the long lease of a flat illustrations are not a great help. A similar situation applies when analysing a new structure where defects have yet to materialise.

Chapter 10
Structural surveys of larger properties, ancillary and office matters

CONTENTS

LARGE DWELLING HOUSES

Introduction The scope of this book has been confined so far to structural surveys of older houses, principally with regard to the medium size house, in order to illustrate the various points concerned in as clear a manner as possible. Before the subject of structural surveys of flats, however, is dealt with it might be advisable to say a word on the subject of surveys of larger houses and one or two points that the surveyor will be asked to deal with, on occasion, that may be outside the normal instructions for a survey. Finally a few points arising in regard to properties which were built as houses but which are now used for commercial purposes will be covered.

Large Houses The survey of an exceptionally large dwelling-house presents problems of its own. The type of property envisaged, in this respect, is a large manor house probably built and added to at a number of different periods, set in parklands with a considerable number of outbuildings used for various purposes within the periphery of the grounds. Let us take for this purpose a particular illustration.

The main structure of the mansion envisaged comprises basement, ground and two upper storeys with a large classical portico on the principal elevation surmounted by a pediment. The main block is rectangular in shape but has a large wing at the rear so that the whole building is in the shape of an "L". The wing is perhaps architecturally the most interesting portion, as it dates from approximately 1450. At the end farthest from the wing, there is a large and substantial stable block, containing residential rooms on the upper floor, built around a cobbled courtyard, enclosed by barns and more outbuildings.

Necessity of forethought Clearly the question of a survey of a property of this size requires considerable thought from the outset. The cost to the client together with the time taken in completing the work by the surveyor are bound to be substantial. There is no question in a case such as this of quoting a fee on the telephone. At the outset the surveyor will have to spend some time ascertaining from his client precisely the information he requires. Once the surveyor has a clear idea of his client's particular instructions, he must then take some pains to ascertain the probable cost of the work involved by himself and the number of specialist firms that will be required to give a full report.

Preliminary visit The surveyor is advised to visit the site personally, even at short notice, to decide, in the first instance, if he can undertake the work and to see what is likely to be involved. If the surveyor decides that he can carry out the survey, he must then estimate the number of days that he is likely to require and allow a margin of safety so that he can complete the whole task in a thorough manner. Experience shows that in a survey of this type, far greater time than the surveyor might anticipate is always taken up by the outbuildings.

Outbuildings The surveyor is apt to look at the mansion as a whole and may be able to estimate with some accuracy the amount of time that this will require, but when looking at the outbuildings these will appear to be small and simple by comparison with the main structure and the surveyor accordingly feels that they will not take him very long to inspect. In fact, of course, the error is a natural one of an optical illusion. The surveyor's eye has become accustomed to the large expanses and ceiling heights of the mansion itself and, accordingly, he does not immediately appreciate the fact that what appears to be a small range of outbuildings may well be approaching the size of a terrace of town houses.

Calculating the time involved

It is suggested that, in calculating the time involved, the surveyor starts with the mansion itself. He should endeavour to estimate the time required for each section of his report covering the mansion, starting with the main roof. The surveyor can then proceed to the main walls and follow with each section until, at last, he has some idea of how long the whole of the main house will take. This process will also assist assessing the time required for the outbuildings.

Overnight accommodation

So far as the practical nature of the survey itself is concerned, once terms are agreed, the surveyor will, if the property is a long way from his office, probably prefer to put up at a hotel for the duration of the time required, so as not to waste too much time in unnecessary travel.

Organising the notes

At the end of each day the surveyor will have accumulated an impressive array of notes. At the end of several days' work these will have amounted to the size of a small book or its equivalent in tapes which will, to say the least of it, be extremely onerous to transcribe. Accordingly the surveyor will need to give some thought to the actual report itself from the outset. It will require expert drafting to keep this a balanced and readable document, in spite of its length, so that it gives the factual information required yet never loses sight of the scope of the instructions.

Initial drafting

It is suggested that each evening, when the work of the day is clear in the surveyor's mind, he prepares further sheets of suitable paragraphs, extracted from his notebook or that he awaits transcribed notes from the tapes dictated from the previous day by a local typing bureau. These can then be written fully and legibly in the correct order for transcription direct into the report itself. Alternatively the surveyor, if practised in this type of work, may care to dictate the appropriate section of his report each evening.

A word of warning, however, might be inserted here. It is always dangerous to write part of a report without having examined the whole structure first. It will be appreciated that a defect in the roof, which appears to be negligible on its own, might be the result of settlement of the structure or part of a major defect, which will warrant a completely different emphasis and style of description in the final draft of the report. In the circumstances it is suggested that the surveyor confines himself at this stage to rewriting or dictating his notes in the appropriate order, as suggested, so that he may then compile his full report, in the light of all the facts ascertained by the time the survey is completed.

Use of Schedules and Appendices

So far as the report itself is concerned, it is by no means easy to produce a document on a very large property that covers the ground adequately without boring the reader. A good deal may be done, however, to make the report readable yet at the same time to deal with all those matters that are of major importance, by providing a number of schedules or appendices at the end of the report.

Such schedules can describe accurately yet in suitably condensed form, a large number of minor matters, the inclusion of which in the main body of the report would diffuse the impact of the important conclusions to such an extent that the document would be liable to be misconstrued. The schedules can cover such matters as sanitary fittings, defects to windows, defects to fireplaces and other relatively minor matters and can, of course, be read in conjunction with the Schedule of Accommodation that will also be provided.

Clearly, of course, it is advisable for the description of identical rooms in every schedule to be the same. This, of course, sounds obvious but it is surprising how often errors creep in. An extract from such a schedule might be as follows:

Sanitary Fittings

Main Structure   *Recommendation*
Second Floor
Bathroom adjoining principal bedroom
> Bath, old roll-top design, enamel crazed and discoloured. Waste pipe too small and damaged. WC adjoining, old valve closet in timber case.

Second Floor Landing
Guest Bathrooms
Bathroom No. 1
> Modern enamelled panelled bath. Modern pedestal lavatory basin and WC of similar pattern.

Bathroom No. 2
> Modern enamelled panelled bath, hardboard panel fractured. WC adjoining, pan fractured.

Servants' Wing
Bathroom
> Bath old, enamel badly worn, wood panelling insanitary. Valve closet WC, inefficient

Schedules for differing purposes

If the survey is of such size that additional schedules are desirable for different purposes, say a different schedule for sanitary fittings, window defects and fireplaces, these should be provided. If possible, however, the surveyor should provide a condensed schedule, rather in the nature of a schedule of condition, which will set out a good deal of information and can be prepared under the heading of each room. For example:

Main Structure
Second Floor
Principal Bedroom

    Ceiling. Lath and plaster. Lined and whitened. One square yard of plaster defective, lining paper loose.

    Walls. Papered. General condition poor, paper old and stained.

    Floor. Boarded. Two boards loose.

    Window. Double hung sash. Fastener missing, one pane of glass cracked.

    Fireplace. Hearth tiles cracked.

Provided that sufficient use is made of the schedules by compressing a large volume of small details taken from the notes in this manner, the main body of the report can be confined to dealing with the major items relating to the structure under the principal headings.

Main body of the report
The headings under the item of services can often be dealt with, quite simply, by referring to the specialist's report attached at the end of the surveyor's report and repeating the final conclusions, together with the estimate of cost. This will assist the reader in that he will not have to turn over a number of pages to find the important conclusion. Accordingly the main body of the report, when read by the client, will provide him with a full and concise picture of the extent of the surveyor's recommendations. When the client

Eminently the large dwelling house which, when taken with its outbuildings overleaf, requires considerable care in planning the survey and the presentation of the report.

subsequently requires further detail, he can turn to the schedules and appendices.

Additional information required kept separate

Very often a client will ask for additional information that does not normally come within the ambit of a structural survey. It is

The side elevation and two of the outbuildings of the large dwelling house illustrated on the previous page.

312

Further outbuildings of the large dwelling house illustrated previously.

important in these circumstances to re-state the client's exact instructions for the additional work in the opening paragraph of the report. The result of the further investigation required should then be included under a separate heading, immediately before the final conclusions of the survey set out at the end of the document.

The reason for this is that it is important, both from the surveyor's point of view and the client's point of view, that the full scope of the additional work expected from the surveyor is clearly understood. If the information required is mixed up with a good deal of other descriptive paragraphs on the first page of the report, not only will the client have to hunt for the information he needs, but the surveyor is not likely to remember afterwards exactly what he was asked to do.

An example of such additional information required might be where the client asks the surveyor to report on the question of the drainage of a large meadow adjacent to the house that he is buying. The client may have been asked to take an option to purchase, and be worried that the ground is waterlogged and sodden. With smaller properties the surveyor may be asked to express and opinion on forming an opening in a partition or other small alterations, such as forming a bathroom having regard to the existing drainage installation.

HOUSES USED FOR COMMERCIAL PURPOSES

A few words on the subject of houses used for commercial purposes

313

Part conversion for retail purposes

might be useful, so far as these are concerned with the subject of this book.

The surveyor will often have noticed, during his inspection of a parade of shops, that it is quite common throughout the country to

Old houses have been adapted for shopping use since time immemorial.

Not to miss out on the retail boom, the owner of the house on the right built out over the front garden to provide two shops.

find that shops, even in main thoroughfares, have been formed and converted from what were at one time, ordinary dwelling-houses. It is still possible to see the red facing bricks and attractive flush casements of the upper part of an elegant 18th-century house which has been gutted at ground level to form a shop.

Again, large numbers of Georgian terrace houses, which originally faced a main road, have been altered with shop extensions built up over the front gardens to the pavement line. Such structures commonly fall to the surveyor's lot for close examination, usually on behalf of a client who is contemplating either taking both the shop and the living accommodation above on a full repairing lease or purchasing the freehold. The particular nature of these structures can sometimes give the surveyor special problems.

Generally with converted houses the original ground floor becomes part of the shop and any basement area becomes a cellar to the shop. Since this is probably used as a store and shopkeepers tend to take little interest in storage accommodation, neglect may have caused a number of defects. The original timber boarding to the floor may be rotted due to the penetration of dampness and insufficient ventilation brought about by the construction of the shop. Alternatively defects may arise due to the fact that the gullies have been allowed to become blocked or that rain-water pipes are fractured. Pointing may have been neglected and the wood windows and cills may be rotted.

So far as the structure of the house itself is concerned, the surveyor should always bear in mind the original purpose as a private dwelling-house, built with the minimum of elaboration,

Building over former front garden

Effect of alterations

The three houses below have for many years been used as offices.

315

flats is conducted. One of the most stubborn problems, of course, has been the question of contribution for the upkeep of the property in respect of such matters as external repairs and maintenance, cleaning of common parts and the provision of any joint services such as hot water.

Conversions into two flats

In a small case such as a two-storey Victorian terraced house, divided into two self-contained flats, the arrangements could be quite straightforward. The cost of the upkeep of the exterior and any areas used in common such as porch and garden areas, could be divided between the two respective lessees. Lighting of common parts would probably not be necessary, apart from perhaps one light bulb and the chances would be with a conversion of this type that any requirement as to cleaning of staircases etc. would also not be necessary. It is furthermore likely that each flat would have its own separate means of hot water supply.

Multi-flat blocks

It will be appreciated however, that the situation is vastly different in the case of a large converted house or a block of purpose built flats. Here, matters of common benefit would include the external repair and maintenance of the building, the maintenance of parts used by all tenants and of gardens, the cleaning and lighting of staircases and passages, the maintenance of lifts, the provision of central heating and hot water and the employment of staff, including perhaps a resident porter or caretaker, together with cleaners, gardeners and possibly others as well.

Such complex expenditure cannot be met by simply making each individual flat owner liable for a proportion of the total cost. It became necessary to have a far more positive approach to the question of the common expenditure and it was soon realised that this could only be effectively dealt with in the case of blocks of flats of any size with expert professional help.

The "service charge"

The umbrella term to include all matters of common expenditure came to be known as a "service charge" and as it soon became the custom to require the payment of service charges in advance of needs, for obvious reasons, the question also arose as to the legal position of the money accumulated since in the case of the sale of individual flats as separate freeholds, a serious difficulty arose.

Freehold property

A covenant to pay a service charge is a positive covenant so that in the case of the purchase of a freehold in England the burden of the covenant would not run with the property so as to bind successors of the purchaser. However, after some head scratching in legal circles, it was decided that since all the owners of the separate "properties" within a block entered into a covenant with a common vendor, the obligation arising in each case was analogous to the payment of a rent charge, although not similar in every respect.

Leasehold property

In the case of the disposal of individual flats as leaseholds, however, the position was different. The covenants as to the provision of services in a lease are almost certain to run with the reversion and the land. A tenant's covenant to pay a service charge would be likely to be subject to a general provision in the lease for re-entry for non-payment of rent or breach of any of the other covenants. Successors to both the freehold and leasehold interests accordingly

332

would have to carry out the various services for the benefit of the premises as a whole. Due to the strength of the legal process behind such obligations, most lawyers in England and Wales have tended to turn to the leasehold rather than the freehold system of disposal for the sale of flats.

Building Society policy on sale of freehold flats

Doubts about the freehold system of disposal for flats has led to a number of building societies and local authorities refusing to entertain applications for advances in respect of flats conveyed as freeholds and this in turn has restricted the use of this method.

The next main difficulty that emerged was a practical one. After the disposal of freehold or long leasehold flats, the interest of the freeholder or reversioner was a very small one. Admittedly he received payments by way of ground rents, rent charges and service charges or contributions for the upkeep of the property as set down in the individual leases concerned, but unless the whole matter was carefully thought out, there might be little incentive by way of profit for him to carry out his obligations.

The "vanishing freeholder"

In the lack of legally practical and binding covenants to make it necessary and worth while for him to continue his relationship with the lessees, he would not be likely to be seen much in evidence around the property. This in fact happened a good deal with early leasehold transactions, many reversions being sold and re-sold again and again, while in a number of other cases freehold reversioners vanished completely. The situation was not very satisfactory to say the least.

"Substance" of the freeholder

This led to another worry over the payment for services. Solicitors were much concerned that there should be a direct contractual link between a lessee and a freeholder who collected his ground rent and service charges and the substance of the freeholder was clearly a material point. If the freeholder turned out to be a man of straw, the lessees would be left in a position where they would find it impossible to enforce the covenants of the lease against him so that they would be left in an extremely difficult position.

Sufficiency of amounts

The way to overcome this dilemma was to reserve a sufficient ground rent or rent charge in respect of each of the flats conveyed so that the freeholder would have a substantial interest in the property remaining so as to make it worth while to carry out his obligations. A horrible variation, however, in the case of rent charges, is that it would be possible for the owner to sell the benefit of their receipt and disappear from the scene without passing on the responsibility for his obligations to anyone at all. This, however, could be overcome by the vendor covenanting not to dispose of the rent charges without transferring the responsibility for the services. However, much depended and in a number of cases still depends, on the probity and goodwill of the freeholder for the continuation of the proper upkeep of the block.

Where flats are sold as individual freeholds, the vendor will be left with only the freehold of common parts such as gardens, forecourts etc. and the rent charges on the flats that are sold. If the flats were disposed of as individual leaseholds, the freeholder would still that it can usefully by sued. Nor can the company enforce the obligations of the owners of the various flats against each other. All such arrangements can only be carried out with the backing of the vendor or freeholder.

However, notwithstanding the difficulties, this arrangement is still regarded as being the best that has been evolved so far for the upkeep of blocks of flats in England and Wales and, with the benefit of a management team chosen by the landlord and his own strong backing, the arrangement is, at its best, both firm, decisive and in the long term interest of all for the upkeep of the property.

OTHER FORMS OF OWNERSHIP IN FLATS

Co-Ownership There are of course other arrangements that have been adopted for the ownership of flats besides those mentioned above. The formation of a co-ownership Society for example registered under the Industrial and Provident Societies Act 1965, has been one way of dealing with management but such a Society must not trade for profit, must be established for the purpose of constructing, improving or managing houses, and must restrict membership to persons entitled, or prospectively entitled, to occupy a house provided or managed by the Society. Various Housing Acts bear on such arrangements and a trend towards such schemes is a possibility.

The main purpose of the arrangement is that co-owners pay, in the form of a rent, the total outgoings for not only maintenance, management and service charges, but enough to cover the capital and interest on loan payments following the acquisition of the freehold by the Society, the loan being advanced by a Building Society subject to the benefit of a separate mortgage from the Housing Corporation. The arrangement is not adaptable in that a co-owner is not allowed to assign or sub-let his flat and if he unfortunately has to surrender his interest in the scheme by way of death, a complicated calculation has to be carried out whereby his deposit is repaid to his executors.

The amount of money refunded by way of deposit is varied according to any improvements made during the tenancy by the co-owner, less depreciation, and is also varied by a share of the increase or decrease in the co-ownership value of his flat, according to the rent at which it will be re-let. Although co-owners are entitled to tax relief in the same way as owner occupiers who make interest payments on single mortgages, or alternatively the mortgage option scheme can be invoked on a communal basis to keep rents down in a time of high interest rates, the arrangement is a rather inflexible one that gives the participant little freedom to come and go and little long term capital benefit.

Commonhold At the time of writing consultation is in progress on whether to establish a new form of tenure in England and Wales to be known as "commonhold". The purpose is to enable the freehold ownership of parts of a property and establish a system for management.

MANAGING AGENTS

Whatever the type of arrangement used for the upkeep of the block once the various individual leases or flats are sold, it has become the rule rather than the exception to employ the services of an established firm of managing agents. In drafting the arrangements for the payment of service charges, solicitors are now careful to ensure that such a firm is given wide powers and that its charges will be paid not only on the basis of a commission on the collection of the rents, but also on the basis of fees for the setting up and running of building contracts for repair work and maintenance contracts for routine attendance to lifts, boilers etc.

Uniform service charges

The objective for which the managing agents will strive will be to collect together all possible items of expenditure both actual and forecasted so as to levy a service charge that is uniform and one that does not vary widely from year to year. This is achieved by splitting the service charge into two elements; current expenditure on the one hand and a reserve for future expenditure on the other. There are also the items of running expenditure, such as wages, as against items of capital cost. Under the latter heading, however, there will be not only matters such as boilers and lifts which have to be replaced, but also items such as motor mowers and vacuum cleaners.

Reserve or Sinking funds

The accountants to the management company will require details of all capital items and provision for their renewal, whether large or small, will have to be decided upon, either out of current income as in the case of small items such as mops, or whether as a reserve created by a sinking fund to meet the larger items of cost in the future. A reserve fund is in any case necessary not only for the replacement of plant and machinery but for items such as external re-pointing and re-painting and in the case of older blocks, substantial roofing repairs and the renewal of out of date electric wiring systems. The managing agents submit accounts in which outgoings are set against the amount in hand in the sinking fund. The advantage of a separate managing company is that the accounts make it quite clear that the sinking fund is the property of the flat owners.

Apportionment of service charge

In early leases the apportionment of the service charge was made by reference to rule of thumb calculations inserted for most part by the solicitors preparing the documents. The owner of a flat might have been made liable for the same sum as that of the owners of all the other flats irrespective of size or amenity. Alternatively, there might have been a complicated proportional formula by reference to the old rating assessments.

It is, however, now common for a somewhat more sophisticated approach to be brought to bear. Fire insurance for example, can be apportioned according to the cubic content of each flat while other services can be related to the individual floor area of each separate flat. The payments in respect of central heating for example, could be further refined by reference to the heating surfaces of the radiators in the individual flats concerned.

337

It should, however, be added that apportionments are indeed often based on old gross or rateable values since it was considered that these had been independently assessed and must therefore be accurate. This is not, however, a very valid argument. It is doubtful if the assessments took into account the many subtle differences in amenity between one flat and another and the system suffered from the cardinal disadvantage that if one particular lessee had carried out improvements, his rating assessment was increased with the result that he could now be penalised by an increased charge for services.

Anomalies New apportionments on the basis of rateable value have not of course been possible since the advent of the community charge from 1 April 1990 but they will still be found enshrined in the less carefully settled leases. Some anomalies, however, are bound to occur even under the best of circumstances but making it all the more necessary that the apportionment be carefully thought out in advance and set out clearly and unequivocally in the lease whereby the premises are held as an aid to the avoidance of future disputes. A ground floor tenant might well complain at the charge imposed for a proportion of the cost of maintaining and servicing a lift and might have to be content with the explanation that a lift is an amenity which increases the value of the flats in the block as a whole and therefore benefits him to some extent, however small.

Agents' need for money in hand It will of course be understood that a competent firm of managing agents will need to have money in hand before disbursing payment in respect of accounts. This provision is not always provided for in leases although it is now customary, as is the need for a managing agent to build up a reserve fund against a forecast of expenditure.

A firm of managing agents will properly ask for a wide discretion in dealing with repairs. One helpful Court case decided that the freeholder is not bound to adopt the cheapest method of effecting repairs as it is open to him to take the advice of a surveyor and carry out an effective long term repair rather than to make a temporary patch.[1] It is essential that competitive estimates be obtained for work in all cases where required by the terms of the Landlord and Tenant Act 1985 irrespective of the lease terms and most firms of managing agents feel that competitive estimates give a certain protection to their actions when it comes to repairs of any size.

Need to see Lease or Draft Lease Those who undertake surveys of flats will see many different types of lease and some very unusual clauses. It should therefore be obvious by now how necessary it is for the surveyor to procure and examine a copy of the lease or other appropriate document, even if this is only in draft in the case of a new development of flats, before the fee is agreed and the survey is put in hand, for the lease tells the surveyor a great deal. He will have the opportunity to learn about the relationship of the various parties and also will be able to gain a clear idea as to his client's probable liabilities.

[1] *Manor House Drive Ltd.* v. *Shahbazian* (1965), 195 E.G. 283.

Examining the document also has an advantage which contrasts with surveys of other property in that a good deal of information about the flat concerned should be known to the surveyor before he finally confirms his instructions. He will know the floor on which the flat is situated and possibly the size and shape of the accommodation if there is a plan attached. He may also, if the building is a comparatively recent one, know the exact age of the structure, and he will further know the nature of the repairing obligations of his client so that he is able to judge in advance the extent of his survey.

The temptation at this stage however, for the surveyor to put the lease in his briefcase and rush off to inspect the property should be avoided. First of all the surveyor should ask himself if he has a complete understanding of the following points:

1. The function of the parties to the lease and their relationship to each other.

2. The term of the lease and the amount of the annual ground rent. As has been seen this can be a material point in assessing the strength of the reversionary interest and the likelihood of the freeholder or vendor to carry out any necessary repairs to the structure or common parts in the future.

Extent of property 3. The definition of the extent of the flat so far as this is relevant to the question of repair and in particular the following:

    (a) Walls and partitions; whether the lessee is responsible only for the upkeep of the interior faces of external walls or walls separating the flat from common parts and whether by contrast in the case of a dividing wall between the flat and any other flat, the liability extends up to half of such partition severed vertically or whether, contrary to these usual and generally accepted provisions, some other arrangement is stipulated.

    (b) The entrance door to the flat and any other doors leading to a balcony or garden.

    (c) The liability for the windows of the flat including frames, sashes and casements and the particular position relating to glass.

    (d) Ceilings and floors; whether the liability for ceilings extends merely to the decorative surface or whether it includes the ceiling plaster or plasterboard or whether, even further, it includes the fixings. So far as floors are concerned, whether the liability extends to floorboards only, or whether the lessee is responsible for the joists and sub-structure below.

    (e) The liability for electrical, water and sanitary apparatus inside the flat, including wires and pipes.

    (f) The responsibility for pipes, generally termed "conduits, pipes, wires and cables" which carry electricity, water and soil to and from the flat. This liability can also extend to matters such as ventilation ducts, television and telephone cables including "hall porter" telephone systems

Repairing covenants 4. The exact nature of the repairing covenants under which

339

lessor and lessee are bound. The lessee is likely to be responsible for the upkeep of the interior of the particular flat concerned, but the surveyor should note the exact words since these are obviously important. Is the lessee, for example, as is most common, liable to "well and substantially renew, repair, uphold, support, maintain, cleanse, amend ..." etc. or is he merely responsible for "keeping the interior of the premises in tenantable order and condition"? Similarly are any matters such as sanitary fittings or glass particularly specified under this covenant?

The surveyor should also check to see if the lessee is bound under a specific painting and decorating covenant and, if so, its nature and extent. By the same token, the exact liability upon the lessor or vendor should be noted to ensure that he is specifically bound and that requirements as to external painting etc., common parts, foundations, roofs and walls, boilers, water tanks, lift motors and cables etc. are not left uncomfortably vague or are missing entirely from the lease.

Service charge   5. The surveyor should examine the arrangements relating to the payment and calculation of the appropriate proportion of the annual maintenance cost, whether this is termed a service charge or not. The surveyor is concerned here not only with his client's liability but the liability of other lessees as they will affect his client's occupation and quiet enjoyment of the flat. Among the points to look for are:

(a) Whether the calculation of the appropriate proportion of the service charge is not only fair but whether it is ascertainable and the arrangements for its payment, whether in advance or arrear.

(b) To whom the service charge is paid and the payee's relationship with both the freeholder and lessee, assuming the payee is not the freeholder. Whether a firm of professional agents is concerned with the levying of the service charge and their standing and powers in the lease generally to maintain and be responsible for the services and whether its decision on such matters is final and binding.

(c) The exact nature of the responsibility for the provision of hot water and central heating; whether this is specified in detail or whether it is not specified at all as is sometimes the case.

(d) Whether exact standards are specified for the lighting and cleaning of common parts or whether these are also left vague.

(e) The arrangements that are proposed in respect of the cleaning and upkeep of the driveways, paths, forecourts, landscaped areas and grounds and whether reference is made to boundary walls or not.

(f) Any special arrangements relating to plant such as lifts and specific facilities such as garages together with access drives.

(g) Whether there is a clause for arbitration in the case of dispute or difficulty.

340

Provisions for dealing with other tenants

6. Whether there are specific arrangements to overcome practical problems between the lessees of the various flats. Are there arrangements in the lease covering the need for notice by the occupier of one flat as against another before works of repair or renewal are carried out? Are the lessees as a whole restricted from making structural alterations, or from altering the appearance of the various flats for example by the removal of internal partitions or main timbers or from tampering with the hot water or heating installations? Is each lessee responsible for the financial consequences of burst pipes inside his flat and the overflowing or stopping up of any baths or fittings due to his own negligence?

"Rules of the House"

7. Is there a schedule of regulations applicable to the occupants of each flat throughout and are these practical and reasonable?

Enforcement of Covenants

8. Finally the surveyor should check to make sure that covenants can be enforced not only against the vendor or freeholder but against other lessees as well.

Need to read complete lease

It will be appreciated that it takes some considerable time to read the often very lengthy close typed lease document relating to the sale of a flat, to sift and understand the contents and to make notes which will be of use on the inspection and when the time comes to draft the report. The surveyor should be under no illusion as to the importance of the lease. He must see it and he must read it from beginning to end. Working from extracts or reading only "the important parts" is likely to be fraught with danger.

In the case of extracts being supplied many assumptions would have to be made as would be the case if no information at all was supplied on the terms and this in itself can lead to misunderstanding. In the second instance, there is little doubt that if it came to the test a surveyor would be held negligent if, having been supplied with the document, he failed to read it through and as a result missed something of importance.

Effect of lease study on fee

An hour or even two is not by any means an untoward time for the surveyor to devote to the lease and ideally the surveyor will wish to be sure of recompense for this amount of time spent on a client's affairs. Accordingly circumstances will dictate whether the thorough examination of the lease is carried out before the total fee for the survey is settled or afterwards. When the surveyor is dealing with a client well known to him or taking instructions from solicitors it may well be that the course recommended below can be followed and the scope of the survey and consequently the fee decided when the lease has been carefully studied.

Allowance in quoted fee for time to study lease

In other circumstances the surveyor may be asked to quote a fee in advance, being told only the address, the floor on which the flat is situated and an outline of the terms. In these cases the surveyor in his all-inclusive fee should allow for his study of the lease and make it quite clear, in writing, the extent to which his survey will be taken. However, having obtained a clear idea as to the precise terms of the lease, the writers recommend that the best procedure is for the surveyor then to refer back to his clients either by telephone or

Many of the multi-storey Georgian and Victorian, as here, terraced, semi-detached and detached houses have been divided into flats, often one to a floor.

Victorian properties

bedrooms above and servants' bedrooms in the attic, remains thus and the basic strength or weakness of each part may remain the same.

The fact that the top floor rooms are converted to a self-contained flat and are being sold on a long lease to a concert pianist, may or may not be an advance from the social point of view, but nevertheless the size and span of the joists will probably not have been altered, so that the surveyor may have to warn his client after carrying out quick rule-of-thumb calculations as to floor loading that the original structure was designed for maid servants rather than a baby grand piano.

So far as services are concerned, the Georgian property may doubtless have been re-drained to a sound standard but its hot and cold water and central heating installations may be of practically any date. There are cases where the absence of any inspection chambers leads the surveyor to realise with incredulity that the drainage system has never been altered or modernised, but such cases are rare due to the by-law requirements which arise during conversion.

So far as the remaining services are concerned, the usual wide range of installations of various ages will be encountered and with a property of this period, the survey is bound to be arduous. It will be necessary for ancient pitched roofs, whether tiled or slated, to be investigated and elderly mansard slopes to be examined together with the very old and inconvenient box and secret gutters that may not have been inspected for years.

Distorted brickwork will require careful analysis and, in particular, the need to decide as to the original form and design of the structure having regard to all the subsequent alterations will be paramount. Perhaps, however, the saving grace of surveys of this type is that as Georgian property becomes more and more in demand every year and the prices reflect this trend, the client is able to allow the surveyor more and more latitude in terms of time for effective investigation and to make a full and efficient survey thoroughly worth while.

So far as Victorian structures are concerned, these too can vary enormously in terms of possible liability to the purchaser of an individual flat. In 1887, the Victorian building boom was at its height but it is too often forgotten that by that time Queen Victoria had sat on the throne for exactly 50 years. The reader should remember therefore that early Victorian properties will have the same characteristics in many ways as Georgian property, and from 1837 through to about 1914 the amount of development was prodigious and the types of structure employed for the larger houses of infinite variety.

All of these were, and are, potential meat for conversion and vary from a badly built house with poor design characteristics, of say 1880, to a much better type of structure built in, say, 1908. In the former case, the roof structure may be shallow and the slated coverings sagging and imperfect, the walls may be bulged due to poor design and the bricks may show signs of general failure.

Internally, the layout may be inconvenient and a partial or hasty conversion may have led to all the problems of poor sanitary facilities, inconvenient room sizes and insufficient means of escape in case of fire as already discussed.

On the other hand, in the latter case, the position might be quite different. The tiled roof may be sound and of excellent weatherproof characteristics, the main walls may be both sturdy and with excellent facing brickwork, slate damp-proof coursing and good ventilation for ground floor timbers. With a new brick back addition for sanitary and kitchen purposes, many conversions of houses of this period are excellent. The surveyor can often reassure his client that in many ways the risk element of anything going wrong is probably less than that of a new structure though, as with all conversions, the effect that any new alterations may have on the existing structure will require consideration.

Purpose built blocks of flats, erected prior to 1914

Many blocks of flats were built before the outbreak of the First World War and, as might be expected, these were built in ways that reflected the many layers of Victorian Society. The blocks of flats of this period now left to us vary from the small blocks of artisan developments to the large pretentious structures housing what are now known as "mansion" flats. In the latter case we now see these buildings with affection tinged with an element of romanticism but nothing can conceal the stark and unsympathetic qualities of the smaller blocks built for workers in the big towns.

Flats for artisans

The surveyor will undoubtedly encounter a number of these smaller blocks in his work and while sympathising with the ingenious efforts of developers to disguise concrete staircases and landings and gloomy passages and entrance halls with floor coverings of

The inner area of most cities contain blocks of flats built in Victorian times for artisans, often by charitable trusts and some, as here, with balcony access from the rear.

Victorian mansion flats can be of substantial floor area with large elegant rooms and facilities in proportion to match even extending at times to accommodation for living-in staff. Porterage, central heating and hot water, and a lift service were standard. The construction was often very substantial.

first-class construction, even quite tiny projections are often protected with lead or zinc cappings, but this is not invariably the case.

Often, in order to preserve a particular ideal of design, the architect on such a block will have treated the question of rain-water disposal with disdain so that rain-water gutters and pipes, the pipes often being rectangular in section, may be hidden, or carried round awkward angles so that their efficiency is much reduced or worse carried internally in concealed ducts or chases. The penalty of a cracked section of cast iron pipe can often prove formidable especially if this particular fault is hidden to the eye and thus neglected over a long period.

Many of the best quality Victorian mansion flats are sold for very high prices and the surveyor accordingly needs to take care in estimating the efficiency or otherwise of the various services offered. The purchaser of a large Central London leasehold flat does not expect to shiver throughout the winter or to suffer an electric shock when trying to install his hi-fi. Nor does he wish, and indeed nor does anyone for that matter, to suffer the consequences of the back flow from an insufficient number of drainage outlets. In flats of this type, special care should be allocated to the arrangements relating to services, common parts, grounds and the like.

The block of Victorian mansion flats top right was built in an elaborate style with round and faceted slate covered turrets and a fairly liberal use of terra-cotta over the entrances, in broad band courses and as balustrading for some of the balconies. With elaborate common parts and the provision of a full range of services maintenance costs on such a building must be high and would be reflected in the annual amount of service charge on which the surveyor would need to give proper advice.

The block bottom right is a modern equivalent of the mansion flat which while providing rooms and facilities considered in tune with modern requirements is luxuriously appointed. The buildings' problems however will be quite different from those in the block above reflecting the difficulties of construction in the 1960s when the block was built.

Purpose built blocks of flats built after 1920

It is commonly supposed that blocks of flats built between the two World Wars and after the Second World War are superior to those in the previous classification and certainly the Building Societies used to subscribe to this view, placing an almost mystic importance on the age of buildings. It is, however, by no means the case that blocks of flats in this group are free from serious faults. The block of flats built between the two World Wars often displays the same faults as those found in the smaller scale domestic construction of that period. Poor quality roofing tiles are commonplace and although the covering to a good many roof slopes will have been renewed, many have not.

In addition, the "modern" look of the period which demanded steel casements and whitened rendering, very smart when the block was built, wears badly by comparison with the brickwork of earlier periods. Sulphate attack from poor design and detailing will have made a sorry mess of chimney stacks and parapets while the early steel casements, made when an adequate galvanising process was in its infancy, will have surely rusted to the point where they need renewal. Although such blocks are likely to have purpose built kitchens and bathrooms, these are often cramped, ill planned and awkward by modern standards. Serious faults will also be commonly found with drains. These are, like the house construction of the time, often shallow, of narrow bore, and with imperfect beds so that they have become defective.

So far as modern blocks of flats are concerned, it is hoped that the chapter on structural surveys of new dwellings will be sufficiently convincing to show that the easy assumption of a "modern is best"

Even from a distance the surveyor would be put on guard if carrying out a survey of a top floor flat. What has gone wrong at roof level to spoil the designer's trim detail on the right and necessitate its replacement by the rather awkward looking parrapet?

358

The right to buy legislation has brought surveyors the task of advising purchasers of flats in blocks such as this. These blocks exhibit the characteristics of their period and it may be necessary to advise the client to engage an engineer.

The detailing around and above the entrance and the positioning and type of windows are points that a surveyor would need to investigate on a survey of a flat in this near new block.

The gables and fibre slated roof on the near new block of flats below were no doubt provided to blend with the typical inner suburban street scene of which it now forms part. The surveyor would need to consider all details of construction to advise a purchaser of a flat including the likely length of life of the slates.

"Queen Anne" details at the front of blocks of flats as here in both private and local authority sectors are often let down by "Mary Anne" detailing at the back.

attitude can be misplaced. Cases of settlement in newly constructed blocks of flats with all the consequent problems that this can cause are not infrequent and in particular the failure of adequate design in the provision of effective vapour barriers in flat roof construction can cause very heavy expenditure not long after the defects liability period has ended.

The host of detailing faults and other problems associated with new construction make the survey of a newly constructed flat a more onerous undertaking than is often assumed by the lay public. There is not likely to be much money available for detailed investigations and accordingly the surveyor will be limited firstly to what he can see with his own eyes and secondly as to what information he can acquire from the developers and local authority as discussed in Chapter 12.

This period does, of course, embrace the substantial number of local authority blocks of flats built before the Second World War and subsequently as part of slum-clearance programmes the occupiers of which may now be exercising their right to buy a long leasehold interest.

The older blocks of medium height are more often than not built of load bearing brickwork with concrete floors and exhibit many of the characteristics of pre-1940 blocks built in the private sector although as to be expected units are generally much smaller, there is an absence of trimmings and the common parts may be a bit grim. Nevertheless some have been modernised more than once. Whilst the basic structure is in many instances sound, it is the aspects of modernisation that are often dubious with poor windows affected by rust if metal or wet rot if of timber, inferior joinery, poor sanitary fittings and plastic plumbing, inadequate electrical installations. When it comes to external parts of the building for which the prospective purchaser will have a proportionate liability, inferior roofing materials, inadequate rainwater disposal and drainage provisions are not uncommon.

The post Second World War period began to see framed construction being used more often, both steel and reinforced concrete and later still the spread of the now decried high rise structures of the 1960s and 1970s with their novel prefabricated concrete cladding panels. To give useful and appropriate advice to a prospective purchaser of a flat in one of these blocks requires very great care indeed in view of the many defects for which these blocks are renowned. Indeed the use of High Alumina cement and calcium chloride in the concrete mix all occurred to a large extent with this type of construction and even though structures may have been given a clean bill of health by the local authority's engineers in recent years it will almost certainly be necessary to recommend the use of an engineering consultant to carry out appropriate tests to identify probable hazards and establish the strength of the concrete.

THE COMPILATION OF THE REPORT

Check on Maintenance Programme

Having completed his survey of the flat whether new or old, the surveyor has one important final step to take before sitting down to draft his report. This is to acquire from the managing agents or person responsible for the collection of the ground rent, as much information as he can relating to the maintenance programme.

Very often following the survey of a flat, much information can be obtained from managing agents regarding work which has been or is proposed to be carried out and it is surprising how often an inquiry of this sort repays the effort in adding to the surveyor's knowledge of the property.

Drafting the report

The final operation will, of course, be the drafting of the report. Here is it not proposed to be dogmatic as to any particular form but some guidance is suggested and a specimen of a possible report is included as Appendix 3 at page 523. The selection of report headings is a matter for the circumstances of the case and the priorities of the individual surveyor concerned, but a form is needed that will ease the task of the client in reading the document and carry him logically from point to point without the need for turning back to check on points badly made or turning over the pages ahead to find out some fundamental information which has not been given in proper sequence.

Order of contents

Accordingly it is suggested that the surveyor commences the report as for any other structural survey by repeating his precise instructions and then gives a factual account of the situation and a brief description of the property supplemented with photographs if possible. This can then be followed by a schedule of accommodation with or without measurements in the usual way.

At this point, however, the report can be varied if desired from one relating to a house by introducing at this stage a new main heading entitled "The Lease" or, where appropriate, "The Draft Lease". On the other hand it is a perfectly valid arrangement to continue the report on a similar basis as the report on a house by dealing next with the condition of the block in which the flat is situated and the flat itself and including the section dealing with the lease towards the end of the report. If covered early in the report the surveyor should summarise in clear non-legal language the main provisions of the Draft Lease or Lease as seen from the surveyor's point of view in such a way that the report, when referred to subsequently, can give reasonably full information as to those main points in the lease which relate to repair and maintenance.

The relationship of the parties, the term of the lease and the amount of the ground rent should first be stated, the demise considered in detail so as to define what is being purchased and the repairing covenants then summarised together with any information that there may be as to how these are related to such matters as windows, doors, walls and partitions, ceilings and floors and the liability for services.

STRUCTURAL SURVEYS OF FLATS AND MAISONETTES

The exact terms of the lessee's responsibility should be dealt with, firstly as to the full liability and secondly, as to the part liability and its concern with the arrangements relating to the calculation and payment of the service charge. The arrangements for the up-keep of the common parts, services, garden areas and provisions relating to staff and lifts, if any, should be dealt with and also the point as to the method for the settling of disputes and the procedures that are to be adopted between respective lessees in the event of repairs being required to one flat which may have an effect on another.

There is, of course, a limit to the amount of space that the surveyor can devote to summarising the provisions of the lease or draft lease for obvious reasons. Some matters which are of obvious concern to the lessee, but which are set out in the document in comparative clarity are best not summarised although the surveyor should draw his client's attention to them. An example of this might be a full schedule of regulations that are particularly stringent affecting the occupant of each individual flat.

In whatever way the surveyor drafts his summary of the lease, he should recognise that this, to some degree, must involve a process of selection and he should make it quite clear that his summary is for a particular purpose and he should also use a form of words in the report to confirm that he makes his comments strictly from the surveyor's point of view rather than the legal point of view.

The important point is that the surveyor's summarising comments on the lease or draft lease are related in plain and simple language to the prospective purchaser's liabilities both in the physical and the financial sense and also be directed to drawing his attention to the salient points that may have some effect on his use and enjoyment of the flat in future years. Only the surveyor will be able to treat the lease in this way as the client's solicitor is unlikely to inspect the property unless specifically asked to do so.

Body of the report

The body of the report, dealing with the surveyor's findings, should relate itself as far as is possible to the ground work that is appropriate to the circumstances. Here of course the surveyor has a choice. He might either take the view that full liability under the terms of the lease for a small area takes precedence over a partial responsibility for a wider area or he may, alternatively, consider that the important matters relating to the main structure should come first.

Reports drafted with both points of view in mind are equally valid according to circumstances but ideally the latter type of report lends itself best to a block of flats or a flat conversion in a decaying or imperfect structure while the first type of report is best for a flat in a purpose-built block or converted house where very little is found to be wrong. The reasons for this are obvious. It is always best to start with the matters which are and sound as if they are of the greatest importance. The danger in some types of layout is that for example a good deal of space is devoted to minor plaster cracking while the last page and a half of the report covers enormous defects. The survey may be exact and thorough but a badly

Importance of stressing that comments on lease from a Surveyor's point of view

balanced report can given the contrary effect and the surveyor should try to avoid this.

Structural elements

Accordingly, therefore, it is suggested that within the framework proposed the normal report should deal with the structural elements, separated into external and internal matters (or the other way round according to preference), the external matters comprising main and subsidiary roofs and main walls while the internal matters comprise ceilings, partitions, floors, windows and doors etc.

The decorations, whether internal or external can be dealt with within this framework or alternatively as a separate item if required and the services can again be dealt with separately under individual headings relating to drains, cold water supply, electricity, gas, hot water and heating installations. Matters relating to boundaries and other external items can be dealt with finally, if this is logical, or alternatively in the body of the report if this is preferred.

Limitations

Towards the conclusion, the surveyor should, under an appropriate heading, near his final summing-up, set out the limitations of the survey as agreed in the conditions of engagement. He should include a proviso relating to parts of the structure which are covered, unexposed or inaccessible and he should also outline those areas that he inspected and refer to those areas that he was unable or not instructed to inspect. Thirdly he should set out the nature of the floor coverings, and other claddings such as casings and the like which are very common in Victorian flats which prohibit inspection of the basic structure.

Conclusions

Finally in the same way as with any other structural survey report, the surveyor will wish to draw the threads together in the form of his advice on the proposed purchase. He may perhaps have to advise that further investigations are carried out before a decision on purchasing is taken.

On the other hand he may be able, with a degree of confidence, to advise that repairs costing an approximate sum of money are necessary to the flat for which the purchaser will be solely liable as against other repairs required costing approximately a further figure, to the structure, common parts or services, for which the purchaser may be liable for only a small percentage of the cost over the next few years.

The surveyor may also have comments on the level of the current service charge and whether it is adequate or likely to be increased, having regard to the need or otherwise of repairs for which all tenants will be liable in proportion.

There may, furthermore, be specific points in regard to the lease which the surveyor might wish to reiterate at this point as being particularly likely to affect the client's future comfort and convenience in occupation and correspondingly the ease with which a re-sale of the interest in the flat might be effected in the future. Possibly in the light of the inspection there are points in the lease which require further advice being taken from the client's solicitor before the purchase is completed.

Other forms of layout

It is considered that the basic layouts suggested above will cover most cases but there will, of course, be occasions where the circumstances are abnormal and where another form of layout is required. An obvious case in point might be a recently built pair of maisonettes standing on their own, or a vast rambling flat or maisonette formed from two or more units with a number of bedrooms, several bathrooms, servants' quarters etc. occupied by a captain of industry with a large personal staff. Here the importance of appendix schedules to deal with routine smaller defects should be considered in order, firstly, to cut down the tedium of reading a long involved document and, secondly, to give due weight to the important matters with which the surveyor's client will be mainly concerned.

On the survey of a flat in this near new block the surveyor would need to ascertain what precautions had been taken in the construction to guard against the effect of tree roots.

Chapter 12
Structural Surveys of New Dwellings

CONTENTS

EARLIER PRACTICE BY THE PURCHASERS OF NEW HOMES

The flight to the suburbs between 1920–1940

The first edition of this book, published in 1964, speculated on the reasons for the increase in the number of requests for structural surveys since the early 1950s. It found that this was mainly due to an increase in the purchase of older houses as compared with new houses, a factor in complete contrast to conditions which existed in the period 1920 to 1940.

At that time, the unrestricted building of new estates of houses for sale caused a flight to the suburbs, leaving the older houses nearer the centre of the towns for renting to those who could not afford to buy. Up to the middle 1960s it was comparatively rare for a surveyor to be asked to carry out a structural survey of a new house and accordingly that aspect of the subject received but a passing mention in the first edition of *Structural Surveys of Dwelling Houses*.

Buyers of new houses tended to follow previous custom, relying on such factors as position, design, price and the reputation of the developer or builder to guide their choice. This was a reasonable course to follow since only a small number of new houses seemed to show alarming faults within a few years of their construction.

New houses at this time were assumed by purchasers and solicitors alike to be built not only with all the normal standards of quality but with the benefit of new improved by-law control as well. The consequences of this innocent approach became apparent in the later 1960s when the changes which had been taking place in the building industry began to come home to roost and resulted in widespread publicity not only for cases of comparatively minor defects arising from poor materials and finishings but also for more serious defects arising from major faults in design and construction. There has been no decline in this publicity since and every few years some new horror story emerges.

FACTORS CONTRIBUTING TO FAILURES IN HOUSE BUILDING SINCE THE 1940s

The private house building industry in this country has undergone numerous changes in the period since the 1940s. These changes taken individually were possibly insufficient in themselves to account for the spate of publicity on defects which began in the late 1960s, but when all are taken together, it is not very difficult to see how a situation conducive to defects arose. Among the factors involved were:

Less desirable sites

1. The need to make use of less desirable sites became more pronounced as long as the policy of retaining the Green Belts around the big cities was maintained. This situation led to

367

developments on land never before contemplated, such as houses being built on steeply sloping sites and on land with drainage problems as well as on land previously used for other purposes, for example mineral extraction and waste dumping. A skilled analysis of the precautions necessary in building on such sites needs to be taken, in advance of building, to ensure future stability. Such an analysis has not always been carried out on new developments with dire results in some cases.

Less experienced developers

2. The continuing high demand for new housing and, accordingly, the high degree of profitability in boom times which has tended to draw the less experienced developer into house construction. Unlike the larger nationally known organisations who, with their substantial resources, can buy up tracts of land well in advance of requirements and look to the maintenance of their good name over an extended period, the less experienced developer can be tempted, and indeed may be forced, into the purchase of the less desirable sites. In order to maximise profits over a shorter period, he may then be inclined to cut corners. There are obvious dangers here for the unwary purchaser.

Shortage of materials

3. Since the 1940s there have been periodic shortages of some of the basic materials of building. Economic circumstances, for example, have led to the use of much timber of comparatively poor quality, particularly for joinery purposes. As a corollary to these shortages, many new materials have been developed to take the place of the old. Whilst the results of initial testing have often been good, experience in the long term has not always been up to expectations.

Government policy

4. The vagaries of government economic policy have been particularly severe on the building industry and the private house building sector has had alternating booms and slumps with the result that the size of the labour force fluctuates wildly. In bad times good and bad workmen are displaced, but whereas in boom times the bad are immediately drawn back by the high wages obtainable, the good, remembering past experience, may not be tempted to return. The same thing happens in the supervisory grades and the result is a lack of consistency both in standards of workmanship and supervision.

Speed of construction

5. The speed of modern construction tends to work against a good finish. The pressure to finish a house started in a period of boom conditions before the boom subsides is considerable and various short cuts can be taken with modern materials and additives to ensure that work proceeds whatever the conditions. The result is a marked reduction in the time taken from commencement of construction to completion, although a heavy price may be exacted later when the defects start to appear.

Economy of construction and innovation

6. The inevitable desire to keep down the selling price of new houses on large estates consistent with maximum profitability, has meant an increasing trend towards cost economy in construction and the use of innovatory methods and cheaper materials. The penalty for this may take some time to appear but in today's economy minded, low rise construction, the effects can be far more

368

extensive and costly to remedy than might have been the case if a greater margin of safety had been maintained.

THE HOUSE BUILDING INDUSTRY'S RESPONSE TO CRITICISM

Pressure

The spate of publicity on the defects in new houses in the mid-1960s had its effect. The predictable response that it ought not to be allowed and that the government should do something about it, came from some M.P.s and Consumer Protection Organisations, particularly when it was found that if the builder went bankrupt, there could be no remedy at all.

The principle of "let the buyer beware", *caveat emptor*, was found to apply to new houses as well as old (except in so far as it was possible to claim for defects rendering them uninhabitable, provided the claim was made within the limitation period of 6 years from the date of construction). Furthermore the guarantees offered by some builders under the old "National House Builders Registration Council" scheme covering about a quarter of the new houses being built at that time were slow in operation and difficult to enforce.

The more reputable organisations in the house building industry became worried that their own image might be damaged by the rogue element in their midst and also by the possibility that the government might impose much stricter controls on building. Even more important, however, was the effect on the Building Societies who became alarmed that the value of their security, wrapped up in so much new building, might suffer.

NHBRC reorganised as NHBC and Building Society policy

Pressure was brought to bear and the National House Builders Registration Council was reorganised in 1967. The Council was and still is, despite the change in name to the National House Building Council in 1973 and the importation of non-builder members to the extent of two thirds of the council, a contractors' protection association and not primarily concerned with consumers' protection. Recalcitrant contractors were however expelled from the Council's Register and the Council's Requirements on the design and construction of houses were raised, on advice taken from the Department of the Environment. The Building Societies Association also agreed that in future its members would only advance money on new properties which obtained the Council's Certificate and which in turn enabled the purchaser to secure the protection of the House Purchaser's Agreement.

The "Buildmark" scheme

From 1 April 1988 "Buildmark" became the name and trade mark of the Council's combined ten year warranty and protection scheme. It requires the builder to put right at his own expense any defect which may arise as a result of the builder's failure to comply with the Council's Requirements for standards of workmanship and materials within a period of two years from the date of the Council's Ten Year's Notice. There is provision in the scheme for arbitration and the Council will honour any arbitrator's award if the builder fails to do so or should the builder become bankrupt or go into liquidation. Beyond the end of the second year, the purchaser is covered by insurance in respect of damage due to major defects in the load bearing structure and defects in the drainage system including subsidence, settlement and heave unless this is already covered by legislation e.g. for mining subsidence, or by household insurance, during the next eight years.

Once again this is consequent upon failure to comply with the Council's Requirements and there is a limit of compensation at the time of writing to the original purchase price or three times the national average purchase price (about £220,000 in 1989) increased in line with inflation up to a maximum of 12% per annum compound. There is no provision under the House Purchaser's Agreement for the remedying of normal shrinkage defects, though of course this may be covered by the builder's own "after sales" service on the contract for sale, equivalent to the six months defects liability period in a normal building contract.

Defective Premises Act 1972

A feature of the arrangements made by the National House Building Council is that they do not detract in any way from the purchaser's rights under a contract for sale or under Common law, unlike some guarantees of manufactured articles. Conversely, however, the rights of purchasers of a dwelling in England and Wales under Section 1 of the Defective Premises Act 1972 (which states that the duty of a person taking on the work of providing a dwelling, be he builder or developer, is to see that it is completed in a workmanlike manner so that it will be fit for habitation) are withheld when the National House Building Council's arrangements operate, since this is an alternative scheme of protection for the purchaser. This is approved under Section 2 of the Act by the Secretary of State for the Environment, once the Council issue their Ten Year Notice in respect of the particular dwelling.

Limitation Acts

If the Council does not issue its Notice then, of course, the provisions of the Act would apply, but these provisions are far less comprehensive, would probably involve proceedings in Court and are governed by the Limitation Acts since the breach of duty can only arise before completion of the work. Actions must therefore be brought within six years (three years if damages are claimed for personal injuries) of the completion of the dwelling.

NHBC requirements for builders

An examination of the reassuring publicity put out by the National House Building Council might make the layman ask why it should be necessary to have a structural survey of a new house at all, now that all these additional safeguards are available. He is told that the Council's registration system excludes all "jerry builders" from the National Register of House Builders by assessing their financial stability, insisting on the requisite technical competence and the serving of a probationary period while a reasonable number of new houses are completed. Good standards are encouraged by the operation of a "no claims" discount on the annual membership fee.

The builder is required to build houses at least to the minimum standards laid down by the Council's Requirements and he must allow spot checks during the course of construction if he wishes the house to obtain the Council's Certificate on completion. Following satisfactory completion there is the two-year warranty against defects already discussed and beyond the second year additional insurance provision up to the end of the tenth year for major structural defects is obtained, while there is further protection against the bankruptcy of a builder where a purchaser actually suffers loss.

Spot checks during construction

While it must be admitted that the arrangements made by the National House Building Council are better than none at all, they are by no means sufficient to ensure the prevention of defects. The fact that a builder is on the Register is no guarantee that he will carry out good work and the spot checks which are carried out on average once every three weeks and amount in all to about one to four hours of inspection during the course of construction, are quite insufficient to prevent the incidence of bad work in all cases even though they may in some instances be responsible for preventing defects which would be hidden by the time the house was completed.

Example of remedies under NHBC scheme

The Council quotes as examples of defective work which has been dealt with, or compensation paid to aggrieved purchasers, under its scheme, renewal of the roofs on twelve houses, major subsidence to six houses, incorrect filling over the site of twelve houses causing sulphate attack, breaking of concrete raft foundations and severe dry rot in a three year old house.

Purchaser's anguish

The Council cites these examples of work remedied and compensation paid as an illustration of the value of its ten-year guarantee warranty in protecting the purchaser against major failure in the load bearing structure. This may be so and it is arguable that purchasers would probably not have done any better in a Court of Law, but it is not difficult to imagine the anguish which the purchasers must have endured before matters were resolved and repairs were carried out in order to allow them to move back into their, no doubt, hard earned home (or in some cases their "compensatory home"). Others, apart from the Council, may be forgiven if they cite these examples as revealing something rather more disturbing than merely the value of a guarantee or warranty. Certainly it would not be surprising if prospective purchasers and their solicitors draw less benign conclusions.

Failure by builders to put right defects

The Council also published the result of a study of items which builders had failed to put right in the first two years after construction and which gave rise to complaints to the Council. While many of the defects complained of such as shrinkage cracks, ill-fitting doors, loose wall and floor tiles and leaks in pipes were comparatively simple to put right, amongst the most frequent of the more serious defects were settlement in concrete slabs, failure in wood floors, subsidence, damp penetration through walls and floors, faulty flues and missing damp-proof courses.

NHBC requirements for design and the construction of houses

As time has gone on, further and more stringent clauses have been added to the Council's Requirements for the design and construction of houses in an endeavour to solve not only the

371

property as with old and are as described in Chapter 14 which discusses the legal position of the surveyor.

It is when the surveyor is put on guard and comes to warning a purchaser against some particular aspect of the property, that we see the differences in technique. In the survey of an old property, the surveyor will see some defect or indication that all it not well and proceed to warn his client of the likely consequences who will then either not proceed with the purchase or ask for permission to carry out further investigation depending on the circumstances.

Projecting possible defects

It is unlikely, however, that in surveying a new property the surveyor will be put on guard in precisely the same way by seeing something actually wrong. What the surveyor needs to do is to examine all the evidence from whatever available source and express an opinion as to what is beginning to go wrong now or what is likely to go wrong in the future. In other words, the surveyor will be accepting the very onerous task of weighing up all the necessary considerations in order to provide his client with a critical analysis of the design and construction of the dwelling and speculating on the ability of the structure, services and finishings to fulfil his client's expectations for the future.

Let no one assume that this is an easy task, either physically or mentally. It is often more demanding on both faculties as well as more time consuming than the survey of an older property. The objective will be to ensure in so far as is possible that the client and his family will be spared the fearsome worry and the awful disruption and inconvenience that can be involved by the purchase of a house with a major defect. There is an old saying that "no one wishes to buy a lawsuit" and this is certainly more true in relation to a home than anything else. This sentiment can equally be extended to include the purchase of the arbitration and insurance procedures provided by the National House Building Council, however fair and unbiased their manner of administration.

Definition of new properties extended to those up to 10 years old

Before proceeding to discuss the settlement of the instructions, it is appropriate to discuss what is meant by a new property in the context of a structural survey. For this purpose it is convenient to divide new properties into two categories, those built as part of an entirely new estate (or those single properties far removed from other earlier development) as against properties built essentially as an infilling process amongst existing older property. In the former case, there is every reason for following the new house technique when instructions are given to survey a house within ten years of its completed construction date.

In the latter case it is suggested that any property under five years old should be surveyed by the new house technique. In certain circumstances this might be extended to a property in the 5–10 year old range, for example where knowledge exists of defects in properties nearby, or where sub-soil conditions are particularly difficult, or the house is built on a steep hill or on an area of land previously filled.

It is possible to envisage with some properties in the 5–10 year old category that the survey might well start off as one appropriate

374

to an old property and develop into one along the lines of a survey for a new property. It should be remembered that the surveyor must pursue his investigations to the extent necessary to complete his instructions, hence the necessity for it to be clearly understood from the start just what those instructions are within the scope of the agreed fee.

Initial ascertainment of information

In any discussions with a client on the survey of a near new property, sufficient information should be ascertained initially so as to enable the surveyor to decide whether it is to be a survey conducted as for an old or a new property having regard to the circumstances set out above. In discussion it may be possible to contrast the two types to the clearer understanding by the client of the surveyor's work.

If the survey is to be carried out as for an entirely new property, then it would be appropriate to discuss the following points, bearing in mind the principle discussed in Chapter 1 to this book; this is that the client should be given the opportunity to decide what he will have done, within certain limits consistent with the surveyor's own views as to the minimum scope of instructions acceptable so as to enable him to carry out an adequate structural survey to satisfy his own standards.

Basic requirements for survey for new and near new properties

In relation to the survey of a new property just what should the standard for an adequate survey be? To begin with, a structural survey of a new property must surely provide, so as to avoid the client's comment, "I could have done this myself", not only a good description of the site and its surroundings, the property, its accommodation, services, finishing and special features, but also a detailed commentary on its elements of construction. This information will be mainly factual and the client should be informed, when discussing the instructions, that comments on the adequacy or suitability of layout are excluded as these do not, in the normal course of events, become matters of consequence on a structural survey since they are items on which the client and his family must satisfy themselves.

Comparison with original drawings

However, to give comments and opinions on the suitability of the elements of construction to fulfil their proposed function will be dependent upon various circumstances. For example, with a brand new property the surveyor will also wish to compare the original drawings and the specification with the property being surveyed so to advise his client on whether he is to obtain the whole or part only of the original bargain. In this respect it is not unusual for the documents and the facts to differ. There are many reasons for this, some genuine, some not so genuine but all are worth exploring by the client or his solicitor if it is decided to proceed.

If ascertaining the reasons involves correspondence, it might be said at this stage that this is beyond the scope of the survey, it being sufficient for the surveyor to note the discrepancy and to comment on the possible effect this may have, if any. On the other hand, with a property a few years old, the client will be buying in all probability from the vendor in occupation and therefore the property, as in any

All the near new houses shown on this page include forms of construction which require investigation particularly flashings to cavity brickwork, stepped construction, odd insertions and projections, novel windows.

Right to buy surveys are now common. A full site investigation would have been economic for a large outer suburban estate development as above. Was one carried out? Can the surveyor see it? The remaining photographs illustrate infill developments in inner suburban areas.

contractor, then a copy may have been deposited with the local authority as part of the material submitted to prove the design and in order to obtain approval under the Building Regulations and it should be possible to consult this at the local authority offices.

A deposited sub-soil investigation with the local authority would probably be the only evidence available in relation to a house a few years old as to detailed conditions below ground. If this was not available, the surveyor would need to ascertain whether any geological survey maps were available for consultation either at the local authority office or at a local museum or the Geological Museum at South Kensington, London.

Discussion with Building Inspector

Next the surveyor will wish to discuss the matter with the particular Building Inspector who dealt with the scheme at its approval stage and who carried out the site inspection on behalf of the local authority during the course of construction.

With the aid of the records, the Building Inspector can often contribute useful information as to the site before and during construction and whether any unusual factors or unique conditions necessitated any special precautions being taken in relation to the house under consideration. Information of this nature may be kept on record cards or some other form of filing system, even though alterations or additional annotations may be lacking on the drawings deposited with the authority.

The surveyor should keep a careful note of all the information gathered in relation to the sub-soil, a note of its source and also in some circumstances an estimate as to its reliability. This information is very vital as the surveyor will now have to consider whether he has enough information of sufficient reliability to put himself in the designer's shoes, design the foundations and to relate his design to what he has been led to believe exists below ground.

Inadvisability of assumptions

It might be thought that all new building schemes would be built on foundations that have been designed having regard to all the circumstances of the site, but this is still unfortunately far from the case. It is the unexpected which catches everybody out. Should a site have dubious characteristics which are well known in the locality, usually every precaution will be taken when building to cope with these characteristics and probably all will be well. It is when everybody believes, often quite genuinely, that this site is "just like the last", or "it has always been done like that in this area" that unwarranted assumptions are made. This is particularly likely to arise on a small development of say 10–15 houses, when it may be felt that a soil investigation is an unnecessary expenditure not likely to add to one's knowledge, but likely instead to put up the cost of the houses or alternatively eat into the profit.

It is perhaps as well to remember that 80 per cent of all new houses are built by small local builders in just such limited numbers at a time. Similarly in regard to individual houses or small groups of houses on a very large development, circumstances will be anticipated as being just like those appertaining to the rest of the development and time and trouble for individual consideration will very often be lacking, particularly when it may involve delays.

383

inspection. Of course, so much would depend upon the precise instructions in a particular case but in relation to a survey of a newly constructed house or one within ten years of construction, it is considered that a surveyor must do more than just make a visual inspection of the property, however close and intense that inspection may be.

Case examples of a new flat survey and four- and eight-year-old house surveys

Some might cite *Bishop v. Watson Watson and Scoles* (1972)[1] where a surveyor succeeded in defending a case against him of negligence involving damp penetration to a near new flat arising from defective detailing. There was no real evidence to suggest on an inspection of the flat that anything was wrong and as the surveyor had only been instructed to carry out a "visual" inspection he succeeded in his defence.

The correct conclusion to be drawn from this case however is of the near worthlessness to the client of a survey report based on a visual inspection only, when by extending the inquiry to an examination of the plans and details the faults would have been revealed, analysed and anticipated. If the plans had been detailed correctly in regard to damp precautions and the workmanship had been at fault, the client's remedy would have been against the vendor, not the surveyor.

The above case can be contrasted with *Daisley v. B.S. Hall and Co.* (1972)[2] where it was held that on a survey of an eight year old house a surveyor should have taken steps to ascertain the type of trees forming a line along the boundary of the plot, together with the type of sub-soil and warned the purchaser of possible movement due to the roots of Poplar trees depriving clay soil of moisture and inducing shrinkage. The surveyor having seen some cracks had attributed these to "minor settlement and bedding down" making no mention of the trees or the sub-soil. Mr. Justice Bristow is reported as having said in that case:

"In my judgement, it follows that any surveyor who finds a house under 10 years old built as close to a row of Poplars (25 feet), where two of those trees had been felled for no apparent reason other than to reduce the risk of root damage, is under a duty to ascertain by effective means the nature of the sub-soil whether or not he finds evidence of settlement of the house which may be due to sub-soil shrinkage. If he finds that the sub-soil is shrinkable clay, then it is clearly his duty to consider whether damage which may be due to this cause has already taken place, because this must affect the seriousness of the risk of damage of which it is his duty to warn his client. If circumstances are such that the risk is high, clearly he should warn his client not to go on with the purchase. If circumstances are such that the risk is very small it must, in my judgement, be his duty to say so. Between the two extremes, the price which he advises it is sensible to pay must take account of the extent of the risk as he

[1] Estates Gazette, 16th December, 1972, p. 1881.
[2] Estates Gazette, 3rd March, 1973, p. 1553.

sees it and the possible cost of putting things right if damage does occur."

The judge was also reported as saying that for surveyors "it really is essential to make sure of your tree recognition, because Poplars are not the only trees of which there is more than one species". In this case the Poplars were of the species *Populus canadensis* Moench, a close relation of the black poplar. The judge was sympathetic towards a young inexperienced surveyor who failed to recognise the trees as Poplars but the damages were assessed at £1,750 plus costs, all the same.

In another case relating to the structural survey of a four year old house built on the side of a steep hill[1] the surveyor submitted a report which contained no reference to a defect of any kind, according to the reported judgement, apart from minor hairline plaster cracks, their locations not mentioned. The judge commented upon various defects on which evidence had been brought to show existed at the time of the survey and said:

"The defendant failed to notice the repointing. He failed to notice the shape and extent of the crack over the kitchen door. He failed to notice in-filling in the cornice in the south east bedroom or to observe that the cupboard doors were not running freely. He failed to notice the over-papering. It must be well known that, human nature being what it was, from time to time vendors would take steps to cover up defects. That was at least part of the reason why the purchaser employed a surveyor. The totality of what was there to be seen considered against the known potential dangers of a steeply sloping site to which the defendant appeared to have given no real thought, ought undoubtedly to have aroused his suspicions and led him to a close examination of the house. This would have revealed the slope in the floors; he would have been led also to look at and think about the highway outside. An examination and consideration of the road would have further aroused his suspicions and led him to the highway authority."

Evidence was brought to show that the local authority had experienced considerable trouble with its road and that the divisional surveyor had expressed concern to the builder (who was also the vendor at the time of the survey) in connection with his building operations because of the instability of the road. Subsequent to the survey when more cracks appeared it was ascertained by sub-soil investigation that the house was built on 3.35 m of weathered soil which was slipping on the consolidated clay beneath and that slope stabilisation should have been carried out prior to special foundations being provided for the house. Damages were assessed in this case at £11,400, since the house was gradually breaking up and was worthless and it was held that a surveyor, without making any guesses but using his intelligence, should have come to this conclusion at the time of the survey.

---

[1] *Morgan v. Perry* (1973), Estates Gazette, 23rd March, 1974, p. 1737.

would be as well for the surveyor to be aware of the timber industry's endeavours to reinstate itself favourably in the house building sector in so far as ground floor construction is concerned. The Timber Research and Development Association pointing to the comfort due to resilience in a timber floor, its warmth, freedom from surface condensation and its potentially pleasing and long lasting appearance, has investigated cheaper alternatives to the traditional form of suspended hollow floor.

That the recommendations tend to favour Scottish practice in construction would probably come as no surprise to readers from north of the border who have always suspected that building affairs are ordered better in northern climes (as witness the higher standards in the Building Standards (Scotland) Regulations 1981). In the south, much reliance is placed on the oversite concrete to support a traditional hollow ground floor but in Scotland the oversite concrete is often omitted, the site covered with pitch and the floor formed of joists spanning between structural walls, much in the same manner as first floor construction.

Adoption of the Scottish practice would therefore tend to follow and support the recommendations for timber floors over deep fill made by the National House Building Council and thereby overcome the problem of settlement in oversite concrete slabs irrespective of the depth of fill. In fact, TRDA recommend the use of a heavy gauge polythene, in lieu of the pitch used in Scottish construction, which they indicate as having a far greater resistance to moisture and vapour penetration than concrete.

The proposal which has been prepared in conjunction with the Building Research Establishment, provides for a hard core oversite to be blinded to take the polythene which is weighted down by sand. Even the polythene is omitted when sites are steeply sloping or are liable to flooding and instead in these cases all the timber is treated or alternatively an insulating barrier of bituminised fibre insulation board or draped building paper is placed below the actual floorboards.

Surveyors must therefore expect to see construction along these lines in fairly new houses. Indeed it has been postulated that on a suitably dry site, the only excavation need be a mechanically excavated trench. Once excavated, the trench would be filled with concrete, whilst the area within the external walls is weed treated and covered with polythene below a suspended floor. Lack of proper supervision and bad workmanship could combine to produce a splendid crop of failures, coupled with luxuriant growth, with these new forms of construction.

Main structural walls

The main structural walls will probably be the next concern of the surveyor and here again in the case of a house where the construction has been completed, as distinct from one in process of construction, the surveyor will need to examine plans in conjunction with his site survey. Modern construction for brickwork, with its almost universal reliance on cavity work, requires the surveyor to pay attention to the design of those hidden details known to be a frequent source of trouble.

394

Traditional brick construction

In particular, the level of damp-proof courses in both external and internal walls, the details for closing cavities at the sides and tops of window and door openings will necessitate close attention while the construction of inner leaves, the distribution of loads from the roof and floors and the type and disposition and quality of wall ties will also require consideration. Cavity work undoubtedly requires greater consideration by way of design, greater care in workmanship and correspondingly better supervision than comparable solid work, and it is of course in just these features that much new work has been found wanting.

The NHBC survey of defects found that a large number of complaints were related to damp penetration around openings in external walls and through general areas of main walls. While the use of 150mm wide damp-proof courses around openings would help by permitting more flexibility in the positioning of frames in openings, much of the trouble has been found to be due to wall ties being built in with a slope down towards the inner leaf and mortar droppings accumulating on wall ties and on the tops of trays over window and door lintels.

Unfortunately there is little the surveyor can do in regard to poor workmanship and lack of supervision as exemplified by these two examples and the surveyor, of course, must include a disclaimer to this effect in his report. Nevertheless, it is important to stress that signs of these defects can become apparent remarkably soon after the completion of construction although possibly requiring fairly diligent inspection in the absence of pronounced staining.

Furthermore, the standard of workmanship and supervision on the site in general can often be gauged from an examination of visible features in the same house or in a house partly completed nearby. An indication of poor standards on parts left visible to the surveyor might lead him to assume that the same standards applied in hidden parts sending him back, perhaps, for an even more detailed examination of the critical parts of the structure for the possibly minute tell-tale signs which would provide verification of his assumption. Absence of proof, however, must leave the surveyor with his disclaimer covering the limits of his inspection, since the presence of cavity work in itself is insufficient grounds for suspecting that the safeguards essential to that mode of construction have been omitted or botched.

Novel forms of construction

The surveyor will be particularly concerned in regard to any novel forms of construction or any unusual juxtaposition of differing forms which, although not novel in themselves, can produce difficulties when used in conjunction with each other. In regard to the latter aspect, so much architectural trimming is carried out by mixing timber framing and for example tiles or some other material with traditional brickwork or in other cases with reinforced concrete or rendered block work. Horizontal and vertical junctions with other materials introduce potential weak points to which careful attention must be given by the designer to obviate damp penetration.

The higher these junctions the more exposed they are to driving

395

The new house, all ready for the surveyor's inspection! By completion much will be hidden from the surveyor's eyes and permission is unlikely to be forthcoming from the contractor or developer to open up. Having inspected, a glance around might reveal, if the surveyor is lucky another house of the same design in process of construction. Even better if the estate is large, a number in different stages of construction. Alternatively, but not quite so good, the surveyor may have to make do with another house in process of construction of different design as here below, but nevertheless being built by the same contractor on the same development.

rain and the more susceptible to trouble. Much difficulty has been experienced over the years in dealing with just such troubles in blocks of flats where there is a concrete or steel frame and infilling panels of comparatively traditional design. The difficulties have

On this part completed house the surveyor can see a great deal more of how it is being put together as well as the quality of materials being used and the standard of workmanship.

Further houses on the same development as on the page opposite. Even more can be seen here of important structural details before the roof covering is put on.

been even greater where the design is based on an infilling or cladding of prefabricated panels and when these sections are also used on low rise housing, the troubles can still be extensive. With low rise housing, however, the troubles are related more to the

With the advantage of being able to inspect at this stage the surveyor can see the construction of party walls, the top of external walls, the arrangement of roof timbers and their fixings and probably details of lintels, damp proof courses and floor construction.

397

It is not often the surveyor will see a near new house with a timber exterior of this type. Apart from commenting on the aspects of maintenance this will involve, the surveyor will need to ascertain and assess the type of overall construction. Timber frame perhaps on a brick plinth?

System building

degree of exposure, a factor which the surveyor must of course take into account in his report in all cases.

It is none too easy a matter to speculate on trends in construction for external walls. When it remains a fact that for ordinary two-

The surveyor will also need to establish the type of overall construction employed on this house which might not be all it seems, particularly in view of the curious detail at the far end.

A near new house of comparatively simple basic design but nevertheless showing influences in detail from earlier styles.

story housing, traditional brick wall, timber floor and tile covered pitch roof construction still remains the cheapest, it will require something very innovatory indeed to achieve general acceptance. The hopes of the 1950s and early 1960s that the use of system

Another near new development which also suggests that care and attention has been paid to detail with in part a sympathetic use of local stone and roofing materials. The surveyor will need to establish how the relationship of the two differing walling materials has been dealt with.

building with prefabricated panels would provide substantial economies have proved illusory and not only because of a lack of big orders to encourage large scale production, but also because of the technical difficulties which have already been touched on.

Timber frame construction

There were those who pinned their faith on timber frame construction which remains the traditional form in North America as well as Northern Europe and Scandinavia for low rise housing. The old bias against such construction in building legislation has been overcome and it is undoubtedly true that many of the grumbles which arise with traditional construction do not apply to timber framed construction. For example, once a start is made on site, the construction will take about an eighth of the time to complete in comparison with a traditional house. There need be no compromise on comfort or durability standards in the design and at the end there is a product which, owing to its essentially dry nature in construction, will be free of those teething troubles by way of shrinkage cracks which so beset the house of traditional construction.

There is sufficient flexibility with timber framed construction to satisfy the requirements of most developers producing variants with an eye to the private market, but the enthusiasm which had been generated for this form of construction was nearly nipped in the bud by some very unfavourable TV and press publicity. Some developers cut back on this method of construction for a while following the criticism but, when it was shown to be mainly alarmist and that timber frame construction was no more prone to defects than other methods, have now restored its use to former levels.

As timber framed construction has now for long been a non-traditional method of building in this country, the National House Building Council has required that all such designs for which their Notice is to be granted shall, since 1st January, 1974, be designed by a competent person (defined as a consulting chartered civil or structural engineer with appropriate experience in timber engineering). The Council has also laid down requirements as to vapour and waterproof barriers for the framing and preservative treatment for the lowest horizontal timber in contact with the sub-structure, in order to preserve the durability of the framing against fungal attack.

There can be no criticism of this step and indeed if the surveyor is presented with a survey of a timber framed house, not so designed, he would have no alternative but to advise the engagement of someone competent to check the design, as it is unlikely that any surveyor, not also qualified as an engineer, will make much headway with BS 5268 Code of Practice for the Structural Use of Timber Part 2 1984. On the other hand, there is available a *Design Guide on Timber Frame Housing* published by the Timber Research and Development Association, containing about 270 design and data sheets, embodying the Association's experience in the design and construction of timber frame housing which might prove useful as a rough check, but by no means as a substitute for an engineer's opinion.

Pitched roofs   Mention of the Timber Research and Development Association brings to the fore the benefits which have accrued from the Association's work in the field of pitched roof design. No surveyor carrying out surveys of new or near new properties will have failed to have come across the designs put forward by the Association for making the most economic use of the timber available. The trussed rafters and trussed designs for roofs have been a boon to estate developers and the sight of recognised and approved designs of this nature at the correct spacing is, to some extent, a guarantee of future stability, particularly since in most cases the workmanship of assembly and erection can be examined in the roof-space.

Departures from the norm, such as excessive spacing or a lack of the required bracing between members may put the surveyor on guard and necessitate much further consideration of the design and its ability to transmit loads without undue deformation. As before, it may be necessary to advise a purchaser to take specialist advice on really difficult problems of timber engineering if it is beyond the surveyor's ability to determine the outcome with confidence.

On the other hand defects in workmanship, such as the use of unsatisfactory timber with an excess of knots, poor quality or badly fixed timber connectors giving rise to the possibility of failure or eventual corrosion, or even, as has been seen on occasions, the cutting of a timber to facilitate the running of, for example, an overflow pipe, may allow the surveyor to give more immediate positive advice.

Over the years, some disappointment had been expressed that the Timber Research and Development Association concentrated so much on the design of shallow pitch roof structures which made it impossible to utilise the space within the roof for living accommodation. However, in recent years trussed rafter designs have been introduced for roof structures which incorporate rooms within the roof-space. Pitches have become steeper, but this is probably no bad thing because shallow pitches generally bring additional problems of weather proofing. On the other hand, the formation of rooms in the roof-space as part of the original design may restrict access for inspection to constructional timbers as it does in many old houses.

Flat roofs   Fortunately flat roofs, in view of their propensity to failure if badly designed, are comparatively rarely found in normal two-storey domestic work although they do make an appearance on the larger house, on the taller narrow fronted town house and, of course, they also appear on additions and garages, although sometimes in the latter case the omission of a ceiling tends to reduce the problems encountered, both in performance and on the survey, to manageable proportions. Flat roofs are, however, often encountered these days on blocks of flats.

Faults in flat roofs   The National House Building Council as previously mentioned acknowledges paying out millions of pounds in claims for defective flat roofs before raising its standards in 1980 and there is no shortage in other reports of information on flat roof failures; for example the Building Research Establishment reported in 1972 that of 323

401

Crown buildings with flat roofs, 101 leaked. These latter were no doubt reinforced concrete roofs on framed buildings in many cases, but there are also plenty of examples of very serious failures in flat roofs of timber construction due to incorrect placing of insulation, vapour and water barriers, lack of ventilation and bad detailing to abutments, often necessitating entire renewal of structure and covering within the space of two or three years of the original construction.

Clearly flat roof design requires close attention by the surveyor both on site and to the plans when found on new dwellings. This problem is symptomatic of numerous aspects of modern construction methods relating both to roofs and walls. Waterproofing the external surface is carried out before the structure is dry, which thereby entraps moisture. This moisture coupled with that arising from interstitial condensation produces very damp conditions which even if it does not cause an outbreak of dry rot in unventilated organic material such as timber, timber based products, strawboard or the like, disturbs the dimensional stability of other materials and can cause failure in the structure.

Timber floors   It seems hardly credible, in view of the long standing tradition, but one of the most frequently encountered defects found by the National House Building Council has proved to be failure in joisted floors. The defect was found mainly in comparatively narrow fronted terraced or semi-detached houses and arose from a combination of undue shrinkage and deflection on deep joists used to span from party wall to party wall, poor jointing of trimmer joists to trimming joists and trimmed joists to trimmer, overloading from the partitions and the hot water storage cylinder at first floor level and yet more localised shrinkage due to the heat emanating from the cylinder. The results of the basically bad design giving rise to this combination of circumstances, even apart from the serious danger of eventual collapse, are sagging floors, untidy gaps around, or cracks in, first floor partitions, ill fitting doors and sometimes the precarious loosening of the fixings for the hot water storage cylinder.

The general view of the Council was that, to improve the situation, it was better to use joists of lesser depth spanning shorter distances from main walls to load bearing partitions, to ensure sound jointing around openings in the floor, to avoid load concentrations from the cylinder and to insulate the cylinder effectively and isolate it from the floor. Having regard to the incidence of this reported defect the surveyor will wish to pay particular attention to details of construction for upper floors particularly around the stairwell even apart from the usual matters such as joist sizes, bearings and load distribution.

It is not the purpose of this chapter, to cover all those aspects of design, construction and workmanship which have to be taken into consideration in order to produce a successful building from the structural point of view, let alone in the matter of the finishings and services (since these are matters for books on building construction of which there are many). However, it is hoped that those mentioned so far will be of sufficient magnitude to dispel any lingering suggestion that the survey of a new dwelling is an easy matter.

The factors of quality and durability

As to the visible items such as bricks, tiles or joinery, the surveyor will be relying in the main on his own eyes, but supplemented with information derived from the specification or other information supplied by the contractor or developer. In particular, quality will be uppermost in the surveyor's mind having due regard to the asking price of the property since it is unrealistic to expect top quality materials in a less than top price house. It is sufficient to say that materials are of a reasonable quality having regard to all the factors involved, but of course those materials backed up by a certificate that they comply with a British Standard will tend to reassure the surveyor, within certain limits, of their likelihood to satisfy over a period of time. It is at the very cheapest end of the scale that the surveyor is placed in difficulty and he may find himself having to make sharp comments on, for example, the extremely cheap and shoddy fittings or even just expressing doubt that some new product may not prove the boon that its advertisers would wish us to believe.

Even at the top end of the scale, it is quite astonishing how the surveyor will at times find the poor quality mixed with the good, in total contrast to the image which the developer is hoping to create. The layman cannot usually distinguish between the good and the bad in regard to many building materials and fittings (although the growth of the "do-it-yourself" movement has meant that many have a far better idea of the subject than hitherto, a trend likely to continue) and he employs a surveyor to do just that for him.

Preservative treatment for non durable external joinery

In regard to external joinery such as claddings, window frames, casements and sashes and external door frames, the National House Building Council requires treatment against fungal attack with an approved preservative, or preservative and paint system, except where an approved durable timber is used. This requirement, introduced in 1969, is clearly a sensible one in view of the many failures reported of window joinery due to wet rot. Even on the cheapest house, one would expect nowadays to find joinery manufactured at least to British Standards and, unless made up of one of the durable timbers, treated with preservative.

The Services

As to the services, here again the surveyor will look to materials produced in accordance with British Standards and installations in accordance with relevant Codes of Practice as a recommendation to suitability for the intended purpose and trouble free service for the reasonably foreseeable future.

Hot and Cold Water Services

As to the cold water and drainage services, the surveyor will be able to deal with these himself together with a hot water system not combined with central heating. It is of interest to note that in a schedule setting out important defects selected on a basis of frequency of occurrence multiplied by a points allocation for seriousness, the National House Building Council found that over half of the 13 items included were concerned with either plumbing or drainage, ranging from leaks at the joints of W.C. pans to soil stacks and defective manholes.

Most of the items quoted are of a nature easily ascertainable on inspection, provided the water supply is turned on at the time of the survey, a basic essential, but they are all very vital items which could be the cause of much more serious defects, fungal attack for example, if not caught in time. Defects of this nature will be found by assiduous site inspection and provide material for the schedule of items to be put right before the purchaser moves into occupation in the case of a brand new house, or for which an allowance should be made, in the case of the near new house, off the purchase price.

Of more note here is the consideration of the materials used and the design of the installation. In plumbing installations one must expect to find p.v.c. cisterns and polythene pipes for the cold water system on houses in the cheaper range and even on some medium priced dwellings. The important aspect in this regard is that polythene pipe is to the appropriate British Standard and jointed and supported correctly. Pipes of polythene must not of course be used for hot water installations, so that copper is still the most likely material to be found in service for conveying hot water, although one must expect to find stainless steel becoming increasingly common.

For sanitary pipework above ground the British Standard BS 5572 Code of Practice for Sanitary Pipework provides the main guideline to sound procedure and of course it is to be expected that wastes and soil pipes will nowadays also be, in the main, of plastic to say nothing of gutters and rain-water pipes. The surveyor needs to be familiar with the various types of plastic pipe available and their suitability for use under varying circumstances. BS 5572 provides much information and it would seem that anything not covered by the current edition of 1978 would require very careful consideration indeed and certainly much more than total acceptance of publicity material issued by even the most well-known national companies.

Drainage   In regard to the underground drainage system, much of the information assembled for a consideration of foundations in relation to the sub-soil, will prove essential when the merits or otherwise of the drains are considered. Surveyors will be aware of British Standard Code of Practice C.P. 301, Building Drainage, and perhaps also aware of the difficulties which were experienced in producing the 1971 edition following research work carried out on underground drainage lines in the decade following the publication of the 1950 edition. The conclusions drawn from the research were not universally accepted, so that in the realm of underground drainage a certain amount of confusion exists. Although the National House Building Council's Requirements lay down some minimum standards for pipes and jointing, protection and workmanship, no reference is made to either edition of the Codes and the general idea seems to be that what satisfies the local authority will satisfy the Council. Unfortunately this is not necessarily a guarantee of soundness since the Building Regulations also ignore the Codes and are content with a pious re-statement of a few high-sounding principles which can be interpreted, and indeed are, in practically any way according to the fancies of the local Borough Engineer and Surveyor.

Therefore what is acceptable in one area is not necessarily so in another and, of course, it is always open to the bigger estate developers to produce a convincing case for a novel system which the local authority might have difficulty in resisting in the case of a very large development. The surveyor must therefore be familiar with all the advantages and disadvantages of both the traditional methods and also the new methods, particularly if installed at variance with the Codes, if he is to comment with any degree of confidence on the underground drains.

Fascinating though it is, the subject is far too extensive to cover adequately at this point and it must remain sufficient merely to point the contrast between rigid and flexible pipes, rigid and flexible joints, materials for both pipes and joints with the possibilities of deterioration in both, depth of pipes in ground, loads thereon, support by concrete or granular material, cover, gradients etc., etc. Whatever methods are used, of course, site characteristics will loom very large in the consideration by the surveyor of whether the system is likely to be satisfactory.

Electrical and Central Heating Installations – Tests – Safety

In regard to other service installations, such as electrical and any central heating system, unless the surveyor is an expert or at least confident that he can draw the correct conclusion from any tests he carries out, he should limit himself entirely to factual description. The desirability of tests has already been mentioned but of course, the decision as to whether they are carried out or not, rests, with the client. The surveyor may, of course, wish to reinforce this advice rather heavily in the circumstances of finding much dubious design and construction elsewhere in the property and which suggest an aspect of safety in relation to the services.

It is hoped that the foregoing pages have provided some indication of possible lines to be taken in certain circumstances in the survey of a new or near new house, but they can do no more than this. As in all cases of structural surveys the surveyor's method of approach to his work should be that which will ensure that all aspects of any particular property are covered. Furthermore, the knowledge that it is essential to pursue his inquiries just as far as it is necessary to obtain the answers or to warn his client if it is not possible to do so, will guarantee the production of a reasonable report irrespective of the fee being charged.

In contrast to surveys of old houses, it is considered necessary with surveys of new or near new houses to carry out more than a mere visual inspection in order to provide something of value for the client, and it is hoped that this has, by now, been abundantly demonstrated. A sample report for a new house appears on page 537 as Appendix 4 incorporating the method of treatment suggested in this chapter. The sample report should, as stressed in Chapter 9, be taken as a broad guide only since any report must be tailored to suit the property in question and, in any event, there are a number of different ways of setting out reports to produce the same effect. Each surveyor should decide on the form of report which suits him best for a survey of a new house, as for any other.

Chapter 13
House Buyers' Reports and Valuations

CONTENTS

INTRODUCTION

Initial reaction to launch of RICS House Buyers Report Form 1981

It is hardly surprising that the introduction of any new schemes, particularly those introduced in some haste to a surveying profession already made wary by a spate of adverse cases of negligence against its members, should attract comment. Those who piloted through the first edition of the RICS House Buyers Report Form were, however, understandably taken aback at the volume of criticism. Every aspect of the scheme came under fire from the way the forms were drafted to the nature and extent of the limitations. But the strongest area of concern centred on the basic question; what was the extent of the surveyor's duty to his or her client and, most importantly, what would the Courts make of it?

RICS publication "Buying a House" 1981

Misunderstandings amounting in many cases to bewilderment were not allayed by the pamphlet entitled "Buying a House" published by the Royal Institution of Chartered Surveyors which explained the purpose of the House Buyers Report and Valuation Form at the same time. This said as follows:

> "The difference between this standard form of report and valuation and a structural survey is that the latter is based on a very detailed examination of the house. It is essentially a technical examination and report which can be time-consuming and may involve the occupier in some inconvenience. The RICS standard form of report, however, which is particularly attractive when time is short or economy important, involves a less comprehensive inspection and a concise report, being sufficient to enable a chartered surveyor to give a general opinion on the quality and condition of the fabric. It aims to assist a prospective buyer in deciding upon the soundness or otherwise of the proposed purchase. On the other hand, a structural survey will provide a detailed report on the condition of the property setting out structural and other defects, but would not normally include a valuation."

As a statement this was less than helpful.

Since there are few occasions when time is not short and economy unimportant, the inference deduced from this wording is that the survey for a House Buyers Report answers all questions economically and fully, while the surveyor carrying out a structural survey spends added time looking for what are, in effect, minor defects. The reverse is, of course, the truth. The whole of the time on a structural survey is, or should be, spent in assessing the structure. Finding out how the roof framework is supported and the relationship of outer walls to floors and partitions forms a major task while incidental notes, either room by room or externally, are added as supporting evidence to the main investigation and general conclusions. If a structural surveyor does not concentrate on the structure first and deal with small problems in their due order he is, as already discussed, likely to land himself in trouble.

House Buyers Report Forms and
Structural Surveys

This contrast between the House Buyers Report Form and a structural survey has never been clearly explained to or, indeed, understood by the general public. A number of distinguished surveyors have said that they are in fact hard put to describe the difference between a Structural Survey and a House Buyers Report. A number of building surveyors in particular take the rather gloomy view that the basic requirement of a House Buyers Report Form is to carry out a normal structural survey, putting in outline answers to the questions on the form, mostly by way of description, and including a whole bundle of appendices.

In no other way, say such surveyors, can one be certain that one is free from liability. This viewpoint, however, while understandable to the many practitioners who work in urban areas developed before 1900, has been hotly criticised by others on the grounds that this outlook undermines the whole point of the RICS Scheme which offers, against traditional structural surveys, the benefits of speed and reduced cost. The scheme is, they say, particularly suited to those large inter-war and post-war estates up and down the length of Britain. It is therefore relevant to consider the basic thinking behind the scheme and its origins but to do this it is necessary to go back some way in time.

Origins of the "restricted survey"
Scheme

The clear forerunner of the House Buyers Report and Valuation Form was the Inspectahome Scheme started by Messrs. Jordan Impey & Co. in the late 1970s. Whatever the RICS thought of this scheme, and a large number of members had misgivings, it was, nevertheless, the first real attempt to pinpoint and try to deal with the central problem that has now, with hindsight, become clear. This is the fact that there is a strong and continually growing demand for the services of surveyors and valuers coupled with an equally strong reluctance to pay the level of fees which allow for anything but limited time spent at the property concerned.

The Inspectahome Scheme was considered by the RICS but was thought to be dangerous on the grounds that the inspection did not go far enough. "The Scheme", said the Committee concerned in a press release, "was not comprehensive enough to provide a thorough service to those seeking to establish the condition of a property and it was essential that a full structural survey should be carried out to perform the task in a thorough and professional way." This was in July 1979. A fuller version of the RICS view was released to the public in the September of that year.

RICS Guidance Note on Structural
Surveys

About the same time, the Building Surveyors Division of the RICS was giving thought to the production of a Guidance Note on Structural Surveys. This was launched in December 1979, its production possibly hastened by the introduction of Inspectahome. It was therefore at about this point that the profession began to talk seriously about the implications of a full survey on the one hand and a general inspection and valuation on the other.

At one end of the scale, a building surveyor who has carried out a full structural survey and who was also asked to provide a valuation could, it was felt, perhaps fall into the trap of making too many deductions from his valuation due to defects which might lead to

410

bad advice. At the other end of the scale, a valuer who was asked to carry out a general inspection and valuation might not go far enough in his investigatory inspection which could lead to the risk of a claim. This oil and water situation of surveys and valuations has always been a source of confusion but the doubtful aspect was that the Courts had not at that point been asked to define the duties of a surveyor under the "half way House" type of scheme. They have since done so.

Purpose of the restricted survey scheme

It was the General Practice Division of the RICS which conceived the House Buyers Report and Valuation Scheme with Building Surveying representatives on the Committee. Understandably, they took it as an established fact that there was pressure from the great consumer lobby to produce a scheme which preserved the benefits of a structural survey but was simpler and basically cheaper. Furthermore, there could be an added advantage if a prospective purchaser did not have to pay separate fees to both a Building Society on the one hand and a private surveyor on the other. The Building Societies responded with alacrity.

The Chief Surveyor to the Abbey National Building Society wrote in early 1980 "I believe that there is a real need for an alternative to the structural survey and I consider that there is a moral and practical responsibility on the part of the Building Societies towards mortgage applicants in the survey and valuation sphere. The Building Societies Inspection, Report and Valuation is a vehicle which could be developed for the use of mortgage applicants ... A report and valuation form, designed to have an acceptable balance between a Society's requirements and the need for the applicant could be developed, and the report form could be made standard for all the Societies". The words "a report and valuation form" were significant in this context. He was also to add on another occasion that it was ludicrous for people to rely on £50 or so of professional advice, for the most important transaction in their lives.

Building Society involvement

The next stage was that various Building Societies started discussing and drafting report forms; some Societies offering different "services" and the RICS still bogged down by understandable difficulties came to the view that something must be done fairly quickly. The decisions to be taken were of necessity awkward ones. How should the fee, for example, be calculated; particularly in the light of the findings of the Monopolies Commission in other similar and recent cases? Should the emphasis be on the valuation side with surveying as an adjunct, or on an abbreviated survey with valuation as an adjunct?

Finally, however, the scheme was launched on May 20th 1981 being of mixed background from Inspectahome, public pressure, the attitude of the Building Societies and the aims of the RICS General Practice Division with assistance from the Building Surveyors Division. Certainly, the scheme came as a surprise to most members who, opening their morning paper at the breakfast table suddenly found that this new scheme was launched on the general public with, so far as they were concerned, no consultation to obtain individual views. Reaction varied on the one hand between practitioners who thought that the scheme was dangerous and risky and, worse, retrogressive, and others who said that, whether we liked it or not, the mood of the country was becoming more and more consumer orientated and that a framework had to be found to comply with public needs.

The attitude of this latter group was enormously strengthened by the fact that a recent survey at that time showed that only some two per cent of house buyers procured a structural survey and that this service was, in the main reserved for a minority of purchasers who were buying the most expensive houses. Those practitioners who held that the structural survey was the only answer retorted that added publicity from the RICS (what were our subscriptions paid for for goodness sake?) on the merits of the structural survey and spreading the message of its true value would be far better than rushing to meet a public demand that was, to say the least of it, not necessarily in the best interest of either the house buyer or his surveyor.

It cannot be emphasised enough, however, that the scheme was originally thought out on a deliberate and carefully restricted basis. The objective was first to provide a vehicle for the general practice surveyor to give a report with valuation advice as against a full and time consuming structural survey and secondly to satisfy public demand by offering an alternative option, at a definite saving in money, to house buyers who would not or could not pay for the full or traditional structural survey.

As such the scheme was restricted to houses and bungalows of up to 200 sq. metres or 2,000 sq. ft. in floor area and of not more than three storeys in height. It excluded period properties construed as those built before 1875 and the report form was drafted primarily to satisfy the requirements of houses built since the early 1900s whether terraced, semi-detached or detached in suburban areas. "Three up and two down", as one might say.

However, the carefully worked out limitations of the House Buyers Report Forms were soon forgotten in the rush of events that followed. Building Societies, seeing the commercial potential of offering three different options to their applicants; either a Valuation, a House Buyers Report Form or a "full" Structural Survey pressed the middle option with enthusiasm, and some Societies reproduced the RICS style of report almost exactly but omitted the limiting notes. The report and valuation form came therefore to be offered to all applicants for all types of property of whatever age often without any real explanation of the difference. This has led to problems.

Often the only interview with the applicant when he or she is asked what type of inspection he or she requires is conducted in the office of the Building Society. The work is then referred to a staff or panel surveyor who simply has to answer whether he can carry out the inspection or not. The result is that a number of applicants subsequently wished that they had asked for something other than what was obtained. A large number of surveys in the larger cities and towns are obviously in respect of nineteenth century buildings which, as we have seen, would have been the last type of category envisaged by the RICS as being suitable for House Buyers Reports. Problems were then encountered over converted buildings and it was to deal with the whole aspect of flats of various types that the Flat Buyers Report Form, a much improved version of the original House Buyers Report Form, was introduced.

Original fee scale

The RICS House Buyers Report and Valuation Form was originally tied to a fixed fee scale. On a purchase price of, say, £40,000, the surveyor was entitled to a fee of £102.00 for a post-1945 house, £115.00 for a house built after the First World War and £128.00 for a house built before that time. The scale has now long been abandoned since it disappeared with the abolition of scale fees in general but, the scale, which was inflexible, is little mourned. In fact, scale fees still have relevance since House or Flat Buyers Reports are often linked to Building Society Valuations and agreement of fees with the client bear in mind the scale valuation fee of the Society.

ISVA Home Buyers' Standard Valuation and Survey Report

Subsequent to the introduction of the RICS House Buyers Report, the ISVA produced their own Home Buyers Standard Valuation and Survey Report. Like the RICS Forms, the ISVA Forms have also undergone some modifications but when the RICS Flat Buyers Report Forms were introduced the ISVA was content for a time to allow their Home Buyers Report Forms to serve for both houses and flats. The form's use for both purposes was recognised in the Guidance Notes where it was stated that "the state of external repair and the repair of the parts (including the services) used in common are relevant to the degree of financial responsibility undertaken by the purchaser of an individual flat. In the circumstances, the nature and extent of the inspection to be made beyond the confines of the flat in question will need to be clearly identified and agreed beforehand ..." Now, however, the ISVA have introduced their own Flat Buyers Standard Valuation and Survey Report Form.

For reasons which have already been discussed, the House, Flat and Home Buyers Reports of the two Institutions are now used for properties of ages and types far different from those originally contemplated. It is perhaps interesting to read in the Guidance Notes that while "No specific recommendation is made as to the circumstances in which the ISVA Home Buyers Standard Report may be offered ... it is considered unsuitable for new dwellings under construction, for dwellings containing more than ten rooms in all and for period properties. Sub-standard property may be included although special care will be needed to identify the respects in which it is not of conventional construction".

RICS & ISVA Survey Report Forms

The package of documents issued by each Institution include Guidance Notes, Terms of Engagement and the report forms. The RICS produce separate report and valuation forms for houses and flats and the Conditions of Engagement are both separate and in each case printed on the inner side of the first page. The RICS consider it so important to emphasise that the House Buyers

413

Report and Valuation is not a structural survey that this information is printed at the head of page 1.

The ISVA Home and Flat Buyers' Standard Valuation and Survey Report Forms include the Building Society/Bank supplement sheet and applies to both houses and flats.

RICS HOUSE BUYERS REPORT AND VALUATION (4th Edition)
CONDITIONS OF ENGAGEMENT

Before discussing the RICS and ISVA Report Forms themselves it is first necessary to emphasise than, since the inspection is proclaimed as being less comprehensive than a full structural survey, the Conditions of Engagement are of vital importance and the client must consent to these to ensure that a binding contract is set up.

What the surveyor will provide Originally the Conditions of Engagement were set out in nine separate clauses which have now, in the current fourth edition of the RICS House Buyers Report Form been increased to eleven. Under Clause 1 the Surveyor, "who will be a Chartered Surveyor or an Incorporated Valuer, will advise the Client as to his opinion of the state of repair and condition of, and the value of, the property specified by the Client on the standard form of House Buyers Report and Valuation published on behalf of the Royal Institution of Chartered Surveyors". This Clause is of obvious generality but it is intended to focus the attention of the Client on the particular report form involved. It is interesting to note the increasing association between the RICS and ISVA since the first report forms were produced.

The scope of the valuation Clause 2 is interesting. "Unless otherwise specifically agreed, the surveyor will advise whether or not the price agreed for the property reflects the current open market value with vacant possession taking into account its repair and condition and market conditions generally." This clause pre-supposes that the price agreed is known to the valuer. In Building Society Valuations the price that has been agreed is always disclosed whereas for valuations required by Banks this is not necessarily the case. Accordingly, it is desirable for the surveyor/valuer to press for information as to the agreed price.

Work to be reasonable Clause 3 "save as hereinafter provided, the surveyor will carry out such work as is reasonable in his professional judgement, bearing in mind the limitations of the inspection" appears to be rather bland but is nevertheless the basis of the contract should any action for negligence be contemplated. It does postulate the judgement of the ordinary general practice surveyor or valuer inferred in the words "reasonable in his professional judgement" rather than any specialist skills.

Inspection of surfaces Clause 4 which has been retained intact in the fourth edition states "the Surveyor will inspect as much of the surface areas as is practicable, and will lift loose floorboards and trap doors where accessible, but he will be under no obligation to raise fixed floorboards or to inspect those areas of the property that are covered, unexposed or are not readily accessible. Inspection will therefore exclude both the roofspace, if there is no or no reasonably accessible roof hatch, and the outer surfaces of the roof if they cannot be readily seen. Similarly, inaccessible flat roofs over three metres (10 ft.) above ground level will not be inspected". This clause is designed to make it quite clear to the client what the surveyor can or cannot be expected to see and it is interesting to note that the introduction of the three metre ladder also referred to in the RICS Guidance Note on Residential Structural Surveys is now universal and any surveyor without such a ladder would be considered negligent if he failed to spot some accessible defect from this height.

Testing of services only if specifically instructed

Clause 5 states that "the Surveyor will not be responsible for arranging the testing of services, unless specifically instructed to do so. Specialist tests can be arranged at an additional fee". This has been introduced in the fourth edition as a separate clause whereas previously the first sentence was included at the end of clause 4. The fourth edition therefore expects that the surveyor/valuer will be able to call upon expert specialist help in carrying out tests should his client so desire. The term "services" might be open to several interpretations and has not, so far as is known, been discussed in the Courts but would presumably for houses cover drains, gas, electrical, cold water, hot water and central heating installations. The question of services to flats will be considered later.

Covered, unexposed or inaccessible areas not to be inspected

Clause 6 is, in effect, a saving clause familiar to many surveyors but not now included as a requirement of the surveyor's insurers. It says "Except where the contrary is stated, parts of the structure and of the woodwork which are covered, unexposed or inaccessible, will not be inspected, and will be assumed to be sound and in good repair". This, as a Condition of Engagement at the outset, or in other words as a term of the contract, has obvious legal force.

No opinion on uninspected parts or list of minor defects

Clause 7 states "The Report will not purport to express an opinion about or advise upon the condition of uninspected parts and should not be taken as making any implied representation or statement about such parts, nor will it list minor defects which do not materially affect the value of the property. Any such defects that may be referred to should not imply that the property is free from other such defects". This clause which is at first glance a little obscure to the surveyor has the clear imprint of legal advice. The validity of the clause does however depend upon the surveyor not making statements which could imply comments about those parts of the property or structure that he cannot see and which could be unwise.

Exclusiveness to client, mortgagee, etc.

Clause 8 is what might be described as the "for your eyes only" limitation. The clause states that "The Report is provided for the sole use of the named Client and, where the Surveyor is so notified, his Mortgagee, and is confidential to the Client and his professional advisers. The Surveyor accepts responsibility to the Client alone for the stated purposes that the report will be prepared with the

415

skill, care and diligence reasonably to be expected of a competent Chartered Surveyor or Incorporated Valuer, but accepts no responsibility whatsoever to any person other than the Client himself. Any such person relies upon the Report at his own risk". Whether in fact the contents of the Report can be limited in this way or not is a matter of legal discussion, but as clause 8 does, in fact, state this particular limitation as a Condition of Engagement it therefore, presumably, has legal force. The surveyor of course needs to be aware of the problems in this connection that relate to structural survey reports.

Assumptions about the property   In Clause 9 four assumptions are made; firstly that no deleterious or hazardous materials or techniques have been used and that it is impracticable to comment on the state of any wall ties; secondly, that the house is not subject to any unusual or especially onerous restrictions, encumbrances or outgoings and that a good title can be shown; thirdly, that the house and its value are unaffected by any matters which would be revealed by a Local Search (or Search in Scotland) and Replies to the Usual Enquiries, or by a Statutory Notice, and that neither the property, nor its condition, nor its use, nor its intended use, is or will be unlawful; and fourthly that inspection of those parts which have not been inspected would neither reveal material defects nor cause the surveyor to alter the valuation materially. Finally, the clause states that the surveyor will be under no duty to verify these assumptions.

Clause 9 illustrates as no other clause can do, the changing scene in which the surveyor and valuer operates. Under the similar clause 8 in the earlier edition, High Alumina Cement Concrete and Calcium Chloride additives are specifically mentioned but have been sensibly discarded so that "deleterious materials" are included as a general term. Such a phrase would presumably include such unfortunate horrors as a cavity fill which burns issuing toxic fumes. It is interesting that under this clause wall ties are specifically mentioned but it is confidently expected that this clause will change during coming years as each new edition of the Conditions of Engagement is produced.

The fee   Clause 10 "The Client will pay the Surveyor the agreed fee for the Report and Valuation, and any expressly agreed disbursements" expresses a sentiment with which all surveyors and valuers would applaud. It should be noted however that any disbursements should be prior agreed in writing.

Conditions to be agreed in writing   Finally, Clause 11 has been introduced in the fourth edition and states that "these (above) terms to be agreed in writing". The introduction of this clause suggests a sad history whereby the Conditions of Engagement have not always been agreed between the Surveyor and the Client with consequent misunderstandings on one or both sides as to what had been contemplated. The purpose of the clause is to draw the attention of the parties to the importance of agreeing terms.

416

RICS FLAT BUYERS REPORT AND VALUATION
(4th Edition)
CONDITIONS OF ENGAGEMENT

Inspection confined to flat, common parts and garage(s)

The Conditions of Engagement for the Flat Buyers Report and Valuation are similar to those of the House Buyers set out above with some obvious amendments and additions. Clause 3 of the Flat Buyers Conditions of Engagement states that "Save as hereinafter provided, the Surveyor will inspect the subject flat, together with the related common parts, and any relevant garage(s). Other flats or property will not be inspected, the object being to advise on the standard of construction and maintenance of the specific flat, indicating repairs required to maintain the fabric of the flat. The surveyor will carry out such work as is reasonable in his professional judgement bearing in mind the limitations of the inspection". This clause alerts the client to the fact that, if he did not already know it, the surveyor will not inspect every flat in the block but only the "subject" flat.

The provision that the object of the inspection is to "advise on ... repairs required to maintain the fabric of the flat" obviously gives the surveyor a wide freedom of action which is underlined by the last sentence of this clause. Obviously, it would be extremely difficult for brief guidelines to be more specific than this due to the enormous variety of flats. This clause does however, put a strong professional duty upon the surveyor to be aware of the extent of his or her client's liability for the boundaries of the flat comprising ceilings, walls and floors together with the extent of the maintenance liability for external walls, roofs, common parts, services and environs.

Limitation of roof inspection

One of the main problems in the inspection of flats concerns the roof or roofs particularly where these are of a complex nature and where the block of flats is a large one. This difficulty is dealt with under clause 5 which states "inspection will exclude the roof space unless there is an access hatch from the common parts or arrangements have been made by the purchaser for access through the top floor flat to an access hatch. Such roof inspection will be restricted only to that part of the roof over the subject flat to which access has been made available. If a separate visit is necessary an additional charge will be made. The inspection will also exclude outer surfaces of the roof or elevations if they cannot be readily seen. Similarly, inaccessible flat roofs over 3 metres (10 ft) above ground level will not be inspected". This clause is a helpful one to the surveyor/valuer since it overcomes the problem where the client assumes that the surveyor will, as part of his or her duty, gain access to other flats as part of the service. This clause envisages the fact that where access to the top surface of the main roof is impossible without entry through another flat, and where an inspection is obviously highly desirable that firstly the client has the duty of obtaining access and, should a further visit be necessary an additional charge will be made.

417

ISVA HOME BUYERS STANDARD VALUATION AND SURVEY REPORT – TERMS OF ENGAGEMENT

Standard of work and exclusiveness to client etc.

The printed Terms of Engagement for the ISVA Home Buyers Standard Valuation and Survey Report are not numbered and differ in form and content from the Conditions of the RICS Form. The first clause is as follows:

"Responsibility is accepted in the preparation of this report for the skill and diligence reasonably to be expected of a competent surveyor and valuer but the information it contains is for the confidential information only of client(s) for whom it is prepared and of any Building Society, Bank or other lender to whom written application for a mortgage advance has been made or will be made within twenty-eight days after the date of this report."

This clause at the outset of the Terms of Engagement shows the value placed upon it by the ISVA. The guidance notes suggest that the client is asked to sign the printed Terms of Engagement to which the member should add his own signature. One signed copy should then be handed or sent to the client and the other signed copy retained. Thus the client is identified and this "for your eyes only" clause has due force.

Purpose of the Report

"The sole purpose of the report is to provide a concise and readable account of the general condition of the property to which it relates, to assess its value and to identify essential repairs. Dimensions and data of a technical nature are excluded unless such information is a necessary element of the advice to be given or recommendations to be made."

Under this clause dimensions of rooms are specifically excluded whereas under the RICS Form such exclusion is inferred by the setting out of the printed form. Presumably, "data of a technical nature" applies to descriptions ranging from roof trusses to services which could not only take up too much space but unbalance the main message of the report.

Extent of the inspection

"The property was examined as it stood, and it must be assumed, unless otherwise stated, that furniture, fixtures, fittings, carpets and other floor coverings have not been moved and the under-floor areas have not been inspected except (with the vendor's consent) to the limited extent permitted by the lifting of un-covered and loose floorboards (if any). Flues have not been examined. No opinion can be expressed on, or responsibility accepted for, the condition of those parts of the property which remain hidden, inaccessible or unexposed. In this context, (i) the adequacy and condition of wall ties, if any, is not known, and (ii) the extent, efficiency and condition of any thermal insulation (other than in any roof void where easily accessible) has been disregarded unless the material used and/or the manner in which it has been injected/installed is readily visible and obviously defective to a material degree."

418

Unlike the RICS form, this clause deals with the problems of furniture and fixtures. It defines the extent to which the surveyor/valuer is expected to proceed in examining timber flooring and the provision relating to the vendor's consent is a cogent one to remind both surveyor and purchaser that the vendor has the right to a voice in the matter as well.

Inspection with aid of binoculars and ladder

"Roofs, chimneys, parapets and gutters, together with projections and elevations above first-floor level, have been examined externally, where visible, with the aid of binoculars where required. Only reasonably accessible roofs or parts of roofs over single-storey structures not exceeding 10 ft in height have been examined with the aid of a ladder."

The introduction of binoculars is hardly new in surveying terms since binoculars are an essential item of equipment included in the RICS Guidance Note for Residential Structural Surveys but nevertheless their inclusion here makes it mandatory for ISVA Surveyor/Valuers to carry binoculars with them. Woe betide them if they leave them in the office.

Exclusion of foundation inspection and drain test

"Foundations have not been exposed and unless instructions have been given for a drains test, drains have not been examined because no reliable opinion on condition can be given unless a test is applied."

It might seem at first sight unnecessary to explain to a client that foundations will not be exposed but the writers have known cases where clients have assumed that surveyors have some magic technique for examining foundations. This is perfectly understandable. The fact that the surveyor and valuer does not examine or comment upon foundations and that he obtains his notes to comment upon the stability of a structure from above ground level only, must seem very odd to a number of lay people. The comment that "no reliable opinion on condition (of drains) can be given unless a test is applied" is absolutely accurate and well worth stating.

Exclusion of lifts, escalators etc. and security systems

"No responsibility is accepted for the efficiency or state of repair of any lift, escalator or other form of mechanised transit system or any security system or security arrangements."

This clause is introduced due to the need to cater for flats and is self-explanatory.

Inclusion of cold water storage cistern but exclusion of central heating and hot water systems, gas and electrical installations

"The condition of any cold water storage tank has been checked. No assessment has been made of the suitability, method of installation, condition, efficiency or capacity of any central heating or hot water system, boiler or other equipment. The safety, standard or workmanship and state of repair of the gas and electrical installations are also outside the scope of this report."

This clause is a later amendment to the original terms which stated that "the flow of hot and cold water supplies (including the condition of any cold water storage tank(s)) has been checked ..." which was of extremely doubtful value since it implied that the surveyor/valuer would turn taps on and off but that would end his involvement. This rather redundant exercise has now been deleted from the current Terms of Engagement and the clause is now quite specific.

Inclusion of garages but exclusion of other separate structures and leisure installations

"Garages and other outbuildings wholly or mainly built of brick, stone or concrete have been included in the survey subject to the limitations on inspection previously described. The existence of other separate structures, if any, (e.g. greenhouses, sheds, workshops, summer houses) and leisure installations (e.g. swimming pools, tennis courts, ponds, lakes and water courses, together with ancillary accommodation/equipment have been taken into account only for the purpose of completing section 15 and their state of repair is specifically excluded from this report."

This clause suggests that the ISVA Home Buyers Standard Valuation and Survey Report will be extensively used for quite large properties. In the event that this is so it is certainly wise to deal with the question of "leisure installations" since the assessment of swimming pools (to say nothing of saunas) is a specialist matter and the surveyor/valuer is well-advised to make no comment except to suggest the need for further advice.

Boundaries included but exclusion of paths, drives etc.

"Readily visible, significant defects to boundary structures (walls, fences, entrance gates) have been noted, but the condition of drives, hard standings, terraces, paths, steps and garden structures (e.g. screen or retaining walls, inner gates and fences, tanks, butts and wells) is not within the scope of the survey."

In the original Guidance Notes, it stated that boundary structures "have been examined only to the extent necessary to establish their stability" but this clause, presumably intended to separate comments on condition from those on ownership has wisely been dropped. The provision to exclude drives, hard standings etc. is to exclude the bulk of description which could apply, say, to a relatively small 1920s house with a large garden and attractive environs. The report might well appear to be totally unbalanced in that the environs would take up much too much space and importance.

Contrast with structural survey

"The examination carried out differs from a full structural survey in that, although no lesser degree of care has been exercised, inspection has been restricted to the identification of major deficiencies or failures as distinct from items of disrepair which cannot reasonably be classified as serious. Specific reference to any repairs coming within the latter category shall not be taken as implying that the property is necessarily free from other defects which cannot be reasonably classified as serious."

This clause tries hard to explain to the client the difference between an ISVA Home Buyers Standard Valuation and Survey Report and a "full structural survey". It appears to get into the same tangle as the wording used by the RICS in this connection but the point will not be laboured. It has been dealt with elsewhere.

Age and character, deleterious materials etc.

"Finally, observations on condition take into account the age and character of the property and the building practices and methods prevailing at the time of construction, but it has been assumed (unless the contrary is stated) that the property is asbes-

420

tos free and that (i) no deleterious or unsuitable materials have been used in its construction; (ii) those parts that have not been inspected by virtue of the exclusions contained in these Terms of Engagement and in this report do not contain defects in the quality, or in the suitability, of the materials used, or in structural design or in repair, such as materially to affect the valuation."

It is as well for it to be pointed out in the Terms of Engagement that observations on condition take into account the age and character of the property and the building practices and methods prevailing at the time of construction. A surveyor/valuer will often reassure his client concerning defects to an older property. The client may nevertheless be taken aback if he or she is used to new property only to find distortion in roofs and walls, uneven plasterwork and draught from windows. Otherwise this clause which has been extended from that in the original Terms of Engagement rather shows the hand of the lawyer.

Exclusion of checks on title, use, outstanding notices etc.

"Intending purchasers or their legal advisers, will be deemed to have satisfied themselves that, inter alia, the conveyance or transfer, lease or other deed does not contain onerous restrictions or covenants, that a good title can be adduced and that the usual enquiries are made for the purpose of ensuring that there are no outstanding statutory notices affecting the repair, use or enjoyment of the property and that its use or intended use does not conflict with any statute, regulation or planning provision."

The above clause is another comparatively recent addition and its incorporation in the Terms of Engagement is to make it quite clear where the liability of the surveyor/valuer ends and that of the client or legal adviser commences. There have been a number of cases relating to problems of enquiry particularly in the case of flats and this clause is no doubt designed to make it clear where the responsibility for making enquiries lies.

The current Terms of Engagement issued by the ISVA illustrate, when compared to the original terms, how the field of the surveyor/valuer is constantly changing. Some of the new provisions were probably never thought of when the original terms were drafted such as the condition of wall ties or thermal insulation but other additions such as the exclusion of flues from examination are likely to have been the result of experience. One wonders whether the addition of lakes and water courses to swimming pools, tennis courts and ponds is also the result of experience and if so, the imagination boggles.

ISVA FLAT BUYERS' STANDARD VALUATION AND SURVEY REPORT

Terms of Engagement

The printed Terms of Engagement for the ISVA Flat Buyers' Standard Valuation and Survey Report are, as in the case of the Home Buyers' Report, not numbered and follow the same format although there are a number of necessary modifications. The first of these is as follows:-

"It may not be reasonably practicable to identify as such, flats which are of timber framed, concrete framed or steel framed construction."

With the bewildering range of flats whether purpose built or converted of various era's, one would have thought that if this clause was to be included at all, it might reasonably be taken further but it does serve to point out that identification of the structural elements may not be practicable under certain circumstances.

Modifications

The clause in the Home Buyers' Report dealing with the matter of the inspection with the aid of binoculars and ladder has been modified as follows:-

"The state of repair of the property (Being a block of flats or any complex of dwellings or residential or other building(s)) of which the flat forms part has not been inspected except where the structure of the flat is integral. To that extent only, roofs, chimneys, parapets and gutters, together with projections and elevations have been examined externally where visible from ground level. Where the flat is at ground level, reasonably accessible roofs or parts of roofs over single storey structures not exceeding ten feet in height have been examined with the aid of a ladder." "Foundations have not been exposed and drains have not been examined".

It should be noted that it is stated specifically that drains have not been examined. There would appear to be slight conflict with clause 8.2 where rainwater goods, soil and waste pipes need comment and clause 10.5 where foul drains (main or other) suggest, according to the space allocated to this item, reasonably detailed comment. Presumably the clause is meant to cover those drain runs that are hidden below ground.

Common parts

The question of common parts is dealt with as follows:-

"To the extent that access to the flat is by way of staircases and passage ways used in common, the apparent condition of these common parts has, where relevant, been taken into account for valuation purposes. No responsibility is accepted for the efficiency or state of repair of any lift, escalator or other form of mechanised transit system or any security system or security arrangements."

The clause relating to the cold water storage cistern in the Home Buyers' Report together with the exclusion of central heating, hot water systems and gas and electrical installations has been retained intact with the amendment that "the condition of any cold water storage tank within the flat has been checked." This again might conflict with the provisions of clause 10.3 services (water) where the surveyor and valuer should presumably inspect the rising main and cold water storage cistern in the roofspace where this serves the flat in question and possibly other flats as well.

422

Exclusions   Finally, the Terms of Engagement state as follows:-
"Intending purchasers, or their legal advisors, will be deemed
to have satisfied themselves that

(*a*)   The lease or other deed does not contain onerous restrictions
or covenants.

(*b*)   A good title can be adduced and the usual enquiries are made
for the purpose of ensuring that there are no outstanding
statutory notices affecting the repair, use or enjoyment of the
flat and that its use or intended use does not conflict with any
statute, regulation or planning provision.

(*c*)   The property of which the flat forms part is adequately insured under comprehensive terms or such other terms as are
deemed acceptable having regard to the provisions of the
lease and otherwise, (including the requirements of any
lender).

(*d*)   The lease includes provision for management arrangements
that are satisfactory both in terms of effectiveness and cost.

(*e*)   Enquiries are made to establish whether or not any large
items of expenditure are to be anticipated within 5 years.

(*f*)   The landlords are not in breach of any obligation to their
tenants which may give rise to the appointment of managers
by the Court under Part 11 of the Landlord and Tenant Act
1987 ("the Act").

(*g*)   No notices have been served under Part I of the Act
(qualifying tenant's rights of first refusal on a relevant disposal).

(*h*)   No notices have been served under Part III of the Act
(qualifying tenant's right to acquire the landlord's interest
without the latter's consent).

(*i*)   No application has been made to vary the terms of the lease
under Part IV of the Act.

(*j*)   All relevant information is disclosed relating to service
charges (Part V of the Act) and otherwise (Parts VI and VII of
the Act.

FORMS FOR THE RICS HOUSE BUYERS REPORT AND VALUATION

Fourth edition revisions   The fourth edition of the House Buyers Report and Valuation
Forms issued by the RICS is substantially similar to its predecessors
amended in minor respects only such as the introduction of item 6;
"Personal Community Charge, per person".

Descriptive clauses   The forms have thirty-five clauses, the first seven of which are
informative or descriptive. The first three clauses deal with the
name and address of the client, the address of the property inspected
and the date of the inspection, while clause 4 deals with weather
conditions. A common view among surveyors, in relation to the
weather, is that if the inspection is carried out in pouring rain the
client or ultimately the judge might have some pity on the surveyor
in the event of an error but it is considered dubious to take this

sanguine view. It is more likely that this clause would have effective force if, in the event of heavy snow lying on the house and grounds that some element of liability in examining roof claddings on the one hand or discovering inspection chambers on the other might be relieved. Such limitations should in any event be confirmed in writing elsewhere in the report.

Clause 5 deals with tenure and tenancies while clause 7 invites a brief description of the property in terms firstly of age and type, secondly of any unusual factors regarding location, and thirdly, accommodation. The printed note on unusual factors suggests remote (position), steep hill, liability to flooding etc. but there seems to be a certain confusion and thought at this point. A steep hill to the surveyor/valuer suggests the possibility of structural movement while it is doubtful if liability to flooding should appear under the heading of "description". Any signs of structural movement due to a steep hill or flooding should certainly be dealt with elsewhere in the report.

Clauses for the structure

The main heading of "STRUCTURE" carries with it eight separate clauses. These comprise chimney stacks, flashings and soakers (clause 8), roofs separated into two sections; exterior and roofspaces (clause 9), parapets, parapet gutters, valley gutters (clause 10), gutters, down pipes, gullies where visible (clause 11) and main walls (clause 12). The final three clauses under the main heading are damp-proof course and sub-floor ventilation (clause 13), external joinery including window and door frames (clause 14) and exterior decorations and paintwork (clause 15).

Apart from the roofspaces, accessible internally, the term "STRUCTURE" relates, broadly, to the exterior. Although internal partitions, chimney breasts and floors might reasonably be regarded as part of the structure, nevertheless these are relegated to a later heading.

Difficulties with the layout for structural items

There are two difficulties in this form of layout. The first is that, in order to inspect structural items with any degree of adequacy, the surveyor/valuer has to complete his full inspection before completing the section on main walls (item 12). An example of why this must be so is the familiar case of the flank wall of a semi-detached house which has moved outwards to a substantial degree affecting the internal stability of ceilings, partitions, staircase and flooring. Accordingly, to adopt the House Buyers Report and Valuation Form simply as a questionnaire to be filled in in the order of items set out without a backward glance is not, obviously, desirable, but to be fair the RICS never intended that procedure should be linked with format.

The other difficulty, which is equally cogent, is that the numbered sections and sub-sections occupy somewhat similar spacings so that gutters, down pipes and gullies (clause 11) might, in many cases, have a disproportionate amount of space while main walls (clause 12) might well have insufficient space. Having said this, one should add that in many cases of post-war low rise houses, the layout and spacing of the form will prove perfectly satisfactory but in other cases, mainly earlier properties in town or city centres,

424

they may not. In the latter case surveyors have found ways to overcome this problem which will be dealt with later in this chapter.

Clauses for the interior

Under the heading "INTERNALLY" there are nine separate clauses. The first three relate to main elements in the structure such as ceilings, walls and partitions (clause 16), fireplaces, flues and chimney breasts (clause 17) and floors (clause 18). Here again the space devoted to each clause is somewhat similar. The final clauses relate to dampness (clause 19), internal joinery—including doors, staircases and built-in fitments (clause 20), internal decorations (clause 21), cellars and vaults (clause 22), woodworm, dry rot and other timber defects (clause 23) and thermal insulation (clause 24). With this section, particularly if there are no cellars, vaults or timber defects, space is not at such a premium. The surveyor/ valuer should remember, however, for the sake of completeness that the section of the report headed "INTERNALLY" may have to include a number of items not specifically referred to in print. A curious omission is windows, for example. External joinery, including window frames, is mentioned under clause 14 while internal joinery, including doors, staircases and built-in fitments, are mentioned in clause 20. Windows themselves, which occupy a good deal of descriptive space in any type of report are not specifically mentioned.

Clauses for the services

Under the heading of "SERVICES" five clauses are included ranging from electricity (clause 25), gas (clause 26), cold water, plumbing and sanitary fittings (clause 27), hot water and heating (clause 28) and underground drainage (clause 29). A sub-note to this section of the House Buyers Report makes it clear that the services have only been inspected visually where they were accessible and tests have not been applied. It also makes it clear that standards and adequacy of installations can only be ascertained as a result of a test by an appropriate specialist and it states that a general comment only is made under clauses 25 to 29 inclusive.

Presumably the inspection is limited to description, albeit brief, a record of any obvious signs of shortcomings noted and recommendations for test(s). A sub-note to clause 28, hot water and heating, says that "other than balanced flue outlets, internal heating appliances normally require a flue liner, but a visual inspection does not always reveal that one has been fitted" but the importance of a lining to an old flue is such that it would be as well if the need for further enquiry or investigation be carried out by the client.

Otherwise some demarcation line problems of a minor nature exist between items 11, gutters, down pipes, gullies where visible and item 29 underground drainage, since this section is divided into two separate parts (a) foul drainage and section (b) surface water drainage. A sub-note says that inspection covers have only been raised where visible and possible and this suggests that the surveyor/valuer should remove such covers to discharge his duty.

General clauses

The final clauses in the RICS House Buyers Report and Valuation under the heading "GENERAL" relate firstly to garage(s) and out-building(s) (clause 30), the site (clause 31), Building

425

Regulations, Town Planning, Roads, Statutory, Mining, Environmental matters and Services (clause 32), Summary and Recommendations (clause 33) and lastly Valuation (clause 34). At the end of the final page the Limitations set out under clause 9 of the Conditions of Engagement are repeated.

The sub-note to item 30 (garage(s) and out-building(s)) should not be overlooked since it states that "comments are restricted to important defects only. Other buildings, swimming pools, tennis courts, etc. are excluded". This comment is less than specific and it is doubtful how much legal force this sub-note carries. It will be preferable for such a clause to be contained within the Conditions of Engagement since, as we have seen, such a clause is included in the ISVA Terms of Engagement.

Under clause 31, the site, a sub-clause says that "general reference is made and only significant defects in boundary fences, walls, retaining walls, paths and drives are reported. Reference to flooding, tree roots, and other potential hazards is included where applicable". Here again one can see why the ISVA devote such care to limiting the surveyor's duty on the environs. Clause 31 as it stands leads to some perplexity. What for example is a "significant defect"? Obviously a high brick boundary wall that is about to collapse is defective to a significant degree but does weathered pointing count as a "significant defect", or not?

This point is not so carping as it sounds since many properties will have complex boundaries in different ownership of various types ranging from brick to close boarded or other wood fencing panels and the description of defects may take up considerable space. Presumably a general note such as "maintenance is needed to boundaries" would suffice with the warning that ownership should be investigated but when one considers that the Environs are contained within the short space of the Site (clause 31) with all the problems of terraces, trees, drives and retaining walls, the Conditions of Engagement could be more specific in what is expected of the surveyor/valuer.

FORMS FOR THE RICS FLAT BUYERS REPORT AND VALUATION

Fourth edition revisions and descriptive clauses

The RICS Flat Buyers Report and Valuation Forms (fourth edition), like their predecessors, follow the format of the House Buyers Forms. Clause 7 (description) is enlarged to five sub-sections to describe whether a flat is purpose built, converted or self-contained or otherwise, the date of conversion, the number of flats in the block, number of storeys and the floor on which the flat is situated. The surveyor/valuer should also state whether access is provided by staircase and/or lift and include a description of the garage and outbuildings that relate to the particular flat under consideration.

Clauses for the structure and interior

Clauses 8 to 28 follow the similar headings contained in the House Buyers Report and Valuation Forms with the proviso that the internal headings 16 to 28 are applicable to the subject flat only. Under "services" however, some obvious modifications have been made to cover clause 29 (common services including central heating, hot water and cold water main services), clause 30 (drainage), clause 31 (lifts) and clause 32 (entrance door and other security system(s), T.V. aerials). Finally, the general items include common parts (clause 33), garages and out-building(s) (applicable to the flat only) (clause 34) and the site (clause 35). Hot water and central heating, together with cold water are separated between items 28 for sole use of the flat and item 29 common services. In the former case a sub-note says that the installation would be inspected but not tested and in the latter case the installations have not been inspected. Under item 30, drainage, surface water drainage is specifically included (as it may be to soakaways or other form of system) but it is difficult to explain why this clause appears in the Flat Buyers and not the House Buyers Report and Valuation Form.

General clauses   The final clauses under the RICS Flat Buyers Report and Valuation format are comprehensive. Under "GENERAL" common parts (clause 33), garages and out-buildings (applicable to the flat only) clause 34 and the site (clause 35) are included as is the clause dealing with Building Regulations, Town Planning etc. (clause 36). A new clause 37 dealing with Fire Precautions and Means of Escape alerts the surveyor/valuer to this important aspect of the inspection.

It is generally considered that clause 38 dealing with management arrangements is an excellent one. It sets out in printed terms the steps that should be taken by the legal adviser to look into the aspects of management. Should the surveyor obtain answers to oral enquiries which might be assumed to be correct for the purpose of the report, nevertheless these should be checked by the client's legal adviser.

Finally, clause 39 deals with deleterious materials which is a repeat of clause 10 in the Conditions of Engagement while questions 40 and 41 Summary and Recommendations and Valuation complete the work of the surveyor.

The limitations to the surveyor/valuer's inspection are again set out under clause 42. These again repeat the exclusion clauses that relate to deleterious materials but, as an interesting note, also exclude cladding fixing.

FORMS FOR THE ISVA HOME BUYERS STANDARD VALUATION AND SURVEY REPORT

Descriptive and environmental clauses   The ISVA Home Buyers' Standard Valuation and Survey Report Forms commence in a very similar manner to those of the RICS. Similar information on the property, name and address of the client and the date of inspection is followed by "climatic" or "physical" restrictions (if any) by which, according to a sub-note, such items as snow, dangerous structures, property that is vacant, occupied, furnished or part furnished, locked or otherwise inaccessible, is to be

427

miscellaneous information should be included on supplementary sheets. In the former case the report form if completed with single line answers can look grudging, while in the latter case, a proliferation of supplementary information can not only look confusing but destroy the purpose of the forms.

If the surveyor/valuer merely records defects the forms are likely to have an unbalanced effect thus under clause 9 (roof-exterior) of the RICS House Buyers Report:

"Some tiles are uneven and some are broken and the bituminous felt covering between the tiled roofs is wrinkled but evidently watertight"

might be re-stated as follows:

"There are two separate roof structures of pitched design, the roofslopes being covered with plain machine made clay tiles with half round tiles to hips and ridges. The two structures are separated by a small central flat roof formed of timber covered with bituminous felt which is wrinkled but evidently watertight. Slight unevenness of the tiles was noted to the roofslope over the garden elevation and some tiles are uneven to the eaves of this same roofslope but the condition is basically acceptable. Six tiles are broken to the roofslope over the front elevation where the T.V. aerial was recently fitted."

Again, under "roofspaces"

"The tiles are laid on battens nailed to timber rafters of conventional pattern with an underlay of roofing felt. The rafters are supported by TRADA type timber trusses comprising principal rafters, horizontal beams at the head and base, each truss having three pairs of angled struts. Hip braces are evidently original but additional braces have been added to the trusses fairly recently to strengthen them against wind and storm damage. Joints between truss members are formed with galvanised metal connectors and the condition is fair. The roofing felt is torn at one point over the access hatch but this is a minor matter. It was not possible to inspect the timbers below the felt covering to the small flat roof."

Similarly, under clause 12 (Main Walls) the following:

"There is evidence of some minor shortcomings due to haste in workmanship but the basic condition is fair."

This might be better re-stated as

"The main walls are of cavity design with external facings to the outer skin formed of stock bricks with red brick decoration to external angles, window and door heads and sides. The inner skins to the cavity walls are, judging from the main roofspace, likely to be formed of blockwork. There is evidence of minor shortcomings due to haste in workmanship but the basic condition is fair."

It is as well for the surveyor/valuer to follow the printed sub-clauses under each heading thus, where the RICS Flat Buyers Report states that "the general condition only has been noted" in the case of item 13 (exterior decorations and paintwork), 18 (joinery—including doors, built-in cupboards and kitchen fittings) and 19 (internal decorations) it is as well to keep the comments short.

> "Internal decorations are provided in emulsion paint over plain lining papers to the walls and ceilings with white oil paint to the joinery. The decorations are in clean and acceptable condition, but have been provided to a fairly basic standard."

In the case of services it is desirable for descriptive comment to be given and if any problems are observed, these can be added to give reasons for a test thus

> "The electrical wiring is in p.v.c. cable and the electricity meter and fuse box are contained inside a high level fitted cupboard to the first floor landing. The electric socket outlets are of different types and surface wiring was noted where the installation has been extended by the vendor. An electrician's inspection is recommended."

A similar clause could be inserted in respect of hot water and central heating.

> "The flat is supplied with central heating and domestic hot water both provided by a Princess Superflow balanced flue gas boiler situated in the kitchen. There are pressed steel radiators in the main rooms but the valves show some signs of rust. There is no hot water storage tank and domestic hot water is supplied from the heating boiler. The installation should be examined by a heating engineer."

Or, in the case of the drains:

> "Rainwater, waste water from fittings and the discharge from W.C.'s is taken by down pipes to gullies and branch drains which connect with a main drain taken to a public sewer. The drain is shared with the upper flat. The inspection chamber in the rear garden is in satisfactory order and in clean condition but the deeper front inspection chamber needs attention as the interceptor cap is broken and the drain is partly blocked. Added waste water outlets from the kitchen project over a side gulley and this arrangement is unhygienic and should be modified."

PRACTICAL CONSEQUENCES ARISING FROM THE INTRODUCTION AND USE OF THE FORMS

Claims – lack of communication

The RICS and ISVA Forms are now in wide use. It is, however, a fact that their adoption has produced a spate of complaints and a number of claims have been settled out of Court. A disconcertingly high number of these show clearly that far from the surveyor and valuer being ill-equipped from the technical point of view to carry out the work, uncertainties and misunderstandings have arisen regarding the appropriate use of the forms.

Very often the client will have expectations which are not realised. It is, for this reason, vital that the surveyor and valuer has direct contact with his client so as to clear up any misunderstandings at the outset of the whole operation. Enough has been said, it is hoped, in this chapter to illustrate that reliance upon the printed publicity from the two Institutions will be insufficient to clarify the differences between a mortgage valuation, a House or Flat Buyers' Report or a structural survey (or "full" structural survey as it is often termed) in the applicant's mind. It is unfair, also to expect a staff member of a Bank or Building Society through whom instructions may be issued to the surveyor if a mortgage is involved, to spend additional time in explanations as to the differences with the applicant, a subject which he or she might themselves imperfectly understand.

Locality   A further problem concerns the question of locality. It is quite common for general practice firms to restrict their instructions for structural surveys to a fairly small area surrounding their office or offices. The introduction of the House and Flat Buyers' Report Forms has meant that rather than restricting the inspections for these to within the same smaller geographical limits, the reverse, understandably, has happened with House and Flat Buyers' Reports following the pattern of mortgage valuations over a much wider area thus leading the surveyor into fields that might be relatively unknown to him relating to different types of structure, whether by age or type, or varying types of land formation or sub-soil.

Uncertainty   Again, until recently, there has been uncertainty, perhaps forgiveable, in the mind of the surveyor and valuer as to the nature and extent of his duties under the House or Flat Buyers' Report Forms. There has been a tendency to assume that the "half-way" concept of the scheme applies to all aspects, from the amount of time spent in liaison with the client and the preliminaries, the amount of time spent on the site including the extent of investigations and the amount of the fee. All these aspects were, it was assumed, directly related to each other and each, in equal measure, must therefore lie somewhere between the ambit of the mortgage valuation on the one hand and the structural survey on the other. Again, it is easy to see why this idea was at the back of the minds of surveyors and valuers since it was, after all, the basic concept behind the scheme in the first place. However, it should be remembered that the scheme was intended to be strictly related to simple houses when it was first introduced and its growth in terms of all types of houses and flats, never envisaged. It is this factor that has also led to difficulties.

Doubts as to the surveyor's duty on site however, have been clarified by two cases which will be discussed in some detail both in this chapter and also in the next chapter on the Legal Position of the Surveyor.

The view of the courts

In the case of *Howard v. Horne and Sons* (1989)[1] where the case related to the condition of electrical wiring and is more fully discussed in the next chapter, the surveyor no doubt felt it was safe to rely on the Terms of Engagement referred to earlier in this chapter. Quite obviously however, the Judge felt that a far more painstaking visual examination, of the type some surveyors might consider more appropriate to a structural survey, should be carried out. This points to the danger of relying too closely on the printed clauses in the Conditions of Engagement and the comments in parentheses under the various clause headings of the report forms if there is any doubt about the condition of the property. Much misery and heartache can be saved in relation to the service installations if the surveyor and valuer makes use of his obvious right to recommend tests of services before exchange of contracts if there is something that strikes him as being wrong, odd, or even unusual. If this is justified, as clearly it is under the terms of a full structural survey, there is even more justification in the case of a House, Home or Flat Buyers' Valuation and Survey Report.

In the case brought by Mr. and Mrs. Cross against David Martin and Mortimer[2] heard in the Queens Bench Division of the High Court in November 1988, the comments of Mr. Justice Phillips are illuminating. The matter concerned defects following a House Buyers' Report and Valuation on the terms of the standard RICS form in respect of a semi-detached house, 13 Dane Acres, Bishops Stortford, Hertfordshire. This had been purchased by Mr. and Mrs. Cross in 1984 for the sum of £52,675. Following purchase, certain defects were alleged which formed the substance of the case and which, broadly, concerned: firstly, settlement of the solid slab that formed the ground floor; secondly, misalignment of a number of doors on the first floor; and thirdly, alteration of the roof trusses in order to enable the loft to be converted into a room.

As a preliminary to his judgment, Mr. Justice Phillips said as follows (his abbreviations):-

"The HBRV is now a common form of survey for the domestic house purchaser, but no reported case yet gives guidance as to the nature and extent of the duty of the surveyor who carries out such a survey. It has been suggested apparently in some quarters that an HBRV constitutes a more perfunctory survey than that which is described as a structural survey. In July 1984, a Report of the Joint General Practice and Building Surveyors' Division Working Party on Structural Survey Advice to the Profession on Residential Property expressed the view, under the heading 'expertise';

"We are convinced that the same level of expertise is required from the surveyor in carrying out an HBRV as that for a structural survey."

"Having heard the expert witnesses in the present case and

[1] Estates Gazette Law Reports 1990 Volume 1, p. 272.
[2] Estates Gazette, 11th March 1989.

considered the HBRV form, it seems to me that this conclusion is well founded. The HBRV form has 32 heads against which the surveyor makes his entries. Most of these heads consist of specific features of the house surveyed. Against some heads, the form notes limitations on the extent of the survey that will be effected, but I doubt if these do more than state expressly what would be the limitations reasonably implicit in the structural survey of a domestic house ..."

After a long and detailed commentary upon the nature and extent of Mr. Mortimer's investigation, the Judge added at the conclusion of the case:

"I have found Mr. Mortimer in breach of his duty of care on three counts. My judgment might suggest that he is a slap-dash surveyor and that this was a slap-dash survey. If so, I would like to correct that impression. Mr. Mortimer's notes show that he took a lot of care over this survey. I believe he attempted to apprise the Plaintiff of the effect of the loft conversion; his failure in that respect was in the form of his report. As to the first and ground floors, Mr. Mortimer had inspected many houses before in Dane Acres. His firm had inspected this very house on the occasion of its previous sale. Familiarity perhaps lulled Mr. Mortimer into a slight sense of false security. The result of this action should not be taken as a reflection on his general competence."

A number of the problems previously outlined, leading to complaints, did not apply in this case. According to the Judgment "prior to purchase, the Plaintiffs instructed the Defendants to advise them and, having regard to the age of the house, which was built in or about 1968, it was considered that the appropriate type of survey would be the House Buyers' Report and Valuation on the terms of the standard RICS Form." Accordingly, there was no failure of communication on this aspect of the matter. Secondly, Mr. Mortimer was not only an experienced surveyor but knew his locality extremely well since, as the Judgment stated ... "Mr. Mortimer had inspected many houses before in Dane Acres." It therefore remains that Mr. Mortimer was found in breach of his duty of care, according to the Judge, in two respects: firstly that "familiarity perhaps lulled Mr. Mortimer into a slight sense of false security" and secondly that "his failure ... was in the form of his report".

Difficulties and necessary care

If anyone believes that, as Phillips J. said, "it has been suggested apparently in some quarters that an HBRV constitutes a more perfunctory survey than that which is described as a structural survey" that belief should now be dead and buried. One of the enormous problems that lies in the path of those who attempt to categorise houses into types whether by age or size, for the benign purpose of producing formats or proformas to speed up surveys and make them more cost effective, lies in the fact that quite small newly constructed houses built to an up-to-date standard will exhibit alarming faults while other older and neglected structures which are confidently expected to have a limited life will stand, virtually

434

unchanged, through the decades. All surveyors and valuers are at risk of being lulled into a false sense of security which they must try to guard against but, in particular, it is obvious that with the introduction of the House, Home and Flat Buyers' Report Forms that a good deal of experience is needed to become wholly at ease with the form of expression needed to convey the surveyor's message.

Surveying within the terms of a House or Flat Buyers' Report, is, as has been said, as equally exacting as that within the terms of a full structural survey. The Courts will decide as to whether a surveyor has discharged his duty not only in the nature and extent of his inspection but as to whether he has passed the appropriate facts and findings to his client. Rather therefore than risk a claim for negligence, it would be best, in cases where a structure shows signs of complicated faults, to revert to the procedure of a structural survey and swallow the resulting financial loss. This can be the only approach in view of the need for site work thoroughness.

The only saving in surveyor's time relates to compiling the report and it is not therefore difficult to see why the Consumer's Association found that fees for House Buyers' Reports not very different from those of structural survey reports. It can be seen now that any expectation that they would be significantly less was misplaced. Whether now that this point has been established beyond doubt, it will have any effect on the willingness of surveyors to carry out the work or the willingness of clients to pay say, three quarters or more of the fee charged for a structural survey, remains to be seen. Paying that bit more and obtaining a proper detailed report, as the Consumers' Association recommend, represents much the best buy.

Finally, where the use of the House, Home and Flat Buyers' Report Forms is mutually agreed with full understanding between the parties, the surveyor should polish and re-polish his skills in drafting to become totally conversant with this type of format. However, he is advised to remember the words of Mr. Justice Phillips and to remember that, however much he is under pressure pending his client's exchange of contracts, that he always has the right, indeed duty, of advocating further time for investigations or tests. If he does not, and a serious fault is discovered later, he may well pay the piper but it is the client who will experience the consequent inconvenience and misery.

Chapter 14

The Legal Position of the Surveyor

by PAUL MURRELLS
SOLICITOR

CONTENTS

INTRODUCTION

Surveyor's liability   As with members of all other professions, a Surveyor can be liable to two groups of people, namely:
– his employer, in the law of contract;
– all people, where there is a sufficient relationship of proximity or "neighbourhood" such that in the reasonable contemplation of the surveyor carelessness on his part may be likely to cause damage to such people. This liability arises normally in the common law tort of negligence. In Scotland, this is known as delict.
Liability may be in both contract and tort/delict.

Liability in contract   With most surveys there will be a contract in that in return for payment of a fee or some other form of consideration by the client, the surveyor has agreed to inspect the property and, generally, prepare a written report. Conditions of Engagement may define the basis of such contract. These will be looked at later in some detail. To succeed in a claim, the client must show that there has been breach of such contract and that damage has been suffered as a consequence.

Liability in tort   This may seem fairly clear cut. Liability in tort is a different matter. Here, to say the least, the width between the goal posts is elastic. For a claim to succeed three principles must be established, namely:

1. a duty of care in accordance with the "neighbourhood" principle is referred to already. This was defined by Lord Atkin in the House of Lords more than 50 years ago in *Donoghue v. Stevenson* [1932] AC 562. This was the sorry tale of the snail with a craving for ginger beer. Sadly, the lady who found the remains of the snail in her drink did not recover from the experience;

2. there must be a breach of such duty. Negligence must be established. This includes liability for negligent mis-statements in accordance with the principles laid down by the House of Lords in the well-known case of *Hedley Byrne & Co Ltd v. Heller & Partners Ltd* [1964] AC 465. Advertising Agents asked their bank about a company's financial standing and were given a reply "without responsibility". The reply was wrong. As such, there was the basis for a claim in negligence. This will be the case even if the advice given is simply verbal and not confirmed in writing. The claim failed in Hedley Byrne because the bank had given an express disclaimer of responsibility. However, clear guidelines were laid down. Subsequent legislation has made reliance upon disclaimers extremely difficult (*see post*—confirmation of instructions);

3. damage must have been suffered as a consequence of such breach. Lack of a fee in the form of a gratuitous service may mean that there is no contractual liability but there may be liability still in tort.

Limitation

In carrying out a survey, the main liability will arise under contract with the client. However, as stated already, there can be liability in both. It is important to bear this in mind because a claim may be time-barred in contract but not in tort. The effect of the Limitation Acts will be considered later. Likewise, for contribution to be claimed from some other person, a concurrent duty of care in tort must be established. Breach of contract may be insufficient.

In common with other professions and trades concerned in the building industry, surveyors have been involved in many court cases which have attempted to explore the minefield of limits of liability for negligence. In the words of Lord Donaldson, the current Master of the Rolls, there is a "measure of authoritative chaos". Further developments in case law are imminent. The law relating to professional liability can be described charitably as being in a state of flux. Unless one has the attributes of a prophet, it is difficult to predict future events with any conviction.

Insurance

This is hardly a conducive working arrangement for the surveyor and his client. Each is seeking certainty and security so that they both know exactly where they stand. With the outcome of litigation being so difficult to predict, let alone the expense of it, insurance becomes increasingly a means of sharing liability for any loss. Most claims which are pursued with vigour will be settled, particularly where it seems clear that the surveyor has been negligent. To a limited extent, this creates certainty.

The surveyor's professional indemnity and liability insurance policy will provide an indemnity in respect of legal liability for errors and omissions committed in the course of his business. This is the most commonly known of insurances but there are others developing which may be relevant in the context of dwelling houses. It may be possible to insure the property rather than the surveyor in the form of Defects Insurance. Inevitably, the cost of insurance will have to be reflected in the survey fee. Professional Indemnity policies will be considered later in more detail.

STANDARD OF CARE

Surveyors no different from other professions

For liability to be established, it must be determined that the surveyor has fallen below the standard of care. The law does not differentiate between one profession and another. A surveyor's liability is governed by the same principles as those applying to Accountants, Architects, Doctors, Engineers, Solicitors and others. The standard of care may be expressed as under a contract or implied as under Section 13 of the Supply of Goods and Services Act 1982. The standard is one of reasonable care and skill. What would a reasonably competent member of the same profession have done in the same circumstances? Inevitably, the standard is set by the evidence of independent experts. As such, it is an objective standard.

Reasonable competence–no hindsight

In considering the standard of care of the professional man in the

440

case of *Eckersley & Others v. Binnie & Partners* [1988] CILL 388, Lord Justice Bingham said in the Court of Appeal:-

> "He should be alert to the hazards and risks inherent in any professional task he undertakes to the extent that other ordinarily competent members of his profession would be alert. He must bring to any professional task he undertakes no less expertise, skill and care than other ordinarily competent members of his profession would bring, but need bring no more. The standard is that of the reasonable average. The law does not require of a professional man that he be a paragon, combining the qualities of polymath and prophet. In deciding whether a professional man has fallen short of the standards observed by ordinarily skilled and competent members of his profession, it is the standards prevailing at the time of his acts or omissions which provide the relevant yardstick. He is not ... to be judged by the wisdom of hindsight."

Standard determined by work not surveyor

The standard will not be lower for a surveyor with no professional qualifications. *Freeman v. Marshall & Co* (1966) 200 EG 777 is an example of this. Here, it transpired that condensation was in fact rising damp. The surveyor's defence that he was not qualified did not succeed. The law makes no distinction between a newly qualified surveyor and one who has been qualified for many years. The standard is determined by the work and not by the surveyor carrying it out.

Examples of Court judgments

A recent example of a senior Judge's interpretation of the standard of care expected of a surveyor is to be found in the judgment of the Vice Chancellor, Browne Wilkinson, in *Strover v. Harrington & Others* [1988] 1All ER 769 and [1988] 09 EG 61. The survey of an East Sussex property was carried out early in 1986. The report was in a standard form and dealt with the property's drainage system in paragraph 23:

> "The property is drained to the main sewer via drain lines through the adjacent property. The drains are in good order where visible".

It was of some significance that three inches of snow was lying at the time of the surveyor's inspection. It transpired, so the purchasers maintained AFTER they had purchased the property, that drainage was by means of a cesspool.

The surveyor said in evidence that one of the vendors told him in answer to a specific question that the property enjoyed mains drainage. The surveyor maintained that it was normal practice with matters of drainage to ask the vendor what the position was. The ultimate destination of the drain could be ascertained only by means of a detailed inspection which was outside the scope of the surveyor's instructions.

The plaintiff purchasers did not produce any evidence to suggest that this was anything other than normal surveying practice. This leaves a slight question mark over the decision that the surveyor was not liable. It is not known whether the purchasers attempted to obtain a report which may have indicated different surveying practice.

Relying upon information given by a vendor will not always prevent the surveyor from being found liable. It must be questionable for instance whether a surveyor could succeed in defending a claim having relied upon information given relating to timber infestation treatment under guarantee.

The purchasers suggested that the surveyor should have qualified his report by saying "it is thought that—it is said that—in accordance with my instructions the drains have not been tested but the vendors tell me that ...". This would have put the purchasers on notice that further investigation might be required. With the benefit of hindsight the surveyor accepted that it might have been appropriate for him to qualify his report in such a way. In very clear terms, the Judge said that to impose such hindsight would set too high a standard.

In the context of house purchase, it is known to the surveyor and presumably, to the client as well, that it will be part of the conveyancer's function in making preliminary enquiries to verify the position regarding drainage. There is a common printed enquiry form which relates to the nature of drainage made on every house purchase. The surveyor's report is not the principal means for verifying the nature of the drainage. Indeed, in land registry papers supplied to the purchasers' solicitors prior to exchange of contracts, reference was made to a drainage easement. Not only did the claim fail against the surveyor but against the vendors as well. The Judge was satisfied that the true position was in fact known to the purchasers' solicitors PRIOR to exchange of contracts and that this should have been conveyed to the purchasers by their solicitors.

In *Eley & Another v. King & Chasemore* [1989] 22 EG 109, one of the allegations made against the surveyor related to a roof defect. In his report, the surveyor said the main roof slopes were covered by natural slates. It was possible that the roof may have suffered bomb damage during the last war because there had been a fairly major overhaul which would have involved the complete stripping of the whole roof and re-felting. This had been done in a most unusual way, the felt having been laid over rather than under the battens. It was suggested that the surveyor should have pointed out that lack of ventilation could be a problem.

The surveyor's general impression was that the roof covering was proving to be effective. He would have felt happier if he had got up onto the valley gutters so as to inspect them. This would have required the use of a long ladder which was outside the scope of the surveyor's instructions.

In the absence of any sign of water penetration, the Court of Appeal was satisfied that the surveyor did not need to go up onto the roof and, as such, was not negligent. None of the independent evidence produced by the unsuccessful plaintiffs reached any substantially different conclusions to those of the defendant surveyor. Indeed, in another survey of the same property carried out only some six weeks previously, there had been no mention at all of any problem with the roof. Replacement of the roof by the plaintiffs may have had a cosmetic effect but was not necessary so far as water penetrating into the property was concerned.

The *Strover* and *Eley* decisions are recent examples of the current way in which the Courts are attempting to keep the standard of care in its proper context and not extend the parameters of negligence towards a standard of perfection.

BREACH OF DUTY

Typical defects resulting in claims

In the last 20 years there have been a number of occasions upon which the Courts have been asked to rule whether the surveyor was in breach of his duty of care and therefore negligent. Some examples may help to show defects in properties which can result in claims.

Damage from tree roots

In *Daisley v. B.S. Hall & Co* (1973) 225 E.G. 1553, the Judge accepted expert evidence that it was notorious where poplar, willow or elm trees were growing on clay soil, that the very high transpiration through the leaves of these trees tended to dry out the clay round their root systems. This causes the clay to shrink. It was part of a surveyor's training to be familiar with this. A Building Research Station digest was available at the time of the survey in 1968.

In failing to recognise as poplars a row of trees along one of the boundaries of the property, the surveyor was negligent for not warning of the risk of such trees. These were some 40 feet in height and the nearest 25 feet from the corner of the property. Two trees had been felled already and the property was less than 10 years old. The property was called "High Trees". Perhaps, this should have given the surveyor a clue!

Settlement cracks

In *Hingorani v. Blower & Others* (1976) 238 EG 883, the surveyor's terms of employment were to report on observable defects. The surveyor maintained that as at December 24 1969, there were no such defects. He maintained that, along with any other competent surveyor carrying out a proper and thorough survey, he was deceived by the fact that the vendor had fixed the property up so successfully that defects which were undoubtedly there were not observable. Underpinning was needed.

On the evidence, the Judge was satisfied that the North London property had a large crack on the rear elevation which had been filled in. Although persons "faking" a property can colour the mortar so as to make it more difficult to see, the fact is that anybody looking at the whole length of the wall, even if the mortar had been coloured, would have seen a wide band of filling. The house was empty at the time of survey and had been redecorated from top to tail internally. A careful surveyor should have been put on suspicion that there might have been reasons for this, such as disguising defects in the property. Had the surveyor been put on guard he would have seen a long crack which carried the straightforward telltale of having a much wider line of mortar than ought to have been there. Perhaps, the moral of this particular decision is to be careful when carrying out surveys on Christmas Eve!

Leakage from pipes

Fryer v. Bunney (1982) 263 EG 158, is a decision which brings particular anguish to surveyors. A 1979 survey report on an Essex property indicated that it had been checked for damp with a Protimeter. No reading of dampness was registered. Whilst the property was being decorated soon after purchase, tests showed that water was being lost from the central heating tank. When part of the hall floor was taken up, leaks were discovered in defective piping. The Judge was satisfied that a more extensive use of the Protimeter would have revealed the existence of dampness. It was not apparent to the human eye or by placing hands against walls.

Having found that the surveyor had been negligent, the Judge made some interesting comments regarding the surveyor's general standard of competence. There was no deliberate intention by the surveyor to "skimp" his work. Perhaps it was a case of a man doing a job of standard type too frequently.

"Everyone makes mistakes, everyone forgets and can be guilty of carelessness and I think that is what happened to Mr Bunney in this case. I think it was a non-deliberate omission, but I am sure that he did omit to check properly. It may be that Mr Bunney as a result of this experience will be a better surveyor in future. I think he is probably a very good one now, but having had the experience of having made a mistake, I am fairly confident that he will be even more careful in future."

The moral of this decision must be for surveyors to prepare a very simple sketch plan of a property as it is surveyed marking roughly where the Protimeter was applied. It may be a long time after the survey before a complaint is received and many other surveys may have been carried out on other properties in the meantime. It can be very difficult to remember one property clearly from another without some form of sketch to rely upon. Some surveyors keep photographs.

Defects in flat roofs

Hooberman v. Salter Rex (1985) 274 EG 151, concerned a surveyor's knowledge of ventilation problems associated with flat roofs in 1977. The survey was of an upper maisonette formed by the conversion of a five storey Victorian house in North London. The property had a flat roof terrace of timber construction which the Plaintiff turned into a roof garden.

As a result of defects not mentioned in the survey report, water leaked from the terrace into space above the Plaintiff's bedroom ceiling. This led to an outbreak of dry rot.

The surveyor concerned said in evidence that it was desirable not to alarm a client who was keen to purchase a property. The surveyor's job was limited to warning of defects which might make the client change his mind. The Judge was not impressed:

"He was there to inspect the property so far as reasonably practicable, so as to report candidly upon its condition. No doubt he has to be selective and determine what aspects are important and

444

what are unimportant but whether his conclusions are comfortable or uncomfortable to the client is immaterial."

The felt upstands at the walls of the terrace were inadequate. There were neither zinc nor lead wall flashings. The edge of the felt was turned into a groove in the perimeter walls and bonded. There were no timber angle fillets at the junction of the perimeter walls and the decking. The Plaintiff was given no warning.

Presence of mundic *Marder & Another v. Sautelle & Hicks* [1988] 2 EGLR 187 concerned a 1979 survey of a bungalow at St Agnes in Cornwall. The Defendants failed to detect that the outer skin wall was constructed of "mundic" blocks. This material is a cement aggregate made from tin mine waste and may have an arsenic content. Literally, it was freely available during the 1920s and 1930s. With time, and especially if exposed to moisture or damp, the blocks tend to lose cohesion and become crumbly. They can come apart in a person's hands.

The defective walls were discovered in 1982 when extension work was carried out. On the evidence before him, the Trial Judge had little hesitation in finding that the surveyor should have been alive to the problem at the time of his survey. The surveyor was in breach of contract and negligent. It was not necessary to establish whether the precise constituent of the blocks was arsenic or something else, thus leading to rapid deterioration. All that was necessary to be noted was that the blocks were prone to degradation in this way and, so far as this property was concerned, the process was already underway to a serious extent as early as 1979.

An attempt was made at the hearing of the appeal to produce fresh evidence to the effect that the blocks were not "mundic" and therefore less liable to decay. Such attempt failed. The evidence should have been produced at the trial. Even if such evidence had been produced, it is thought unlikely that this would have made any difference to the outcome.

Shrinkable sub-soil Where a surveyor believes that there may be a structural problem, then gives practical advice as to overcoming this and the client acts to his benefit upon such advice, it is unlikely that the surveyor will be in breach of his duty of care. This is exactly what happened in *Eley & Another v. King & Chasemore* [1989] 1 EGLR 181 to which reference has been made already.

The property concerned was at Burgess Hill in West Sussex and was built in approximately 1850. A number of additions had been made to it since, some of which were quite recent to the surveyors report in 1984. The report went into considerable detail. Cracks in the rendering on the walls of the structure were noted as well as cracks to features in other parts of the property.

The report stated that the property stood on a shrinkable clay sub-soil which would be liable to be affected by seasonal changes in its moisture content. This was not unusual for the area. Detailed comment was made as well upon a very tall fir tree close to the property. As a result of the surveyor's advice, such tree was removed by the Purchasers.

The practical advice given by the surveyor regarding the property's construction was to say the following:

"All houses on clay are more at risk than those constructed on a more stable sub-soil. It would be a good idea to see if you could obtain insurance protection against subsidence, ground heave, settlement and land-slip although with so many present and previous cracks in the walls, such cover might not be easy to obtain."

This is exactly what the Purchasers succeeded in obtaining prior to proceeding. The Insurance Company concerned did not call for further investigations before taking on the risk. Within a year of purchase, structural engineers reported that the property had suffered structural movement because of the soil substance and recommended underpinning. A large part of the cost of this was met by insurance. However, insurers did not pay full remedial costs because there was an element of improvement to the property in the work carried out.

Evidence was given for the Purchasers by another surveyor who had inspected the property for another Purchaser who did not proceed. He noted that underpinning might be needed in the future. He did not advise the taking out of specific insurance but indicated that a reduction of approximately £8,000 in the purchase price would be a fair contribution towards underpinning costs. The Purchaser recovered substantially more than this from the insurance taken out on the property. Thus, the Court of Appeal was satisfied that rather than suffering loss as a result of the surveyor's advice, the Purchasers benefited financially from such advice.

The *Eley* decision is very much upon its own particular facts and, as with all decisions affecting the surveyor's standard of care, does not create any form of precedent which might be binding in other cases. To advise the obtaining of specific insurance cover will not be an effective answer in all cases. Nevertheless, it is something which should be considered carefully where circumstances warrant this. It is most important that the surveyor advises in terms which his client should be able to understand.

CONFIRMATION OF INSTRUCTIONS

Misunderstandings between surveyors and clients

By far the largest cause of claims against surveyors is a misunderstanding with the client as to what was to be included in the survey inspection and report and, more importantly, what was not to be included. Written Conditions of Engagement have become fairly common now. However, as examination of a few Court decisions will show, this has not always been standard practice. Sometimes, the report is required urgently and time does not permit confirmation of instructions which are given upon a verbal basis. This is dangerous as misunderstanding can arise as to what was expected of the surveyor. Wherever possible, verbal instructions should be avoided.

Stewart v. H. A. Brechin & Co [1959] S.C. 306, is one of only a few reported Scottish decisions involving a surveyor's liability for anything more than a valuation. Such is the property system in Scotland that it is fairly unusual for structural surveys to be carried out, largely because of the speed at which a house purchase normally takes place. In this case, solicitors for a prospective purchaser of an 18th century country property instructed surveyors verbally as a matter of urgency to carry out a valuation and report upon the property's general condition. After the offer was accepted, parts of the property were found to be visibly infested with woodworm. The Lord Ordinary (Cameron) was satisfied that woodworm would have been apparent at the time the property was inspected and the surveyor's unexplained failure to detect this was negligent. Regarding the surveyor's contractual obligations, Lord Cameron said:

> "I am of opinion that all that the defenders were under contract to do was to make such valuation of the property and to carry out such visual inspection as was reasonably practicable in the circumstances, reporting anything of significance to their client if such should be found. 'Anything of significance' in this context, in my opinion, means anything so material as would or might influence a reasonable man in fixing a price to be offered by him for the subjects or anything which to the skilled eye of a surveyor would be an indication of possible and material defect, structural or otherwise, in the property such as would or might reasonably be expected to affect its value to a prospective purchaser or cause him to reconsider an intention to make an offer for it."

In *Fisher & Another v. Knowles* (1982) 262 EG 1083, the Judge had to interpret exactly what the surveyor's instructions were. From the brief report it is not clear whether there was anything in writing recording such instructions but this must be very doubtful. The Judge decided that the surveyor's instructions were:

1. to provide a report on the general state of the property;
2. to draw attention to those matters which might give rise to suspicion, such as springing floors or a musty smell which might require further investigation;
3. to report any matters which might cause the Plaintiffs to withdraw or to bargain for a lower price.

The report did draw attention to some minor defects but gave a valuation at the asking price for the property. Some four years later the Plaintiffs complained of many defects in the property.

However the Judge found that the surveyor was liable only for failure to report on rot in window frames and defects in ceiling joists and door joinery. There was doubt as to whether the rest were defects. Nominal damages were awarded which did not justify the commencement of High Court proceedings.

Limited instructions *Shankie-Williams & Others v. Heavey* (1986) 279 EG 316, is an interesting example of limited instructions relating to inspection of part only of a property. The case concerned a North London house which was converted into three flats in 1981. The Plaintiffs wanted to buy a lease of the ground floor flat. A surveyor who inspected for their bank found dry rot and advised that no money should be lent until this had been eradicated. As a result, some of the timbers were replaced. Then, the Vendors instructed the Defendant to inspect the ground floor flat. He was a dry rot surveying specialist. He found no evidence of dry rot in the area he was asked to inspect. As a precaution, he sprayed the timbers and gave a 30 year guarantee. The accompanying report did not distinguish between this flat and the remainder of the property. The Defendant said this was the extent of his instructions. The Vendors relied upon the report. Not only did the sale to the Plaintiffs proceed but the first floor flat was sold as well. The Purchasers saw the guarantee but not, it would seem, the report. Some two years later extensive dry rot was discovered. The Purchasers incurred considerable expense in carrying out remedial works and sued for recovery of this.

The Court of Appeal held that the Defendant did owe a duty of care to the Plaintiffs because he knew that the Vendors wanted a guarantee which could be shown to Purchasers of the ground floor flat. However, if that was the limit of the surveyor's instructions, he could not be under any duty to the Purchasers of any other flats in the same building. If the Purchasers had seen the report the position might have been different. One has to stop somewhere! If the Court had held that there was a duty of care to a Purchaser of the first floor flat then what about the second floor? Likewise what about adjoining occupiers? The Vendors might have been converting a row of five houses in the same street. Purchasers of flats in these other houses were too far removed from the surveyor to have any legal rights against him. Perhaps, this surveyor was lucky! Even though his instructions were limited to the ground floor flat, should he not have made some recommendation regarding inspection of the remainder of the property? Dry rot can spread very fast.

Limitations to be agreed before inspection. Unfair Contract Terms Act 1977

If a surveyor wishes to impose any conditions regarding the limitation of his inspection and report, and this is a most wise course to adopt, such conditions must be agreed in writing with the prospective client before the inspection takes place and a contract is made. This is because of the effect of the Unfair Contract Terms Act 1977. Under Section 2 of this Act a person cannot by reference to any contract term or to a notice given to persons generally or to particular persons, exclude or restrict his liability for negligence except insofar as the term or notice fulfils the requirement of reasonableness. It is not possible in any circumstances to exclude or restrict liability for death or personal injury resulting from negligence.

Section 11 of the Act discusses the requirement of reasonableness. For a contract term to be fair and reasonable it must have been in the contemplation of the parties when the contract was made. This is why Conditions of Engagement must be agreed before the survey inspection takes place. Slightly different provisions apply so far as reliance upon a notice is concerned restricting liability to non-contracting parties. Regard must be had to all the

448

circumstances known when the liability arose or would have arisen but for the notice, such as the bargaining power of the parties involved and the difficulty of the task being undertaken. These provisions do not apply in Scotland, as confirmed by a recent decision effecting surveyors' liability to non-contracting parties for a mortgage valuation. (See *Robbie v. Graham & Sibbald* [1989] 2 All ER 504 [1989] 2 EGLR 148.)

Conditions of Engagement

Most surveyors have prepared Conditions of Engagement to meet their own individual requirements, based upon the service they are able to provide. Surprisingly, there are no standard Conditions of Engagement available at present for the carrying out of surveys, if only for guidance purposes. It is possible this will be remedied soon. The RICS Guidance Notes on Structural Surveys contain a section regarding Conditions of Engagement and their confirmation.

As a minimum, Conditions of Engagement should include the following:

— name and address of the client;
— property address;
— purpose of the survey—whether for purchase, lease or some other purpose;
— type of property and its tenure;
— date when the surveyor hopes to inspect;
— date when the surveyor hopes to report;
— fee and any method of extending this;
— size of the property, as advised by the client so, if it is larger, the fee can be extended;
— what will be included in the inspection;
— any limitations of the inspection, such as length of any ladder which may be used, and non-inspection of exposed parts or of outbuildings, swimming pools being an example;
— limitations as to whom the report is intended for and that it is not to be produced without the surveyor's written approval. It is vital to repeat this at the beginning of the report itself just in case the report does find its way into the hands of another person who might attempt to rely upon its content. This way, such person is on clear notice as to the terms under which the report was prepared;
— the position regarding the carrying out of specialist tests on such matters as drains, electricity, gas and water.

Wherever time permits, it is most important that the client should be asked to sign, date and return one copy of such letter or conditions as confirmation that they have been received and, hopefully, understood. This should help considerably in preventing any possible misunderstanding arising later.

A recent example of the importance of confirming instructions in writing is to be found in *Strover v. Harrington & Others* [1988] 1 EGLR 173 which has been discussed already. In his letter accepting instructions, the surveyor expressly pointed out that if the clients wished arrangements could be made for specialist tests to be carried out on the drainage amongst other services. Mr Strover wrote back to the surveyor saying that no specialist tests were required.

This must act as a timely reminder of the importance of confirming instructions as protection against the whims of litigious clients and their legal advisers.

Insurance requirements

Professional indemnity policies available to Chartered Surveyors do not insist now as a condition of insurance cover that any specific clauses are included in the report, such as non-inspection of exposed parts. The current tendency is that the limitations of inspection are a matter for the judgment of each surveyor based upon his own particular experience. Naturally, it is important for a surveyor not to expose himself to any greater liability than is necessary which could result in too many claims on his indemnity policy. This could have a dramatic effect upon future premiums. On the other hand, if in his Conditions of Engagement the surveyor gives details of many matters which will not be covered by his report, this may make many prospective clients wonder what they are paying for and consider instructing another surveyor.

All surveyors who are members of the Incorporated Society of Valuers and Auctioneers (ISVA) or the Royal Institution of Chartered Surveyors (RICS) must have professional indemnity insurance. This is for the protection of the house buying public in the event of breach of duty being established. To a certain extent this may explain why more cases go to court so far as the surveyor's liability is concerned. The only specific condition in the RICS's Professional Indemnity Collective Policy relating to the carrying out of surveys is that these should be made:

(a) by a Fellow or Professional Associate of RICS; or
by a Fellow or Associate of ISVA; or
by a Fellow or Associate of the Faculty of Architects and Surveyors (FAS); or
by a Fellow or Associate of the Royal Institute of British Architects (RIBA); or
by a Fellow or Associate of the Royal Institute of Architects of Scotland (RIAS); or

(b) by anyone who has not less than five years experience of such work or such other person nominated by the Insured Surveyor to execute such work subject always to supervision of such work by a person qualified in accordance with (a) above.

HOUSE AND FLAT BUYERS' REPORTS AND VALUATIONS

Conditions—Intermediaries

Until recently, there were no reported decisions regarding a surveyor's liability for these. Claims have been settled out of Court but guidance upon the extent of the inspection has been awaited eagerly. There is no doubt that since the first House Buyers scheme was introduced in 1981, many purchasers have commissioned such reports in circumstances where they will have not felt the cost of a full survey was justified. Two recent cases demonstrate clearly that the extent of inspection required for the House or Flat Buyers' Report is very much the same as for a full survey. The difference is to be found in the extent of the report.

The importance of written Conditions of Engagement and confirming instructions in writing has been emphasised already. Provided the Standard Conditions are drawn to the client's attention before the contract is made then there should be no problem so far as the Unfair Contract Terms Act 1977 is concerned. In many instances the surveyor's instructions come from an intermediary such as a building society. The surveyor has a contractual relationship with the purchaser client. This makes matters all the more important for the surveyor to be sure that the client understands the limitations. Problems can arise when the surveyor proceeds with the inspection of a property prior to completing a House Buyers' Report where because of its age or size the property may not be suitable for such scheme.

It should be stressed that the House and Flat Buyers' schemes do not contain any conditions excluding liability as has been the case sometimes with mortgage valuations. The success of the schemes is that a limited report is provided. The limitations are explained clearly in the Conditions of Engagement and in the margin notes and headings of the Report itself. These may explain why so few cases have gone to court.

Examples of Court Judgments

Cross & Another v. David Martin & Mortimer [1989] 10 EG 110 concerned an RICS House Buyers' Report and Valuation carried out upon a semi-detached property in Hertfordshire. This was built in the late 1960s. The Judge made it clear that the extent of the survey inspection was indeed the same as for a full survey and that the same level of expertise was required. In his opinion, a purchaser could properly expect to be informed of any feature of the property which involved uncertainty as to its condition, present or future, even if the surveyor's opinion as to its significance was reassuring.

Subsidence

When considering whether the surveyor should have reported on any feature of the property, it is necessary to have regard not merely to the surveyor's opinion of the probable significance of the feature but also to any significant alternative possibilities that the surveyor could not affirmatively rule out. So far as this property was concerned, there were three factors which should have made the surveyor consider the possibility of subsidence, namely:

— the house was built on clay;
— there were poplar trees nearby and
— the property was built on a 9° slope which would require an unusually large amount of fill under the floor slab. There was settlement of solid slabs forming the ground floor. The day after the Plaintiffs moved into the property, a carpet layer found the lounge floor to be irregular.

Also, the surveyor was held to be in breach of his duty of care for not commenting upon distortion to first floor doors. The Judge

451

went to great pains to stress that the surveyor was not slap-dash. He had shown a lot of care. In respect of the defects listed above the surveyor may have been too familiar with the estate of which the property formed part. He may have assumed a slight sense of false security.

Loft conversion

A third complaint was that the surveyor failed to comment fully on a loft conversion and whether it was structurally strong enough to sustain live loading if used as a room. The Judge envisaged the possibility of a vigorous party taking place in the loft room while the roof was laden with snow and a gale was howling outside. A comment to the effect that the construction was sound but that further enquiries should be made with regard to planning permission or building regulations for the conversion was insufficient. It was the surveyor's form of words which let him down. The Judge said the Plaintiffs should have been informed that unless building regulation approval had been obtained for the conversion, it would not necessarily be safe to use the loft as other than a light storage space.

Electric cabling

The other decision is *Howard v. Horne & Sons*. Judgment was given on 10th May 1989 and was reported in the Estates Gazette Law Reports 1990 Volume 1 page 272. It concerned a 1986 inspection of a property in Maidenhead. The Judge referred to the standard note printed at the top of the first page of the report:

"The inspection is to provide a report on the general state of repair of the property described below. It is not a structural survey but a report by a Chartered Surveyor on those matters expressly set out in his report, together with valuation advice."

Regarding the property's electricity supply, the surveyor stated "electrical wiring is in PVC cable". In the Judge's opinion that implied the wiring was modern and that there was no cause for concern about it. The printed standard marginal note beside the Services Section of the report states:

"These have only been inspected visually where they were accessible and tests have not been applied.

Standards and adequacy of installations can only be ascertained as a result of a test by an appropriate specialist."

The statement about the wiring was wrong. The wiring in the kitchen was PVC covered but much of the rest was not and, indeed, was dangerous. The whole system was rewired and the cost of making good paid for as well. The Judge was satisfied that it was proper to have the work carried out. Photographs showed that the wiring was a mixture of old and new. A most important part of the evidence given concerned a board on which several junction boxes were mounted. Some had PVC cables at one side but not the rest. Although not easy to examine, the Judge held that the surveyor should have been able to overcome the difficulties of bad light and dust. The surveyor had to pay damages.

DAMAGES FOR BREACH OF DUTY

Compensation not punishment

Where a surveyor is found to be in breach of his duty, what damages must he pay? The main principle is that the plaintiff must be put, so far as money can do so, in the same position as he would have been if the surveyor had discharged his duty properly. The plaintiff must not be placed in a better position than he would have been if the breach or negligence had not occurred. He must not make a profit. The objective of awarding damages is to compensate the plaintiff and not to punish the surveyor.

Principles for determining a surveyor's liability for damages were laid down in *Philips v. Ward* [1956] 1 All ER 874. Damages will be assessed in accordance with the difference between the price actually paid for the property on the basis that the surveyor's advice was good and what should have been paid for the property in its actual defective condition. Thus, damages will be assessed as at the date of breach or negligence and not as at the date of trial. In this case, the plaintiff paid £25,000 for a property in 1952. The cost of repairs at the time of purchase were £7,000. The value of the property at such time with defects was assessed at £21,000. Damages of £4,000 were awarded (£25,000 minus £21,000) and not £7,000.

However, there is authority to suggest that where the plaintiff pays more for the property than it is worth, then the measure of damage remains the difference between the lower price he should have paid for the property, in good condition, and what he should have paid for it in a defective condition. In *Hardy v. Walmsley-Lewis* (1967) 203 EG 103, the plaintiff paid £4,600 for a property for which, in good condition, he should have paid around £4,300. In a defective condition, the value of the property was assessed at £3,500. £800 damages were awarded (£4,300 minus £3,500) and not £1,100 (£4,600 less £3,500).

Inflation, out-of-pocket expenses, distress and inconvenience

As compensation for the effect of inflation, interest will be awarded upon such damages together with other out-of-pocket expenses and distress and inconvenience. As will be seen from later cases, this means modest compensation rather than excessive sums. It may be reasonable for a plaintiff to delay carrying out repairs, thus adding to his inconvenience, where there is a strong denial of liability by the defendant surveyor. It should be stressed that damages for inconvenience are not awarded for the stress of being involved in a legal dispute. Such aggravation is experienced by most litigants. Damages are awarded because of the physical consequences of the breach which were forseeable at that time.

The principle of diminution in market value, as it has come to be known, was confirmed by the Court of Appeal in *Perry v. Sidney Phillips* (1981) 260 EG 389. However, the effect of the Perry decision is weakened somewhat by the fact that the property had been sold between the date of the trial and the appeal hearing. The "difference" in value approach remained in favour with the court. The cost of repairs could no longer be an issue as the property had

Courts views on diminution in value

been sold at a price considerably in excess of what the plaintiff paid for it some 5–6 years previously.

A review of some court decisions since the Perry case will show that many Judges are uneasy about the diminution in market value principle. Wherever possible, on the basis that liability has been established, Judges will find ways of ensuring that the plaintiff is adequately compensated. This may have an unfortunate effect when consideration is given to the calculation of premiums so far as the surveyor's professional indemnity policy is concerned.

The surveyor's liability for commenting on dampness has been considered already in *Fryer v. Bunney* (1982). In effect, the Judge equated the cost of repair with diminution in value. Expense of approximately £5,000 was allowed following damage caused by a leaking central heating pipe. This figure was made up of cost of repairs, redecoration and the reduced value of carpets. The Judge held that if the house had been put back on the market for sale, no-one would have paid the price which the plaintiff paid for it without deductions of the cost of repairs and redecoration. This was the true figure for diminution. In addition, the Judge allowed £500 for distress and inconvenience.

In *Bolton v. Puley* (1982) 267 EG 1160, the surveyor was held to be negligent for failing to warn the plaintiff of the defective and unstable nature of an old boundary wall which collapsed subsequently. The Judge took cost of repair as the starting point for assessing the difference in value but held that the plaintiff might have agreed to a 25% reduction in the cost of repairs as his own risk. Otherwise, the plaintiff would have incurred no expense and had the benefit of a wall in good condition. His liabilities for future repair would be less as the wall would have had an "increased life". Here again, the sum of £500 was awarded in addition for distress and inconvenience.

In *Treml v. Ernest W. Gibson & Partners* [1984] 272 E.G. 68, the plaintiff paid £21,000 for a property which was found later to have defects in its roof and a wall. These were undetected by the surveyor. The Judge accepted evidence that the property was worth in fact £8,000 at the date of purchase. The cost of repair was a factor in this approach. The Judge considered what would a property developer have been prepared to pay for the property allowing for cost of repair prior to re-sale.

In addition, the Judge awarded £1,250 for distress experienced by the plaintiff and her family as they had to move into a hotel for 10 weeks whilst repairs were carried out. The plaintiff had the benefit of a repair grant under Schedule 12 to the Housing Act 1980. The Judge refused to deduct this as a benefit which did not have to be taken into account. It was felt that a negligent surveyor should not be allowed to benefit from a council's generosity. Hopefully, the position would have been different in the case of an improvement grant. Likewise, where money is recovered by a purchaser from property damage insurers this should be deducted before considering what other damages may be appropriate. It is unfortunate that this decision has not been challenged in any subse-

454

quent reported cases as it represents a novel departure in the award of damages.

In *Wilson v. Baxter Payne & Lepper* (1985) 273 EG 406, a property had been purchased in 1981 for £45,000. It transpired that the property was suffering from settlement damage resulting from inadequate foundations for the London clay on which the house was built. There was a clear conflict between the independent experts as to whether underpinning was necessary. As a consequence, estimates of the diminution in value of the property varied considerably. £8,000 might have to be spent on repairs to the property if no underpinning was necessary. However, £17,500 might have to be spent if underpinning was necessary. With the wisdom of Solomon, the Judge arrived at a figure of £12,500 which was virtually in the middle of the two figures. There was no evidence that underpinning had to be carried out of necessity. So far as distress was concerned, £500 was awarded to Mr Wilson and £700 to Mrs Wilson who had to endure the problem all the time.

The surveyor's liability in *Hooberman v. Salter Rex* (1985) has been considered already. So far as damages were concerned, the Judge found little difficulty in assessing the figure for diminution in value as a nominal sum of £875. However, the real issue concerned the cost of rectifying the dry rot which had taken a real hold before it was discovered some four years after the survey. However, the Judge held that diminution in value as at the time of the survey was the sole test for assessing damages. Nothing was awarded for this. A further head of claim in respect of damaged plants on the terrace of the property was dismissed. The plaintiff did recover £600 for distress and inconvenience.

The surveyors failure to detect "mundic" construction in *Marder v. Sautelle & Hicks* [1988] has been considered already. Diminution in market value was assessed at £19,500 being the difference between the price paid of £33,000 and what the property was believed to be worth in its defective condition, namely £13,500. Shortly after the trial of the case in November 1986 the property was sold for £70,000, having been purchased in 1979. The receipt of the sale proceeds did not destroy the basis of the award of damages. The fact that the subsequent purchaser of the property may have paid too much for it was no argument for reducing the damages. Also, it must have been of some significance that extension work to the property costing £26,000 was carried out in 1982.

Steward v. Rapley [1989] 15 EG 198, is the most recent example of the way in which a court, conceding that diminution in value remains the normal measure of damage, has found a means of awarding what was effectively the cost of repair. It is a Court of Appeal decision and, as such, is of particular significance.

In 1984 the plaintiffs bought a property in Mid-Glamorgan for the negotiated price of £58,500. The defendant firm had been instructed to carry out a House Buyers' Report and Valuation. This described the property as having been constructed apparently in 1870 and gave a valuation of £60,000. Recommendations were made regarding repairs to the roof covering but nothing so

455

significant as to deter the plaintiffs from purchasing. A year later, dry rot was discovered. This was a cause of considerable anxiety to the plaintiffs as their family had increased by then. Following a preliminary report from timber specialists, an independent surveyor was consulted. He was of the view that the dry rot should have been pointed out prior to purchase and that the property's value then would have been £50,000. When builders were opening the damaged areas, the dry rot was found to be far worse than had been anticipated. The final cost of eradication was £26,800. The plaintiffs' expert then gave a further report in which he said the value prior to purchase would have been £33,200.

Was the correct measure of damage:
£8,500 (£58,500 less £50,000) OR
£25,300 (£58,500 less £32,200)?

Inevitably, the Plaintiffs maintained that if the true extent of the problem had been pointed out to them prior to purchase they would not have proceeded. On this basis they argued that cost of repair might be the correct measure of damage. Before the trial a formal admission was made to the effect that the defendants were negligent in having failed to point out the likely or possible presence of dry rot in the cellar, front bedroom, dining room and one of the toilets. As such, the plaintiffs were not advised to have the property inspected by timber specialists prior to purchase. The Trial Judge held that £8,500 was the correct measure but the Court of Appeal decided otherwise. The Court accepted that the principle of diminution laid down in *Philips v. Ward* applied. However, there was nothing in such decision which dealt with a situation where there is a condition in the property which may be worse than it appeared at first sight but which could be identified with reasonable prudence and further investigation. This was the distinguishing feature.

If strict application of the diminution rule will create a financial hardship to the plaintiffs then it will not be applied mechanically. The plaintiffs might not have bought the property at all if they had known the full extent of the problem before purchase. In reaching this conclusion, the Court relied upon another Court of Appeal decision involving a claim against solicitors, namely *County Personnel (Employment Agency) Ltd. v. Alan R. Pulver & Co* [1987] 1 WLR 916, [1986] 2 EGLR 246.

It was argued for the defence that hindsight could not be used in assessing market value at a given date. The Court said that market value in this context takes account only of defects which are discoverable with reasonable diligence and not those which are concealed. "What the eye cannot see, the pocket does not care about. Mutton dressed as lamb may well have the market value of lamb, until somebody discovers that it is mutton. A house with a defective foundation which nobody can discover until the day it falls down will, until that day, have the same value in the market as a sound house ...".

An award of £2,000 made by the Trial Judge for distress and

inconvenience to the plaintiffs remained. This reflected interference with family life at a time when another child had just been born.

Fee recovery

If a surveyor is found to be in breach of contract or negligent, is he entitled to recover his fees for the survey? Following *Hill v. Debenham, Tewson & Chinnocks* (1958) 171 EG 835, a surveyor will be able to recover such fees unless his advice was so wrong that it could be described as worthless.

LIMITATION OF ACTIONS

Limitation Act 1980. Prescription and Limitation of Actions (Scotland) Act 1973

This is a principle of public policy which bars a cause of action if proceedings are not commenced within the prescribed legal limitation periods. The intention is to prevent stale claims from being made. So far as the Courts of English jurisdiction are concerned, limitation periods are laid down in the Limitation Act 1980. In Scotland, the principle is known as Prescription and involves a total extinction of a right or an obligation after a prescribed period of time. The limitation periods are set out in the Prescription and Limitation of Actions (Scotland) Act 1973.

In both the 1973 and 1980 Acts, there is a common limitation period of three years in respect of claims involving personal injury or death. Otherwise, the limitation periods are different and must be considered separately.

In contract

So far as English Courts are concerned, the limitation period in respect of claims in contract is to be found in Section 5 of the 1980 Act. An action founded on contract shall not be brought after the expiration of six years from when the cause of action accrued. This means from when the breach occurred and not when damage was suffered. In effect, this means that time starts to run from the date of the survey report. Where the contract is entered into under seal (most unusual for surveys) the limitation period is 12 years.

In tort

The position regarding claims founded in the tort of negligence is different. Such claims are discussed in Section 2 of the 1980 Act. An action in tort shall not be brought after the expiration of six years from the date on which damage is suffered and not the breach. This is a lot more open ended. Normally, the limitation period will begin to run from when the plaintiff acts in reliance upon the survey report by entering into a contract for purchase of a property. It is possible that this might not be until some considerable time after the survey report.

A good example of the distinction is to be found in *Secretary of State for the Environment v. Essex, Goodman & Suggitt* [1986] 2 All E.R. 69 and (1985) 276 EG 308. The sequence of events was as follows:

— survey carried out in February 1975;
— plaintiff entered into contract for a 25 year lease in July 1975;
— first signs of defect noticed in February 1976;
— Writ not issued until January 1982.

457

There was no doubt that a claim in contract was time barred (by February 1981). However, what was the position in tort? The Judge held that proceedings should have been commenced by July 1981 being six years from when the plaintiff contracted to enter into the lease. As such, the proceedings were time barred and were struck out.

Latent Damage Act 1986

In many cases, a prospective plaintiff may not be aware of the fact that he has the basis for a claim because the defect may not have manifested itself. It may be many years later before it is realised that there may be a defect. It was with this in mind that the Latent Damage Act 1986 came into force on 18th September 1986. Originally, it applied to England and Wales only but was extended to Northern Ireland at the end of 1987. It does not apply to Scotland. The Act is not retrospective which means that any claims which were statute barred before the Act came into force remained so barred. Likewise, the Act does not affect actions commenced before the Act came into force. It does not apply to breaches of contract for which the six year period remains.

The 1986 Act has the effect of adding various sections to the 1980 Act. It introduced an overall "long stop" period of 15 years from the date of breach after which proceedings would be time barred in any event. Only in cases of fraud or disability (involving infants or those of unsound mind) can the 15 year period be extended. Within the long stop period the basic rule of six years for accrual of a cause of action remains.

Still within the 15 year long stop period, but as an extension to the six year rule, is a new period of three years known as the "starting date". This is defined as the earliest date on which the plaintiff or any person in whom the cause of action was vested before him had both the knowledge required for bringing an action for damages in respect of the relevant damage and a right to bring such an action. "Knowledge" is defined extensively in the Act—that in itself would form a discussion in a separate chapter! It involves knowledge of both the material facts about the damage and also the identity of the defendant.

The limitation period is best summarised as follows:

— damage plus six years;

OR

— knowledge plus three years

UNLESS

— breach plus 15 years has occurred already.

Scottish differences

The 1973 Act provides for two different Prescription periods in Scotland. Firstly, there is a five year period, known as short negative prescription, for the bringing of actions for reparation, including property damage. This is the period within which the pursuer could with reasonable diligence have become aware of the damage. Secondly, there is a 20 year long stop or long negative Prescription period after which no claim can be pursued. The longer period has been under review with the possibility of it being reduced to 15 years to fit in with English legislation.

Indeed, the Scottish Law Commission published a report in October 1989 recommending that the 20 year long stop provision should be reduced to 15 years. The report contains a further recommendation that the short negative prescription period should remain at five years. Although the report includes a draft Parliamentary Bill implementing the recommendations it is not known when this may become law.

Mention was made of persons under disability. The limitation period does not commence until the cessation of the disability or death, if earlier. In cases of deliberate concealment, the limitation period does not commence until the date of reasonable discoverability of the concealment.

CLAIMS PROCEDURE

What is a claim?

Notifying possible claims

"A demand for something as due; an assertion of a right to something."

This is the Oxford Dictionary definition relied upon by Mr Justice Devlin in the Accountants case of *West Wake Price v. Ching* [1956] 3 All ER 821.

This may seem fairly clear cut. However, where an indication is given that a claim may be made at some time in the future, depending upon intervening events, then this may amount to a circumstance. As a precaution, it may be advisable for surveyors to notify circumstances to their insurers. Certainly, this is a requirement under the wording of the RICS professional indemnity collective policy. It is a question of looking at the policy wording and seeing what benefits are available. It is most important to take legal advice as soon as possible. This may be available under the terms of the surveyor's indemnity policy.

It is vital that a surveyor should not worry all the time about the cost of next year's insurance premium. It is folly to imperil a current insurance policy by delaying notification of a possible claim or circumstance for the sake of the cost of next year's premium. Likewise, it can be very dangerous to change insurers whilst there are claim circumstances outstanding. The wording of insurance policies can differ. As such, it is possible that a surveyor might be uninsured for a particular claim even though he has had continuous insurance. A new insurer may take the line that a claim should have been notified to a previous insurer and decline cover as a consequence.

Policy to be in force when claim made

It should be stressed that professional indemnity policies are upon a claims made basis which means that a policy must be in force at the time a claim is made and not when the survey was carried out. This could have been some years ago.

Regarding allegations of negligence, a surveyor should be frank, open and self critical. If an insurer is not given sufficient information then he may react unsympathetically. It is possible that the less an insurer is told about a possible claim then the extent of

459

wall ventilator, fitted shelves, double 3 pin power point and fitted carpet to floor.

Landing	With fitted carpet.
Rear Room	8'10" × 11'7" (net) with range of built-in wardrobe cupboards with hanging rails, central dressing table recess and additional compartments at head and base of wall cupboard unit. Single panel radiator, two single 3 pin power points and fitted carpet to floor.
Bathroom	7'10" × 7'5" (overall) with panelled bath with chromium plated mixer with shower fitting, accessories including plastic curtain and rail. W.C. with plastic seat and ceramic cistern, Twyfords pedestal hand basin with chromium plated taps, single panel radiator, mirror faced toilet cabinet, cupboard with lagged copper hot water cylinder with electric immersion heater and shelf above. Sundry accessories and fitted carpet to bathroom floor.

Ground Floor

Entrance Hall	With part panelled front door with decorative leaded pane and leaded sidelights in timber framing, Yale lock, Mortice lock, letter box, bolt and chain. Inner hall area with single panel radiator and cupboard under stairs with gas intake and meter and electric intake, meter, main switch and fuses. 3 pin power point and electric light. Fitted carpet to hall floor and recess with hat and coat hooks.
Main Through Living Room	
Front Section	13'2" (overall) × 11'6" with bay window in addition. Chimney breast with shelf and shaped alcove with semi-circular head and two shelves below. Single panel radiator to bay, three double 3 pin power points, television point and fitted carpet to floor.
Rear Section	12'0" × 10'9" (overall) with chimney breast and alcove with shelves similar to front section, fitted serving hatch, double glazed casement doors to kitchen with mortice lock and bolt, single panel radiator, two double 3 pin power points and fitted carpet to floor.
Kitchen	7'4" × 9'0" with stainless steel sink unit with chromium plated mixer with drawer and cupboard under. Fitted shelves to alcove under staircase, decorative tiled working top below serving hatch with wall cabinets above and drawers and floor cupboards under. Recesses for existing electric cooker and refrigerator. Wall ventilator, wall mounted Ideal W (Selrad Group) gas fired boiler with Landis & Gyr timer below. Electric wall mounted cooker point and two wall mounted power points, sundry accessories including Easiclene waste disposer and floor covered vinyl tiles.
Rear Dining Room	15'3" × 9'5" (approximate overall dimensions) with tiled shelf/working top with cupboards with louvred doors below and wall mounted shelves above. Double radiator, two double 3 pin power points and solid floor covered fitted carpet.

Externally

Rear Terrace	15'3" in maximum depth.
Rear Garden	82'7" from edge of terrace to back boundary.
Small Conservatory	With aluminium frame, glazed panels, brick plinth on concrete base and adjacent fletton brick and concrete barbeque structure.
Single Garage	9'3" × 18'9" (net opening 7'2") of pre-fabricated pre-cast concrete units with corrugated asbestos roof and solid concrete floor. "Up and over" metal door with single access door at side, two striplights, double 3 pin power point, shelf and rear fixed window.

THE STRUCTURAL CONDITION AND STATE OF REPAIR

The Main and Subsidiary Roofs

The Main Roof

The main roof is of pitched design and consists of three separate tiled slops, joined at the apex by a central ridge which runs parallel to the frontage of the building.

Access to the main roofspace is obtained by means of a hatch formed in the ceiling of the top floor landing. This, in fact, appears to be of solid board construction but consists of four glass panes in a large wood surround painted over below, so that care is needed in opening this unit. A purpose made trap door with loft ladder would be preferable as an improvement in the future, the hatch and surround being remade.

Inspection in the main roofspace shows that the tiles with which the roof slopes are covered are laid on wood battens nailed to timber rafters of conventional pattern. These measure 4″ × 2″ in thickness and are placed at intervals apart of 1′2″ or thereabouts. The rafters rest, at their lower ends, upon timber wall plates formed over the head of the front and rear walls of the main structure and are formed, at their upper ends, to meet the central ridgeboard. Intermediate support to the rafters is provided by a single 4″ × 3″ purlin to each roofslope, the front and rear purlins being braced by two angled struts, while the side purlin has a single angled strut. Two 4″ × 2″ timber ties run from front to rear of the roof structure.

Roof space

Inspection shows that some minor unevenness and deflection has occurred in the timbers which comprise the roof structure. The purlin to the side roofslope slopes slightly to the front and rear corner abutments and the bedding of the front and rear purlin ends in the solid fletton brickwork of the party wall shows some disturbance. Some minor splits were noted to timbers and it is evident that what has happened is that some very minor distortion and bedding down of the roof structure under the weight of the tiled coverings has occurred. I do not however, consider that this is serious. I recommend that the disturbed brickwork at the point where the purlin ends into the party wall be made good but this is a minor matter.

One further matter however, that should also need attention, although again, relatively minor, is that the rafters adjacent to the chimney stack and party wall are discoloured due to old damp staining and I recommend that some preservative treatment of the timber be carried out at the head of, and adjacent to, the stack.

Inspection in the main roofspace shows that the solid fletton brickwork to the party wall is basically intact and in sound order and the chimney stack, which has a coating of rendering, is also in reasonable condition.

The timber joists which support the first floor ceilings are similar in size and spacing to the rafters and run from front to rear of the house structure. The joists are stiffened by timber binders running from side to side and the structural condition is satisfactory. Glass mineral fibre has been laid between the joists so as to provide adequate insulation and this is a good feature. The surface of the fibreglass sections however show signs of dust and debris and some cleaning and vacuuming of the roofspace is ideally desirable.

Cold water cistern

A plastic cold water storage cistern of adequate size is installed in the roofspace on timbers bearers and this is obviously of fairly recent provision evidently replacing an earlier cistern. A small circular balance tank is situated nearby. The cistern is provided with a cover and side casing of

1. Front and side elevations showing entrance drive.

2. Disturbed brickwork in roofspace to end of rear purlin.

3. Slight deflection of side purlin each side of central strut.

4. Missing nib to tile viewed from roofspace.

5. View of back addition and garage roofs.

6. A further view of the back addition roof.

7. Rear elevation of building.

8. Rear view showing boundaries.

*9. Original boiler flue cut away and balance
flue to boiler provided in its place.*

10. Minor crack indicating a small amount of differential movement between main and back addition structures.

11. *Cracking between porch structure and front wall of house.*

upper flat containing electricity fuses and meter and bracket lighting point. Further small door to cupboard at high level below stairs containing gas meter. Door to

Lobby   Range of fitted cupboards containing shelves and hanging space, also slatted shelving above a 20 gallon electric water heater with double element. Permanent ventilator.

Note: The second dimension given for each of the Front Rooms has been taken into the square bay windows as their width is only between 2′ and 4′ less than the full width of the rooms. Even so, you will note that there are a number of discrepancies in the selling agent's particulars in regard to the dimensions of the rooms.

Fittings are described as seen on the day of my inspection. You should agree with the vendor, if you decide to proceed with the purchase, a list of those which are to be conveyed with the property, particularly gas fires and kitchen appliances. When asked during my inspection the vendor was uncertain as to which fittings he would be taking with him.

THE MAIN AND SUBSIDIARY ROOFS

The Main Roof   The main roof is of pitched construction with the ridge parallel to the frontage and is provided with gables over the two storey square bay windows at the front. The red machine made clay tiles which are fixed to boarding are supported traditionally on a timber framework comprising 4″ × 2″ softwood rafters at 14″ centres fixed to an 8″ × 1¼″ ridge and tied at the feet by 4″ × 2″ ceiling joists. Over their length the rafters are provided with intermediate support from 7″ × 2″ purlins spanning from side to side which in turn are supported by 4″ × 2″ struts taken off a continuous length of 4″ × 2″ bearer at the front and shorter lengths at the rear.

The general arrangement is shown on photograph 3 below, which shows the purlin and struts supporting the rafters to the front slope which is on the left of the photograph. The purlin and strutting to the rear slope

3. General arrangement of roof structure looking east.

rafters are shown on photograph 4 and another view of the general arrangement looking west is shown on photograph 5.

4. Purlin and struts to rear slope of main roof.

5. General arrangement of roof structure looking west.

The tiled slopes do not extend to cover the triangular area at the rear since the front and rear walls are not parallel. This triangular area comprises a flat roof with its greatest depth at the western end of the property from where photograph 6 below was taken. All that can be seen of this section of flat roofing is that the ceiling joists extend into this area beyond the ends of the rafters to the rear slope, as shown on photograph 7, overleaf.

6. Area of flat roofing covering triangular area at rear looking east.

7. Plate taking feet of rafters to rear slope showing ceiling joists extending into triangular area at rear forming flat roof.

9. Western end of main roof showing parapet wall with zinc flashing and lead flashing to tiling.

8. Buckled bituminous felt to triangular area of flat roofing at rear.

Measurements taken confirm that the construction consists of 4″ × 2″ ceiling joists with probably a layer of 1″ boarding to support the bituminous felt, now extensively buckled and which must be considered at or very nearly approaching the end of its useful life, as seen on photograph 8 above. This type of covering is more in the form of a temporary expedient with a life normally of about 15 years if properly laid. It is probably a replacement for an original covering of zinc since there are sections of zinc flashing to the short length of parapet wall at the west end as shown on photograph 9 on the left hand side and around the chimney stack shown on the right of photograph 6 on the previous page.

The tile covering to the roof slopes is basically the original, now some 80–90 years old, and typical of the quality of tiles used, though much repaired over the years and now presenting a very patched appearance. The vendor informed me that it had been necessary to carry out some recent repairs following the winter gales. These included tile replacements, resetting ridge tiles and refixing loose flashings. These repairs have been carried out in a fairly crude manner and there are still a number of broken and laminating tiles and open joints to ridge tiles at the front of the property where these are difficult to reach.

Although it would no doubt be possible to continue patching the roof, the risk of damp penetration would remain high. The time has therefore come for a major scheme of repair and renewal so that the roof can be left in a condition to provide the occupants with years of trouble-free service.

Such a major overhaul would need to include a thorough examination and renewal, if necessary, of all the lead. This is used extensively as gutters, flashings and soakers at the four valley junctions of the roof slopes at the front and where the tiling abuts other features such as the flank wall of the studios next door. Lead is the best material used in building for this

10. Inadequately strutted joint to purlin of rear slope.

11. The same as 10 above but showing more clearly how the two halves of the joint are out of alignment.

purpose and well worth retaining and renewing where necessary. The work should also include the replacement in lead of the old zinc flashings where these occur at the rear.

There are no signs of undue waviness in the tiled slopes from external examination apart from slight unevenness around the central area of the rear slope. This indicates that in general the timber structure is satisfactory for carrying the load of boarding and tiles. Indeed the clear span of the rafters at between five and six feet is well within the normal maximum span for these timbers and the purlins are clearly of a satisfactory size and strutted correctly in the main.

An examination in the roof space, however, shows that the purlin for the rear slope has been inadequately strutted where it is jointed at the centre point of its length. This has meant that the two sections do not fit together tightly in the same plane as can be seen in photographs 10 and 11 on the left. The settlement which has resulted in at least one rafter adjacent is not sufficient to cause dampness to penetrate. Nevertheless, the strut should be wedged to the purlin and similarly the two halved sections of purlin also wedged so that no further movement occurs.

A close examination of the accessible and visible timbers in the roof space was made for signs of attack by wood boring insect or for signs of wet or dry rot. None were found, even although there is some staining from previous damp penetration as for example in the area below the valley gutter, shown on photograph 12 below. The damp penetration at this point has caused the staining on the ceiling in the Front Room Left, the Sitting Room of the First Floor Flat, near the fireplace, as shown on photograph 13 overleaf. The vendor said this dampness was caused by tiles

12. Staining of timbers below valley gutter at west end of roof space due to blockage and cause of staining on ceiling shown on photograph 13.

could be ideal for dry rot to occur. Damp from condensation is prevented by a vapour barrier. However, it remains vitally important to ensure that damp does not penetrate the balcony surface or get into the structure through defects in the asphalt skirting around the roof as could be the case if the defect mentioned on page 495 and illustrated on photograph 15 is not repaired.

I have been able to see the vendor's plans but I have not been able to see whether the construction as built is identical because of the presence of the asphalt surfacing and the fixed ceilings below. There is no evidence however to indicate that the construction is not as shown and there is no indication of damp penetration even below the defective skirting on the renewed section of ceiling in the Ground Floor Rear Bedroom.

Flat Roofs to Rear Oriel Windows

According to the vendor's plans these small roofs are constructed basically in the same way as the Balcony roof except that the joists measure $3'' \times 2''$ and are carried on hangers from the lintel above the opening and cantilevered outwards. The same remarks on verification and performance apply to these roofs as to the Balcony roof as they were constructed at the same time and photograph 16 shows that a similar defect is beginning to develop with the asphalt skirtings which will also require repair.

Chimney Stacks

There are five chimney stacks serving this property, three containing two flues and two stacks containing a single flue. The three stacks containing two flues serving the Front and Rear Rooms Left and the Front Room Right at both floor levels are in fair condition, although the front stack at the western end leans in towards the roof slightly. This is not serious but the pointing, cement fillets to the oversailing courses and the flaunching around the rather mixed collection of different types of chimney pot used could all do with attention at the same time as the major overhaul to the main roof is carried out. Alternatively, those not intended for continued use for gas fires could be reduced in height and capped off, provided through ventilation is left to the interior to prevent condensation.

16. Small flat roof over one of the oriel windows at the rear showing similar defect developing as shown on photograph 15 in skirting.

The single flue stack to the ground floor Kitchen/Dining Room at the rear takes the flue gasses from the gas fired central heating boiler and is attached to the first floor rear wall. It projects about 4' above the flat roof section of the main roof, as shown on the right of photograph 6 where, also, the pronounced lean to the left can be clearly seen. In conjunction with the bulge in the rear wall at first floor level, to be referred to later, the stack is bowed and leaning about 2'' out of plumb over its height. This is not sufficiently serious as to warrant rebuilding at this stage but the stack will need monitoring over the years to ensure that the condition does not worsen and present a risk of collapse.

The top of the single flue boiler stack is finished with a metal cowling confirming the vendor's statement that the flue was provided with a stainless steel liner four years ago, when partial central heating was installed to the ground floor flat. The statement however cannot be verified in total without removing the capping and examining the interior of the flue.

The remaining stack serving the Dining Room to the first floor flat is formed within the party wall separating the property from the studio/workshop premises to the east, as shown on photograph 17 opposite top left. Although the brickwork and pointing are generally fair, the section which extends above the party wall has developed a slight fracture which should either be repaired and the brickwork repointed or the stack reduced in height and capped off if the flue is not required.

Rainwater Disposal at Front

At the front of the property rainwater is collected from the roof slopes

17. Chimney stack serving First Floor Dining Room fireplace formed within party wall to adjoining Studios.

Rainwater Disposal at Rear

mainly by cast iron gutters fixed to fascia boards forming part of the deep overhanging eaves. Because of the presence of gable roofs over the projecting square bay windows there is a need for separate sections of guttering and rainwater pipes at both the east and west ends and in the centre as well. Gutters cannot be inspected on this elevation without the aid of a long ladder and accordingly no detailed indication can be given of their condition. It is significant however that the central gutter section above the first floor Bathroom window and the associated rainwater pipe has been replaced in plastic. The need for this replacement is obvious from the damp staining to the walls of the Front Rooms Left, the Sitting Rooms of both flats and the staining to the brickwork externally in the area of the rainwater pipe. The other gutters and rainwater pipes on this elevation are probably still the original and should now be considered at the end of their useful life and in need of renewal.

If gutters or rainwater pipes develop faults it is important that they are renewed promptly or, better still, in regard to this elevation, renewed entirely at the same time as the recommended major overhaul of the roof. If they are not, and brickwork becomes saturated, there is always a danger of rot developing in timberwork of floors where there is no through ventilation. In regard to this property, there is softness and waviness in the skirtings of both the Sitting Rooms where dampness can be seen to have penetrated in the past. Floorboards were raised in both rooms adjacent to the affected skirtings but there were no indications of rot to the joists or boards. The damage from the past damp penetration can therefore be shown to have been limited to attacks of wet rot to the skirtings which require renewal. The adjacent brickwork was tested with a moisture meter and found now to have dried out completely so that there is no danger of any wet rot spreading to other timbers.

At the rear the discharge of water from the main roof is collected by a cast iron ogee shaped gutter fixed to a wood fascia board. The gutter is in two sections because of the intervening chimney stack and there are outlets at both east and west ends. At the west end there is a 3″ cast iron rainwater pipe with a right angled bend at its foot, as shown on photograph 18, left. Apart from the untidiness of the detail there is nothing inherently wrong with this arrangement and the appearance is probably better and less liable to the complications of blockage than would be the case if the pipe were to be extended round the chimney stack and along the parapet wall at the west end of the balcony to discharge, with attendant bends, into the gutter at the top of the ground floor rear wall. Nevertheless both gutter and rainwater pipe are old and approaching the end of their useful life. At present the gutter is clogged with debris which should be cleared to prevent overflowing in the meantime before renewal.

At the east end the rainwater is taken by means of a plastic rainwater pipe to discharge into the plastic half round gutter at the foot of the small lean-to roof over the first floor larder. It was understood from the vendor that this pipe was renewed when the felt roof covering over the larder was repaired about 2–3 years ago. The present arrangement is adequate and evidently effective if somewhat untidy in appearance. From here the rainwater is taken by means of a 3″ cast iron rainwater pipe to discharge over a gulley situated at the rear of the side entrance to the workshops next door.

18. Bend at foot of rainwater pipe discharging rainwater from rear of main roof on to balcony.

Rainwater disposal from balcony

Rainwater flows off the balcony at the rear into an ogee shaped pressed steel gutter, visible on photograph 16, thence to discharge into a 3″ steel rainwater pipe with a shoe at its foot over a gulley by the double doors leading from the ground floor Kitchen/Dining Room. This arrangement has the appearance of having been installed about 7–8 years ago when the alterations to the ground floor flat were made and is satisfactory.

THE MAIN WALLS

Description

The main walls to this property are of solid brick construction and, as is typical of most of the properties in this area and of this size and age, are 9″ in thickness. This thickness of brickwork is generally satisfactory for a two storey building from a structural point of view. It is not however as efficient either at keeping out the weather when exposed to driving rain or at insulating the building against heat loss as a brick wall of cavity construction.

Brickwork of this thickness when used for two storey construction needs adequate restraint from the possibility of sideways movement and this aspect, together with the condition of external pointing, are vital factors in maintaining satisfactory performance. Close attention was paid to these aspects during my inspection.

In properties of this age, wall restraint is normally provided by the building in of floor joists, by the bonding to other walls at the corners and by the weight of the roof which, if properly braced and with correctly nailed joints, will assist in preventing outward movement.

With this property the timber floor joists at first floor level run from side to side, i.e. from east to west, and therefore the only restraint to the main part of the front wall of the property is provided by the weight of the roof and the fact that the wall is divided into three sections along its length by the presence of the square bay windows. Because of the bond at the corners these tend to make the wall stronger than would be the case if the wall was constructed in one continuous length.

19. Looking up at front wall of bay window showing that bowing outwards is barely perceptible.

Nevertheless in the front walls of the bay windows there are signs of slight movement since these are not only extended to a higher level to form the apex of the gables but also do not have the benefit of restraint from the roof load. In consequence they have bowed out slightly in the centre, as evidenced by the opening of the joint at the centre of the sills to the windows and cracking to plaster internally above the windows in the cornice to the ceiling as shown on photograph 20. As decorations have been renewed a few years ago in one room and the cracks show no sign of re-opening it can be assumed with reasonable certainty that the bay window front walls have reached a position of repose and are unlikely to move further. As will be seen the movement is just perceptible on photograph 19.

There is similar slight movement to the west flank wall of the property which although restrained at first floor level rises as a gable to follow the line of the roof. Again, the movement is only just perceptible externally, see photograph 21, opposite top right, because some additional support is provided by the two chimney breasts. A slight crack is evident internally at the end of the partition separating the Front and Rear Rooms Left, where it meets the flank wall.

Neither of the two foregoing wall movements are serious and they are not unusual or untoward in a property of this age. What is more serious is the evident outward bulging of the rear wall, together with the single flue

498

20. Cracks internally to Ground Floor Living Room (Front Left) are visible where left unfilled and undecorated to ceiling due to bowing of front wall to bay window.

21. Movement barely detectable externally in west flank wall above first floor level but inducing cracks visible internally.

boiler stack, at first floor level, as shown on photograph 22 on the left. So far as the chimney stack extends above the level of the flat roof the bulging is also very evident on the right of photograph 6.

The outward bowing of the general walling is more evident by way of the half-inch crack shown on photograph 23 overleaf at the junction between the rear wall internally and the partition separating the Dining Room from the staircase landing of the first floor flat. That this bulging movement may well be of a slow but continuing nature can be gauged from the gap between the outer brickwork and the window frames in each of the windows to the Dining Room and Rear Room Left Bedroom, the latter shown on photograph 24 also overleaf. As can be seen from the photograph the gap has been filled with mortar at some time in the past but has continued to open as the brickwork moves away from the window frame.

As the rear wall at first floor level is a mere 10′ or so in height it is not immediately evident as to why it should bulge in this manner. The wall at its base is built off steel beams 9″ deep carried within the depth of the ceiling to the ground floor flat and spanning from the flank walls to the single brick thick structural partition wall separating the rear Bedroom from the Dining Room/Kitchen. Due to the existence of the asphalt roofing externally and the ceilings below it is not possible, without opening up the structure, to ascertain the width of these beams. Nevertheless they show no sign of deflection along their length and it is therefore fair to assume that they are adequate for their purpose.

22. Outward bulging of rear wall and single flue boiler stack at first floor level.

23. *Crack at junction of rear wall and partition separating Dining Room from Staircase landing at first floor level.*

24. *Gap between brickwork and frame to Dining Room window at first floor level.*

Possibility of further movement

The wall is therefore firmly held at its base and, accordingly, it is probable that there must be a sideways thrust at the top from the feet of the rafters comprising the rear part of the main roof. This may be due to the way the lower ends of the rafters are carried on a plate running along the top of the ceiling joists, as shown on photograph 7. Even though the fixing of the three timbers at this junction may be sound and secure, there could still be an eccentric thrust through pressure on the ceiling joists since there is no real support from below as there would be if the feet of the rafters were carried on the top of a brick wall.

The bow in the wall and the chimney stack at the rear of the first floor is not so serious in my view at the present time as to warrant immediate rebuilding, but this is a possibility that cannot be ruled out for the future in view of the evidence of continuing movement. Since the section of flat roofing at the rear and the tiled slopes need stripping and re-covering the opportunity should be taken to examine all the joints at the feet of the rafters to ensure that all fixings are secure and, if not, to renail or preferably provide screw or bolted connections. The joint between window frames and brickwork will need to be remade when the windows are replaced (see the need for this in the section on windows and external doors), as will the joint between any internal partitions and the rear wall. These remade joints can then be monitored to check whether movement is continuing or not. If it is, then it will be necessary eventually to rebuild the wall in a strengthened form to prevent a re-occurrence of the bulging.

Other than the movements described above there are no indications of settlement or other movements in the general surfaces of the main walls or in the piers of brickwork between window and door openings or move-

500

ment associated with defective beams or arches above such openings. It is significant that all the movements noted derive from causes high above ground level so that the foundations to the walls of whatever form they might be (and they cannot, of course, be seen without digging down) may be considered satisfactory for their purpose as must the subsoil on which the property is founded.

Bricks and Pointing

Three different types of brick are used for this property. On the front and east flank elevations yellow London stock bricks are used with smoother red facing bricks on the corners and for band courses. These, together with the pointing, are in satisfactory condition as is the stonework around the openings in the square bay windows and which is also carried up as strips to the rendered brick gable walls.

To the rear, however, cheaper Fletton bricks have been used at first floor level with brick arches to windows and doors. Although generally bricks and pointing are in fair condition they are more prone to weathering on this elevation and the pointing will need renewal, perhaps sooner than on the front and flank elevations, possibly within 10–20 years or so. Minor local repairs are required which should be dealt with where earlier attachments to the brickwork have been removed.

At ground floor level the brickwork has been painted and the vendor informed me that in carrying out the alterations seven years ago, a mixture of rough and smooth bricks was used and the concrete lintels installed above the door and window openings were left exposed. These provided a poor appearance which the vendor subsequently disguised by painting the surfaces and then fixing a heavy quality wood trellis on wood battens, both secured with brass screws so that the trellis could be taken down when the wall required repainting. All these features as described are in fair condition.

Damp Proofing

Near the base of brick walls enclosing a building there is now, and has been for many years, a requirement that a damp-proof course be installed. This is a thin layer of impervious material, which, when installed, prevents the rise of dampness in the wall by capillary action from the ground.

At the time this property was built some local properties were provided either with damp-proof courses of an inferior type of material, or alternatively with the damp-proof course in the wrong position. Apart from the merest trace of some form of bituminous material in a brick joint near the entrance door to the ground floor flat, however, there is no evidence remaining of any damp proof course which may have been installed originally in the external walls.

The vendor informed me that when he first saw the property there was extensive damp staining internally to the lower sections of the external walls. Subsequently, Pentokil were employed to provide a damp-proof course of silicone material injected into the base of the walls and for the stained plaster to be hacked off and renewed. The work, he said, was carried out to Pentokil's usual guarantee, the documents for which are held by his solicitors. The date when the work was certified by Rentokil as having been carried out satisfactorily, the period of the guarantee and the arrangements necessary for the benefit of the guarantee to be transferred are matters which should be verified by your solicitor before contracts are exchanged, assuming you wish to proceed with the purchase.

In the light of this information, a careful check was made with a moisture meter for the presence of rising damp in the lower sections of the external walls. None was found and there is, therefore, every indication that the work was carried out in a satisfactory manner. Indeed in the ground floor front room left, the sitting room, the new plaster can be seen along the base of the front and flank walls where the walls have yet to be decorated, as shown on photograph 25 below left. This also shows the waviness in the skirting caused by earlier defects in the rainwater pipe adjacent, referred to in the first paragraph under the heading of Rainwater Disposal.

Windows

At the front of the property the windows are all of the wood casement type in wood frames with glazed leaded lights. They are not exposed to the prevailing weather and are protected to some extent by being well set back from the face of the brickwork, as well as by the projecting eaves detail to the roof and the barge boards. As a result they have remained in fairly good condition, apart from the window to the kitchen at first floor level which is ill-fitting and requires rehanging.

The original furniture to the windows at the front is of painted metal. Fasteners, stays and pins, where present, are barely serviceable, being bent and corroded, and some sections have broken. They could with advantage be replaced by the type of new brass fittings used in the Front Ground Floor Bedroom which are functional but in character with the building.

At the rear, the windows provide a contrast between the two floor levels. At first floor level the original wood casements with fanlights are larger than at the front and consequently weaker. They have also been badly neglected and are now in need of total renewal. One half of the larder window is shown on photograph 26 below and the Dining Room

25. New plaster at the base of the front wall in the Ground Floor Living Room undecorated since the installation of an injected chemical damp proof course. Photograph also shows waviness in skirting due to earlier damp penetration.

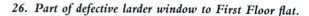

26. Part of defective larder window to First Floor flat.

27. Defective window and sill to First Floor Dining Room.

window on photograph 27 above. The cement sills to these and the other window at this level are cracked and defective allowing damp to penetrate causing bulged plaster and stains internally. This plaster will need hacking off and renewal following repair or renewal of the sills. Skirtings were tested with a probe, but the dampness has not extended downwards sufficiently to affect these in the areas concerned.

At ground floor level the original windows have been replaced by metal casements in wood frames. In the Dining Room/Kitchen and Bedroom they have been framed up as small oriel windows with cylindrical angle posts. These are all in satisfactory condition and are provided with lockable stays and fasteners.

A further fixed light window is formed in the flank wall of the Rear Bedroom. From the inside it appears in satisfactory condition, but it is not possible to see the exterior without gaining access to the side entrance passageway to No. 8 adjoining and on the day of my inspection there was no reply to my approach to the occupier next door. As the window appears to be original, I would suspect that the condition externally is poor. Clearly there are problems of access for cleaning and maintenance. Such a window would not be permitted under the current regulations on the boundary line and it could with advantage be bricked up, since it does not provide a great deal of additional light and cannot be opened.

External Doors   Both front entrance doors are in a satisfactory condition, although that to the ground floor flat is warped. At the rear the door to the balcony from

503

28. Defective door leading from First Floor flat on to balcony.

the upper flat is old and defective, as shown on photograph 28 above, and needs renewal as do the double doors from the ground floor flat leading out from the Bedroom. The other pair of double doors from the Kitchen are comparatively new, the glazed sections are double glazed and in good condition.

Support to Brickwork above Windows and Doors

Openings for windows and doors in external walls need to be provided with beams (lintels) across the top, to support the brickwork above. At the front of this property, as can be seen from the photograph on the cover to this report and from photograph 1, these are of stone except to the two smaller windows at first floor level.

The stone beams probably do not extend to the full thickness of the wall and typically, in a property of this age, it is to be expected that a second timber beam would be provided to support the inner half of the one brick thick walls. These timbers cannot be seen and are prone to attacks of rot through damp penetration and lack of ventilation. No defects were noted in the immediate vicinity of these lintels or any signs of rot by way of fungal growths or strands, but nevertheless it remains a possibility that such timbers are unsound and would require to be replaced in concrete if disturbed either now or at some future date.

It is probable that timber beams also support that section of the main roof immediately above the two smaller windows on the front elevation. These too cannot be seen but, as they are well protected by the deep projecting overhang of the roof, they are less vulnerable to wood rot and, provided gutters are kept in good order, they should remain satisfactory.

504

At the rear of the building, the same form of wood beam would be used behind the brick arches above the windows and doors at first floor level, as shown on photograph 14, and also over the windows in the west flank wall overlooking the side entrance passageway to No. 8. In view of the evident need to renew all these windows and the door the opportunity should be taken to check the condition of the beams. Because of the fact that the brickwork in front of these beams is exposed to driving rain by the prevailing wind it would be as well to allow for complete replacement of these five beams.

The drawings of the rear wall at ground level shown to me by the vendor indicated that all the openings for windows and doors were now spanned by reinforced concrete lintels of appropriate depth for their span. The external faces of these can be seen by inspection and there are no indications of defects, which would have become apparent by now if the beams had been badly made or incorrectly installed.

INTERNALLY

Ceilings   The ceilings throughout the first floor are of wood lath and plaster, as can be seen from the roof space and photographs 4 and 7. There is a loss of key of plaster to laths in a number of places judging from looseness when pressed. Most pronounced is a section of bowed ceiling over the staircase, as shown on photograph 29 below. This could be due to pressure from the plate taking the feet of the rafters to the rear slope of the main roof, photograph 4 again, but seems more likely to have been caused by leakage from the water cistern to the first floor preparatory to its renewal. Elsewhere in the two rooms on the east side of the landing there are a fair number of cracks to the ceilings and damp stains and a hole in the Bedroom ceiling suggesting that it may have been necessary to let water out from above the ceiling to relieve the pressure again perhaps if the water

29. Bowed ceiling plaster to First Floor flat above staircase landing.

30. Flaking decorations to First Floor Rear Bedroom ceiling.

cistern had suddenly burst. Photograph 30 above shows another part of the rear Bedroom ceiling with flaking decorations and photograph 31 below further damp staining in the Front Room.

Unfortunately, when plaster loses its key on ceilings there is no saying how long it will be before it falls. For certainty's sake the only solution is to take down and replace all loose and bulged areas and this is the course of

31. Damp staining to ceiling and frieze in First Floor Front Room Left, Sitting Room due to defective rainwater pipe now replaced.

506

32. First floor; impact damage.

Partition Walls

33. First floor; absence of making good.

Floors

action which is recommended for the landing and the two rooms on the east side. Against this there is the characteristic that many loose and bulged ceilings stay in place for many years provided they are not disturbed. The fact that most of the ceilings are first floor level are divided by small timber mouldings into squares may well help towards restraint, but it would not be wise to rely upon the mouldings as they are really too light for that purpose and a budget for replacement is the only prudent course.

At ground floor level the ceilings of the Front Rooms and the Entrance Hall and Lobby are probably the original and, where seen at one point, of lath and plaster construction. In the Bathroom and Kitchen/Dining Room the ceilings are of matchboarding, in the former at a lower level than the remainder of the flat which is appropriate for the narrow width of the compartment. In the rear Bedroom tapping the ceiling from front to back indicated that from about half way the construction was different as was to be expected in view of the renewal of the balcony above as explained by the vendor. I have only been able to see the vendor's plans, not the actual construction which is hidden, and which shows plasterboard and a skimming coat of plaster to line up with the existing lath and plaster section. Apart from some cracking associated with wall movements already described and small sections of missing cornice mouldings where the ceilings have not been redecorated recently there are no major problems visible to the ground floor ceilings.

All partition walls at ground floor level sound solid when struck and measure about 6″ overall. From the age of the building and the evidence obtained from the cupboard below the stairs to the first floor the partitions are almost certain to be of half brick construction, i.e. 4½″ thick, with a layer of plaster either side. Apart from areas of making good required, i.e. where electrical wiring has been installed and along the edge of door architraves, tops of skirtings, etc. there are no indications of defects.

In contrast, all partitions at first floor level sound hollow although still about 6″ in overall thickness. The age of the property suggests that these partitions are likely to be of timber construction with a covering of lath and plaster. This form of construction is visible where the rear wall has pulled away from the partition separating the Dining Room from the staircase landing on photograph 23.

There are areas of impact damage to the plaster of these first floor partitions which require making good as well as damage caused by re-wiring and the repair of those cracks already mentioned in relation to the flank wall and rear wall movements. These defects are shown on photographs 32 and 33, as well as a curious defect causing bulging on the short length of partition separating the Kitchen from the inside of the cupboard by the fireplace in the Dining Room. This is shown on photograph 34 overleaf and since the hot water storage cylinder in the cupboard is fairly new it is possible that the defective plaster may be the result of earlier leakage from the old cylinder before it was replaced.

There were no indications of rising damp to the partitions at ground floor level, either visibly or by extensive testing with a moisture meter. It may well be that whatever form of damp proofing was originally installed to keep dampness from rising internally in the partitions it has remained effective for its purpose. Certainly at the time of my inspection the property was free of rising damp.

At first floor level the floors are of hollow timber construction, except in the larder and kitchen where they sound solid since at this point they are above the side entrance to the adjoining premises.

Boards were lifted in the Front Room Left and on the landing at the top

34. Bulged plaster on partition separating kitchen from Dining Room at First Floor level.

of the stairs. It was found that the floor is constructed of 9″ × 2″ timber joists at 14″ centres with 6″ × 1″ boards. The joists span from side to side and the longest clear span is across the Front Room Left, about 13′6″. The size of joist used is satisfactory for such a span in domestic construction and no undue level of vibration was found to be present. There are, however, a number of loose floorboards which could be a source of irritation if not refixed. There is no provision within the depth of the floor for sound insulation between the two flats so that carpeting would normally be considered essential to deaden the sound of footsteps.

The first floor construction is, of course, supported off the external walls and the internal partition walls at ground floor level. These latter are all of brick construction and in good condition and there are, in consequence, no sloping areas or tilting present in the floor construction.

It is not possible to ascertain the construction of the solid sections of flooring but the surfacing is of cement screed in the kitchen and larder, well worn and uneven in the Kitchen. Access was gained to the adjoining premises below the Kitchen but here a smooth finish is presented. This sounds solid when tapped but gives no indication of what form the construction might take. Apart from the wear to the surfacing no other defects were apparent.

Part of the Dining Room to the First Floor flat is also over the passageway and the timber floorboards of this section are likely to be fixed to the solid construction. It was not possible to take up a floorboard to ascertain the method of fixing because of the fitted carpet in this room, but there are, however, no indications of defects of a structural nature in this area.

At ground floor level, the floors in all compartments are of hollow timber construction with the exception of the area within the cupboard below the stairs to the upper flat. This has a cement surfaced floor about a foot lower than the top surface of the wood flooring and provides a vantage point from which the construction of the wood flooring can be seen. This is of 4″ × 2″ joists at 14″ centres with 1″ boarding of various widths. The joists span approximately 4′6″ and are carried on sleeper walls comprising two courses of bricks and a 4″ × 3″ timber plate.

There is no evidence of a damp proof course below the timber plate, where it would normally be expected to be found, but also no evidence of untoward dampness in the timber plate or the joists. It would seem that the site is well drained and correspondingly not prone to dampness.

The present owner informed me that when the new Bathroom was formed for the Ground Floor Flat a new wood floor was installed to replace the old solid floor. At the same time additional new air bricks were inserted at the base of the rear wall so that there are now sufficient air bricks in both front and rear walls to provide adequate through ventilation. The lack of this may have caused a problem of rot at some time in the past because it can be seen, where the present owner has left the boards bare, that certain renewals have had to be carried out in the Front Room Left. It is not possible to say why it was necessary for this to be done; rising damp, a blocked rainwater pipe or gulley at the north-west corner, coupled with inadequate sub-floor ventilation are possible causes, but the vendor said it was before his purchase. There are no indications now, however, of any problems likely to lead to a reoccurrence.

In addition to a close inspection for rot and damp, timbers were inspected for attack by wood boring insects. Apart from evidence of flight holes, in one or two floorboards near the entrance to the ground floor flat and in the skirting between the Front Bedroom and Lobby doors, there were no indications of any severe attack at Ground Floor level. The inspection was, however, limited at first floor level by the presence of fitted carpet and linoleum and I must therefore advise that the timbers be treated against insect attack.

Staircase The staircase from the ground floor entrance up to the first floor flat is in one long straight flight and constructed of softwood timber comprising $8\frac{1}{2}" \times 1"$ treads and $6\frac{1}{2}" \times \frac{3}{4}"$ risers housed and wedged to wooden strings either side, each tread being provided with three triangular blocks for firmness.

The condition of the staircase is sound and there is no undue vibration in use. There is a handrail to one side and a balustrade at the top.

If the staircase had been constructed today in this position it would have been necessary to provide it with a fire resisting lining to the underside to protect it as an escape route for the occupants of the first floor flat. Such provision would be a desirable improvement if it was proposed to continue the use of the property as two flats.

Joinery Both flats still have the original joinery of panelled doors with moulded architraves to the main rooms and moulded picture rails and skirtings throughout, all typical of the period of construction. The original joinery extends to include the ornamental moulded fireplace surrounds with mirrored overmantels to the Sitting Rooms of both flats and the entrance doors with leaded lights and leaded light fanlights. Although some wear and abrasion damage is apparent the condition generally is fairly good, apart from the absence of the lock and latch to the Bathroom door to the First Floor Flat and replacement of the original round fluted brass door knobs at that level with white plastic lever handles.

At first floor level the joinery is painted but at ground floor level the vendor has stripped, sanded and applied a matt varnish finish to most of the joinery, except the picture rails.

THE SERVICES

Cold Water Service The cold water main enters the property from the street below ground level near the entrance to the ground floor flat and there is a small access pit in the front garden with cast iron cover and stopcock, the turn key to which is broken and should be replaced. The mains pipe from the stopcock is in copper, suggesting a replacement for the original lead, and rises through both flats by the staircase to feed first the cold water galvanised iron storage cistern in the roof space above the first floor landing of actual capacity 30 gallons serving the ground floor flat and shown on photograph 35 overleaf. This cistern is very rusty, as can clearly be seen, and should be replaced forthwith as it could burst at any time.

Before reaching the cistern a branch in copper is taken to serve the sink in the ground floor Kitchen. In the roof space there is connection to a lead pipe which continues across the roof space to feed the glass fibre cistern at the east end, which supplies cold water to the first floor flat. A branch partly of lead and partly of copper serves the Kitchen sink in the first floor flat. The glass fibre cistern, also of an actual capacity of 30 gallons, with its lead pipe connections is shown at photograph 36 also overleaf, from where it can be seen to be raised above the floor level in the roof space (and also on photograph 3), presumably to increase the pressure available at the taps of the various fittings. Why this should have been done is unclear, since there are no fittings at first floor level which would not have functioned satisfactorily if instead the cistern had been positioned on the floor of the roof space.

509

35. Rusted galvanised iron cold water storage cistern serving Ground Floor flat.

Down services from both cisterns are respectively in copper to the ground floor flat and lead to the first floor flat. Lead has been superseded for plumbing installations by other materials in new buildings, initially because of cost but, more recently, because of the health hazard which can arise from the use of lead pipes in soft water areas and when the pipes are new in hard water areas.

36. Fibreglass cold water storage cistern serving First Floor flat.

This property is situated in an area of hard water and because of their age the pipes are likely to be heavily furred with lime deposits. Accordingly, while there is little likelihood of any danger to health from this source, all the lead pipework must be considered to be approaching the end of its useful life and could cause problems from pinhole leaks at any time if not renewed. There is an unsatisfactory arrangement in the area of the first floor Kitchen brought about by just such a pinhole leak which necessitated the untidy replacement length of copper tube being inserted. Old and untidy lead pipes can be seen below the basin in photograph 37, on the left, in the first floor Bathroom.

Irrespective of the material used and the condition, the size of cold water pipes is satisfactory throughout for the purpose for which they are installed including, importantly, the size of overflow pipes from cisterns. The latter from the cisterns in the roof are taken to discharge over the roof tiling and can be seen on the photographs. Their positioning is not ideal as they can discharge for a long time before being noticed. The stains on the tiling indicates that this has been happening in the past. They should be repositioned when the cisterns are renewed so that their discharge is instantly noticeable if anything goes wrong with the ball valve controlling the intake supply of mains water.

Hot Water Installation

37. *Old lead water supply pipes, waste pipe (with cleaning eye) and anti-syphon pipe to first floor lavatory basin in Bathroom. Note also old type bayonet gas point.*

For the first floor flat hot water is supplied to the Kitchen sink by a small unit electric water heater of about 2 gallons capacity. This is very old. The sink, as well as the bath and basin in the Bathroom, have hot taps which are supplied from a 20 gallon copper hot water storage cylinder situated in the cupboard by the fireplace in the Dining Room. This cylinder has a jacket of insulating material and is fitted with an electric immersion heater controlled by a switch with pilot light in the adjacent Kitchen. An adjacent similar switch controls the unit water heater mentioned before.

It is probable that an earlier cylinder in this position was heated by a back boiler behind the slow burning open fire adjacent, but this has now been disconnected. There is no visible rating on the immersion heater to judge its capability for heating adequate amounts of hot water. At the time of my inspection the heater had been left on and water of adequate temperature was being delivered to all fittings, but it is not possible to say without a test how long it takes for a tank of water to heat from cold. Clearly, with the minimum amount of insulation to the tank and the fairly long lengths of insulated pipes this is an expensive system to run. All lengths of pipe for hot water in the first floor flat are in lead and accordingly the same remarks apply to these as for the lead cold water pipes mentioned previously.

Hot water for the ground floor flat is supplied by a proprietary 20 gallon fully insulated hot water storage tank positioned on the floor of the airing cupboard in the Lobby. This is fitted with two electric heating elements, a smaller one for full time use and a larger element for bathing purposes. The installation dates from the time the flat was altered about seven years ago and with the short runs of copper pipe, insulated where seen, to the various fittings, it should be serviceable. As with cold water pipes, the sizes of hot water pipes are satisfactory throughout for their purpose irrespective of other considerations.

Central Heating

There is no central heating for the first floor flat but the ground floor flat is provided with a gas fired small bore copper pipe system with white enamelled steel radiators. The system was installed in 1985 by Servowarm Ltd. and according to the papers shown to me by the vendor the system has been maintained by that firm every year since.

511

The boiler for the ground floor system is fitted out of sight in the old fireplace opening in the Dining Room/Kitchen. It utilises the flue from that fireplace and is fitted behind a radiant/convector gas fire of which it is an integral part, access to the boiler controls being via a removable panel at the bottom of the front of the gas fire. There is an electric timer control adjacent to the chimney breast and the system can be simply operated to be on for 24 hours, all day or for two periods a day. The electric pump necessary for circulation and the small black plastic cold water storage cistern supplying the water for the system are positioned in the bottom and top cupboard respectively at the end of the dresser fitment. The cistern is fitted with a ball valve and the overflow, which is in plastic tube, is taken down through the floor to discharge out through an air brick below the double doors leading from the Kitchen/Dining Room out into the garden.

The vendor says the system has been trouble-free and is simple to operate. It was in use at the time of my inspection and all radiators were hot. It was not, however, possible to see the boiler and no comments can be made about it or the system's safety and efficiency without employing the services of an independent heating engineer to carry out the appropriate tests. This is a course which must be recommended before the exchange of contracts, particularly as with the presence of a number of gas fires it must be assumed that the system provides background heating only.

Electrical Installation

The two flats provide a distinct contrast in the character of their respective separate electrical installations.

On the first floor, although the plastic covered wiring may be no more than 10–15 years old, it is mainly on the surface, and there is only one 13 amp power point in each room, except the Dining Room where there are two. There is a cooker control panel in the Kitchen, but again this is surface wired. No test on the installation was carried out, but this is not really necessary in the circumstances as the system is inadequate by modern standards and it is assumed you would wish to rewire the installation to provide an appropriate range of power points etc. and to reprovide the meter and controls, currently arranged in an untidy fashion at high level on the landing by the door to the balcony, in a better position.

At ground floor level, an entirely new installation was provided about seven years ago when the flat was modernised. There is a good provision of lighting and power points, as can be seen from the Schedule of Accommodation, and the wiring is concealed to the white plastic power and lighting points and the lighting and power switch plates.

It will be noted that there are no ceiling lighting points in each of the Front Rooms at ground floor level, although a lighting point at skirting level controlled by a switch at the door in each room enables a standard or table lamp to be used without compromising safety.

If you wish to be assured of the safety of the installation you should have it tested by a qualified electrical engineer. In my view this is essential before contracts are exchanged, particularly as a notice in the cupboard under the stairs where the meter and fuses are positioned indicates this should have been carried out two years ago.

Gas Installation

A separate gas supply is provided to both flats with a meter on the staircase landing for the first floor flat and one in the high level cupboard in the entrance hall for the ground floor flat.

As in the case of other service installations there is a contrast between the two flats. Little has been done to the installation of the first floor flat for many years and indeed there are a number of gas points of a type requiring a "push and turn" type of bayonet connector, including one in the

Bathroom below the basin, visible on photograph 37, which have long since been declared obsolete by the supply company. There is one modern radiant gas fire which is functioning and properly connected to the supply in the Front Room Left, the Sitting Room, but the gas fire installed in the other Front Room, a Bedroom, is extremely old and still with an unsatisfactory turn key gas control. I would advise that you anticipate for the complete renewal of the gas installation at first floor level.

At ground floor level I was informed by the vendor that the gas installation was renewed when the flat was modernised seven years ago, not only to provide for the connection of the vendor's various gas fires, all of which are functioning, but also with a view to ensuring that a gas fired central heating system could be installed at a later date, as indeed it has been. While I have no reason to believe that the installation to the ground floor flat is other than sound it would, nevertheless, be advisable to have a test carried out by an engineer to be sure that it is safe in all respects.

The property was originally lit by gas and the sealed off stubs of gas pipes for the gas brackets still project from the walls in places.

Waste Water Disposal and Drainage System

The head of the drainage system is a surface water gulley in the paving outside the double doors to the rear Bedroom of the Ground Floor Flat. From this the drain passes along the rear of the property in a west to east direction below the paving and the end part of the Bathroom, where it projects beyond the general line of building, to connect to the end of a brick built inspection chamber below the paving at the rear of the side entrance to the adjoining workshop premises.

Along its length at the rear the drain picks up the outlet from a trapped gulley adjacent to the double doors leading from the Dining Room/Kitchen. This receives the discharge from the sink by means of a copper waste pipe with cleaning eyes and also rainwater from the 3″ cast steel rainwater pipe bringing rainwater down from approximately half of the main roof via the balcony at first floor level.

Chambers and Branch Drains

The chamber at the rear of the side entrance has three branches. The first is a direct connection to the WC fitting in the ground floor Bathroom, and the second is to the trapped gulley situated against the wall of the Bathroom. This receives the discharges by means of copper waste pipes from the bath and basin, together with rainwater from the small pitched roof over the larder to the first floor flat as well as the other half of the rainwater from the main roof by means of a cast iron rainwater pipe. The third branch at high level connects direct to the foot of a ventilating pipe partly in 4″ cast iron and partly in 4″ plastic pipe.

The drain then passes below the paving of the side entrance to the front of the property, where it connects to another chamber within the ground level curtilage of the workshops and studios of Nos. 11 and 12 next door. There are also three branches to this chamber. The first is connected to a trapped gulley nearby which in turn receives the discharge from the old sink in the First Floor Kitchen by means of a lead waste pipe connected to a 2½″ cast iron waste stack. This is carried up as a vent on the front elevation and also, by means of a 3″ cast iron rainwater pipe, the surface water from the easternmost section of the main roof. The gulley also receives rainwater and waste water from a drain which passes along the front of the property below the narrow garden. This drain carries rainwater from the westernmost section of the main roof, brought to ground level by a 3″ cast iron pipe, rainwater from the central section via a 2½″ plastic pipe and waste water from the old bath and basin in the First Floor Bathroom through lead wastes connected to a 2½″ cast iron stack.

The second branch within the chamber is connected by an underground branch drain to the foot of the 4″ part lead, part cast iron, soil pipe taking the discharge from the W.C. in the First Floor Bathroom. This soil stack is carried up above roof level as a vent.

The third branch at high level is to a 4″ cast iron fresh air inlet just within the front boundary of Nos. 9 and 10 at more or less ground level. Such inlets are very prone to damage and this one is no exception, the mica flap and its grille being broken and in need of renewal since it is needed as a method of drawing fresh air into the system while preventing unpleasant odours. Considering the number of pipes on the front elevation (six all told, as can be seen from the unnumbered photograph on the cover and photograph 1) it is surprising that another ventilating pipe could not have been added in preference to the air inlet at ground level which is of a type not now permitted.

Waste pipes, traps and anti-syphon pipes

To prevent the entry of foul air into the property the outlets from sinks and baths need to have traps provided with a water seal immediately adjacent to the fittings. All fittings at this property have proper sized waste pipes and proper traps are fitted (one can be seen below the basin in photograph 37) with access plates to enable blockages to be cleared. Where more than one fitting is connected to a waste pipe the traps should be provided with anti-syphon pipes to prevent the water being sucked out from the trap of the fitting not in use. Anti-syphon pipes are provided where necessary for this property, but they are taken merely into the open air and not connected as they should be into the waste water stack at a higher level. This will need to be corrected when fittings are renewed.

Inspection chambers

Both covers to the inspection chambers were raised during my inspection and sanitary appliances turned on within the flats. It was found that all drains were free running and that there were no blockages. The chambers were found to be clean with sound benching to the white glazed channels and smooth unbroken rendering to the sides. The undersides of the cast iron covers were however rusty and both should be wire-brushed, primed and painted to prevent further rusting.

It must be anticipated with a property of this age that rainwater, waste and soil pipes where made of cast iron can develop leaks through rust spreading from the interior where they cannot be painted. Short of renewing all such pipes which will, perhaps, guarantee a trouble-free future for a time, depending on material selected and workmanship, there is no way of being sure that defects will not arise at any time. What is important is that, as with defective rainwater pipes and gutters already mentioned, they are renewed promptly.

Desirability of Test

The vendor stated that the drains had been trouble-free during his seven years in occupation, apart from the need to clear gulley blockages on occasions. However, only a water test can indicate whether drains are watertight or not. Although there are no signs to indicate that the drains are leaking, in view of their proximity to and the fact that they run parallel to both the front and rear walls as well as one flank wall, it would be advisable to have them tested (subject to the vendor's permission) before contracts are exchanged so that you can be assured of their soundness before contemplating purchase.

SECURITY

Windows to the ground floor Front Rooms are fitted with Banham security bolts as well as the normal stays and fasteners, while the front doors have good quality dead locks and bolts as well as a night latch.

At the rear on ground floor level, both sets of double doors have Banham security bolts, top and bottom on both leaves as well as ordinary bolts, while all metal windows have lockable fasteners and stays. At first floor level the old casements have been bolted shut with the exception of the larder window, while the door leading on to the balcony has a rim lock and two bolts, one with additional padlocking arrangement.

EXTERNAL DECORATIONS

The external decorations are only in fair condition; better at the front than at the back, which is more exposed to the prevailing south-westerly winds. They are now due for complete renewal.

There is evidence of inadequate preparation when the external decorations were last renewed, particularly at the rear, and additional attention will need to be paid to areas where paint is flaking.

INTERNAL DECORATIONS

Only the Front Bedroom, the Entrance Hall and the Bathroom at ground floor level have decorations which can remotely be described as adequate, subject to views of taste. The ground floor Rear Bedroom, although redecorated a few years ago may not be to your taste. Elsewhere complete renewal is required which will entail more than just normal redecoration in view of the additional preparation which will be required by way of making good to cracks and damaged areas of plaster.

THE SURROUNDINGS

Front At the front of the property, the boundary fences are of wood construction, with posts and feather edged boarding about 3′ high and there is a wooden gate. The condition is very poor throughout, although some concrete spurs have been provided to give additional support. The hedge is best described as "straggly", paving is minimal and the narrow area of ground is uncultivated and subject to the undesirable attention of the local animal population. You will no doubt wish to effect substantial improvement to this area to enhance appearance if you decide to purchase.

Rear At the rear the small triangular garden is supported some 3′ higher than the bottom of the railway embankment by a timber post and boarded retaining wall. The vendor told me he constructed this himself six years ago at a fraction of the amount he had been quoted for a corresponding brick retaining wall. It is fulfilling its purpose at present and the posts remain firm, even near the bole of a tree with a diameter of about 2′–3′ which, I was told, had been cut down at the time. How long the retaining wall will remain effective is I believe a matter for speculation. Its pliability to some extent works in its favour and its lining of polythene if unbroken should help to keep damp at bay, but inevitably the timbers will decay and renewal may need to be contemplated in, say, five years even though at present there is no evidence of defects.

In view of the evidence of what must have been quite a large tree being cut down a few years ago, a close examination of the ground floor rear wall and the adjacent paving was made. This was to ascertain whether there was any evidence of ground heave after the soil recovered its former volume once the extraction of moisture by the roots of the tree ceased. Although the paving is cracked and worn and could with advantage be renewed, it is still sloping down and well away from the base of the rear wall and there was no evidence in the wall itself of any untoward movement due to soil recovery. If such an effect was going to take place it would have happened by now so that the presumption must be that the tree was not of the type taking an undue amount of moisture from the subsoil.

Garden fences The enclosing fences on either side of the garden are of timber post and feather edged boarding and are in sound condition. Elsewhere, the garden is laid mainly to grass which is in fair condition and there are some small areas for plants formed by a rockery, mainly round the tree stump.

ENVIRONMENTAL FACTORS

Mention was made at the beginning of this report in the description of the property of its proximity to a local station. The trains make a fair amount of noise both accelerating from the station and braking towards it. You will no doubt ensure before exchange of contracts that you do not find such noise excessive.

The presence of the Studio/Workshops next door and more business premises further along the street does mean that more lorry traffic is generated than would otherwise be the case if the street were wholly residential. Furthermore, when in operation the loom next door makes a "clattering" noise and the making of stained glass windows evidently involves an element of hammering.

LOCAL TAXATION

The property is situated in an area where the Poll Tax for this year has been set at £425 per head, considered so high by central government as to warrant the Local Authority being capped.

TENURE

I understand that the property being conveyed is freehold. I have drawn your attention at the beginning of the report to the fact that part of the property is in effect a "flying freehold" over part of the ground floor of the adjoining studio/workshop premises Nos. 11 and 12. Your solicitor should be asked to advise you on the rights and responsibilities of the respective owners in regard to support to the upper part, protection to the lower part, together with this property owners right to drainage below the land of the adjoining premises. This situation has arisen probably because of the splitting of the original freehold title.

An aspect of which you may not be aware, since it is not mentioned in the sale particulars, is that the whole of the small garden at the rear, apart from the narrow paved area parallel to the ground floor rear wall, is on licence from the railway and not part of the freehold which is to be conveyed. The vendor told me that the licence has been in existence since the property was built, but you should obtain the advice of your solicitor on the terms which will be of particular concern to you if you do decide to convert the two flats into a single residence. The lack of a garden however small could be a distinct disadvantage for a house, even if it hardly seems to

516

affect the marketability of a two bedroomed flat. My experience is that the railway resists all attempts to part it from the freehold of its land even though it would appear to have had no use for it over the last 80 years or so. Your solicitor should also make enquiries from the railway authority as to whether any works they have in mind for the future would affect this property. It is understood that an extension of the line from the next up station has been planned for many years, but has been held back through lack of funding.

CONCLUSION AND GENERAL REMARKS

1. Being purpose built this property would appear to have had more care taken over its design and construction than perhaps would have been the case if it had been but one of an estate. For example, it is a little unusual to find steel used as a beam to support the brickwork of the rear wall at first floor level and the use of brick throughout for the ground floor partitions. The fairly good quality of joinery and timberwork in the main roof is nevertheless more typical of the type of construction commonly found from the early part of the century. However the property has been neglected.

2. Irrespective of any considerations of the possibility of converting the property into a single family house there are a number of items of essential repair required to put the property into reasonable condition having regard to its age. These are:

   (a) The major work of stripping and recovering the main pitched roof slopes with clay tiles and the flat section of the roof at the rear in a durable material, such as asphalt, together with the renewal, where necessary, of ridge tiles, soakers, flashings, gutters and rainwater pipes so that when the works are completed the roof can provide sound service without attention for some years.

   (b) The reconstruction of the small pitched roof over the larder and its covering in a durable material.

   (c) The repair and repointing of brickwork where necessary to the chimney stacks, parapet walls above the flat section of the main roof and elsewhere at the rear.

   (d) The renewal of the three defective windows and the door to the balcony at the rear of the First Floor Flat, together with the glazed double doors to the Bedroom of the Ground Floor Flat.

   (e) The renewal of both water cisterns and all sanitary fittings and pipework to the First Floor Flat.

   (f) The rewiring of the electrical installation at First Floor level and the renewal of the gas installation.

   (g) The treatment of the structural timber with preservative against wood boring insects.

   (h) External redecoration and complete fence and gate renewal at the front of the property.

In my view it would be wise to allow for the expenditure of about £10–£15,000 on the above work. This must be considered only the most approximate order of cost, since the only way to obtain an accurate figure is by the preparation of a detailed specification and the obtaining of competitive estimates.

3. You will note that the above figure does not include internal decorations of any description to any part as the cost of these is so much dependent on individual requirements. You will perhaps have a rough idea yourself how much it costs to decorate a room from your own experience but, if not, I should be happy to discuss the subject on the telephone.

4. The approximate estimate does not include either for any work which may eventually become necessary in regard to the bulged rear wall at first floor level. As mentioned in the report, the evidence suggests that the movement is of a continuing nature, albeit slow, and therefore requires careful and accurate monitoring to establish the rate if this is so. The property is 85 years old and the movement to date is no more than to the order of 1″ at the maximum of the bulge. While it would not be wise to assume a uniform rate of future movement it nevertheless seems unlikely that the need for rebuilding will arise within the next 10–20 years and I do not therefore consider it reasonable to include the cost (which could be to the order of £2,000 to £3,000 at current prices) or a proportionate part at this time.

5. As to the possibility of conversion into a single family residence, you should first be sure that you do not find the fact that the small garden is only on licence inhibiting. If you are satisfied on this then I see no reason why such conversion should not prove to be a comparatively simple matter to produce a three/four bedroom house with two (one en suite) or even three bathrooms if the one on the ground floor is retained. It would not be too difficult to remove the present separate entrances and provide a single entrance further forward in a porch. Making the staircase look attractive might prove to be more difficult and, of course, nothing can overcome the restricted nature of the site.

6. This report has been prepared for your private and confidential use and for the use of those acting directly on your behalf. It shall not be reproduced in whole or in part or relied upon by third parties for any use whatsoever without my express written authority.

7. I trust this report provides you with the information you require and answers any points or doubts you may have about the property. I shall be pleased to discuss its contents if you wish or to answer any queries. An additional copy is enclosed for your use.

Yours faithfully

Chartered Surveyor

APPENDIX

10th April 1990

Dear Sir,

Nos. 9 and 10 Wasp Street, Antsville

Following our telephone conversation, when we discussed the scope of your requirements and I explained what it would be practicable to do, I set out below the terms and conditions upon which I shall be pleased to carry out on your behalf an inspection of the two storey block containing two 2-bedroomed flats at the above address and to report to you upon its structural condition and state of repair, together with providing you with advice in general terms, on the possibility of converting the property for use as a single family dwelling. You have informed me that you do not require tests to be carried out on the drainage, electrical, central heating or gas installations and that you are hoping to purchase the freehold interest with vacant possession.

If instructed, I shall make a thorough inspection both internally and externally of all parts of the property where visible and readily accessible with the use of a 3 metre sectional ladder. My inspection will extend to include the drainage, electrical, central heating and gas installations serving the property.

In most cases the close and detailed visual inspection, which I shall carry out is sufficient to provide enough information to form a view of whether the property is likely to provide satisfactory accommodation for the foreseeable future, having regard to its age and character. To assist you to reach a decision I shall provide a list of any necessary repairs which I consider should be carried out in the near future to preserve the value of the property together with an estimate of their very approximate cost within a range of figures. The list will not contain any items of improvements to the property or alterations.

Although no parts of the structure will be opened up, fitted carpets or floorboards raised, heavy furniture moved or the contents of fitted cupboards cleared and you will appreciate that my responsibility cannot extend to reporting on parts of the property which are covered, unexposed or inaccessible, I will, nevertheless, advise where I consider it necessary to expose hidden features or carry out tests on the service installations to establish the true condition before you assume liability by way of purchase.

My fee for the inspection and the provision of two copies of my report, prepared under the above terms and conditions, will be £800 inclusive of all travelling and other expenses, but exclusive of VAT. In the unlikely event that such further enquiries or investigations are considered necessary as envisaged in the previous paragraph, or it is necessary to visit the offices of the local authority, and you wish me to undertake such work then I shall be happy to agree an appropriate fee in advance at that time.

Subject to access being made available by the vendor, I aim to carry out my inspection on Wednesday 18 April and would anticipate being able to send you my report within the following three working days.

My report will be provided for your own private and confidential use and the use of any other professional advisers you may employ. It must not be reproduced without my express written authority and no responsibility

519

can be accepted to any other person to whom it may be shown or who may rely upon its contents.

Because of the implications of the Unfair Contract Terms Act 1977 it is necessary for me to ask you to indicate your acceptance of these terms and conditions by signing, dating and returning to me the attached copy of this letter. Its receipt in my office will confirm your instructions and I will then contact the vendor.

Yours faithfully,

Chartered Surveyor

I hereby confirm my instructions to carry out an inspection and report upon Nos. 9 and 10 Wasp Street, Antsville, in accordance with the above terms and conditions.

Signed .... Date ....

First Floor Flat, N°. 4 Blenheim House,
Lancaster Street, London.

Miss Florence A. Spitfire,
c/o Lady Hurricane,
3 Vampire Walk,
Venom Way, London.   7th April, 1989

Dear Madam,

Flat No. 4 Blenheim House,
Lancaster Street, London

INSTRUCTIONS

In accordance with the instructions contained in your letter of the 1st April, 1989 and with which you returned a copy of my Conditions of Engagement sent to you previously duly signed, I have inspected the above flat and now set out, as requested, my report on the STRUCTURAL, DECORATIVE AND SANITARY CONDITION having regard to the proposed sale to you of a long leasehold interest in the flat in place of the short term agreement which has now expired. I also enclose the report submitted by the electrical engineer in respect of the wiring system inside the flat.

SITUATION AND DESCRIPTION

Blenheim House consists of a block of what are usually termed mansion flats, built on the southern half of an area of land bounded by Hampden Road on the North, Stirling Way on the South and Lancaster Street and Wellington Street on the East and West respectively. The block is within a mainly residential area and within a quarter of a mile of the Underground Station of Heyford Street and within a few yards of bus routes in Hampden Road and is accordingly in a very central position from the point of view of public transport.

The block has frontages to all the streets previously mentioned except Hampden Road but the principal frontage is to Lancaster Street where the main entrance to all except two of the flats in the block is situated. It is a little difficult to be certain of the precise number of flats in the block as the numbering on the name plates is not consecutive, but there would appear to be a total of twenty-seven. The accommodation is situated on basement, ground and five upper floors, but there appear to be no flats in the basement.

The block is separated from the street by a narrow basement area with a rendered brick pavement retaining wall surmounted by a stone coping with cast iron balustrade. The main entrance is approached by a flight of five mosaic tiled steps and a landing and is set within an ornamental stone porchway.

The elevations to the three streets are constructed of red facing bricks with stone sills to the timber framed metal windows and stone key-stones to the red brick arches. There a number of ornamental stone band courses but there is not the amount of ornamental brick and stone work normally associated with mansion blocks, and this factor together with the use of metal windows, suggests the date of construction either shortly before or immediately after the First World War.

On the Lancaster Street frontage there are four bay windows rising to the full height of the building and directly above these, the elevation is finished with a series of small gable ended roofs with stone details. A feature is made of the angle between Lancaster Street and Stirling Way where there is a square bay window, the detailing at the corner being topped with a cupola. Similar details extend round to the Stirling Way frontage but on this elevation there are two bay windows only. The elevation to Wellington Street, however, is much plainer and there are no bay windows at all and this is where the tradesmen's entrance is situated.

The main roof of the block of flats is of flat construction covered with asphalt, although on the Lancaster Street and Stirling Way frontages there are extensions above main roof level to provide a background for the small ornamental gables and other details which form an architectural feature to the top of these elevations.

Flat No. 4 is situated on the first floor of the block and extends from the main entrance in Lancaster Street along to the junction of and round to include part of the Stirling Way frontage. The flat is approached through a ground floor entrance hall which is carpeted and mahogany panelled, and by means of a flight of stairs which are also carpeted and mahogany panelled to the first floor marble surfaced landing. There is also a fully automatic lift giving access to all upper floors in the block.

ACCOMMODATION

Note. In this Schedule the rooms of the flat are numbered from the entrance door of the flat, in a clockwise direction. The first dimension given in each case is taken parallel to the Lancaster Street frontage and dimensions given are approximate and for descriptive purposes only.

First floor

Flat No. 4. First Room. Study
About 13'4" (4.06 m) × 11'9" (3.58 m). Fireplace with wood and tiled surround, fitted gas fire. Bay window with glazed door on to small balcony over the main entrance.

Second Room. Lounge
About 15'0" (4.57 m) × 20'0" (6.10 m). Fireplace with wood surround and tiled hearth, the fire parts removed and a metal back plate fitted to form an opening for the tenant's electric fire. Gas point capped off. Bay window. 2 No. night storage heaters. Ceiling and walls plaster panelled.

Third Room. Dining Room
About 13'6" (4.12 m) × 20'0" (6.10 m). Fireplace with wood surround, marble interior and hearth, the opening blocked and fitted gas fire. Bay window. Fitted cupboards.

Fourth Room. Bedroom
About 12'0" (3.66 m) × 15'6" (4.72 m). Original fireplace removed but no permanent ventilator fitted to flue. Lavatory basin (H.&C.) with resealing trap. Textured plaster finish to walls between skirting and picture rail.

Fifth Room. Bedroom
About 17'9" (5.41 m) × 13'3" (4.04 m). Fireplace with wood surround, the opening blocked but no permanent ventilator fitted. Bay window. Night storage heater. Fitted cupboard with double doors.

524

Sixth Room. Bedroom	About 13'3" (4.04 m) × 13'9" (4.19 m). No fireplace or permanent ventilator. Lavatory basin (H.&C.) on chromium plated stand.
Seventh Room. Bedroom	About 19'0" (5.79 m) × 11'6" (3.51 m). No fireplace and no permanent ventilator fitted. Lavatory basin (H.&C.). Night storage heater. Range of fitted cupboards with three single doors. Glazed screen in rear wall to adjoining Kitchen, painted over.
Entrance Hall	About 60' (18.29 m) × 6'3" (1.91 m), but a section 9'0" (2.74 m) wide by the entrance door. Automatic hall porter telephone. Two cupboards each with double doors. Further fitted cupboard. Two night storage heaters. Two single doors on double swing hinges giving access to Lobby and usual domestic offices all overlooking an internal light well, as follows:
Bathroom	5'6" (1.68 m) cast iron panelled bath (H.&C. on mixer fitment, with shower attachment). Lavatory basin (H.&C.) in wood casing. Fitted cupboard with slatted shelves. *Separate W.C.* High level W.C. suite with plastic water waste preventer. Extractor fan fitted to window.
Shower Compartment	Low level W.C. suite with vitreous china water waste preventer. Plastic shower cubicle with tray (H.&C.). Permanent ventilator in window.
Kitchen	About 16'0" (4.88 m) × 14'3" (4.34 m). Double bowl single drainer stainless steel sink unit (H.&C. on mixer fitment). Gas point for cooker. Plumbing and waste for washing machine and dish-washer. Night storage heater. Fitted cupboards. Cupboard containing electricity meters and controls. Door to tradesmen's staircase. Door to landing.
Outside W.C.	High level W.C. suite with cast iron water waste preventer. Fair faced brickwork. Concrete floor. At present used as store room.
Further Small Store Room	On landing to tradesmen's staircase 4'0" (1.22 m) × (0.61 m). Fitted shelves. Permanent ventilator. Gas meter over.

THE DRAFT LEASE

The draft Lease which you have sent to me is, as usual in these matters, long and complicated, and my comments strictly from the surveyor's point of view are as follows:

The demise is to be shown on a plan which is not attached to the draft but is also closely described in the First Schedule on page 14. The lessee's liability extends only to include plasterwork, doors, frames and windows of the external and bounding walls and plasterwork of ceilings above and floorboards below but not the brickwork, ceiling or floor joists which are expressly excluded.

The surfacing of the balconies is included but not the structure or railings, so that this item presumably includes the balcony opening off the Study even though this is shared, and possibly the balcony, or more precisely flat roof approachable through the window from Room Seven. In my view the reference to balconies should be deleted from Part 1 of the Schedule and item (iii) near the top of page 15 amended to "all parts and railings and parapets of any balconies". The demise also includes all pipes, wires, etcetera expressly for the flat and sanitary and water fittings.

The term is for 125 years from the 24th June, 1989 and there is provision for the rent to rise every 25 years but the amounts are not stated. In addition, a basic maintenance charge for an unstated amount is to be paid to cover insurance costs for the building (in this respect it should be noted that the loss of rent referred to is the Lessors' only, and accordingly apart from the fully comprehensive contents and occupier's insurance, the tenant will have to insure for loss of accommodation for himself, for say three years) the repair in good and substantial order of the remainder of the building not demised, repainting the outside in 1990 and thereafter every four years and the inside common parts in 1990 and every seven years.

The basic maintenance charge is extended by Clause 4 to include all those other items of services, such as repairing, cleaning and lighting the lift and common parts, maintenance of the hot water system, payment of rates other than those on the flat, refuse disposal, the "Entryphone" system, employment of staff and their accommodation, employment of managing agents etcetera, etcetera. If the amount of the basic charge is insufficient an excess charge at the rate of 4.64 per cent of the total extra cost as certified by the managing agents is payable. It is stated that the basic maintenance charge is to be calculated at the same rate on a total sum of £45,000. The charge is payable half yearly in advance and any surplus is to be held over by the Lessors. On the first full year therefore, there will be a payment of £2088 for services.

The Lessee's covenants include for a specific internal redecoration in 1990 and in every seventh year and the usual clause to well and substantially repair and maintain the flat. There are also the usual covenants in regard to use of the flat as a single family dwelling, against alterations without consent, and to yield up well and substantially repaired at the end or sooner determination of the term. The covenants in regard to assignment and sub-letting appear to me a little less stringent than usual, but your Solicitors should advise you on any difficulties that may arise in regard to these, as well as the significance of Clause 2, paragraph (xxvii).

The "rules of the house" as set out in the Third Schedule on page 17, are similar to those contained in most Leases of this type. It is noted that the passage of the Flat should be carpeted to comply with the Schedule, which it is not at the moment. Despite para. 19 of this Schedule there is a profusion of television aerials on the chimney stacks of the block.

STRUCTURE. EXTERNAL

Main roof The main roof of the block was inspected and was found to be mainly of flat construction covered with asphalt and with asphalt skirtings to red brick parapet walls on the north and east elevations, and asphalt skirtings to the brick structures and chimney stacks, rising from the general roof line. It is not possible to say with certainty the form of structure supporting the asphalt, but having regard to the age of the property, it is probably of timber, although it is not possible to say without opening up whether it is provided with the refinements of a vapour barrier and insulation. These are considered necessary to prevent condensation and possible outbreaks of dry rot within the thickness of the roof structure. The asphalt is not new and is probably some 10 to 15 years old. Some minor cracks occur in the asphalt and need repair and some of the pointing around the top edge of the skirting has fallen out in places, requiring renewal. Asphalt generally is considered to have a life of about 25–30 years and accordingly, renewal of the asphalt must be anticipated within about 10 years, though its life may be extended by treating it with some form of light reflective surfacing.

To the parapets on the north and west elevations, there are a number of shaling bricks and sections of open and loose pointing and in particular, on the west elevation there is a small fracture near the north-west corner. The top of the parapets is finished with a brick on edge coping and a damp-proof course consisting of two courses of tiles in cement. Pointing to the brick coping is generally open and loose and a considerable number of the tiles forming the damp-proof course have been damaged, or, where exposed, show signs of shaling. A section of the parapet along the west elevation appears to have been rebuilt in the past but the reason for this is not apparent.

Over the extent of the roof, a number of chimney stacks extend above the general roof level. Although some of these have been capped off, others appear to be still in use and in most instances, shaling bricks are apparent together with open and loose pointing and also cracked and defective flaunching to the tops of the stacks. One has been partly rebuilt at the top and at least two have been tied back to the main structure with steel bands.

On the elevation facing Lancaster Street and Stirling Way, each of the small gabled roofs is provided with access by means of double doors, and from the interior spaces it is possible to see sections of the roof timbering, which where observed were of sound construction and in satisfactory condition. However, the condition of the doors and frames is poor in that a number are hanging off their hinges and these features have clearly not been painted for many years.

It is not possible to inspect closely the condition of the slated slopes which form part of the architectural features to these two frontages, but where observed, there are a number of slipped and broken slates which require refixing or renewal. The asphalt has been extended to cover various of the remaining ornamental features and where observed this was in a satisfactory condition. On the other hand, the stonework where this is exposed, is showing signs of slight shaling.

The structures containing the cold water storage cisterns and the lift motors are generally neglected although part of the lift motor room has been rebuilt fairly recently, possibly at the time when the lift was changed to automatic operation. Generally, however, the brickwork needs re-pointing and the joinery to doors and windows is old and in urgent need of re-painting, and again, some doors are hanging off their hinges and glazing is broken.

Sections of the main roof along the Wellington Street frontage are at a lower level than the remainder and appear to be used as roof terraces by the occupants of the top floor flats. These sections have a covering of cement but it was not possible to see whether this is laid over asphalt or not. The cement work is cracked but I have no way of ascertaining whether this is causing dampness to penetrate to the flats below at the present time.

There is one glazed skylight in the main roof, constructed of patent glazing bars covered with lead and glazed in wired cast glass. This is in good condition.

Main walls The block of flats is substantially built in brickwork and the thickness of the external walls at first floor level on the Lancaster Street frontage, Stirling Way frontage and around the internal light well, is 18″ (457 mm) of solid brickwork. In my examination of the elevations I found no indication of settlements, bulging or leaning in any of the walls apart from very slight gaps which arise around window frames to the windows of this flat. These gaps have been pointed up and there are no indications of any movement subsequent to the pointing which must have been carried out many years ago. The gap is more in the form of a wide joint rather than due to movement.

The condition of the bricks themselves is generally satisfactory although a few are showing signs of shaling towards the top of the elevations, as is to be expected with this type of facing brick. The pointing generally is also satisfactory but again, at high level, there are indications of loose and open pointing in places and this also occurs at lower levels, sometimes in the areas of pipes, where there are indications of past leakages. There is always a danger of dry rot arising when pipes leak, but as no leaks have occurred on the external walls of this flat, but only on the walls of other flats, I am unable to comment on whether any outbreaks arose or not, or whether proper steps were taken to deal with cases of rot which have arisen. Enquiries should be made of the managing agents on this aspect.

At basement level, the condition of the rendering to the retaining wall of the pavement is fairly poor in that there are a number of cracked and loose areas and on the Wellington Street frontage a section has fallen off. The area paving is also cracked in places and requires repair.

On the Lancaster Street frontage the small balcony over the main entrance of the block, which is approached from a glazed door in the first room, Study, is covered with asphalt which is in good condition, and there is a brick parapet which is capped with sections of stonework forming the top of the porch around the main entrance. The stonework is eroded slightly and the joints between the sections require repointing.

On the Stirling Way frontage, there is a further small balcony over the secondary entrance on this elevation which is approached through the window in the Seventh Room. This balcony is also covered in asphalt which is in good condition and has low brick parapet walls and stone copings. The brickwork to the parapet is satisfactory but the coping stones are chipped and damaged to some extent and the joints require pointing.

The stonework to the sills of the windows to this flat is generally satisfactory, being well moulded and possessing correctly formed throatings on the underside. However the brickwork in the panels below the windows is only 9″ (228 mm) thick and accordingly, in one or two positions where sills are chipped and there are slight gaps between the wood and stone sills to windows, dampness has been penetrating and this has caused the plaster below the windows to be uneven and soft, and to register a high moisture content.

The dampness is particularly apparent in the Fourth and Seventh Rooms and it may also arise in the remaining rooms, but the interior face of the walls at this point, in all except the Fourth, Sixth and Seventh Rooms, is covered over with wood panelling. There are no signs of rot on the faces of these panels but I cannot guarantee that dampness behind the panels may not be affecting the timber which cannot be seen. In any repair of window sills it will be necessary to ensure that all joints are sound and that mouldings are repaired so that they continue to perform their function of throwing water clear of the brickwork below.

STRUCTURE. INTERNAL

Ceilings The ceilings throughout the flat are of lath and plaster construction and there are some slight cracks, unevenness and making good apparent in the surfaces. None of the defects however are serious and even the slight crack which occurs on the ceiling in the Fourth Room and which runs from the fireplace to the front wall, could be filled on subsequent redecoration and is unlikely to open again.

Partitions The partitions within the flat are of substantial construction and are solid-sounding. Having regard to the age of the block, it is probable that these are of brick construction or some form of partition block where the size is below that of normal brick dimensions. There are structural partitions of an overall thickness of 10 in. (254 mm) separating the Second, Third and Fourth Rooms from the Entrance Hall, separating the Second and Third Rooms, separating the Hall and Kitchen, together with a further structural partition around the common staircase. Between the Sixth Room and the Hall, the structural partition measures 14″ (356 mm) overall.

There are no signs of movement or settlement in any of the partitions within the flat with the exception of the thin partition, probably non-structural and about 4″ (100 mm) overall thickness, separating the Third and Fourth Rooms which has a slight crack in the frieze. There is also slight movement in the partition separating the Fourth Room from the Entrance Hall, where again there is a slight vertical crack in the frieze by the door opening. Both these cracks are small and should be filled on redecoration, when it is unlikely that they will re-appear.

Floors

All the floors throughout the flat are of hollow timber construction, but at the time of my inspection were fully covered with layers of carpet and underfelt, linoleum or in the case of the Entrance Hall panels of chipboard. It was accordingly not possible to take up sections of flooring to ascertain sizes of the structural members, but there was no evidence of settlement or undue vibration throughout the flat to suggest that this was necessary, or that there is anything wrong.

It is noted from the Lease that there is a direct liability only in respect of the floorboards and not the structural joists, so that accordingly the direct liability is fairly limited. There is however, a section of flooring in the Fifth Room by the fireplace, where it is apparent that the flooring has sunk slightly, but this may only be due to a defective or poorly fixed floorboard. Having regard to the fitted carpet and the heavy night storage heater adjacent, and furniture, it was not possible to expose this for closer examination.

Windows

The windows throughout the flat consist of metal casement sashes in timber frames. These sashes are generally in good condition, but in the First Room the fanlight is rusty, the cord missing and the opening section cannot be closed; and in the Fourth Room a window stay is broken. In the W.C. the glass to the window is cracked.

The windows should be well maintained and painted otherwise rust will attack the metalwork and cause expansion, thus breaking the glass. This has occurred to the neglected window of the outside W.C. As mentioned previously, defects in the window sills are causing damp penetration and it was observed that a number of the sills are almost bare of paint, which has resulted in a certain softening of the timber.

The putty joint between the wood and stone sills is open in places and this is a contributory cause to the damp penetration, which is also aggravated by the absence of a damp-proof course below the sills. The provision of such a damp proof course was not usual in structures of this period. In the Third Room it was noted that the timber window sill boards are split to the two side windows of the bay, possibly due to past damp penetration.

Doors

The doors throughout the flat are the original doors from the time the block was built, with the exception of the door to the Shower Compartment which is a comparatively new flush door. The remaining doors are of timber panel construction, but those to the First, Third and Fourth Rooms are slightly warped, and those to the Fifth and Seventh Rooms and the W.C. are badly warped.

In particular, the door to the W.C. needs renewal. Other minor defects occur, for example the fittings are loose on the door to the Seventh

529

Room, the frame to the door of the First Room is split, and in the door between the kitchen and the tradesmen's entrance, three squares of glass are broken. Doors to the original cupboards in the flat are a poor fit.

DECORATIONS. EXTERNAL AND INTERNAL

The external decorations to the block are beginning to show signs of wear, and, as noted previously to some of the window sills of this flat, are flaking. Towards the top of the elevation the decorations deteriorate and it is noted from the draft Lease that the block is due for repainting in 1990.

The internal decorations to the flat are good throughout and at the time of my inspection, the Kitchen was in process of redecoration. The draft Lease requires an internal redecoration in 1990 and thereafter every seven years, but having regard to the flat's present condition, the redecoration next year could not be enforced.

SERVICES

Main water, main drainage, gas and electricity are connected to the Authorities' mains. The electrical installation was tested and the electrician's report is attached.

Drainage system   It will be appreciated that no test can be carried out on the underground drains servicing the block, or on the waste and soil pipes in view of the fact that these are used in common. Accordingly no comment can be passed on their condition or on whether they are satisfactory in use. The repair and maintenance of the drains used in common is the Lessor's responsibility under the draft Lease, but the Lessee of this flat has of course to contribute to the cost. Certainly at the present time, waste and rain-water pipes on the elevations require attention.

It was noted that traps to basins throughout the flat are in lead and that all except one trap are ventilated to anti-syphon pipes. The remaining trap is of the resealing type, so that problems of syphonage should not arise in regard to these fittings. Fittings are generally rather old and worn apart from those in the Shower Compartment and the Kitchen.

As you have now held this flat on short term agreements for some years, you will no doubt be aware whether any troubles have been experienced in regard to the drainage system, for example, blockages necessitating the attendance of plumbers.

Cold water system   Cold water is stored at roof level in cold water storage cisterns, situated in three structures built above the general roof line. These cisterns are all old and I would anticipate that in a few years' time, substantial renewals will be necessary. In addition, the cisterns, although enclosed in the brick structures, are unlagged and I would have thought in the circumstances that there might be a danger of freezing in exceptionally cold weather.

Hot water system   Hot water is supplied to all the fittings in the flat as a common service from installations positioned in the basement, comprising the boilers and the hot water storage cylinders. At the time of my inspection, the oil tank was in the process of being renewed.

By the run of pipes at present in position it would appear that new boilers are not intended, merely the provision of oil burners to the existing old boilers. The large hot water storage cylinders in the basement are well lagged, so that it is not possible to comment on their condition, but it is clear that they, too, are old. There may well be a future liability here.

Gas installation

A gas supply is laid on to the flat, but this was not tested. If a test is required it will be necessary to engage the services of British Gas plc. The pipes are probably old, but in the positions where they are situated they are unlikely to have been affected by dampness, which is the usual cause of deterioration in gas pipes.

Electrical installation

The electrical installation was tested and the electrician's report is attached hereto. You will note that the wiring where original, is poor, and that the test is unsatisfactory, so that it is recommended that this be renewed at an approximate cost of £2000. Renewal of the electrical installation, however, presents some difficulty, as to rewire satisfactorily it will be necessary either to have access to the flat above in order to take up floorboards, permission for which is unlikely to be forthcoming, or alternatively to cut away a substantial amount of the plaster.

If cutting away had to be carried out, it would be necessary to redecorate the flat entirely, besides facing the additional cost for making good to plaster. Accordingly rewiring would be an expensive operation but would have to be carried out at an appropriate time. On the other hand, providing the installation is not tampered with or disturbed it may give satisfactory service for some years.

Heating installation

There is no space heating provided as part of the services to this flat and accordingly it is noted that some night storage electric heaters have been installed and the remainder of the flat is heated either by gas fires or individual electric heaters. I take it that you installed the heaters as it was noted that the wiring for these is fairly new and run on the surface of plasterwork and skirtings.

GENERAL CONCLUSIONS

1. In considering the terms of the draft Lease, your Solicitors should be advised of the fact that it is highly probable that not all the flats will be sold on 125 year Leases. It may well be that many of the existing tenants will opt to continue renting their accommodation on short Agreements and accordingly the basis that the Lessor lets all flats on identical terms, as happens in a new block, will not necessarily follow here.

   As such, enforcement of the terms might be complicated. It is probable that no more than half of the flats are comparable with this one and outside the scope of the Rent Acts and no doubt a proportion of the tenants may well consider it advantageous to take a chance on the continuance of the protection afforded by these Acts both from eviction and untoward increases in rent.

2. As will be seen from this report, various matters of repair require attention to the remainder of the block retained in the control of the Lessor. The "fair rent" procedure for those flats still let on short term Agreements tends to keep the income from these fairly low and the present owners are seeking to dispose of long Leases at prices reflecting the full market rental value, rather than those which would be determined by the Rent Officer. By this method, the burden of all repairs is being transferred directly on to the Lessees in proportion, including all those necessary due to past neglect.

3. The block is more than fifty years old and, for this very reason will require more expenditure than a block recently built and this factor must be borne in mind when considering the purchase of a long Lease. On the other hand, the block gives every indication of having been substantially built originally and although the Bathrooms and

531

Kitchens, by way of arrangement around the internal light well, are somewhat inadequate by modern standards, improvements could be carried out, and the accommodation provided in the principal rooms has at least spaciousness and a certain amount of character.

In regard to this flat, I understand that you have taken advice on value, so that I am not asked to comment on this, but possibly some allowance on the price might be obtained in view of the need for repairs to the parts retained under the control of the Lessor.

If I am right in believing that the terms of the present Lease on this flat require you to well and substantially repair the interior of the flat, then clearly no allowance can be expected on account of dis-repair internally. In other words, for example, you may already be liable for rewiring the electrical installation, but I would appreciate a sight of the present Lease to verify this point.

In order to give you a very approximate idea of cost, your immediate proportion of liability for those matters set out in the draft lease for items other than the interior of the flat itself would probably amount to approximately £8500–£10,000.

4. In addition to the matters of repair of those parts of the block retained by the Lessor and the comparatively minor repairs, apart from the rewiring to the Flat, as set out in this Report, there are two matters which might be indications of future trouble. These are –
   (a) The defects in the sills which may give rise to rot in the panels below the windows in the principal rooms.
   (b) The need for the adequate painting and maintenance of the metal windows.
   (c) The evidence of past leakage to pipes on the external walls of other flats. Your solicitor should obtain an assurance from the lessor's managing agents that any consequential dry rot problems which may have arisen were properly dealt with and that no liability will fall upon you.

I shall be pleased to give you any further information or assistance in regard to this Flat, and I should be pleased to comment on the present lease if this could be sent to me.

I return herewith the draft for the proposed 125 year Lease, and I also enclose two additional copies of this Report.

Yours faithfully,

Chartered Surveyor

APPENDIX

30 March 1989

Dear Madam,

Flat No. 4, Blenheim House
Lancaster Street, London

Following your call at my office, I now enclose two copies of my Conditions of Engagement for inspecting and reporting on a single flat in a block containing other flats.

If you wish me to proceed with the inspection and to prepare a report on the above, I would be glad if you would sign, date, indicate your requirements as to tests of the service installations and return one copy to me. I shall then immediately make the necessary arrangements to carry out my inspection.

Yours faithfully

Chartered Surveyor

Conditions of engagement for inspecting and reporting on a single flat in a block containing other flats.

1. Address of flat: No. 4 Blenheim House, Lancaster Street, London
2. Accommodation: 3 living rooms, 4 bedrooms, kitchen and bathroom
3. Interest being acquired: 125 year lease
4. Examination of lease:
   I shall examine the lease or draft lease purely from the surveyor's point of view so as to advise you accordingly.
5. Extent of the inspection:
   A thorough inspection will be made of all parts of the interior and exterior of the subject flat where visible and readily accessible with the use of a 3 metre ladder. The visual inspection will extend to include the drainage, electrical, central heating and gas installations within the flat.

   A more general inspection will be carried out to the exterior of the block containing the other flats together with the common parts and a visual inspection of service installations, lift, boilers and the like serving all the flats. Although it is not part of a normal structural survey to carry out detailed inspection of other flats in the block, endeavours will be made to make an inspection of features adjacent to the subject flat where a fault or faults appear to be present.

   In most cases the inspection of the flat and the general inspection of other parts of the block in which it is situated, should be sufficient, along with advice on the terms of the lease, to provide enough information as to whether the flat will provide comfortable and relatively trouble free accommodation for the foreseeable future having regard to its age and character. I shall provide a list of essential repairs necessary to remedy any existing defects within the flat (but excluding any alterations or improvements) together with an estimate of their very approximate cost within a broad range of figures.

   I shall also indicate where there is likely to be an undue proportionate liability for the exterior, the structure, the common parts or common service installations due to previous neglect.

   Although no parts of the structure will be opened up, fitted carpets or floorboards raised, heavy furniture moved or contents of fitted cupboards cleared and you will appreciate my responsibility cannot extend to reporting on parts of the property which are covered, unexposed or inaccessible I will, nevertheless, advise where I consider it necessary to expose hidden features or carry out tests on the service installations so that you can be advised on the true condition before you assume any liability.
6. Tests of services:
   Tests of service installations can be arranged on your behalf if you wish and indicate below by ticking the appropriate box(es). The

reports of any specialists employed will be attached to my report and if necessary commented upon. No responsibility can be accepted for the contents of specialists' reports as I shall act only as your agent in arranging for tests to be carried out.

Tests required:–

☐ Electrical   ☐ Gas

☐ Central heating

You will appreciate that it is not possible to test the drainage installation where it serves more than one flat without obtaining the consent of all concerned and making arrangements for non-use of the facilities for some hours.

7. Confidentiality:

Inspections are carried out and reports submitted on the basis that they are confidential to the instructing client but may be shown to and used by other professional advisers employed by the client. Reports must not be reproduced without my express authority and no responsibility will be accepted to any other person or persons to whom it may be shown or who may rely upon its contents.

8. Provision of service:

Proposed date of inspection 5 April 1989 or by other prior arrangement. The report will be prepared and despatched within three working days of the inspection or, if later, by prior arrangement.

9. Fee:

My fee for carrying out the inspection and providing two copies of my report under the above Conditions of Engagement is £400.00 exclusive of travelling, other disbursements and VAT and the charges of any specialists employed on your behalf.

In the unlikely event that I need to advise further investigations, opening up, visits elsewhere, etc, and you wish me to undertake these on your behalf, a further fee agreed by prior arrangement will be chargeable. Should the property prove to be substantially different from the description quoted to me as above the right is reserved to make an additional charge.

I hereby instruct you to carry out an inspection and to report upon the flat described at the commencement and in accordance with the Conditions of Engagement set out above for the fee quoted in paragraph 9. I further authorise you to arrange for the specialist test(s) indicated in paragraph 6 to be carried out on my behalf.

Signed .... Date 1st April 1989...........................

18. Ford Close, Jaguar Gardens, London, W12.

J.W. Austin Esq.,   22nd March, 1989
7 Morris Road,
London W8.

Dear Sir,

18 Ford Close
Jaguar Gardens London W12

In accordance with the instructions contained in your letter of the 12th March, to which we replied with our Conditions of Engagement dated 17th March 1989 and to which you agreed the following day we have inspected the above property in order to advise you firstly upon its structural condition and secondly upon the result of tests carried out to the electrical installation, the hot water and central heating systems and also the underground drainage system.

SITUATION AND DESCRIPTION

The property consists of a brick built dwelling-house with a tiled roof forming one of a terrace of six somewhat similar properties on one side of Ford Close, which forms part of a large development of Georgian style town houses constructed over the last year or so. The development consists of planned blocks of two and three storeyed terraced houses placed so as to form residential closes surrounding lawns and paths and the whole development is situated on the edge of Vauxhall Common facing Triumph Ride to the northern side and Jaguar Gardens to the southern side.

The dwelling-house is approached by means of an access road and a communal lawn forming the forecourt to the house itself, which has a frontage of approximately 18 ft. (5.49m), the main structure having a depth of some 33 ft. (10.06m). There is a garden at the rear of the dwelling-house which has a total depth in the region of about 35 ft. (10.67m). The front elevation is faced with yellow stock bricks and there is a projecting single-storey portion comprising the porch and front cloakroom which is rendered.

The surrounding area is mainly residential in character consisting of detached houses of various periods. The houses adjacent to the development fronting Triumph Ride are detached and of good quality, constructed since the Second World War, while the houses to the south and eastern sides of Jaguar Gardens are mostly of the Victorian or Edwardian period being either detached, semi-detached or terraced. The common land extends to the north of Triumph Ride and on the eastern side of the development.

The nearest local shopping facilities are approximately a half mile away although better and more varied shops are available at a distance of about a

537

mile. The terminal point of a local bus route to the West End of London is within approximately three hundred yards across the Common and a local suburban British Rail Station is within a quarter mile of the house.

The development of which this house forms part consists of 30 new houses with three separate garage blocks, these being landscaped to be as unobtrusive as possible and the whole development has been built on the site of four large Victorian houses, now demolished, and their extensive gardens.

ACCOMMODATION

In the schedule below the dimensions given are approximate and for descriptive purposes only. The first dimension given in each case is taken parallel to the frontage.

First floor

Front room — 10 ft. 11 in. × 11 ft. 6 in. (3.33m × 3.51m). Double radiator. Hand basin. Two power points. Large hanging cupboard with four shelves and full width upper shelf and 3-leaf door.

Bathroom — 6 ft. 8 in. × 7 ft. 1 in. (2.03m × 2.16m). Bath with ornamental wood panels and mixer fitment with shower attachment. Low level W.C. suite. Pedestal hand basin. Electrically heated towel rail. Fitted cabinet with 3 shelves. Glass shelf. Infra-red heater fixed to wall. Half tiled walls.

Landing — Large cupboard over stairs containing hot water storage cylinder, fitted electric immersion heater and fully lagged.

Rear room — 11 ft. 0 in. × 15 ft. 6 in. (3.35m × 4.72m). Range of fitted wardrobe cupboards. Radiator. Two power points.

Small rear room — 6 ft. 9 in. × 10 ft. 8 in. (2.06m × 3.25m). Built-in cupboard with shelf and hanging space. Two power points.

Ground floor

Hall — Radiator. Two cupboards under stairs one with shelves and electric light, electric meters and fuses. Hardwood flooring.

Cloakroom — Low level W.C. suite. Small corner hand basin. Thermoplastic tiled floor.

Kitchen — 9 ft. 8 in. × 11 ft. 0 in. (2.95m × 3.35m). Stainless steel sink unit with mixer fitment, single bowl and double drainers. Range of plywood faced fitted cupboards with plastic faced worktop and including tall broom cupboard. Five power points. Gas point. Thermoplastic tiled floor. Permanent ventilator to window. Serving hatch to rear room. Electric point and plumbing for washing machine. Gas fired boiler.

Large rear room — 17 ft. 5 in. × 17 ft. 9 in. (5.31m × 5.41m) (excluding bay). Ornamental fireplace with green marble slab cheeks and hearth and wood surround, fitted electric point in opening but no flue. Two alcoves each side of fireplace each with curved heads, two shelves with cupboards below. Semi-circular bay window. Glazed double doors to garden. Fitted book shelves. Double and single radiators. Five power points. Hardwood flooring.

THE STRUCTURAL CONDITION

The main roof — The main roof of the property is of pitched construction with the ridge parallel to the frontage and the slopes draining to eaves gutters at front and rear. The roof is covered with machine made clay tiles laid on battens and roofing felt and carried by a series of ten pairs of trussed rafters of a design developed by the Timber Research and Development Association since the end of the Second World War so as to economise on the use of timber.

The trussed rafters are made up of timber sections $3\frac{3}{4} \times 1\frac{3}{4}$ in. (95mm $\times$ 44mm) and joined together with special connectors and metal plates. We have checked that for the span involved, for the weight of the roof covering and the pitch adopted, the design of the pairs of trussed rafters is in accordance with the recommendations of the TRDA including the specification for the metal connectors and their coating against damage from rust. We also checked in the roof-space that the timber used and the workmanship of assembly, carried out no doubt away from site by a specialist joinery manufacturer together with the installation including all the necessary on site bracing is in accordance with recommended current practice.

What in our opinion is not entirely satisfactory is the number of pairs of trussed rafters used. For the roof to function properly there is a maximum recommended spacing for these trussed rafters and here this maximum has been exceeded by a small margin. To have used one extra pair of trussed rafters would have brought the space very well indeed within the recommended limits so that it appears that the contractors have taken a risk, which in turn is passed on to the purchaser, of omitting one pair and in slightly exceeding the maximum spacing recommended.

Having regard to the quality of timber used and the fact of the workmanship being satisfactory and also that there is always, in any design of this nature, a margin of safety, it is a risk that is not likely to have serious structural consequences but nevertheless there is a possibility that the 2 in. $\times \frac{3}{4}$ in. (50mm $\times$ 19mm) battens to which the tiles are secured (this measurement having been taken from the plans examined in the contractor's office since the battens are not visible, being obscured by the roofing felt) will sag slightly between each pair of trussed rafters producing a "rippling" effect in the tiling.

This rippling may not interfere with the performance of the roof but it will affect the appearance and there is always a possibility of a flaw or knot causing a breakage so that the tiling may sag in consequence more severely and perhaps cause a leak. In the main, tiling is able to accommodate movement of the nature envisaged.

The specification provides for the clay tiles to be up to British Standard quality, which is as good a guarantee as it is possible to obtain for resistance of tiles against frost damage or lamination. While the roofing felt obscures a sight of the underside of the tiles as fixed on this house, some spare tiles left in the cupboard below the stairs and tiles seen elsewhere on the site of this development, all had the British Standard "Kite" mark on the underside so that, in the circumstances, it would be reasonable to assume that tiles of the right quality have been used.

The ridge to the tiling is finished with "V" shaped clay sections and these have been fixed and pointed in a satisfactory manner. The party walls between the terrace houses are not taken up as parapets but are merely designed to meet the underside of the tiling which is carried straight over to adjoining houses thereby avoiding potentially awkward points of construction.

Within the roof-space it was observed that the roofing felt has been correctly allowed to sag between the rafters. This permits any rain which might penetrate the tiling joints under high winds or driven snow to drain away to the eaves gutters without penetrating to the interior.

539

The lowest member of each pair of trussed rafters not only acts as a tie to the feet of the rafters to prevent them spreading apart but also acts as one of the ceiling joists to which the plasterboard comprising the top floor ceilings are fixed. An adequate layer of glass wool insulating material is provided between ceiling joists, which is a satisfactory method of preventing excessive heat loss through the top floor ceilings while the use of foil backed plasterboard provides an effective barrier to the passage of moist air from the top floor into the roof space which, if allowed, could cause condensation.

Construction at the overhanging eaves was examined at both the front and rear of the house and was found to be satisfactory except that two sections of boarding require refixing to the underside of the eaves at the rear and the front cast iron ogee gutter, which has been fixed with an inadequate fall, requires taking down and refixing. A careful check was made to ensure that adequate provision for through ventilation to the roof space has been made and this was found to be satisfactory.

Roofs to front porch/cloakroom and rear bay window

The roofs to the cloakroom projection at the front of the house and to the bay window at the rear are of flat construction covered with lead sheeting and at the rear draining to a cast iron ogee eaves gutter. The lead sheeting and the eaves gutter were examined from above and the materials and workmanship were found to be satisfactory. In particular, the junction between the flat roofs and respective front and rear walls is adequately protected by a turn up on the lead sheeting and a lead flashing tucked in to the brickwork and pointed up.

From above, both the flat roofs sound of hollow construction and an examination of the plans shows that the construction is intended to be of 7 in. × 2 in. (178mm × 50mm) wood joists with wood boards and bituminous felt as an underlay for the lead sheeting and plasterboard for the ceilings with insulation of polystyrene slabs placed between the joists. This form of construction should be entirely adequate for the purpose particularly since the plasterboard specified is foil backed to provide a vapour barrier at ceiling level.

The main walls

The front and rear main walls of the house were measured on site and were found to be just over 11 in. (280mm) thickness overall. This suggests modern cavity wall construction which is confirmed to some extent by the stretcher bond for the yellow stock brick facings used on both elevations and agrees with the plans in the contractor's office. Cavity construction is nowadays the common form of wall construction and consists of two structural leaves with a 2 in. (50mm) gap between, the two leaves being connected together with metal ties. Such construction when compared with walls of one brick solid thickness have improved damp resistant properties and improved thermal insulation qualities, provided they are properly constructed.

The measurement taken here suggests that the inner leaf in this case is of concrete blocks 4 in. (100mm) thick rather than of brickwork and confirmation of this was obtained from the plans and seen when a floorboard was raised at first floor level and a sight of the inner skin obtained where it is unplastered. The use of such blocks in place of brickwork can produce even better thermal insulation qualities for the external walls but it is important that the insulating blocks are made of sufficient strength to sustain structural loads.

Accordingly a check was made on the drawings and specification to ascertain the type of blocks used for the inner leaf. These blocks were found to be of a suitable proprietary form and the contractor's office was able to produce a certificate obtained from the manufacturer showing that

540

the blocks had been made to comply with the appropriate British Standard.

The thickness of the party walls cannot, of course, be measured without gaining access to the properties on either side. Both these properties are now sold and in occupation but for reasons which will be explained later it was found necessary to endeavour to approach the occupiers of both houses and with the co-operation of one owner it was possible to measure the thickness of the party wall on the east side of the house. This was found to measure 12½ in. (317mm) overall the plaster thickness on both sides, suggesting cavity construction but this time utilising bricks in both skins, a point confirmed by the sight of brickwork in the roof-space and from the plans.

A careful study was made of the plans in the builder's office to see whether the recommendations for good practice in cavity wall construction had been followed, particularly in relation to the type and the positioning of the metal ties, the arrangements at the base of the wall for the prevention of rising damp and also around window and door openings for the provision of support to the outer leaf of brickwork and also the precautions taken against damp entry at the head, sides and sills of openings.

We are able to report that in this respect we found no cause to be critical of the arrangements shown on the drawings and specification details and an exhaustive inspection of the property brought to light no signs of damp penetration or other defect likely to suggest that the drawings had not been followed or that workmanship had been skimped. Damp-proof courses, which comprise a layer of impervious material built into the brickwork at various points to prevent the passage of moisture, are shown on the drawings to be of bituminous felt with a thin sheet of lead incorporated.

The damp-proof course is specified as of a British Standard quality which is satisfactory and at various points we were able to confirm it's presence on account of the edge showing, including at the base of the walls where it is important that the damp-proof course is not bridged by a plinth, paving or a flower bed. Although the walls of the house have probably only been completed for about six months it is probable that defects related to the construction of the cavity walls would have revealed themselves by now. This cannot be said to be the case in relation to defects which can be brought about by shrinkage of materials or the initial settling down of a new building on its foundations and it is on these aspects that we now wish to comment.

You will of course be aware that buildings should be provided with foundations suitable for their purpose. However, since it may take some years for any defects in the design of foundations or any poor workmanship in their construction to become apparent, it is necessary to give some consideration to the design and whether the foundations are likely, given the characteristics of the site and the loads which they will have to carry, to prove satisfactory over the years.

Besides being supplied with plans showing the construction details of the house we have asked for and have had the opportunity of studying the soil survey carried out over the site of this development. From samples taken to a considerable and sufficient depth from various points over the site (although none from the immediate locality of this house) the soil survey ascertained that this site is of firm clay with a bearing capacity of about 2 tons per square foot (220kN/m²).

The site is level but the survey and tests on the samples showed that the soil is of the shrinkable type necessitating foundations being taken down to a depth sufficient to avoid the effects of climatic changes and also necessitating particular regard being paid to the effects of vegetation. We asked for and also obtained for examination a site plan showing the layout of the development in relation to existing features, in particular the mature trees in the gardens of the old houses. This plan shows that no trees have been cut down anywhere near this house and we had already ascertained from our site examination that there were no trees, mature or otherwise in existence likely to cause any future difficulty in relation to this house.

We were also supplied with details of the loading on foundations for a typical two-storey terraced house on this development and have been able to verify these calculations from the information taken on site and to satisfy ourselves that the foundations shown on the constructional drawings are of sufficient size and at an appropriate depth for the avoidance of settlement in this house, subject of course to satisfactory workmanship. The Building Inspector's office has kindly consulted it's record cards and have given us details of their site notes which confirm the information supplied by the builder.

We were nevertheless concerned on our close examination of the main walls of this house to observe slight signs of movement in plasterwork and brickwork at one point in the structure which can by no means be attributed to shrinkage. At the rear of the house the brickwork at ground floor level consists virtually of a single pier 13½ in. (343mm) square separating the semi-circular bay window from the glazed double doors giving access to the garden. This pier carries the ends of two beams which support the brickwork of the rear wall at first floor level and on which bears the weight of the rear part of the roof, together with the floor joists of the rooms at first floor level.

Slight cracks are apparent in the plasterwork at first floor level where the rear wall meets the party walls on both sides and there are further slight cracks to the cornice and ceiling plaster adjacent to the bay window and french doors to the large living room. Externally from the garden and from the flat roof over the bay window it is possible to see slight indications of deflection downwards in both beams towards the direction of the pier resulting in a hairline crack in a horizontal brick joint above the beams.

As mentioned above we were satisfied with the design of the foundations having regard to the loading and sub-soil, particularly in relation to this pier which takes a concentrated load and we were also satisfied with the size of the pier itself. Accordingly the evidence suggested either some flaw in workmanship below ground or some disturbance subsequent to completion of the work, perhaps related to this house only. Confirmation of this view was obtained when we were permitted to inspect the same areas in the occupied house next door, to the east, with the co-operation of the adjoining owner.

Despite close examination no signs of a similar defect either internally or externally were visible and although we were not able to gain access to the house on the west side, we were not able to see any similar signs of a crack in the pointing above the ground floor by looking over from the garden of this property. We asked the contractors if they were aware of any unusual circumstances which might account for the presence of these cracks but the view expressed was that nothing untoward had been encountered during construction and that in any event the cracks, which they had not previously noticed, were so slight as to be unimportant.

542

We are unable to share this view and would have had to express some misgivings even if no other information had become available. In the event however we consulted the Building Inspector's office in whose area the house is built and, while the surveyor who dealt with this particular site could recall no unusual aspects relating to this house and whose record cards showed no untoward occurrences, he was able to produce an old Ordnance Survey map of the late 19th century showing the original houses and their gardens in some detail.

Scaling from this plan and measuring on site shows that the foundation for the pier which has settled is approximately on the edge of the site of an ornamental pool. No one to whom we have spoken has any recollection of this pool and it would appear to have been filled in some years ago, since it did not appear on the site survey and layout plan. It is debatable whether any signs of its former presence would have been visible in the excavation for the foundation to the pier but if signs were present, they seem to have been missed by all concerned.

We have formed the view, therefore, that the pier between the bay window and the double glazed doors at the rear of the ground floor of this property has already settled to an extent greater than any other part of the house. It is impossible to say for certain whether this movement is likely to continue or not but, having regard to the evidence available, we consider the likelihood of continuing movement to be considerable, since there is little doubt of the presence of a weak patch of ground below at least part of the foundation to the pier. If you purchase the property you will face the risk of further movement occurring which, if it becomes too serious, may necessitate underpinning the foundation perhaps on reinforced concrete beams and short piles.

On an inspection of the main walls we found no other indications of structural movement although there are one or two blemishes in regard to the finish of pointing and making good which require remedying. These will be included in a brief schedule at the end of the report of items which require the contractor's attention before you accept the house as complete, should you decide to proceed with the purchase.

In regard to the pointing of brickwork, horizontal joints on these houses are recessed providing a strong visual emphasis. While this is often considered attractive in appearance, the nature of the joints provides a ledge for water to collect. Where bricks have a hard exterior skin over a soft interior the practice of recessed pointing can cause rapid deterioration of the brickwork due to frost action but where, as here, bricks are of a homogeneous character the effect may not be too dramatic particularly in two-storey construction provided with a generous overhang at the eaves as is the case with these houses. Even so deterioration and wear is bound to be more rapid than would be the case with a normal flush or a weathered joint.

The windows of the property consist of wood double hung sashes in wood frames and sills. They are recessed in the openings so as to provide a degree of protection against the weather. The quality of the windows is satisfactory and the contractors produced a certificate to show that the timber had been treated against wet rot. The Schedule at the end of the report contains a few items of a minor nature requiring attention, including a broken square of glass. The same remarks as to quality can be taken to apply also to the external doors.

The floors   The suspended first floor of the house is of timber joist construction covered with 1 in. (25mm) plain edged softwood floorboards. The joists were found to be 11 in. × 2 in. (280mm × 50mm) at 18 in. (457mm) centres which, for the spans involved and the domestic loading, is satisfactory. There is a single line of strutting to each of the front and rear sections and the joists are doubled to carry the light partitions at right angles to the frontage separating compartments at first floor level.

Support to the first floor is provided by the front wall and at the rear by the two beams already referred to, while the support in the centre is from the structural partition of half brick thickness running parallel to the frontage. No defects were noted in the first floor except some boards which require refixing.

It would have been preferable for the boards to have been tongued and grooved rather than plain-edged but, no doubt, you will have in mind to carpet the bedrooms and the landing. You are left, as the purchaser, to provide a covering for the bathroom floor but we understand the contractors will lay hardboard and provide a thermoplastic tile finish to your selection for a reasonable charge if you wish.

The floor construction at ground floor level is solid and from the plans this is shown to be of 6 in. (150mm) of hardcore, 6 in. (150mm) of concrete and a damp-proof membrane of bitumastic with a screed of 1 in. (25mm) or more in thickness. The drawings show a connection between the damp-proof membrane in the floor and the damp-proof course in the walls and we checked that the respective levels on the drawings do in fact agree with the conditions which exist on the site.

The finish in the kitchen and the cloakroom is of thermoplastic tiling but the remainder of the ground floor is finished with what is known as a "Windsor" type of floor. This utilises small sections of timber about 3/8 in. (9mm) in thickness and about 4 in. (100mm) long, pre-fixed to a backing panel which is then stuck down on the screed when delivered. The timber used here is of oak and should provide a reasonable surface for many years to come. In view of the settlement in the pier at the rear previously mentioned, we were concerned that sinking might be apparent in the floor adjoining the pier but despite a close examination no evidence of movement was apparent.

The hardwood flooring requires sanding and polishing and the thermoplastic tiles cleaning and sealing before you accept the house as completed.

Ceilings

The ceilings throughout the house are of plasterboard construction with a skim coat of plaster. It is to be expected that as the house slowly dries out some hair cracks will appear along the board joints. Only very slight signs of such cracking are apparent at the moment and it must be expected that the existing cracks will become worse and that more will appear due to further shrinkage. This cracking is not serious and, after a few years, it is customary for the cracks to be filled and a permanent decoration based on lining paper to be put up.

Partitions

The main central structural brick partition has already been described but elsewhere, on both the ground and first floors, partitions are of solid construction comprising, according to the plans, lightweight concrete blocks 4 in. (150mm) thick plastered both sides. These partitions are not structural and merely serve to divide up the space. No defects were observed.

Doors, cupboards, the staircase and other internal joinery

You will have seen the standard of internal doors, door furniture, fitted cupboards, the staircase, kitchen units, shelves etc. and perhaps have formed your own view as to its appropriateness for your requirements. In our view the quality throughout is very reasonable and up to the standard which one hopes to find in the range of new property available at this price. A few minor points require attention and these are included in the Schedule at the end of the report.

544

Decorations

The decorations have, of course, only recently been applied and to the interior wall and ceiling surfaces represent merely an initial treatment in emulsion paint which will allow surfaces to continue to dry out for the next two to three years. After that period has elapsed a different form of decoration such as oil paint or wallpaper can be applied when drying out and any shrinkage can be said to be complete.

The same comment can be applied to the decorative treatment given to the external rendered surfaces but elsewhere woodwork and metalwork have been painted in the normal way with gloss paint. The specification for the work is satisfactory and the workmanship is, in the main, sound. Here and there, however, there are imperfections which in our opinion should be put right by the contractor.

THE SURROUNDINGS

There is paving to both the front and rear of the property in reconstructed stone slabs. At the front this extends for a width of about 3 ft. (1.00m) and connects to the front entrance path which is bounded on either side by a newly turfed area, there being no fencing between the areas belonging to each property in the terrace.

At the rear, the paving extends for about 9 ft. (2.74m) into the garden in the form of a terrace which should drain towards the garden. However a section of the terrace is showing signs of settling towards the pier, a movement no doubt consequential to that already discussed, and water will collect in the angle between the bay window and the rear wall if this matter is not corrected, irrespective of any further movement in the pier.

Feather-edged boarding on timber posts and rails has been provided to enclose the garden. The presumption from the construction would be that the east side fence is the responsibility of the lessee of this property together with the rear fence and this is confirmed by the plan which you sent to us.

THE SERVICES

Cold water service

The rising main which is in ¾ in. (19mm) copper, a material ideal for the purpose, enters the property from the front and passes up through the house in an internal corner of the kitchen and bathroom to the cold water storage cistern in the roof-space. There is a ½ in. (12mm) branch to the kitchen sink with stopcock.

The cold water storage cistern of galvanised steel which is positioned on the top of the central structural partition, is suitably supported, is of adequate capacity for domestic purposes and is correctly covered and lagged with polystyrene sections.

Down services from the cistern are in ¾ in. (19mm) copper and follow the same path as the rising main into the bathroom, where there are stopcocks, and from there branches are taken to the various fittings and to the calorifier on the landing for the hot water supply. All pipes are well lagged in the roof-space including a 1 in. (25mm) overflow pipe which is taken through the roof-space to discharge over the paving at the rear of the property.

The other small cistern in the roof-space, to which the cold water rising main is also connected, supplies any water lost by evaporation etc. to the hot water central heating system.

No defects in workmanship or in layout or design were observed in relation to the cold water system.

Hot water central heating and gas installation

The installations to supply domestic hot water and central heating were tested by a specialist heating engineer and his report and recommendations are attached herewith. As you will see, while he is satisfied that the boiler and radiators will supply adequate full central heating and hot water for an economic outlay, there are some aspects in relation to the safety of the installation which should be corrected before possession is taken.

Drainage system

The drainage system on this development has been arranged on combined principles in that all soil and waste and rain-water are taken by private drains on the freeholder's land before a connection is made to the local authority sewer.

It will be noted with this property that all sanitary fittings are at the front and it is along the frontage below the grassed forecourt that a 4 in. (100mm) combined stoneware drain is run and to which the soil waste and rain-water from each house is taken via an inspection chamber.

The inspection chamber for this property has three branches all of which are in 4 in. (100mm) stoneware. The first branch takes the discharge from the W.C. in the Cloakroom on the ground floor. The second branch connects with the gully adjacent to the base of the main front wall which takes the waste water from the kitchen sink and also from the basin in the Cloakroom, both fittings having copper wastes, together with rain-water from the front slope of the main roof by means of a 3 in. (75mm) cast iron rain-water pipe. The third branch comes direct from the foot of the internal 4 in. (100mm) cast iron soil waste and ventilating pipe which takes the discharge from the W.C. fitting in the first floor bathroom together with waste water from the bath and basin in this compartment and the basin in the front bedroom adjacent. This pipe is carried up through the roof-space to project through the tiling as a vent.

In the bathroom connections are made from the fittings in copper on the principle known as "single stack" plumbing. Branches for this system need to be kept short and all fittings fitted with deep seal traps. Such traps can be seen on the basins but the bath trap is hidden, although shown as the deep seal type on the plans. Because of the direct connection underground to the drain it is not possible to put a water test on this branch drain but both of the other branches were tested with water and were found to be satisfactory.

We are of the opinion, as the drains at this point are some 4 ft. to 5 ft. (1.22m to 1.52m) below ground and even where they rise to the surface are protected from climatic changes in the sub-soil by the paving, that the branch serving the internal soil stack should also be watertight and also that it is unlikely that any of these branch drains, provided they have been properly laid, should develop faults in the future. You will understand that we cannot speak for the workmanship below ground and it is this, to a great extent, which governs the functioning of the drains and whether they remain trouble free and clear of blockages or not.

As to the joints of the internal soil stack, a smoke rocket was used to test the soundness of the joints which were found to be secure.

At the rear of the property the same conditions exist for the disposal of rain-water from the rear slope of the main roof and the flat roof over the bay window, but there is no inspection chamber. We have checked the plans and these show that at the rear of the terrace below the gardens runs a further 4 in. (100mm) stoneware drain to which connections are made for rain-water and surface water only below ground, but with no access for clearing should any blockage arise.

546

We consider that this is bad practice and it would have been preferable for an access eye at least to have been fitted for each branch. As it is at the moment it is not possible to apply a test to this rain-water drain in view of the lack of access.

Having regard to our diagnosis of the movement in the brick pier in the rear ground floor room of this property, it is conceivable that any special precautions in supporting this drain across the area of the former pool which should have been taken have, in fact, been ignored. In our view there is a risk that if the settlement in the pier continues there is a strong possibility that the drain running below the garden might also be affected and we have allowed for the contingency of a liability for a share of the repair costs in paragraph (3) of the General Conclusions at the end of this report.

It will be appreciated that it is not possible to test the lengths of combined drain at the front of the property without obtaining the permission of all the persons who are concerned with its upkeep. In view of the disturbance to occupiers of adjacent premises that this would involve, it is unlikely that such permission would be given. However, even at its top end this drain would still be some 3 ft. (1m) below ground level and accordingly it is not considered that there is a great deal of risk of leakage at this stage. Furthermore the liability for repair would be a shared one, at least among all the owners who utilise the drain and accordingly not the sole liability of the lessee of this property.

Sanitary fittings

The sanitary fittings throughout are of good quality and up to the standard to be expected in a house in this price range. Notwithstanding this there are one or two adjustments which are required and these will be noted in the schedule at the end of the report.

Electrical installation

The electrical installation was tested by a specialist and his report is attached herewith. Generally the installation is satisfactory but a few matters of workmanship need correcting and the fault which prevents a socket outlet from functioning needs investigation.

GENERAL CONCLUSIONS

1. We understand that this property is of Leasehold tenure with a term of about 98 years at a ground rent of £100 p.a. We have not seen the draft lease although we have seen the plan which is to be attached to the lease and this has been referred to in this report. We have assumed that there is full repairing liability in respect of the house which would be usual and we understand also that there is a shared liability with other lessees for the maintenance and repair of the roads, drains and landscaping of the development.

   It is noted that garages are also on sale on long lease at an extra charge, but you have not asked us to survey a garage and we presume that you are not taking one up. We do not know how this might affect your liability for, say, the paved space for washing vehicles in front of the garages or the turning areas but perhaps your solicitor can help you on this. If there are any unusual features in the lease and your solicitor considers it advisable we shall be pleased to study the document and comment upon its contents from the surveyor's point of view.

2. As we have made clear in this report there are two aspects in relation to this property which involve an element of risk should the long lease be purchased. On the other hand although there is an element of risk involved, both aspects would be capable of remedy by the

547

expenditure of money should the need arise so that they are not such as to require us to advise categorically against the purchase.

You may have cogent reasons, of which we are unaware, for taking the risk which we believe to exist and proceeding to purchase but we feel that we will have discharged our duty in providing these warnings. In the first place there is the spacing of the roof timbers, which is in excess of the maximum recommended. On balance we are of the opinion that the likely need for expenditure in this regard in the future is very remote but this is not the case with the second aspect relating to the settlement in the brick pier at the rear of the property. Frankly we are unable to say if this settlement will continue or not as only long term observation will provide this information.

Should the movement continue, as it well might, you may be faced with expenditure to underpin the foundations of the pier and to repair cracks etc. which at current prices might be to the order of £6,000–£7,000 and this may be necessary within 3 or 4 years. Even when repaired in this way the property would still look slightly out of true since it can be dangerous, even apart from the difficulties involved, to try to force the structure back to its original position. Accordingly the property's resale value might be reduced to some degree by this altered appearance, a further factor which you will, no doubt, wish to take into account.

3. If you do decide to proceed with the purchase of the long lease then it would be reasonable in our view to expect the contractors to attend to the following items before the purchase is completed. The list set out below is comparatively short and to this extent reflects the generally high standard of materials and workmanship utilised in the construction of this house in accordance with the original plans and specification and which makes it all the more unfortunate that it has been necessary to include the reservations set out in the previous paragraph.

(a) *Roof*
Take down, realign and refix main roof gutter at front to provide proper fall.
Refix loose sections of boarding to eaves at rear.

(b) *Main Walls*
Make good around waste pipe from kitchen sink.
Rake out and repoint joints of brickwork above porch roof at front and bay roof at rear.
Hack out and renew broken glass to Bathroom window.
Rub down and repaint sill to kitchen window where finish poor.
Replace broken catch to glazed double doors.

(c) *The Floors*
Sand off and polish hardwood flooring.
Clean off and seal thermoplastic flooring.
Refix loose floorboards in all three bedrooms.

(d) *Joinery*
Ease and adjust glazed double doors to garden.
Ditto cupboard doors in Front Bedroom. Clean and oil catches.
Refix loose handle to door of Bathroom.

(e) *Decorations*
Rub down uneven plaster and redecorate interior of cupboard in Small Rear Bedroom.

Apply additional coat of emulsion paint to rear wall of Large Rear Bedroom where missed.

(f) *The Surroundings*

Take up and relay paving to patio terrace at rear so as to provide adequate drainage towards garden.

(g) *Hot Water and Central Heating*

Carry out recommendations of heating engineer in relation to system.

(h) *Sanitary Fittings*

Fit silencer to water waste preventer in Bathroom.

Adjust flushing cistern to Cloakroom W.C.

(i) *Electrical Installation*

Carry out recommendations of electrician to installation as per attached report.

We shall be pleased to give you any further information or assistance in regard to this property, including, if you wish, checking eventually whether the items in the Schedule above have been completed in a satisfactory manner. As requested we enclose an additional copy of this report and return the lease plan.

Yours faithfully,

Chartered Surveyors

APPENDIX

17 March 1989

Dear Sir,

18 Ford Close, Jaguar Gardens
London, W12

We are in receipt of your letter of 12 March and thank you for your instructions to carry out a structural survey of the above newly built property which you are considering whether to purchase.

Following our subsequent telephone discussion when the scope of the proposed work was considered, we now enclose two copies of our Standard Terms and Conditions for carrying out surveys of new properties. These describe what we shall, in normal circumstances, be able to do but also set out the limitations implicit in such work.

If the conditions and the fee indicated are acceptable to you and you sign, date and set out your requirements as to tests and return one copy to us, we shall be happy to proceed.

Yours faithfully

Chartered Surveyors

Standard terms and conditions for the carrying out of structural surveys of new properties

1. The surveyor will make a thorough inspection of all parts of the interior and the exterior of the property including the surrounding grounds which are readily accessible and a 3 metre ladder will be used where necessary for this purpose.

2. The surveyor will endeavour to examine the plans and specification of the property at the office of the developer/contractor and an

opinion will be provided as to whether the construction shown is in accordance with the plans and specification.

3. The surveyor will visit the office of the local Building Inspector to ascertain whether the works were completed in accordance with the plans as deposited and approved and whether any changes in the design were necessitated as work progressed.

4. The surveyor cannot be held responsible for reporting on parts of the property which are covered, unexposed or inaccessible. However, although no parts of the structure will be opened up or floorboards raised, the surveyor will recommend, if considered necessary, that parts of the structure be exposed so that you can be advised on the true form of construction where there is doubt.

5. Tests of service installations can be arranged if you wish, subject to the vendor's written permission, and on your behalf if you indicate below by ticking the appropriate box(es). We shall act only as your agent in obtaining specialist reports and no responsibility can be accepted for the contents.

Tests are required as follows:
☐ Electrical installation
☐ Hot water and central heating installation
☐ Gas installation.

6. The report as submitted is to be private and confidential to you and your professional advisers. No responsibility will be accepted to any other persons or persons to whom it may be shown.

7. Should the property being purchased be of leasehold tenure a general inspection only will be carried out of those structures, roads, paths, drains, etc for which the purchaser may have a proportionate liability and the report prepared accordingly to cover these aspects together with any restrictive covenants affecting the use of the premises. Should the lease be unavailable assumptions will be made and we will give advice as to examination of the lease being offered before any purchase is finalised.

8. Should we be instructed our surveyor will be able to inspect on 20 March subject to agreement with the developer/contractors for access. We would expect to be despatching our report within three working days of the inspection.

9. Our fee for the survey inclusive of all travelling and disbursements other than the payment of specialists to carry out tests on the service installations but exclusive of VAT which will be charged at the current rate will be £800.00. The fee will cover the inspection of the property and surroundings, the examination of plans, a visit to the Building Inspector and 2 copies of the report. Should it be necessary to advise that further work be carried out and you wish me to pursue further investigations or check that works have been completed on your behalf a further fee by agreement will be charged. The fee is based on the property described by you in your instructions.

I confirm the instructions contained in my letter of 12 March to carry out a structural survey of the newly built house at 18 Ford Close, Jaguar Gardens, London W12 comprising 3 bedrooms, living room, kitchen, bathroom and cloakroom on which a 98 year lease is being offered at £100 p.a., all in accordance with the above terms and conditions including the tests of services indicated at paragraph 5 and for the fee quoted at paragraph 9.

Signed .... Date 18 March 1989

Index

Press Comments

On the First and Second Editions of "Structural Surveys of Dwelling Houses":–

"For those carrying out structural surveys on dwelling houses, this book should stand on the bookshelf next to the valuation tables and be referred to frequently."

Chartered Surveyor

"Excellent and helpful illustrations on the particular subject of settlement. If you have the first edition, you need the second."

The Valuer

"Two good chapters dealing with special problems associated with the survey of flats and new dwellings. An Appendix containing four very useful sample reports. 'Nothing if not thorough' guide".

Building

On "The Repair and Maintenance of Houses":–

"Covers in detail all aspects of the structure and its services, from methods of construction to the diagnosis of defects and eventual remedy. Can be recommended to all. For a firm or library unquestionably a 'must'."

Chartered Surveyor

"Over 1000 pages of absorbing informative text. Almost every possible material is discussed in fine detail and practical advice offered on every aspect of old and modern houses. Title does less than justice. A veritable cyclopaedia."

The Valuer

"Treats separately brick walls, stone walls, foundations etc with useful advice on what to look for and what to do after diagnosis. A book useful to any office and especially to young architects and surveyors."

The Architects Journal

"Publication most timely. Intended for the practising architect and surveyor or student of those professions. Well justifies a place on reference shelves."

Building

"A splendid book. Thoroughly researched and presented in great depth in a very readable style. Ranges in detail from stress calculations for timber and steel work (in imperial and metric) to temporary works and demolition. A first class present to oneself or firm.

Building Technology and Management

"Most informative. Includes many useful structural diagrams and very practical and detailed studies of subsidence problems with the repair of brickwork affected by settlement and decay. For the surveyor a 'must'. Well indexed, simple to find requisite information.

Royal Society of Health Journal

On "Professional Practice for Building Works":–

"A well written volume. Guidance offered on a wide variety of practical points. Extensive consideration given to the control of work in progress. Useful reference aid."

Chartered Surveyor Weekly

"Extends into the practicalities born of first hand experience. Far more enlightening than many other books on the subject. Ought to occupy a place in the Library."

The Valuer

"Covers an enormously wide field. Authors obviously have great experience. Covers many matters not available elsewhere."

The Architect's Journal

"Deals with difficult problems combining practical and technical guidance. Book is a mammoth thesis. Clear writing makes book well worth reading."

Building

"Authors highly experienced. An interesting and stimulating book crammed with sound practical advice. Chapter on Inspection of Work is quite fascinating."

Solicitors Journal